Democracies and Dictatorships in Latin America

This book presents a new theory for why political regimes emerge and why they subsequently survive or break down. It then analyzes the emergence, survival, and fall of democracies and dictatorships in Latin America since 1900. Scott Mainwaring and Aníbal Pérez-Liñán argue for a theoretical approach situated between long-term structural and cultural explanations and short-term explanations that look at the decisions of specific leaders. They focus on the political preferences of powerful actors – the degree to which they embrace democracy as an intrinsically desirable end and their policy radicalism – to explain regime outcomes. They also demonstrate that transnational forces and influences are crucial to understand regional waves of democratization. Based on extensive research into the political histories of Latin American countries, this book offers the first extended analysis of regime emergence, survival, and failure for all of Latin America over a long period of time.

Scott Mainwaring is the Eugene and Helen Conley Professor of Political Science at the University of Notre Dame. His research interests include democratic institutions, democratization, and political parties and party systems. Among his previous books are *Rethinking Party Systems in the Third Wave of Democratization: The Case of Brazil* (1999), *The Third Wave of Democratization in Latin America: Advances and Setbacks* (co-edited, 2005), *The Crisis of Democratic Representation in the Andes* (co-edited, 2006), and *Democratic Governance in Latin America* (co-edited, 2010). Mainwaring is a member of the American Academy of Arts and Sciences. In 2007, he was listed as one of the 400 most cited political scientists teaching in the United States.

Aníbal Pérez-Liñán is an Associate Professor of Political Science and a member of the Center for Latin American Studies at the University of Pittsburgh. His research focuses on democratization, political institutions, and the rule of law in new democracies. He is the author of *Presidential Impeachment and the New Political Instability in Latin America* (2007) and has published articles in the *Journal of Politics*, *World Politics*, *Comparative Political Studies*, *Comparative Politics*, and *Electoral Studies*, among other journals. His research has been funded by the National Science Foundation, the United States Agency for International Development, and the Inter-American Development Bank.

For Sue and Magdalena
With love

Democracies and Dictatorships in Latin America

Emergence, Survival, and Fall

SCOTT MAINWARING
University of Notre Dame

ANÍBAL PÉREZ-LIÑÁN
University of Pittsburgh

CAMBRIDGE
UNIVERSITY PRESS

CAMBRIDGE
UNIVERSITY PRESS

32 Avenue of the Americas, New York, NY 10013-2473, USA

Cambridge University Press is part of the University of Cambridge.

It furthers the University's mission by disseminating knowledge in the pursuit of
education, learning, and research at the highest international levels of excellence.

www.cambridge.org
Information on this title: www.cambridge.org/9780521152242

First published 2013

Printed in the United States of America

A catalog record for this publication is available from the British Library.

Library of Congress Cataloging in Publication Data
Mainwaring, Scott, 1954–
Democracies and dictatorships in Latin America : emergence, survival, and fall / Scott Mainwaring,
University of Notre Dame, South Bend, Indiana; Aníbal Pérez-Liñán, University of Pittsburgh.
    pages   cm
ISBN 978-0-521-19001-5 (hardback)
    1. Latin America – Politics and government – 20th century.   2. Latin America – Politics
and government – 2st century.   3. Democracy – Latin America – History – 20th
century.   4. Democracy – Latin America – History – 21st century.   5. Dictatorship – Latin
America – History – 20th century.   6. Dictatorship – Latin America – History – 21st
century.   7. Authoritarianism – Latin America – History – 20th century.   8. Authoritarianism –
Latin America – History – 21st century.   9. Political culture – Latin America – History – 20th
century.   10. Political culture – Latin America – History – 21st century.   I. Pérez-Liñán,
Aníbal S.   II. Title.
JL966.M353   2013
320.98–dc23   2013015859

ISBN 978-0-521-19001-5 Hardback
ISBN 978-0-521-15224-2 Paperback

Replication datasets and ancillary materials for this book can be found at:
http://kellogg.nd.edu/democracies-materials.shtml

Contents

Tables

Figures

Acknowledgments

This book has had a long gestation, and along the way we have accumulated more intellectual debts than we can remember by now. In the late 1990s, Scott Mainwaring published two papers (Mainwaring 1999a, 1999b) that foreshadowed this book and led to our joint decision to write it. Dan Brinks and the two of us wrote an article on classifying political regimes in Latin America (Mainwaring et al. 2001) that was the starting point for this project. Over the next several years, we published three works (Mainwaring and Pérez-Liñán 2003, 2005, 2007) related to this book, but that are not parts of it. We started working on the book during the Fall 2007 semester, when Pérez-Liñán returned to the Kellogg Institute for International Studies at the University of Notre Dame for a semester as a Visiting Fellow.

Countless individuals provided helpful comments on articles that we produced during the early gestation years of this book; here we acknowledge those who have given suggestions since the Fall 2007 semester. Particular thanks to Frances Hagopian, Steve Levitsky, and Kurt Weyland for providing excellent input at multiple stages of our work.

In September 2008, we had a book seminar at the Kellogg Institute to discuss a very early draft of our manuscript. We benefited greatly from the comments of Daniel Brinks, Steve Levitsky, Beatriz Magaloni, Eduardo Posada-Carbó, Kathryn Sikkink, and Kurt Weyland. Our gratitude goes to these individuals; to the Kellogg Institute for International Studies at the University Notre Dame, which provided funding for the workshop; and to Therese Hanlon, who helped organize the event.

In November 2008, we presented Chapters 1 and 2 at the Centro de Estudios de la Sociedad Civil y la Vida Pública of the Universidad Nacional San Martín in Buenos Aires. We thank Gabriela Ippólito O'Donnell for the invitation and organization and Juan Manuel Abal Medina, Marcelo Escolar, Lucas González, Ricardo Gutiérrez, Marcelo Leiras, Guillermo O'Donnell, and María Matilde Ollier for their comments.

In November 2009, the Catholic University of Santiago, Chile, held a book workshop for us, and again, we reaped helpful comments, this time from David Altman, Rossana Castiglioni, Juan Esteban Montes, Anthony Pezzola, Rafael Piñeiro, Nicolás Somma, and Sergio Toro. Anthony Pezzola organized the workshop.

In May 2010, we organized another book workshop at the Kellogg Institute. We are grateful to Sergio Bejar, Taylor Boas, Sandra Botero, Dan Brinks, Michael Coppedge, Tiago Fernandes, Carlos Guevara Mann, Chad Kiewet de Jong, Carlos Meléndez, Cas Mudde, and Mariela Szwarcberg for helpful comments. Therese Hanlon, Peg Hartman, and Esther Horswell helped provide support for the workshop.

In February 2011, Esperanza Palma organized a book workshop at the Universidad Autónoma de México. We are especially grateful to her, Victor Alarcón, and Roberto Gutiérrez for their comments.

In August 2011, we discussed parts of the book with colleagues from the Universidad Nacional de San Martín and the Universidad San Andrés in Buenos Aires. Carlos Acuña and Gabriela O'Donnell organized this workshop. Carlos Acuña, Martín D'Alessandro, Lucas González, Marcelo Leiras, Juan Andrés Moraes, and María Matilde Ollier provided helpful comments.

In March 2012, we discussed some chapters with colleagues at the Universidade de São Paulo. Elizabeth Balbachevsky organized the workshop. José Alvaro Moisés, Rogério Arantes, Eunice Durham, Fernando Limongi, Edison Nunes, Emmanuel Nunes de Oliveira, and Rogério Schlegel offered helpful suggestions.

In March 2013, we discussed parts of the book at a conference at the Woodrow Wilson Center in Washington, DC. Frances Hagopian and Steve Levitsky gave us excellent suggestions. We are grateful to Cindy Arnson of the Wilson Center's Latin American program and Paolo Carozza of the Kellogg Institute for International Studies at Notre Dame for sponsoring the event.

David Altman, Sergio Bejar, Taylor Boas, Sandra Botero, Chad Kiewet de Jonge (on two occasions), Ezequiel González Ocantos, William Keech, Fabrice Lehoucq, Carlos Meléndez, Cas Mudde, Mariela Szwarcberg, and Kurt Weyland provided written comments on different versions of the entire manuscript.

On four occasions, Frances Hagopian gave us detailed suggestions on parts of the manuscript. Thanks to Mark Beissinger, Jaimie Bleck, Erik Ching, Matthew Cleary, María Victoria De Negri, Robert Dowd, Carlos Gervasoni, Carlos Guevara Mann, Krystin Krause, Raul Madrid, Cynthia McClintock, Monika Nalepa, Valeria Palanza, Eduardo Posada-Carbó, Timothy J. Power, Rachel Beatty Riedl, Leslie Schwindt-Bayer, Nicolás Somma, Martín Tanaka, Guillermo Trejo, Ignacio Walker, Francisco Weffort, and the individuals mentioned earlier, who took part in the book workshops, for helpful comments on parts of this book.

In March and April 2012, Kate Bruhn, Stephen Kaplan, Cynthia McClintock, Alfred Stepan, and graduate students at George Washington University offered helpful suggestions on a paper related to this book.

For one of their assignments, Scott Mainwaring's graduate classes in the spring of 2010 and the fall of 2011 had an option of providing criticisms on the manuscript. Douglas Ansel, Paul Avey, Vince Bagnolo, Nichole Best, Jessica Brandwein, Drew DeWalt, Charles Fagan, Cecilia LePero, Esteban Manteca, Soul Park, and Nathan Sawatzky provided helpful comments on the entire manuscript.

Dan Brinks co-authored the section of Chapter 3 on classifying political regimes in Latin America. He also co-authored two earlier versions of our regime classification (Mainwaring et al. 2001, 2007). We initially planned to include an updated and extended (going back to 1900 and up to 2010) version of this chapter in this book, but spatial considerations precluded this possibility. This updated and extended version of our regime classification also can be found on our Web site.[1] Sandra Botero, Andy Bramsen, Claudia Baez Camargo, Ezequiel González Ocantos, Carlos Guevara Mann, Anjela Jenkins, Chad Kiewiet de Jonge, Shea McClanahan, Andrés Mejía, Carlos Meléndez, Carlo Nasi, Javier Osorio, Jessica Price, Pablo Ros, Melissa Rossi, and Kate Schuenke provided suggestions and did research for our regime classifications. We also benefited from expert advice from Andrés Mejía on Ecuador, Eduardo Posada-Carbó on Colombia, and Samuel Valenzuela on Chile regarding the classification of political regimes. The undergraduate students in Aníbal Pérez-Liñán's Political Development seminar at the University of Pittsburgh recurrently tested our regime classification by applying it to new historical sources.

We coded political actors in twenty Latin American countries over an extended period of time (from 1944 to 2010 for eighteen countries and from the early twentieth century to the present for Argentina and El Salvador). Our research team for this effort included Andrew Alea (Honduras), Alejandra Armesto (Chile), Sandra Botero (Colombia and Peru), Miguel Buitrago (Bolivia), Nestor Camilo Castañeda-Angarita (Costa Rica and the Dominican Republic), Peter Cummings (El Salvador), María Victoria De Negri (Argentina and Uruguay), Laura Gamboa (Honduras and Nicaragua), Craig Garcia (Ecuador), Carolina Goncalves (Honduras), Carlos Guevara Mann (Panama), Patrick Hernandez (Honduras), Víctor Hernández (Mexico), Krystin Krause (Guatemala and Panama), Nayelly Loya (El Salvador), Nara Pavão (Brazil and El Salvador), John Polga-Hecimovich (Ecuador, Paraguay, and Venezuela), Kate Schuenke (Haiti), and Cassilde Schwartz (Cuba and Nicaragua).

Krystin Krause and María Victoria (Vicky) De Negri provided many hours of invaluable research assistance, and Vicky drafted some materials in Chapter 5. For several years, she assisted us in countless ways, ranging from doing much of the base research for Argentina to coding actors for Argentina and Uruguay, offering comments on parts of the manuscript, providing advice that helped us write the coding rules for other research assistants, preparing the manuscript for publication, and doing the index. David Altman, Sergio Bejar, Elizabeth Buncher, Rodrigo Castro

---

[1] http://kellogg.nd.edu/democracies-materials.shtml

Cornejo, Peter Cummings, Annabella España, Agustín Grijalva, Chad Kiewet de
Jonge, German Lodola, Juan Carlos Rodríguez Raga, Melissa Rossi, Kate
Schuenke, Ilka Treminio, and Laura Wills Otero provided research assistance on
other parts of the book.

We benefited from feedback from colleagues at seminars at Brigham Young
University; Columbia University; the Congreso Nacional de Ciencia Política in
Córdoba in Argentina in July 2011; Cornell University; FLACSO-Quito;
Pompeu Fabra University (Barcelona, Spain); Princeton University; Purdue
University; the Universidad de Buenos Aires; the Universidad Torcuato Di
Tella (Buenos Aires); the University of Nevada, Las Vegas; the University of
Notre Dame; and the University of Oklahoma, as well as the 2009 Midwest
Political Science Association meeting and the 2009 American Political Science
Association meeting. The colleagues at the Comparative Politics Reading Group
at the University of Pittsburgh offered valuable advice. Peg Hartman helped with
many details.

Scott Mainwaring gratefully acknowledges the support of the John Simon
Guggenheim Memorial Foundation for a grant to work on this book. He thanks
David Collier, Robert Fishman, Tim Scully, Alfred Stepan, and Samuel
Valenzuela for many stimulating conversations about the issues analyzed in
this book. Aníbal Pérez-Liñán thanks the Kellogg Institute for International
Studies at Notre Dame for a fellowship for the Fall 2007 semester, as well as
the Center for Latin American Studies and the Central Research Development
Fund at the University of Pittsburgh for their support. Funding from the Eugene
and Helen Conley Chair at the University of Notre Dame was invaluable,
making it possible to undertake the coding of political actors that is a core
underpinning of the book.

Lewis Bateman, our editor at Cambridge University Press, encouraged this
project from the outset and waited patiently while we improved our manuscript.

Both of us are deeply fortunate to have partners who have been endless
sources of love, good cheer, encouragement, and support. We are incredibly
thankful that our lives have been so enriched by these partners, Sue Elfin and
Magdalena López.

1

Introduction

We began this book because we wanted to understand the evolution of political regimes in Latin America since 1900 and the reasons for the patterns of those political regimes. What explains why democracies have endured or broken down? What explains why dictatorships have survived or fallen? What explains waves of regime change? Even though the literature had many rich case studies, it was not entirely clear how to cumulate knowledge from these existing studies. Nobody had previously undertaken a project to explain the emergence, survival, and fall of democracies and dictatorships for the region as a whole over an extended period of time.

These empirical issues raised theoretical questions. What theories or theoretical approaches gave us the most leverage in understanding the emergence, survival, and fall of democracies and dictatorships in Latin America? From the outset, we were skeptical that some prominent existing theories would give us much leverage for explaining these issues for Latin America. Modernization theory, which posits that more economically developed countries are more likely to be democratic, did not seem promising as a way of understanding the vicissitudes of democracies and dictatorships in Latin America. A decade ago, we published an article that showed a weak and nonlinear relationship between the level of development and democracy in Latin America (Mainwaring and Pérez-Liñán 2003). Our work added to earlier evidence that modernization theory did not go far toward explaining political regimes in Latin America (Landman 1999; O'Donnell 1973).

As we worked on some related articles that paved the way to this book, class theories of democratization enjoyed renewed visibility with the publication of the works by Acemoglu and Robinson (2006) and Boix (2003). These works see democratization as a struggle between the poor, who always favor democracy when it is a viable outcome, and the rich, who prefer dictatorship when stable dictatorship is feasible. For Latin America (and beyond), these theories are problematic. In many cases, the poor and the working class strongly supported leftist and populist authoritarians even when liberal democracy was an alternative outcome (R. Collier 1999; Germani 1974; Levitsky and Mainwaring 2006; Lipset 1959: 87–126). In other cases, elite actors helped spearhead transitions to democracy (Cardoso 1986; L. Payne 1994). Moreover, contra the assumption of the class-based theories, for Latin America from the 1980s until 2003, many democracies distributed income from the poor to the wealthy, and none did the opposite.

Nor did Inglehart's theories of democracy based on mass political culture (Inglehart 1990, 1997; Inglehart and Welzel 2005) hold much promise as a way of understanding the rise and fall of democracies and dictatorships in Latin America. Inglehart's theories have modernization underpinnings, and modernization theory, as already noted, does not explain regime survival and fall in Latin America. Moreover, in many Latin American democracies, large numbers of citizens express indifference about democracy in public opinion surveys. If large numbers of citizens are not committed to democracy, how can a democratic public opinion explain the durability of democracy?

Finally, all of the established major theoretical paradigms in comparative politics focused on within-country variables. Such a focus cannot easily explain *waves* of regime change, in which international influences and actors hold sway.

We found theoretical inspiration in the seminal works by Linz (1978b) on democratic breakdowns and by O'Donnell and Schmitter (1986) on transitions to democracy, as well as in many case studies about political regimes. We build on these works, but they did not attempt to develop a theory in the strict sense (O'Donnell and Schmitter 1986: 3). Linz and O'Donnell and Schmitter focused on quite proximate questions of regime change and survival and on regime coalitions, without specifying why different actors join the pro- or anti-democracy coalitions. Ultimately, our dissatisfaction with existing theories of regimes and regime change and our desire to provide greater theoretical integration than Linz (1978b) and O'Donnell and Schmitter (1986) led us to set forth a new theory of regimes in this book.

We have two primary ambitions. First, we hope to contribute to broader theoretical and comparative debates about the survival or fall of authoritarian and competitive (democratic and semi-democratic) regimes. Second, we aspire to explain regime change and survival[1] of dictatorships and competitive regimes in Latin America from 1945 to 2010, with some glances back at the 1900–44 period.

Because of the inadequacy of existing theories and the advantages that a theory offers, we concluded that it would useful to elaborate an alternative theory based on more realistic microfoundations about what motivates political actors. Our theory looks at systems of actors, posits assumptions about their preferences and about why regimes fall or survive, and deduces hypotheses from these assumptions. In a theory, it is not only the individual hypotheses that can

---

[1] Throughout the book, we use the terms "regime survival," "regime continuity," "regime durability," and "regime stability" interchangeably. As used here, a stable regime is simply one that survives even if it faces other forms of upheaval.

advance social science; it is also the overarching set of integrated and interrelated propositions (Achen and Snidal 1989). Our theory, which we sketch in this chapter and present more fully in Chapter 2, integrates the study of transitions to competitive regimes and of breakdowns of competitive regimes, and by implication, the study of the durability of dictatorships and of competitive regimes.

A BREAK WITH THE PAST

Figure 1.1 illustrates the fundamental transformation of regimes in Latin America, showing the annual percentage of democracies in the region between 1900 and 2010. The first panel depicts the percentage of countries counted as democracies (as opposed to dictatorships) in the dichotomous classification developed by Adam Przeworski and his collaborators (Przeworski et al. 2000; Cheibub and Gandhi 2004). The second panel reflects the percentage of countries with scores greater than 5 in the Polity scale (Gurr, Jaggers, and Moore

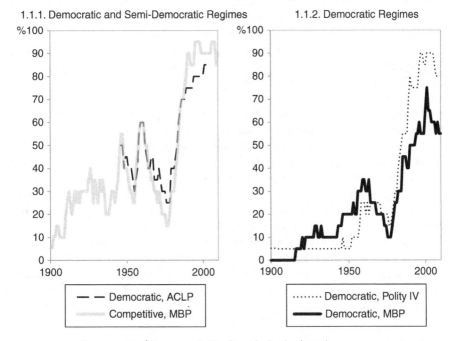

FIGURE 1.1 Percentage of Democratic Regimes in Latin America, 1900–2010
Key: ACLP: Classification developed by Alvarez, Cheibub, Gandhi, Limongi, and Przeworski.
Polity: Countries with scores greater than 5 in the Polity IV scale.
MPB: Mainwaring, Brinks, and Pérez-Liñán trichotomous classification.
Sources: Authors' elaboration based on Cheibub and Gandi (2004), Przeworski et al. (2000), Polity IV 2012 (http://www.systemicpeace.org/polity/polity4.htm), and Table 1.1.

1990; Jaggers and Gurr 1995; Polity IV Project 2012).[2] We also present the classification of political regimes developed for this project, introduced later.

Figure 1.1 suggests that the Przeworski et al. measure is more lenient than a classification based on a score of greater than 5 on the Polity IV scale. Yet all three measures confirm the occurrence of an unprecedented wave of change between 1978 and 1995. They depict a similar trend for the last part of the twentieth century, suggesting reliability in the overall picture.[3] Democracy expanded somewhat in the late 1950s, and then hit a nadir in 1976–77, followed by an unprecedented surge during the 1980s.

Until the wave of democratization that began in 1978, authoritarian regimes were pervasive in most of the region. Many democracies were short-lived, and several countries had had no experience whatsoever of competitive political regimes. The situation changed profoundly between 1978 and 1995. A region that had previously always been predominantly authoritarian witnessed the virtual demise of openly authoritarian regimes. Moreover, since 1978, competitive regimes have been far more durable than ever before. Compared to what occurred in earlier waves of democratization in Latin America, this wave has lasted much longer and has been broader in scope. This transformation is one of the most profound changes in the history of Latin American politics.

The increase in the number of democracies and semi-democracies in Latin America between 1978 and 1995 was dramatic. At the beginning of this period, Latin America had only three democracies, and the other seventeen countries had openly authoritarian regimes. By 1990, the only openly authoritarian governments were those of Cuba and Haiti. By 1995, Cuba was the sole holdout (although Haiti eroded back into authoritarian rule between 1999 and 2006). The shift away from authoritarianism was dramatic in speed and breadth. The trend is even more striking if we consider the total proportion of Latin Americans living under competitive regimes. In 1900, only 5 percent of the regional population enjoyed democratic or semi-democratic politics. In 1950, it was 58 percent. The percentage plummeted to 12 percent of the regional population by 1977, but it had reached 98 percent by 2006.

Figure 1.1 also displays the evolution of political regimes according to our own classification. We classify regimes in Latin America using a simple trichotomous scale developed with Daniel Brinks (Mainwaring et al. 2001, 2007): democratic, semi-democratic, and authoritarian. We lump together the democratic and semi-democratic regimes into a broader category of "competitive

---

[2] The Polity scale ranges between –10 (authoritarian) and 10 (democratic). The threshold of 5 is conventionally employed to distinguish full democracies from other types of regimes.

[3] The Polity score (the only available for the 1900–45 period beside our own classification) does not consider the extension of voting rights, so it overestimates levels of democracy in the early twentieth century. These four measures of democracy are strongly correlated. The series for the proportion of democracies and semi-democracies according to the Mainwaring et al. three-point scale correlates at .98 with the Przeworski series, at .93 with the Polity index, and at .97 with Freedom House scores.

regimes" displayed in panel 1.1.1. We explain our coding of political regimes in Chapter 3.

THE ARGUMENT IN BRIEF

1) **Political actors should be at the center of theories of regime survival and change.** Political actors, not structures or cultures, determine outcomes, even though structures and cultures affect the formation and preferences of actors. We view presidents and organizations such as parties, unions, business associations, the military, and organized movements as the most important actors. These organizations and presidents control political resources and therefore exercise influence in the competition for power.

We locate our theory between structural or long-term cultural approaches, on the one hand, and agency and contingent action approaches, on the other. In many theoretical perspectives, purposeful action is the final step in a long causal chain that is largely determined by deep structural (e.g., Boix 2003; Skocpol 1979) or cultural (Foucault 1972; Inglehart and Welzel 2005) forces that transcend individual actors. In these structural and cultural accounts, actors' decisions are largely determined by macro forces. On the other hand, we emphasize the constraining and structuring of powerful organizations more than approaches that focus on individual leaders' decision making.

2) **We emphasize the role of political factors that help political regimes survive or lead them to fail.** By "political factors" we refer specifically to the impact of actors' normative preferences about democracy and dictatorship, their moderation or radicalization in policy preferences, and international political influences exercised through external actors. We counterpose an emphasis on these political factors to analyses that argue that the survival or displacement of regimes depends largely on structural factors such as the level of development, the class structure, or income inequalities, or on mass political culture.

These political factors have primacy in determining whether regimes fail or remain stable. The empirical evidence for Latin America in the twentieth century supports a primary focus on political factors such as the level of radicalization, actors' normative commitment to democracy, and a favorable international political environment. With a normative democratic commitment on the part of powerful political players and a favorable international environment, democracy can survive in the face of daunting challenges: poverty, significant ethnic cleavages, deep social inequalities, high inflation, and low growth (Linz 1988; Remmer 1996). Indeed, democratic and semi-democratic regimes have survived in post-1977 Latin America in the face of all these unfavorable conditions. This capacity of democracy to survive despite seemingly highly adverse conditions flies in the face of many theoretical expectations before the latest wave of democracy began.

Other analysts have also focused on political factors in understanding regime survival and fall. We add to and modify most previous work by presenting these ideas in an integrated framework and by testing the theory and specific hypotheses in new ways.

2a) Actors' normative attitudes about democracy and dictatorship are important influences in regime survival or fall. If the most powerful actors have a normative preference for democracy – if they believe that democracy is intrinsically the best political regime even if it does not satisfy their other policy preferences – democracy is more likely to survive.

Our focus on the impact of actors' normative attitudes on regime outcomes builds on literatures in political science and sociology that have emphasized the importance of actors' beliefs in understanding political outcomes. Actors' beliefs influence what they view as desirable and how they pursue their interests (Berman 1998; Blyth 2002; Finnemore 1998; Goldstein 1993; Hall 1989; Sikkink 1991, 1993). If powerful actors view liberal democracy as an inefficient, corruption-plagued obstacle to rapid economic growth, as the Argentine military and big business did in the 1960s, when a competitive regime in a poor or medium income country falters in economic performance, it is vulnerable to breakdown. If powerful leftist actors believe that liberal democracy is a facade for bourgeois domination, as most of the Marxist tradition did, they are likely to mobilize for workers' gains even if this mobilization endangers the regime. Conversely, if actors intrinsically value democracy as a "universal value" (Coutinho 1980), they accept policy sacrifices to preserve democracy, and they are more likely to view democracy as an intertemporal bargain (Przeworski 1991, 2006) in which they can compensate for today's sacrifices by gaining tomorrow. We contribute to the literature on the political impact of actors' beliefs or preferences by testing this argument in new ways.

2b) Actors' policy radicalism hinders the probability that a competitive political regime will survive. Policy moderation facilitates the survival of competitive regimes. Several studies have claimed that the content of the policy preferences embraced by powerful political actors (for instance, a preference for or against income redistribution) have important consequences for political regimes. The *intensity* of actors' policy preferences, and not just their substance, is critical for regime survival and fall. Radical policy preferences make actors on the left and on the right of the policy spectrum intransigent and thus unlikely to tolerate the give-and-take of democratic politics.

3) A favorable regional political environment, characterized by the existence of many democracies in Latin America, increases the likelihood of transitions from authoritarian rule to competitive regimes and diminishes the likelihood of breakdowns of existing competitive regimes. Our theory emphasizes the embeddedness of countries' political actors and political regimes in a regional and international context.

Recent work on democratization has emphasized two factors that are at odds with an exclusive focus on domestic factors. First, democratization occurs in wave-like processes; what happens in neighboring countries has a significant impact on a region. Consistent with the arguments of Brinks and Coppedge

(2006), Huntington (1991), and Markoff (1996) at a global level, change in political regimes in Latin America has occurred in waves. It would be difficult to explain wave-like change only on the basis of within-country conditions if there were no transnational effects. The likelihood that political transformations regional in scope could be explained solely by the simultaneous change of domestic conditions in multiple countries is very low. Theories of democratization that are based exclusively on country-level conditions are therefore ill equipped to explain waves of democratization.

Second, these wave-like processes often bring about profound changes in political regimes in a region in a short time. In Latin America, the change from a region that was overwhelmingly authoritarian in 1977 to one that is overwhelmingly democratic or semi-democratic occurred rapidly. Most comparative politics approaches that explain democratization involve long, slow processes. Political culture at the mass level, the level of development, the size and strength of the working class, and income inequality, all of which have been offered as explanations of democratization, usually changes only over the long run. Because the domestic factors that have traditionally been used to explain regime change move relatively slowly, the likelihood that they could account for profound change in a region in a short time is extremely low.

Synchronicity and rapidity of change do not definitively prove that democratization had powerful international causes, but they greatly increase the likelihood that international factors were at work. Many recent works have emphasized the impact of international actors,[4] regional influences,[5] and international organizations[6] on democratization. Consistent with this burgeoning literature, we underscore that battles over political regimes involve not only domestic actors, but also international and transnational actors.

Our work contributes in five ways to the existing literature on international effects on political regimes. First, we include international effects and actors as part of a theory of regime change and stability. Little previous work has integrated domestic and international actors in a theoretical understanding of regime dynamics. Second, an important question has remained unanswered by the existing literature. Because the wave of democratization was more or less contemporaneous with an increasing emphasis by U.S. foreign policy on "democracy promotion," it is hard to disentangle the effects of regional diffusion per se from the role of U.S. foreign policy. We separate these effects in Chapter 4. Third, although the literature on international diffusion of political regimes has burgeoned in recent years, the analysis of the mechanisms behind diffusion is less developed. We analyze this issue in Chapter 7. Fourth, we show that international influences have reinforcing dynamics that help explain the

---

[4] Brinks and Coppedge (2006); Gleditsch (2002); Gleditsch and Ward (2006); Markoff (1996); Pridham (1991, 1997); Starr (1991).
[5] Brown (2000); Levitsky and Way (2010); Whitehead (1986b, 1996).
[6] Pevehouse (2002a, 2002b, 2005).

magnitude and pace of waves of democratization and authoritarianism (Chapters 4 and 7). Finally, in Chapter 8 we show that while international actors facilitate transitions to democracy and prevent the breakdown of competitive regimes, they are not effective at promoting the advancement of competitive regimes once a transition has taken place.

EMPIRICAL CONTRIBUTIONS: UNDERSTANDING
POLITICAL REGIMES IN LATIN AMERICA

Empirically, the book examines democratization and regime change in Latin America over a long sweep of time.[7] We hope to make three empirical contributions. First, we aspire to contribute to understanding the history of political regimes in Latin America from 1900 to 2010. Along with Daniel Brinks, and with the help of sixteen research assistants over the course of a decade, we coded political regimes as democratic, semi-democratic, and authoritarian. We discuss our coding rules and procedures in Chapter 3. Our classification of political regimes lays the groundwork for understanding the evolution of democratization and authoritarianism in the region and provides a research tool that other scholars can use.[8]

Second, this is the first book that tries to *explain* the emergence, survival, and fall of political regimes for Latin America as a whole over a long period of time. There is a huge literature on political regimes in Latin America. However, much of it focuses on single countries or a few countries. Drake (2009), Hartlyn and Valenzuela (1994), and P. Smith (2005) offer valuable descriptive histories of democracy in Latin America, but with little effort to explain regime emergence, survival, and demise.

Third, this is the first book that has attempted to extend an actor-based approach to political regimes to the empirical study of a large number of countries over an extended period of time. Many scholarly approaches agree that political actors (rather than structures or political culture) offer the most fruitful perspective to study political regimes. Such approaches claim that actors' choices determine regime outcomes, and that structures and cultures, even though they influence the actors that emerge and their behavior, do not determine their choices. Actor-based approaches to studying political regimes are common in case studies (Berman 1998; Capoccia 2005; Figueiredo 1993; Levine 1973, 1978; Linz 1978a; O'Donnell 1982; Stepan 1971, 1978; A. Valenzuela

---

[7] By Latin America we refer to the twenty countries in the western hemisphere that were colonized by Spain, France, or Portugal: Argentina, Bolivia, Brazil, Chile, Colombia, Costa Rica, Cuba, the Dominican Republic, Ecuador, El Salvador, Guatemala, Haiti, Honduras, Mexico, Nicaragua, Panama, Paraguay, Peru, Uruguay, and Venezuela. We do not include countries colonized by Great Britain or the Netherlands.

[8] Drake (2009) and Smith (2005) also describe the evolution of democracy in twentieth-century Latin America.

1978; J. S. Valenzuela 1985; Viola 1982). Theoretical frameworks such as those of Linz (1978b) and O'Donnell and Schmitter (1986) also posit that actors (or blocs of actors) are the most useful unit of analysis. Yet given the time-intensive demands of studying a large number of actors across a long period of time in a substantial number of countries, there hitherto has been no extensive (i.e., involving a large number of cases) empirical testing of theoretical propositions about the effects of actors' preferences on regime outcomes.

Working with a different team of nineteen research assistants, we identified the main actors operating under every presidential administration in the twenty Latin American countries from 1944 to 2010 and also coded their attitudes toward democracy and dictatorship and their policy moderation/radicalism.[9] If actors (as opposed to structures or cultures) determine political outcomes, actually examining their preferences and behavior is essential. Some excellent studies have followed this precept for one or a small number of countries, but no previous work has coded actors for so many countries over a long period of time.

WHY DEVELOP A THEORY?

Scholars working on political regimes confront several choices. In terms of the overall analytical strategy, the main question has been whether to develop a theory with an integrated set of hypotheses that is deduced from explicitly articulated initial assumptions (Acemoglu and Robinson 2006; Boix 2003); a theoretical framework that provides a general orientation toward studying political regimes (Linz 1978b; O'Donnell and Schmitter 1986); or a set of narrower empirical hypotheses (Cutright 1963; Morlino 2008: 47–51; Przeworski et al. 2000).[10]

Each of these options has advantages and disadvantages. Theories provide integrative ways of understanding the world – an advantage, given our objectives. A theory makes explicit who the actors are and how they are constituted, what motivates their behavior in regime games, and how they form winning coalitions. Empirical propositions that are not integrated by theories or by theoretical frameworks such as Linz (1978b) and O'Donnell and Schmitter (1986) do not explicitly embed their analyses into an understanding of these issues. In contrast, the empirical propositions that a theory deductively generates are part of an integrated whole (Bunge 1998: 433–43). Some scholars (Coppedge 2012: 49–113; Munck 2001) have commented on the lack of theoretical integration in most work on political regimes and argued that this

[9] To be precise, we coded all presidential administrations that lasted long enough to be in power as of December 31 in at least one year. If a president began his term in a given year and did not serve until the end of that year, we did not include that administration in our dataset.
[10] These distinctions could be seen as a continuum rather than as three discrete categorical possibilities.

constitutes a weakness in this literature. We agree with their judgment; our effort at building a theory responds to their observations.

Notwithstanding the sophistication of some of the work that has inspired us, there have been no previous efforts along the lines presented here to develop a theory of regime survival and fall.[11] The insights of the rich literatures on which we draw do not fully substitute for a theory of regime survival and fall. These insights are not generally connected to each other in a system of cohesive and logical relationships. As a result, work on political regimes has accumulated considerable knowledge, but with less theoretical integration than is desirable. As Coppedge (2012: 49–113) comments, with loose integration, a research finding about the importance of certain independent variables could be compatible with a wide range of theories.

Social scientists want to know not only whether some specific independent variables affect political outcomes, but also what theories hold up (Bunge 1998: 433–43). Because it consists of a system of integrated hypotheses deduced from explicitly articulated assumptions, a theory helps order and organize hypotheses.

Our book integrates previous streams of research into a cohesive theory. The core contribution of our work is not the five discrete hypotheses about regime survival and fall that we present later. Rather, it is the theory, which links these hypotheses in deductively logical ways, and the testing of it. A theory is a way of making sense of the world, of providing an integrated framework. Discrete hypotheses can also advance understanding in the social sciences, but theories help stimulate advances in how social scientists think about politics. The development and testing of theories is a critical part of social science (Achen and Snidal 1989; Bunge 1998: 433–43; Coppedge 2012: chapters 3–4; Ferejohn and Satz 1995; Munck 2001).

Our understanding of "theory" is not restricted to formal models. Our endeavor is a theory because it starts with some explicitly articulated assumptions about the relevant set of actors and the factors that determine their choice of regime coalition, and then we deduce an integrated set of hypotheses from these assumptions.[12]

ACTORS AND REGIME COALITIONS

The notion of political actors forms the first building block of our theory. We focus on a parsimonious set of the most important political actors: presidents,

---

[11] Linz (1978b) and O'Donnell and Schmitter (1986) developed theoretical frameworks that have some of the characteristics of a theory, but without a set of integrated hypotheses.

[12] The formal-theory approaches such as Boix (2003) offer tight integrated theories that provide logical microfoundations for specific macro-hypotheses. Some frameworks (Linz 1978b; O'Donnell and Schmitter 1986) offer heuristics to guide the inquiry of researchers into cases or topics. In this regard, our theoretical discussion follows the second tradition more than the first one.

powerful organizations, and influential organized movements. In democratic regimes, the president and the largest parties are important actors. The government commands many resources, and because it directs the policy process, it strongly influences future resources and outcomes. As head of the government, the president exercises great influence over the government and more broadly over democratic politics. Parties are the primary route to achieving elected office in democratic politics. Democratic politics revolve significantly around the competition among parties.

The military, guerrilla organizations, social movements, nongovernmental organizations, unions, and business associations are sometimes major actors.[13] In authoritarian regimes, the most important actors always include the president and often include a hegemonic party (if there is one and if it is reasonably independent with respect to the president), the main opposition party (under authoritarian regimes with competitive elections), and the military.

In our theory, actors' purposeful action largely determines regime outcomes. Actors form preferences about a political regime based on what they see as desirable outcomes (specifically in terms of policy preferences and regime procedures) and they act on the basis of those preferences. Political actors are instrumental, but they are not always *only* instrumental or narrowly self-interested. The theory does not deny that actors' behavior can have unintended consequences.

Our understanding of who the actors are and what motivates them diverges from some theories. In class-based accounts, social classes are the actors. In contrast, in our view, social classes are usually not sufficiently organized and sufficiently politically cohesive to form political actors. Labor-based political parties and labor unions are actors, but the working class per se is not unless labor organizations or political parties forge political unity among most workers. Similarly, capitalists per se are usually not a unified political actor; they have competing interests and usually lack a single organization that speaks for all of them.[14] When their interests are deeply threatened, business owners might forge a temporary unity that enables them to function like an actor. For short periods, social classes can function like actors when they respond almost uniformly to a political event or process, but such uniformity is the exception. Usually, social classes face difficult collective action problems (Olson 1965); they are internally divided both structurally and politically.

---

[13] Congress is an important decision-making arena in competitive political regimes, but it is not sufficiently united to be an actor. In conflicts about political regimes, legislatures are usually divided along party lines, so we take the parties, not congress per se, to be the actors.

[14] In Chapter 6, we argue that big business in El Salvador usually functioned as a relatively cohesive actor from 1931 until 1977. This exception to the rule occurred in part because of perceived powerful threats from radical popular and/or insurgent movements. In addition, many big business enterprises in El Salvador were diversified across different sectors. For example, big coffee producers typically also owned firms in other sectors, thus reducing conflict among different economic sectors.

Our treatment of actors also diverges somewhat from that of pioneering contingent action approaches such as Linz (1978b) and O'Donnell and Schmitter (1986). Both of these works focus on *blocs* of actors in a manner that is akin to our regime coalitions. They conceptualize the actors according to their positions regarding the existing regime. For example, Linz's loyal, semi-loyal, and disloyal oppositions are *blocs* of actors that share a common orientation toward the democratic regime.

Public opinion is not an actor because it cannot per se act. However, in competitive regimes, public opinion is one of the most valuable resources that actors can employ. It often sways powerful actors one way or the other in regime battles. For example, it is unlikely that a successful coup could occur in the face of solid public support for democracy. Conversely, democracy is more likely to be imperiled if large parts of the public turn against it. In democracies, public opinion routinely limits what leaders can do (Brooks and Manza 2007). Likewise, the fate of dictatorships sometimes hinges on whether citizens turn so obviously against the rulers that it emboldens opposition actors and encourages splits in the ruling coalition. In short, public opinion is important in regime battles, but it is not an actor. Likewise, electoral support is a hugely important asset for parties and the president in democracies, but voters do not constitute an actor; they are divided and are almost never capable of cohesive action.

Actors have different kinds of political resources. "Political resources" are any assets (including material and human capacities, institutional advantages that accrue from formal rules of the game, and for the military, arms) that can be mobilized in the competition for power. Political resources may be highly concentrated or widely dispersed. Actors with intense preferences about the political regime work especially hard to mobilize their resources and to create new ones. For the government, military and state capacity always represents valuable resources.

Whether political regimes survive or are replaced depends on how powerful the coalitions that support them are. Every regime hosts at least two simple coalitions, one that supports the incumbent regime (for example, a democracy) and an opposition coalition that supports its displacement (e.g., the authoritarian coalition). Multiple coalitions (e.g., several opposition blocs pursuing different forms of authoritarian rule) are not unusual in times of great turmoil. Many actors remain on the sidelines and join neither coalition. These regime coalitions are usually not formalized, and the partners in the coalitions shift over time. Regime coalitions win state power when they control enough resources to prevail in the competition for power. In the advanced industrial democracies, the regime coalition that supports the status quo (i.e., liberal democracy) vastly overpowers any other alternatives, and therefore the probability of breakdown in the current historical context is virtually zero.

Once in office, the leaders of a regime coalition adopt policies and build, preserve, or modify the existing political regime. A regime type (a competitive regime or a dictatorship) survives if the size and leverage of its coalition is greater than the coalition working for regime change. The regime changes when the opposition coalition is more powerful.

Most actors are not intrinsically part of either the democratic or the authoritarian bloc. They may change regime coalitions depending on how effectively the existing regime satisfies their instrumental policy preferences and, in some cases, their normative preferences about the regime itself (i.e., some actors prefer democracy even if they believe they might get better policy outcomes under dictatorship). All political actors have policy preferences, and some of them have value preferences about the political regime itself. They support regime coalitions that they believe are likely to maximize their policy goals and their normative preferences about the regime.

BETWEEN STRUCTURE AND AGENCY: THE LEVEL
OF ANALYSIS AND THE CORE VARIABLES

Another issue in the study of political regimes is where to anchor the proper level of analysis for explanations of regime change. Some scholars have emphasized long-run preconditions (e.g., Moore Jr. 1966) while others have emphasized leaders and contingent action in specific historical contexts (Capoccia 2005; Hartlyn 1984; Karl 1987; Kuran 1989, 1991; Linz 1978b; Stepan 1978). Rustow (1970) framed this question as a dilemma between functional theories and genetic explanations, Przeworski (1986) presented it as a tension between macro- and micro-oriented perspectives, and Karl (1990) conceived of it as explanations based on structure and others based on agency. This problem is related to the substantive distinction between explanations of democratization based on socioeconomic conditions and those based on political factors, but it is analytically distinct. Most explanations of regime change based on socioeconomic variables conceptualize long-term processes, but arguments about the impact of economic performance on political stability (e.g., Merkx 1973) often imply causal mechanisms operating in the medium or short run. Most arguments about political factors refer to short-term processes, but claims about political culture (e.g., Inglehart 1990, 1997; Inglehart and Welzel 2005; Wiarda 2001) are based on long-term legacies.

We situate our analysis between long-term explanations such as social structures and short-term explanations based on actors' contingent decisions in quickly shifting conditions. Certainly, long-term factors such as the level of development, the degree of social inequality, and the persistence of profound ethnic, linguistic, or religious fractures affect the viability of democracy. But a fundamental theme in this book is that for our universe of cases, these long-term factors have limited capacity to explain regime survival and fall. To understand why regimes endure or fall, we need to shift the analysis to more proximate causes of regime change.

We do not deny the role of structural forces (patterns of economic development and dependence, class structures, legacies of social inequality, and so on) in the constitution of political regimes. Structural conditions powerfully influence the emergence and development of political organizations and the distribution of resources. These more distant structural causes play a role in the genesis of political regimes. But the effect of structural variables is contingent and diffuse; it ultimately manifests itself in the organization of political actors and in the relative distribution of their political resources.

At the other end of the spectrum, we emphasize causal factors that are more distant than those analyzed by Kuran (1989, 1991) and Lohmann (1994) in their fascinating accounts of the transition to democracy in Eastern Europe and the former East Germany and O'Donnell and Schmitter (1986) in their landmark contribution on transitions to democracy. The short term agency based explanations of breakdowns and transitions of Linz (1978b) and O'Donnell and Schmitter (1986), while richly capturing important processes and interactions, do not tell us under what less proximate conditions breakdowns, democratic survival, and transitions are more likely. We need theories and hypotheses that are situated between structure (or causally distant cultural explanations) and agency to complement existing knowledge. This is the terrain where our theory is located.

Because our theory focuses mostly on fairly proximate variables in the sequence of causation, it is compatible with theories and theoretical frameworks that examine more distant or more immediate causes. For example, modernization theory and our theory could both help explain why democracies and dictatorships survive or fall. The former focuses on more distant causes, and ours on more proximate causes. However, for Latin America from 1945 until 2010, as we show in Chapters 4, 5, 6, and 9, the prominent more distant macro theories have little explanatory power for understanding regime change and survival.

At the meso level of analysis that inspires our effort, three variables affect whether regimes remain in power or fall: (1) whether actors have moderate or radical policy preferences (radical actors tend to be destabilizing in competitive regimes); (2) whether they have a normative preference for democracy or authoritarianism; and (3) how supportive the regional political environment is for competitive and authoritarian regimes. In this section, we introduce the arguments about these three variables.

Radical Policy Preferences. We define radical policy preferences as those toward one pole of the policy spectrum (e.g., toward the left or right when the policy space is effectively unidimensional[15]) in conjunction with an urgency to achieve these preferences in the short to medium term where they do not represent the status quo, or with an intransigent defense of these positions where these positions represent the status quo.[16] They have two main

---

[15] If there is more than one important dimension of competition, the radical/moderation continuum functions in all of them.

[16] In game theoretic terms, these actors have a large discount factor.

characteristics: (1) because their policy preferences are toward one pole of a policy spectrum, the unqualified adoption of their preferences imposes important costs on other actors; (2) their preferences are very intense, so the actors are intransigent (i.e., unwilling to bargain) and impatient (i.e., unwilling to wait for the long term to achieve their policy goals). Radical policy preferences need not be on the extreme left or extreme right, but they must be far enough from the policy preferences of other relevant actors to create polarization. The location of radical policy positions cannot be determined a priori, as it depends on the nature of the policy space.

The argument about radicalism captures the delicate historical balance between conservative actors' demand for security and progressive actors' demand for policy transformation. Put in Dahl's (1971) terms, mutual guarantees among actors increase the viability of polyarchy. For a democracy to survive in poor- and intermediate-income countries, it is helpful that the actors who can destroy the regime – the military and sometimes the economic elite – not fear the possibility of major losses in a short time. If they do, they are more likely to join the authoritarian coalition. At the same time, actors who pursue policy change should believe that transformations are ultimately viable as a result of democratic political competition. If the intensity of their policy preferences leads either conservative or progressive actors to believe that their goals cannot be achieved under competitive rules, those actors might support an alternative regime able to impose their most favored policies unilaterally. Their withdrawal from the democratic coalition often prompts their opponents to do the same, because uncertainty about policy gains will now turn into the prospect of permanent losses imposed by the radical group. The fear of major losses in the short term thus arises when some actors have radical policy preferences.

Actors' Normative Preferences about Democracy and Dictatorship. Some actors have strong value preferences about the political regime in addition to having instrumental policy preferences. These orientations range from a strong value preference for a particular form of authoritarianism to a strong normative preference for democracy, with indifference toward regime type in the midpoint of the scale.

A normative preference for democracy or dictatorship refers to the willingness of political actors to incur policy costs in order to defend or achieve their preferred regime. It means that an actor prefers a kind of regime on intrinsic grounds, as the best possible political regime. When candidates acknowledge their defeat in an election (rather than questioning its results) and gracefully congratulate their opponents, they are behaving in ways that signal commitment to the principles of the democratic regime. When government leaders accept defeat on an important issue that requires a legislative supermajority, even if they could modify procedural rules to impose the preferred legislation by simple majority, they are signaling commitment to existing procedures. This commitment is credible to others because the behavior implies a cost to the actor involved. Observers infer that the player must have a latent normative preference (a favorable predisposition) toward the regime, and that this preference must be strong enough to overcome the short-term losses.

Normative preferences about the regime are part of an actors' belief system or view of the world. They are an example of "procedural utility" – the well-being derived from procedures above and beyond the outcomes they generate (Frey, Benz, and Stutzer 2004).[17] They are consistent with what Max Weber (1978) called "value rationality." This argument builds from evidence that individuals care not only about instrumental gains (outcomes), but also about procedures (Benz and Stutzer 2003; Frey et al. 2001; Frey et al. 2004; Frey and Stutzer 2005; Gangl 2003; Levi et al. 2009; Lind et al. 1993; Sen 1995, 1997; Stutzer and Frey 2006), including the ones that constitute a democratic regime.

A strong normative preference for democracy by powerful actors, especially the president and the major parties, reduces the odds that a competitive regime will break down. Actors' normative preference for democracy can help inoculate competitive regimes from breakdowns. If the key actors are normatively committed to democracy, a competitive regime can survive bad governing performance where it might not survive otherwise (Linz 1988; Linz and Stepan 1989; Lipset 1959; O'Donnell 1986: 15–18; Remmer 1996). Actors with a normative preference for democracy are not willing to subvert democracy to pursue radical policies. And – going back to our previous argument – if radical policies are not on the agenda, it is easier for all actors to accept a competitive regime.

Conversely, actors that normatively prefer a dictatorship readily seize on opportunities to delegitimize a competitive regime and bolster the authoritarian coalition. In moments of poor economic performance or radicalism by opposing forces, actors that are indifferent to democracy can easily be recruited to join the authoritarian coalition if it is already a force to reckon with (Lipset 1959).

A normative preference for democracy by the main opposition parties and leaders also signals to leaders of an authoritarian regime and their allies that the costs of establishing a competitive regime are likely to be bearable. It can help pave the way for a transition to a competitive regime by assuring the actors that support the authoritarian coalition that their interests are not likely to be radically threatened under a competitive regime.

These arguments rest on the assumption that actors' attitudes toward political regimes significantly influence political outcomes. Actors' values about what political regimes are desirable and feasible affect how they behave politically and how tolerant they are of policy failures, of dissent on the part of other actors with strongly opposing preferences, and of political unrest. Normative preferences create a cognitive map that shapes how actors understand political reality and their own interests (Blyth 2002; Finnemore 1998).

Most political regimes hit periods of bad government performance. Actors that are normatively committed to a given regime type accept periods of bad

---

[17] Frey et al. (2004: 381) define procedural utility as "the well-being people gain from living and acting under institutionalized processes as they contribute to a positive sense of self."

performance and blame the administration rather than the regime. In contrast, actors that are normatively indifferent or hostile to that regime might seize on the difficult period to attack the regime and join the opposition regime coalition (not merely the opposition to the government).

Actors' normative attitudes about democracy and dictatorship are not reducible to their economic interests or to cultural predispositions. These attitudes, however, are not perfectly exogenous, a prime mover of political processes. In order to avoid tautology, an explanation of regime outcomes based on normative preferences must be willing to inquire into the origins of attitudes toward democracy and dictatorship, their variance across countries, and their transformation over time. We address this issue in Chapters 2 through 7.

Like Dahl (1971: 124–88) and most authors who have contributed to this literature, we focus on powerful actors because their beliefs have a more direct impact on regime outcomes than mass beliefs. We focus exclusively on actors' value preferences about democracy and dictatorship as opposed to other social or cultural beliefs. Other scholars have argued that nonpolitical beliefs such as trust in individuals (Inglehart 1990, 1997) and religious beliefs (Huntington 1984, 1991; Levine 1992; Stepan 2001: 213–53) affect political regimes. These other beliefs have effects on democracy and authoritarianism, but they are not a central part of this book.

International Actors and Influences. International actors disseminate new beliefs about the desirability (or lack thereof) of different kinds of political regimes and policies, and they prove by example that some political projects are feasible (or not). They provide resources to empower some domestic regime coalitions, and they offer incentives to domestic actors, thereby altering the costs and benefits of different options in the domestic regime game. Where the regional political environment and the U.S. government are favorable to competitive political regimes, the costs and benefits of the regime game shift for domestic political actors, creating stronger incentives for transitions to competitive regimes. Where the United States and the Organization of American States (OAS) adamantly oppose the breakdown of competitive regimes, potential coup leaders and their supporters face higher costs.

International actors exercise indirect as well as direct effects on regime change. For example, external influences may affect domestic actors' radicalization and commitment to democracy, which in turn affect regime outcomes.[18] International actors also influence domestic actors' calculations about their policy benefits under different regimes. For example, if international actors threaten to impose sanctions against dictatorships, most domestic actors will typically lower their expectations regarding their policy benefits under authoritarian rule.

---

[18] There is a related body of work on the impact of the international diffusion of ideas on social policy. See Meseguer (2002) and Weyland (2006).

In addition to operating indirectly, international actors sometimes have direct impacts on political regimes. For example, U.S. or OAS military actions led to transitions to competitive regimes in Panama in 1990 and Haiti in 1995 and 2006. The U.S. invasion of the Dominican Republic in 1965 helped maintain an authoritarian regime in power. On several occasions, including Honduras in 1983, Bolivia in 1984, and Peru in 1989, the United States lobbied against military coups and might have thereby directly influenced regime outcomes.

We summarize these five core empirical arguments as follows:

1. Policy radicalization makes a breakdown of a competitive regime more likely.
2. A normative preference for democracy by important actors (e.g., parties, leaders, the government) makes a transition to a competitive regime more likely.
3. A normative preference for democracy by important actors makes a breakdown of a competitive regime less likely.
4. A regional political environment favorable to democracy makes transitions to competitive regimes more likely.
5. A regional political environment favorable to democracy makes breakdowns of competitive regimes less likely.

None of these empirical arguments is surprising or counterintuitive. The originality of our work rests in an attempt to integrate these arguments through an actor-based theory on regime change and stability and on how we develop and test the theory.

Like all theories about highly complex political realities, ours simplifies reality. Its purpose is not to capture all the complexities of regime change and survival, but rather to call attention to a few highly important issues within an integrated theoretical framework.

TESTING THE THEORY

Most work on political regimes has chosen between extensive and intensive testing. We undertake both kinds of testing because both give us different kinds of leverage for understanding the emergence, stabilization, and fall of democracies and dictatorships.

We followed two overarching principles about testing the theory. First, quantitative evidence across a broad range of cases should support the theory. When it is possible to measure theoretically important independent and dependent variables in a reasonably efficient and valid manner, quantitative analysis is a useful beginning point to assess the causal impact of the independent variables. Otherwise, there is no good way of knowing how extensively a theory travels. In addition, the quantitative analysis tests a wider range of alternative explanations more rigorously for a broader range of countries than our qualitative evidence.

The quantitative analysis in Chapter 4 provides this *extensive* test of our theory. It tests whether our theory holds up for a large number of observations (twenty Latin American countries for 1945–2005, for a total of 1,220 country-years). In the quantitative analysis, the dependent variable is whether a regime breaks down or survives in a given year. Over the course of a decade of research, we collected information on a wide variety of independent variables to test our theory and several competing theoretical approaches to regime change and survival. The dataset contains several original variables (including our regime classification, a novel indicator of U.S. policies toward Latin America, and new indicators of actors' radicalism and normative regime preferences) with varying time coverage beginning in 1900 and ending in 2010. Because of data limitations, our quantitative explanation focuses exclusively on the period since 1945. The quantitative testing is indispensable for seeing how far in space and time a theory travels – that is, for assessing its generality and its scope conditions (Goldthorpe 1991; King et al. 1994).

Our second principle for testing is that structured case studies must fit the theory. Theory building is facilitated by detailed case knowledge (Capoccia and Ziblatt 2010). With large macro processes such as the rise and fall of political regimes, it is not sufficient that quantitative evidence line up behind a hypothesis or a theory. With such processes, several competing accounts could explain the same quantitative findings. Theory that is not informed by the reality of cases is therefore more prone to misunderstand large macro causal processes. The combination of quantitative and qualitative analysis is far better than either alone.

In Chapters 5 and 6 we employ qualitative case studies of Argentina and El Salvador to provide *intensive* testing of our theory. Structured case analyses are an essential part of our testing process for five reasons. First, because structured qualitative case analysis allows for attention to sequences, it is useful for assessing causal mechanisms. Sequences and actors' interactions can help disentangle mechanisms that are not clear on the basis of regression analyses. We can analyze what precipitated regime change or "reequilibration" (Linz 1978b) at crucial historical moments.

Second, the structured case studies enable us to examine interactions among actors. Such interactions are decisive in regime outcomes. Although the quantitative analysis in Chapter 4 provides an essential test of important parts of the theory and of competing explanations, it does not test hypotheses about interactions among actors. For example, in Argentina, from 1930 until 1976, the lack of a normative preference for democracy was mutually reinforcing among actors. President Juan Perón's (1946–55) authoritarian proclivities and radical tendencies generated deep hostility and reinforced radicalism in much of the anti-Peronist camp from 1946 to 1966. Likewise, after 1983, the building of a normative preference for democracy was mutually reinforcing among actors. It is very difficult to capture such interactions in a quantitative analysis involving twenty countries over a long period of time.

Third, part of our theory addresses the formation and dissolution of regime coalitions. The structured qualitative cases help illuminate and test this part of our theory. The case studies revolve centrally around the formation of winning regime coalitions and the stability or lack thereof that results from those coalitions. This key part of the theory is difficult to test quantitatively.

Fourth, the variables for actors' normative regime preferences present challenging problems of endogeneity. Do actors' normative preferences cause regime change, or does regime change causes actors' normative preferences? These problems are both statistical and substantive. We address the econometric problems in Chapters 3 and 4, and the structured qualitative cases in Chapters 5 and 6 also help untangle these problems of endogeneity. They also illustrate more clearly than the quantitative analysis why normative preferences for democracy or dictatorship are important in understanding regime change and stability.

Fifth, the structured case studies allow us to scale down to the level of political actors in each historical period. We can then study actors' attitudes toward democracy and dictatorship and their radicalism or moderation in more detail. These issues create questions of internal validity for which a case study can be particularly enlightening (Gerring 2007: 43–48). The case studies also enable us to explore the actors' reasons for a low normative preference for democracy and radicalization. Such information allows us to reconstruct historical causal sequences that lead to regime breakdown or stability.

We draw on the rich tradition of qualitative research that has enriched the analysis of why democracies emerge (R. Collier 1999; Huntington 1991; Levine 1973, 1978, 1989; O'Donnell, Schmitter, and Whitehead 1986; Rueschemeyer, Stephens, and Stephens 1992; J. S. Valenzuela 1985; Yashar 1997), consolidate or fail to (Linz and Stepan 1996), and stabilize or break down (Capoccia 2005; D. Collier 1979; Figueiredo 1993; Linz and Stepan 1978; O'Donnell 1973; Potter 1981; Santos 1986). We part paths from most of this tradition by (1) trying to be more systematic in coding actors and our core independent variables; (2) working with a larger number of country cases (twenty) than most qualitative studies; and (3) using quantitative analysis to test the extension of our theory beyond the qualitative cases.

The number of countries that we study – the twenty countries of Latin America – occupies an uncommon intermediate niche in regime studies. A majority of the work on political regimes involves a small number of countries, most often one or two, and most of the rest is quantitative work based on a larger number of countries. One of the least developed strategies in studies on political regimes is the intermediate-N strategy (in terms of the number of countries) that we pursue. Region-wide studies of democratization that are sensitive to intra-regional differences are uncommon (for an exception, see Bratton and van de Walle 1997).[19] Both the intermediate-N strategy and the regional research

---

[19] Many works focus on differences across a few cases in a given region, but few simultaneously take a region as a whole and evince a strong interest in intra-regional differences.

design, which in principle are discrete but in our case are combined, are useful compliments to the large-N and small-N studies that dominate regime studies.

This intermediate niche has distinctive advantages. The much larger number of countries and observations than single-country case studies enables us to test hypotheses in a more systematic and extensive manner than a single country or a few countries would allow. The twenty countries display considerable variance in regime types across countries and over time, and offer a broad range of conditions in terms of the independent (and control) variables for this study. At the same time, the number of countries is sufficiently small that we know a reasonable amount about regime dynamics in a majority of them. This knowledge helps generate hypotheses and informs the understanding of causal mechanisms. The mixed quantitative/qualitative, intermediate-N strategy pursued here is not superior to other alternatives, but it is an underutilized strategy that yields distinctive benefits. We try to bridge the gap between qualitative area studies and large-N research through close knowledge of some cases for intensive testing and a more extensive test of hypotheses provided by a quantitative design.

CASE SELECTION FOR QUALITATIVE CASES

In this section, we first discuss why we chose two countries for our qualitative cases as opposed to looking at a similar number of transitions, breakdowns, and regime survivals in a larger number of countries. We then explain the logic for choosing Argentina and El Salvador.

The need to examine actors' interactions and use structured case studies to understand sequences and causal mechanisms precluded a qualitative analysis of more than a small number of cases and dictated a strategy of treating these cases in enough detail to support our primary claims. In light of these considerations, we focus on two country studies over time rather than selecting breakdowns and transitions from a larger number of countries.

The logic of our qualitative analysis of Argentina and El Salvador rests primarily on understanding interactions among actors, processes, and sequences to understand regime outcomes. Because within-country observations allow for close examination of processes, interactions, and sequences, it is generally easier to identify causal mechanisms than in cross-country comparisons. Within-country observations have far less variance in most control variables than observations across countries and thus help clarify which independent variables account for the change in the dependent variable. Finally, given the extensive historiography, focusing on two countries allowed for greater coverage of the secondary literature and for better case knowledge than would have been possible had we chosen the same number of breakdowns, transitions, and stabilizations but with a larger number of countries.

Within-country observations are ideal for process tracing – for close attention to sequences and causal mechanisms (D. Collier 1993; Collier, Brady, and

Seawright 2004: 250–64; Collier, Mahoney, and Seawright 2004; George and Bennett 2004: 204–32; Mahoney 2003: 360–67). Within-country analysis reduces the number of explanatory variables because many change slowly and hence do not explain short-term variations in the dependent variable. We increase the number of observations by looking at multiple administrations within each country. This combination of a smaller number of explanatory variables and multiple within-country observations ameliorates the well-known concern about the indeterminate research design in many small-N studies: many variables, few cases (Lijphart 1971: 685–91). In within-country qualitative analysis, the logic of causal inference is not reducible to a cross-country comparative method based on a small number of observations – a method that is vulnerable to deep weaknesses in causal logic. Unless it is accompanied by within-country process tracing, it is difficult in small-N cross national comparison to weigh competing explanations (Collier, Brady, and Seawright 2004; George and Bennett 2004: 153–66; Goldthorpe 1991; King et al. 1994: 199–207).

In the post-1977 wave of democratization in Latin America, there have been two dramatic changes relative to earlier periods. First, many countries that earlier went through cycles of democratic breakdowns and transitions back to competitive political regimes become stable democracies. Eight countries in the region had at least three breakdowns since 1900: Peru (with seven transitions and six breakdowns), Argentina (six transitions and five breakdowns), Panama (five transitions and five breakdowns), Ecuador, Honduras (five transitions and four breakdowns each), Uruguay, Costa Rica (four transitions and three breakdowns each), and Chile (three transitions and three breakdowns). Notwithstanding the breakdowns in Peru in 1992 and Honduras in 2009, as a group, these countries have been vastly less prone to breakdowns of competitive regimes since 1978 than they were before then.

Second, eight countries have shifted from deep authoritarian pasts, with little (and short-lived) or no prior experience with competitive regimes, to having stable competitive regimes in the post-1977 period. This includes Bolivia, whose experience of competitive regimes before 1978 was limited to the 1956–64 period; the Dominican Republic, which was semi-democratic from 1924 to 1928[20]; El Salvador, which had no experience of a competitive regime until 1984; Guatemala, which was semi-democratic from 1926 until 1931 and from 1945 to 1954; Haiti, which never had a competitive political regime until the one that broke down after a few months in 1991; Mexico, which was semi-democratic from 1911 to 1913 but otherwise authoritarian until 1988; Nicaragua, which was semi-democratic from 1929 to 1936 but then had authoritarian regimes until 1984; and Paraguay, which had dictatorships steadily until

---

[20] The Dominican Republic also had a very short-lived competitive regime for seven months from February to September 1963, but it did not reach our threshold of surviving until December 31 of the year in which it was inaugurated.

1989. Except for Haiti, these countries have gone from largely unchecked and often brutal histories of dictatorship before the third wave of democratization to competitive regimes after the transitions.

The story of the third wave is largely the story of these two sets of countries.[21] Accordingly, we chose two countries that together exemplify the most common regime patterns in twentieth-century Latin America: one (Argentina) that had many breakdowns before the third wave and has been steadily democratic during the third wave, and one (El Salvador) that has shifted from persistent authoritarianism before the third wave to a durable competitive regime. Sixteen of the twenty countries in Latin America squarely fit one of these two patterns.

Argentina had experienced chronic instability of both competitive and authoritarian regimes between 1930 and 1983, including five breakdowns of competitive regimes during this period. We address two questions. First, why did competitive regimes consistently break down before 1983 despite many favorable social and economic conditions? Second, what explains the dramatic change from the chronic breakdown of competitive regimes until 1976 to democratic survival in the period since 1983?

Chapter 6 focuses on El Salvador and asks the opposite questions. What explains persistent authoritarianism for almost the entire twentieth century until 1984? How did a country with a history of consistent and often brutal authoritarianism overcome daunting obstacles and experience a transition to a competitive political regime? Why did this regime fend off threats and become stable? Whereas Chapter 5 explains repeated breakdowns in Argentina during much of the twentieth century and the absence of breakdowns after 1983, Chapter 6 explains the absence of transitions in El Salvador during most of the twentieth century and the occurrence of a transition after 1984.

Although we present detailed qualitative evidence about only two country cases, our analysis was informed by reading about a much larger number of countries and by doing some fieldwork at some point in our careers in twelve countries in the region: Argentina, Bolivia, Brazil, Chile, Colombia, Costa Rica, Ecuador, Mexico, Paraguay, Peru, Uruguay, and Venezuela. This fieldwork enhanced our understanding of these national realities.

LATIN AMERICA AND THEORY DEVELOPMENT

If we cast our argument as a somewhat general theory of regime change and survival, why should we focus on a single region of the world? We have two theoretical and one pragmatic reason for following this strategy.

---

[21] The remaining four countries are Brazil, Colombia, Cuba, and Venezuela. Brazil and Colombia had only one breakdown, so they did not follow the more common pattern of multiple breakdowns. Cuba and Venezuela are exceptions because as of this writing they have authoritarian regimes.

First, as we argued elsewhere, regions have particular dynamics and political processes that are specific to those regions (Mainwaring and Pérez-Liñán 2007). Social science generalizations that are based on large-N, cross-regional, or worldwide units of analysis must be attentive to these regional specificities (Bunce 1995, 1998, 2000). Otherwise, social scientists will generalize where they should not. Causal inferences based on a worldwide sample could lead to a misleading understanding of what factors promote democratization in some regions. Different regions may present distinctive and *systematic* causal patterns that an assumption of worldwide causal homogeneity would obscure. The effect is more substantial and hence the need for caution is greater when entire regions of the world rather than simply a few countries are exceptions to a generalization.

Consider the finding in Chapter 4 that the level of development does not affect the probability of transitions to or breakdowns of competitive regimes. The fact that modernization theory does not hold for a wide income range in Latin America between 1945 and 2005 is important, and it suggests a likely pattern of causal heterogeneity by region. Even though *on average*, wealthier countries are more likely to transition to democracy and less likely to establish dictatorships (Przeworski et al. 2000), the causal effect of economic development may differ across regions in the same broad band of levels of development. Particular causal factors may have heterogeneous effects in different regions of the world. Therefore, an analysis that overlooks regional patterns may impose a misleading assumption of causal homogeneity (Mainwaring and Pérez-Liñán 2003; 2007).

A conventional response to this argument is that regions represent "proper names" that should be replaced by "variable names" in the analysis. In principle we agree, but until all the variables that define regional patterns in world politics are thoroughly identified (which is an extraordinarily difficult task), an assumption of causal homogeneity across regions may induce greater bias in the results of an empirical analysis than the assumption of causal heterogeneity at the regional level.

Second, as we emphasize throughout this book, political developments in one country influence regimes in other countries of the same region. Regions are more than labels for arbitrary sets of countries; they identify geographic networks defined by spatial and cultural proximity. In Chapters 4 and 7, we show that it is impossible to understand regime outcomes without emphasizing region-wide factors. Analyses that fail to consider regional influences would overstate the importance of domestic factors, conclude that regime change and survival are highly idiosyncratic processes, or perhaps commit both mistakes.

Regime change has occurred in region-wide waves: a first wave of democratization from 1902 to 1911; a second wave from 1938 to 1946, a counterwave from 1948 to 1955; a third wave of democratization from 1956 to 1958, another counterwave from 1962 to 1977; and finally, the post-1977 wave of democratization. In Chapters 4 and 7, we show that region-wide influences account for this wave-like behavior. To explain the vicissitudes of democracy and authoritarian regimes, idiosyncratic factors come into play in every country, but there nevertheless have been distinctive region-wide trends, including the post-1977 trend toward democracy. To understand political regimes, we therefore must examine both region-wide trends and explanations *and* country-specific processes.

It is impossible to understand regime outcomes by focusing only on individual countries or only on global trends. Political regimes were traditionally a subject matter for comparative political scientists who focused on domestic processes, but regime dynamics are not exclusively domestically driven. Both because of regional specificities and because of distinctive intra-regional influences, social scientists and historians must be attentive to the importance of regions in politics. International influences on political regimes are especially important within regions (Gleditsch 2002). If we always treat countries as the unit of analysis and fail to pay attention to regional effects and dynamics, we will miss these regional effects and as a result will fail to understand causal processes.

While advocating the importance of regions in comparative politics, we reject the assumption that Latin America is relatively homogeneous in a descriptive sense (i.e., that variance in fundamental conditions across countries in the region is small), and we reject gross generalizations about regions as a whole unless there is empirical evidence to support them.[22] Our approach looks at regional influences, but it treats the countries within the region as distinct. In Chapter 4, we treat each country differently by virtue of assigning each one a different score for most independent variables and for the dependent variable for a given year. We believe that this is the way that regions of the world should be studied. Latin America has important common trends and influences, but it also has huge cross-country differences in everything from political regimes to the level of development. For example, in 2005, Argentina had a per capita GDP of $5,721 in 2000 dollars, more than fifteen times greater than Haiti's ($379), which was one of the lowest in the world outside of sub-Saharan Africa (World Bank 2007). Similarly, seven countries (Argentina, Brazil, Chile, Colombia, Costa Rica, Uruguay, and Venezuela) had lengthy experiences of democracy before 1978 while a handful of others had histories of continuous or nearly continuous dictatorships late into the twentieth century (El Salvador, Haiti, Mexico, Nicaragua, and Paraguay). Our research design is predicated on recognizing these differences across cases and within cases over time.

Our empirical focus on one region does not entail a position against broader generalizations in social science research. We adopt an intermediate position: generalizations are important, but there are few truly universal findings in analyses of political regimes.[23] Most generalizations in social science are

---

[22] Broad generalizations about Latin America as a whole characterize some works that emphasize Iberian political culture.

[23] Universal findings are expected to hold for most representative samples of the same population, but the definition of the population is itself an analytical task (Ragin 2000: 43–63). For instance, "universal" may simply refer to all U.S. voters in the second half of the twentieth century.

bounded by geographic or historical contexts.[24] Regional specificities are not the only way to bound generalizations in social science, but because regions are large parts of the world with distinctive dynamics and intra-regional influences, delimiting some analyses and generalizations by regions is useful. We do not claim that regions should be the primary unit of analysis in comparative politics or that analysis of regions is superior to other research designs. But regions *are* substantively important, and the reasons for this importance have been under-articulated in political science. For developing and testing theories about regime change, it is substantively useful to examine regions.

We also have a pragmatic reason to focus on Latin America. Even though our theory of regime change should travel beyond Latin America, a focus on one region allows for testing hypotheses using better-quality data for a longer historical period, without assuming that some indicators (e.g., U.S. policy toward democracy) would have an equivalent effect in other regions of the world. We coded political regimes in the twenty Latin American countries between 1900 and 2010, and also identified and coded the normative and policy preferences of 1,460 political actors throughout the region from 1944 to 2010. Much of the critical information collected for this project involved labor-intensive coding of political regimes and actors. Nothing remotely similar to this coding of actors is available for other regions. The use of more conventional, readily available indicators would have allowed us to expand the geographic scope of our tests, but would have undermined the validity of the indicators and thus the interpretation of the results.

Consistent with a perspective that emphasizes regional influences and dynamics while underscoring the specificity of individual countries, we deal with two different levels of analysis: countries and Latin America as a region. Our primary analysis of the rise, survival, and fall of political regimes takes place at the country level. However, region-wide actors and influences affect country level actors, processes, and regime outcomes. At the country level of analysis, our theoretical puzzle is to explain the rise, survival, and fall of regimes. At the regional level, it is to explain waves of democratization and authoritarianism. The regional trend is the mere aggregation of country outcomes, but country patterns in turn are influenced by what takes place in the region.

Analysts have used a variety of different theoretical approaches and independent variables to explain why democracy exists in some countries but not others. Many factors affect the likelihood that democracy will exist. One final advantage of focusing on Latin America is that it holds constant a few such factors: predominant religious preference, presidential systems, and Iberian colonial experience (except for Haiti). These commonalities reduce the number of independent variables and thus facilitate the explanatory process.

---

[24] For an excellent example of how presumably universal findings may be historically bounded, see Boix and Stokes (2003) on the historically changing relationship between the level of development and democracy.

PLAN FOR THE BOOK

Chapter 2 outlines our theory of regime change and durability in more detail. Chapter 3 discusses waves of regime change in Latin America from 1900 to 2010. It describes the evolution of our dependent variable over time, focusing on periods of expansion and contraction of democracy. This chapter also addresses the measurement of our main independent variables. We introduce novel indicators of normative regime preferences, radicalism, and international conditions, and discuss the historical evolution of those factors for our sample of twenty countries. In the last part of the chapter we treat actors' normative preferences as an endogenous explanatory variable, showing that dominant preferences may be influenced by incumbent regimes, but they are not a mere reflection of structural conditions.

Chapters 4, 5, and 6 test the theory. Chapter 4 presents a quantitative analysis of the twenty Latin American countries for the 1945–2005 period. A set of survival models allow us to reconstruct the probability of transitions and breakdowns in particular countries and years, and also the overall wave of democratization experienced by the region after 1977.

Chapters 5 and 6 present intensive tests of the theory through qualitative case studies. Chapter 5 examines Argentina, which had chronic breakdowns of competitive regimes before 1978 despite many favorable circumstances and has enjoyed a democracy without breakdown since 1983 despite many unfavorable circumstances. Decreased radicalism, an increase in commitment to democracy, and a more favorable international environment have been crucial in Argentina's post-1983 political transformation. In Chapter 6, we trace the reasons for the breakdown of the traditional very powerful authoritarian coalition and the emergence of a democratic coalition in El Salvador in the 1980s and early 1990s.

Chapter 7 further explores the mechanisms behind our finding that international actors and influences are an important explanation of regime outcomes. This finding has become common in regime studies since 1986, but the mechanisms behind it are not clear in the existing literature. We discuss six mechanisms that help explain the impact of international actors on regime outcomes: (1) the preferences of actors regarding political regimes and policy diffuse across country borders to domestic actors, generating an indirect mechanism of influence on political regimes; (2) domestic actors in one country draw inspiration from events in another country (demonstration effects); (3) international actors sway domestic actors to join a regime coalition; (4) international actors provide resources to strengthen some actors; (5) international actors such as the Catholic Church simultaneously function as domestic actors, and as domestic actors they influence regime outcomes; and (6) international military interventions. The combination of quantitative testing in Chapter 4 and qualitative analysis in Chapters 5, 6, and 7 enable us to add to the existing literature on regional influences on political regimes.

Chapter 8 explores the implications of our theoretical conclusions for the current (and future) direction of Latin American regimes. It describes regional tendencies in the evolution of political regimes after the third-wave transitions. To an unprecedented degree, competitive regimes have survived during this time. However, an analysis of the levels of democracy achieved by those competitive regimes after 1978 indicates, alongside many striking advances, two different problems in the region: democratic stagnation and democratic erosion. Some countries had relatively low levels of democracy after their transitions to competitive politics, and they have been unable to improve significantly over the past three decades. Other countries are experiencing an erosion of political rights and civil liberties.

Current democratic stagnation is partially anchored in historical legacies. In countries where political actors lacked a normative preference for democracy before 1978, they failed to invest in the development of institutions (competitive parties, independent courts, and civic-minded security forces) important for building high-quality democracy. By contrast, democratic erosion is related to more recent trends. Governments in Venezuela (since 1999), Bolivia (2006), Ecuador (2007), and Nicaragua (2007) have revitalized the somewhat radical forces in the region, and they have fostered intransigence in some sectors of the right. Regional political influences are more supportive of leftist radicalism that does not embrace (and often even opposes) liberal democracy. During most of the period since 2001, the United States emphasized antiterrorism more than human rights as the focus of its foreign policy, weakening the credibility of democracy promotion efforts. Because of the opposition of some leftist presidents with dubious democratic credentials to OAS interventions, the OAS cannot act as coherently as it did during the 1990s on behalf of democracy. We test those arguments using a latent growth curve model for levels of democratization in nineteen post-transition countries during the contemporary period.

Chapter 9 discusses the implications of our findings for alternative theoretical approaches to explaining regime change and survival. The Latin American experience creates doubts about some prominent existing theoretical approaches to political regimes: modernization theory, class theory, theories based on economic performance, and theories based on political culture. The evidence presented in this book suggests that some prominent theories of political regimes are not convincing. We argue that a theory can help integrate some of the most important lessons about the emergence and fall of political regimes in ways that are consistent with the historical evidence about Latin America.

2

A Theory of Regime Survival and Fall

This chapter develops our theoretical approach to understanding regime change and survival. Our perspective is situated between structural and contingent action or agency approaches to studying political regimes. We emphasize the moderate or radical nature of actors' policy preferences, their value preferences about political regimes, and the impact of international influences and actors.

Our theory focuses on political organizations, organized movements, and presidents as the most powerful actors. We situate the domestic regime game within an international context. We link regime outcomes (survival and failure) with micro-conditions (the normative attitudes and policy preferences of concrete political actors). Our approach explicitly emphasizes political processes operating in the medium term. Although we do not deny the role of long-term historical factors, specific political actors are responsible for the actions that lead to regime change or survival.

MAKING THEORY USEFUL: ASSUMPTIONS

In our view, theories advance social science only if (1) their assumptions are realistic[1] and (2) they can generate testable hypotheses that are supported by the bulk of the empirical evidence. Theory generated from unrealistic assumptions easily generates unrealistic hypotheses and reaches distorted conclusions. Abstruse theory that does not guide empirical work or theory that is not supported by the evidence likewise fails to adequately explain regime outcomes.

---

[1] On this point, we disagree with Milton Friedman's (1953: 14) well-known position that assumptions need not be realistic. Unrealistic assumptions introduce false premises into an argument. As a result, the theory may be wrong even if its internal logic is correct and its empirical implications are true. The only way to minimize this kind of error is to embrace assumptions that are reasonably realistic.

On both accounts, existing structural and cultural theories of political regimes have shortcomings. On both accounts, we believe our theory holds up.

In this section, we articulate and defend the plausibility of five assumptions behind our theory.

1. Purposeful actors in pursuit of their interests determine regime outcomes.
2. In the era of mass politics, organizations such as political parties, militaries, labor unions and confederations, business associations, guerrilla groups, organized social movements, and heads of government are the most important actors.
3. Most actors are interested in a range of policy considerations, and some also have strong independent normative preferences regarding the political regime.
4. Actors' normative attitudes about political regimes or their policy moderation/radicalism cannot be reduced to their structural position in society.
5. Powerful organizations create some path dependence in political systems in policy moderation/radicalism and normative preferences about the political regime, but countries and individual actors can break from this path dependence.

First, purposeful actors in pursuit of their interests, not structures or cultures, determine regime outcomes. In this respect, we side with rational choice and other actor-centered approaches to politics. Actors have real choices about political regimes; their structural or cultural locations do not determine their regime preferences.

Of course, structures and cultures influence actors' choices of political regimes, and in some contexts, they exert a powerful influence. For example, at very high levels of development, in most countries all powerful actors prefer democracy to authoritarianism. Yet as the statistical analysis in Chapter 4 shows, across a very wide range of levels of development (from $378 to $8,211 in 2000 U.S. dollars), the level of development had no statistically significant effect on regime outcomes in Latin America over a long period of time (see also Acemoglu et al. 2008). For this very wide income band, the level of development does not explain regime outcomes in Latin America.

We agree in principle with Coppedge (2012: chapter 3) that a theory that focuses on more distant causal mechanisms is more satisfying than one that focuses on more proximate causal mechanisms. However, if a theory predicated on more distant causal mechanisms is problematic on empirical and other grounds, and if a theory that focuses on more proximate causal mechanisms provides considerable leverage, the latter is preferable. There is a legitimate space and need for developing theory aimed at very proximate causal mechanisms (Kuran 1989, 1991; Lohmann 1994), at intermediate causal mechanisms such as we engage in, and at more distant causal mechanisms. As we show in Chapters 3, 4, 5, 6, and 9, more distant structural and cultural causal explanations do not hold up well to empirical scrutiny for the Latin American cases.

Second, we make assumptions about what constitutes an actor. As we noted in Chapter 1, we focus on organizations, organized movements, and presidents. When we refer to organizations and organized movements as actors, we include both leaders and followers. Under democracy, the largest parties are important actors because they connect leaders and activists to party identifiers and other supporters. The direction set by the leaders influences activists, party identifiers, and other supporters. Conversely, party leaders derive some of their power from their support at different levels of the organization. Likewise, the military is often a powerful actor because the top brass controls soldiers who carry the guns. All organizations are hierarchical; in most, a relatively small number of individuals make the decisions that determine the organizations' location on our scale from policy moderation to radicalism and their normative preferences for democracy or dictatorship. Even so, leaders owe their position to support from below and must to some degree be responsive to those constituents. The preferences of the rank and file help shape organizational preferences and help determine who holds the leadership positions. Leaders without followers eventually lose their positions.

We treat the emergence of these organizations and their preferences as exogenous to and prior to our theory (although we address endogeneity in Chapters 3 through 6). We analyze causes of changes in actors' preferences, but we generally do not attempt to explain their preferences at the time when they emerge. This moment is an initial "critical juncture" prior to our theory (Collier and Collier 1991). All theories and all social science start with some priors.

Different theories of political regimes have differing views about how to conceptualize the actors. Class approaches tend to assume that the actors (classes) are constituted prior to the formation of organizations. In contrast, we view classes as an important background condition that influences the formation of organizations and movements. Classes per se only occasionally constitute actors.

Linz's (1978b) analysis of breakdowns and Kuran's (1989, 1991), Lohmann's (1994), and O'Donnell and Schmitter's (1986) analyses of transitions focus on regime coalitions rather than the actors per se. We initially focus instead on the actors that form regime coalitions. In this respect, our work is situated between structural approaches and contingent action or leader-focused approaches.

Third, we assume that both a wide range of policy considerations and actors' normative preferences regarding the political regime determine their choice of regime coalition. Conflicts about religion, nationality, and ethnicity are often central in regime outcomes. This assumption stands in contrast to work that reduces actors' interests to material outcomes. Considerable evidence sustains the assumption that actors are interested in a range of policy outcomes (i.e., policies about religion, education, nationality, ethnicity, cultural issues) that cannot be inferred from their material interests (Capoccia and Ziblatt 2010; Lijphart 1977; Sahlins 1976; J. S. Valenzuela 2001).

Prior research has shown that many individuals have normative preferences regarding the political regime and that these normative preferences are not reducible to other interests (Hofferbert and Klingemann 1999; Rose and Mishler 1996). An additional individual-level microfoundation for the argument about normative preferences is that people value procedures, not only outcomes (Benz and Stutzer 2003; Frey et al. 2004; Frey, Kucher, and Stutzer 2001; Frey and Stutzer 2005; Gangl 2003; Levi et al. 2009; Lind et al. 1993; Sen 1995, 1997; Stutzer and Frey 2006; Tyler 1990). As Frey et al. (2004: 383) argue, "Democracy can be expected to have positive procedural utility effects because it enhances individuals' perceptions of self-determination."[2] The extensive prior evidence about individuals' normative preferences and procedural utility helps justify our claim that some actors have normative preferences that affect regime outcomes (Berman 1998; Dahl 1971: 124–89; Ollier 2009).

Fourth, we assume that actors' normative attitudes about democracy and authoritarianism, as well as their policy preferences (moderation/radicalism), are not structurally determined or reducible to cultural dispositions based on religion, ethnicity, or colonial legacies. If actors' preferences could be explained largely on the basis of such structural conditions or broad cultural predispositions, these structural or cultural factors would be the core explanatory variables. However, as we show in Chapter 3, structural variables such as poverty and inequality do not go very far toward explaining preferences.

In addition, a tight relationship between actors' structural position and radicalism is not consistent with the fact that in many countries, most guerrilla leaders – the radical actor par excellence – are middle class (Moyano 1995: 109–13; Wickham-Crowley 1992: 23–28). Moreover, radicalism occurs in waves that are difficult to explain on the basis of structural variables. If actors' structural position, the country's level of development, or the level of inequality predicted actors' normative preferences regarding political regimes or their policy radicalism, we would focus on these variables on the grounds that theories that focus on more distant causes are more satisfying (Coppedge 2012: chapter 3). Of course, structural positions have *some* impact on actors' preferences.

Fifth, although we share with literature on path dependence the idea that organizational carriers are crucial to understanding political continuities (in our case, especially continuities in value preferences about political regimes and policy preferences), we depart from this literature in emphasizing that regime change and political upheaval create opportunities for strong breaks with the past. Traumatic events may induce changes in normative and policy preferences, and new actors may emerge in contexts of political upheaval. Both can generate new dynamics in normative and policy preferences. In addition, actors'

---

[2] The idea that political participation is an intrinsic good has a very long pedigree in the history of political thought, dating back to Aristotle's emphasis on political participation as a condition for human happiness.

normative orientations toward particular regimes and their policy preferences may adjust synchronically in response to the orientations and preferences of other actors in the domestic and international arenas.

The assumptions that underpin a theory inevitably privilege some perspectives on regime survival and fall at the expense of others. With the exception of international influences, our theory privileges factors that are relatively proximate to the dependent variable. Other potentially important influences on regime outcomes such as a country's state capacity (Linz and Stepan 1996; Mainwaring 2006; O'Donnell 1993, 2010), the nature of the prior political regime (Kitschelt et al. 1999; Linz and Stepan 1996), and so forth enter as background conditions whose effects operate through their influence on the independent variables at the core of our theory.

THE MACRO LEVEL: COMPETING REGIME COALITIONS

Our theory relies on a conventional assumption: political regimes survive when the most powerful actors in a society integrate a coalition that accepts the existing regime. They collapse when enough actors join an opposition bloc capable of overpowering those who defend the existing regime. This idea is common in the literature on regime survival and fall (Acemoglu and Robinson 2006; Boix 2003; Casper and Taylor 1996; Colomer 1991; Kuran 1989, 1991; Lohmann 1994; O'Donnell and Schmitter 1986; Przeworski 1986). If the status quo is an authoritarian regime, a powerful democratic coalition will induce regime change; if the status quo is a competitive regime, a powerful democratic coalition will create stability.

We begin with the simple idea of two competing coalitions, one that supports dictatorship and the other that supports a competitive regime. A regime coalition does not usually entail a formal agreement, but rather the effective convergence of actors in support of a competitive or authoritarian regime. In most historical situations, many actors remain on the sidelines.[3]

The competition between democratic and authoritarian coalitions is not always the most important battle about the political regime. Often, battles between different authoritarian coalitions are more important. In some historical settings, intense political competition took place between two radically opposed authoritarian views, for example, between the Marxist left and the Fascist right in late Weimar Germany, or between the Islamic fundamentalists and the shah's government in Iran in the late 1970s. In cases such as Germany under the Weimar Republic, Argentina from 1969 to 1976, and El Salvador from 1979 to 1992, in which two competing authoritarian coalitions are radically opposed to each other and are both very powerful, we analyze three

---

[3] Actors remain on the sidelines when the expected rewards – normative or material – of supporting any coalition minus the cost of mobilization are smaller than the advantages derived from neutrality.

coalitions rather than two. But because our book focuses on regime *types*, the competition between democratic and authoritarian coalitions is our primary concern. For the sake of simplicity in the exposition, we usually focus on the competition between the authoritarian and democratic coalitions. These coalitions are internally diverse.[4]

The political regime that prevails at a given place and time hinges on the balance of power among competing actors. In most times and places, most actors take the regime as a given. Regime change usually results from incumbents being replaced by new rulers who prefer a different regime, although in a few cases, incumbents changed the regime while still in office.[5] Transitions to competitive regimes occur when democratizing coalitions push previously dominant authoritarian coalitions to step down from power or to hold competitive elections. A transition can occur either because the coalition in favor of a competitive regime defeats the dictatorship or because it negotiates the authoritarians' withdrawal from power. Breakdowns of competitive regimes occur when the pro-regime coalition is overpowered by an authoritarian bloc. Competitive and authoritarian regimes survive when incumbents are replaced by leaders with a similar regime choice – or when they are not replaced at all, as occurs with long-lasting dictators.

Different actors use different resources in their quest for political power. The most important resources include money, the support of powerful individuals, arms and coercive power, votes, and support in public opinion. The leverage provided by these resources depends on the formal and informal rules that structure the competition for power. For example, votes and support in public opinion are always important in competitive regimes; they are somewhat less important in most authoritarian regimes.

As part of the competition, actors may challenge the rules that structure the struggle for power. In the absence of widely accepted (if not legitimate) rules regulating the competition for power, force usually trumps other resources. In such contexts, military capacity often becomes the decisive factor shaping the outcome.

---

[4] For valuable ways of conceptualizing intra-coalition differences in authoritarian regimes, see O'Donnell (1979); O'Donnell and Schmitter (1986); Przeworski (1991: 51–99). These three works distinguish between hard-liners and soft-liners in the authoritarian coalition and between moderates and maximalists in the opposition. Linz (1978a, 1978b) distinguished between the loyal, semi-loyal, and disloyal opposition under democratic regimes. These more differentiated portrayals of regime coalitions are useful complements to our theoretical model.

[5] A few breakdowns of competitive regimes occurred when the president violated the constitutional order to impose a dictatorship. Examples in modern Latin America include Perón in Argentina in the 1950s, Bordaberry in Uruguay in 1973, and Fujimori in Peru in 1992. Similarly, some authoritarian regimes held and won relatively free and fair elections, thus creating a new competitive regime. The Sandinistas in Nicaragua in 1984 and the revolutionary Bolivian regime in 1956 are examples. The Sandinistas took power in 1979 in an uprising but first held competitive elections in 1984. The Movimiento Nacionalista Revolucionario (MNR) took power in 1952 but first held competitive elections in 1956.

THE MICRO LEVEL: POLICY AND NORMATIVE
REGIME PREFERENCES

Political actors support the coalition that is most likely to satisfy their demands for two types of outcomes: a broad range of policy outcomes (economic, social, cultural, educational, religious, etc.), which are important to all actors; and normative preferences about the political regime, which are important to some actors.[6] Value preferences about the political regime could be seen as policy preferences of a higher order,[7] but for analytical purposes we distinguish between policy preferences and a normative preference for a certain kind of regime. Normative regime preferences are a source of "procedural utility."

The normative regime dimension does not refer to the specific content of routine policy decisions. However, the procedures embedded in the political regime affect the likelihood that certain policies will be adopted (e.g., the over-representation of poor states favors some policy outcomes; activist judicial review favors others) and therefore may be inimical to some policy outcomes. The regime alters the probability of different leaders coming to office and thus shapes the probability of future policy outcomes.

Different actors in different historical moments weight value preferences about the regime and instrumental policy outcomes differently. Some actors are motivated exclusively by their instrumental policy preferences. They do not have value preferences about the political regime. Linz's (1978a: 149) account of the Spanish parties during the short-lived democracy of 1931–36 provides a clear example of actors whose instrumental policy preferences trumped any normative commitment to a democratic regime: "With the exception of minor parties, all parties, even the less radical ones, were loyal to a democratic regime and constitutional procedures only so long as certain values they held higher than democracy could be pursued within the democratic framework."[8]

We can represent the utility of any regime r for an actor j as a function of policy *and* normative regime preferences, such that $u_j(r) = n_j(r) - \rho_j (x_j - x_r)^2$, where $n_j(r)$ is the (normative) value assigned by the actor to the particular regime (positive if the actor sees the regime as desirable, negative if undesirable, and zero if the actor is indifferent), x_j indicates the policy preference of actor j, x_r is the policy output under the regime, and $\rho_j \geq 1$ indicates the degree of policy radicalism. Following the convention, we have represented policy preferences as single-peaked and subject to quadratic loss (Shapiro 1969). The more distant the policy is from the

---

[6] Along related lines, Magaloni (2006: 175–92) argues that in the 1990s, Mexican parties competed on two dimensions: a regime dimension (democracy versus authoritarian) and a policy dimension that can be mapped on the left-right scale.

[7] Value preferences about the political regime involve policies about how to make policies. In this sense, they are higher-level policies.

[8] Along similar lines, Rouquié (1982b: 341) described the lack of normative commitment to democracy in Argentina between 1943 and 1973: "All political forces prioritized defeating the adversary in power over respecting the institutions."

ideal point in the one-dimensional policy space, the greater the loss suffered by the actor. However, the location of actors in the policy space may be less relevant for their regime choices than their radicalism. We return to this point later.

Differences in policy preferences lead to conflict about the regime when some actors conclude that their policy goals cannot be pursued under the incumbent regime, and that the cost of such a limitation is unacceptable. This problem arises under two situations. First, if some actors want an immediate change of the policy status quo, the compromise and negotiation demanded in competitive regimes may become unsatisfactory. Second, if some actors believe that the incumbent regime will impose irreversible or very costly policy changes to the status quo, they may conclude that the regime is no longer acceptable.

Radical and Moderate Policy Preferences

Our first hypothesis (H1) is that *radical actors increase the risk of breakdown of a competitive regime.* In Chapter 1, we defined radical preferences as intense policy preferences located toward a pole of the policy spectrum. Disputes over policy are most likely to produce conflict about the political regime when some actors have radical preferences. Radicalism translates into an urgency to achieve policy goals in the short to medium term where they do not represent the status quo or into an intransigent defense of these positions where they represent the status quo. In the extreme, it can lead to the use of violence as the ultimate recourse to impose or defend policy preferences.

The government or opposition actors can embrace radical policy preferences. Government policies oriented toward imposing major shifts – toward the left or the right – in the short run without negotiations with the opposition indicate transformative radicalism. Similarly, intransigence in the defense of highly controversial policies, rejecting as a matter of principle an open policy debate, indicates reactionary radicalism. Radical governments are willing, sometimes even *inclined*, to pursue policies that are highly polarizing.[9] These policies tend to create two adversarial camps, one offering strong support and another one offering intense opposition to the measures. If some sectors find government policies costly, radical governments dismiss such criticism as proof of the low moral standing of their critics and of the righteousness of their policies.

Governments with radical preferences face a distinctive dilemma under competitive regimes. If they are radically conservative (i.e., unwilling to admit changes to the status quo), the competitive regime serves their policy goals only as far as no major political party or social movement questions the policies they deem sacred. As soon as this happens, the government confronts the choice of either submitting the controversial policies to the competitive process or limiting the scope of competition to insulate those policies and therefore undermining democracy.

---

[9] Corrales (2011) argues that Hugo Chávez seemingly deliberately used polarization as a political strategy.

Radical governments seeking deep social change confront a similar challenge. Under normal conditions, when important parties and social organizations defend the status quo, the institutions of a competitive regime (the legislative opposition, the courts, subnational governments, and the independent media) impose restrictions and delays in the pursuit of a government's radical policy goals. Radical presidents are thus forced to bargain with the opposition or to undercut the institutions that work as veto players, thus undermining democracy. The latter response often triggers polarization: confronted with government intransigence, many opponents conclude that policy costs will be irreversible and embrace conservative radicalism. The government in turn denounces these sectors as the very reactionary forces that justify its push for radical change. As powerful actors perceive a significant threat to their interests in the incumbent regime's policies, their support for the regime wanes, and they become more likely to join an authoritarian coalition.[10] Some sectors may defend moderate positions, but the escalation of radical preferences rewards intransigent elites on both sides. Moderates may not "abdicate," as Linz (1978b) concluded in his classic study of breakdowns; they are simply displaced from their central role in history by the march of events.[11]

Radical policy preferences on the part of the opposition also have the potential to undermine democracy. Radical opposition groups may pose a serious threat to the interests of some powerful actors, affecting their calculations about the desirability of maintaining the regime. To protect their interests, the entrenched actors may subvert the competitive regime in order to preempt radical elites from dictating policy.

For instance, in Latin America in the 1960s and 1970s, the emergence of revolutionary leftist groups provoked a powerful counterreaction from the right, leading to the breakdown of competitive regimes. The growth of the left contributed to the breakdown of competitive regimes by inspiring fear in the right in Brazil in 1964 (Benevides 1981; Cohen 1994; Figueiredo 1993; Santos 1986), Chile in 1973 (A. Valenzuela 1978), Uruguay in 1973, Argentina in 1976 (De Riz 1987; Viola 1982), and Peru in 1992.

Whether it originates in the government or in the opposition, policy radicalism on one side of the spectrum tends to breed symmetrical responses on the other side, with consequences for competitive regimes. Radical preferences often pose a threat to some powerful actors. Where this is the case, it is more difficult to preserve competitive political regimes (Bermeo 1997). Conversely, if actors believe that a competitive regime is unlikely to impose major permanent losses,

---

[10] Cohen (1994), Figueiredo (1993), and Santos (1986) called attention to the role of radicalization and the conservative establishment's sense of threat in the breakdown of democracy in Brazil in 1964. See Linz (1978b) on radicalization and the breakdown in Spain in 1936 and Yashar (1997) on the impact of radicalization on the breakdown in Guatemala in 1954.

[11] In the qualitative case studies (Chapters 5 and 6), we argue that such a marginalization occurred with the centrist Radical Party in Argentina during the failed democracy of 1973–76 and with the Christian Democratic Party in El Salvador in the late 1980s.

they are more likely to accept democratic politics. Where uncertainty about the consequences of competitive politics is great and the perceived costs might be high because of radical actors, the likelihood that competitive regimes can survive diminishes (Bermeo 1997; Figueiredo 1993; Levine 1973).

Leftist or rightist preferences by themselves are not a problem for competitive regimes. Some actors hold leftist or rightist preferences as long-term objectives. If political actors, even those that are very unsatisfied with the current status quo, are willing to pursue policy goals over a long period of time, they may eschew radicalism in favor of progressive reformism, betting on the accumulation of moderate policy changes over the long run. This was Eduard Bernstein's (1850–1932) strategy for achieving socialism, embraced by the Swedish Social Democrats from an early time (Berman 1998).

From the early 1940s (the popular front era) until 1959 (the Cuban revolution), the communist parties in many Latin American countries combined far left policy long-term objectives and moderate short-term behavior. Their leftist policy preferences and their quest for revolution in the medium term made them a *somewhat* radical actor – more so than the Swedish Social Democrats because they were positioned further to the left and had more intense policy preferences, but not as radical as the revolutionary guerrilla left, which pursued similar long-term objectives but with a much greater sense of immediacy.

Our hypothesis about radicalism is different from Sartori's (1976) well-known argument about polarization in *Parties and Party Systems: A Framework for Analysis*. Sartori posited that democracies with polarized party systems are more vulnerable to breakdown than other democracies. He defined polarization as the ideological distance among relevant parties and asserted that democracy is more difficult to sustain when ideological differences are more intense (see also Sani and Sartori 1983).

We modify Sartori's argument in two ways. First, we examine a broader range of actors, not only parties. Second, we qualify his argument about ideological distance. Democracies with polarized party systems regularly survive and thrive. In their 1983 article, Sani and Sartori identified Spain, Italy, France, and Finland as Western European countries with polarized party systems, yet democracy as a regime type has been stable in all four countries. Sartori (1976: 159–63) was right to point to the perils of polarization in Chile (1970–73), but Chilean democracy survived and recorded many achievements despite persistent party system polarization from 1932 until 1970.

What explains why polarization contributes to breakdown in some cases but is unproblematic in others? The key issue is radicalism, that is, the intransigence and the urgency of actors with policy preferences toward the left or right of the spectrum. Radical actors are not willing to defer their quest to achieve policy objectives into the distant future. Conversely, when actors are willing to achieve their policy objectives over an extended period, we do not expect high polarization to have detrimental effects on democratic durability. In this context, actors do not subvert democracy in order to achieve their policy goals (or to prevent others from achieving theirs). Willingness to achieve objectives over the long term can compensate for polarization, because actors may favor a pronounced shift away from the status quo and yet accept playing by the rules of the competitive regime.

We do not have a strong ex ante theoretical expectation about the impact of radicalism on the probability of transitions to competitive regimes. On the one hand, radical oppositions to authoritarian rulers might foster fear and intransigence on the part of the government, making them less willing to cede power or liberalize. Dictatorships might be unwilling to negotiate with radical oppositions; they often use the existence of violent oppositions to justify increasing repression. On the other hand, radical oppositions can be effective in delegitimizing governments and weakening authoritarian incumbents, and they can catalyze other oppositions. Given these potentially offsetting effects, we do not formulate a hypothesis about the effects of radicalism on the probabilities of a transition to a competitive regime.

Normative Preferences for Democracy or Dictatorship

Our second and third hypotheses summarize our argument about normative regime preferences. We claim that (H2) *a normative commitment to an incumbent authoritarian regime among the main political actors reduces the probability of a democratic transition.* Conversely (H3) *a normative commitment to democracy among the main political actors reduces the likelihood of breakdown.* It follows that a lack of normative preferences for authoritarianism facilitates transitions while a lack of normative preferences for democracy facilitates breakdowns.

Some actors have strong normative preferences for the regime itself, not only preferences over outcomes. Their choice to join a given regime coalition is not determined exclusively by policy interests. They view democracy as an intrinsic value, not only as a regime that can advance their policy interests. They believe that democracy is inherently the best political regime; they accord it legitimacy. As Hofferbert and Klingemann (1999: 23) noted, protestors in Central and Eastern Europe took to the streets in 1989 and 1991 "for freedom, not for a stereo, fresh broccoli, or a new car."

A normative preference for democracy means that an actor is willing to accept some sacrifices regarding policy outcomes in order to establish or preserve democracy. A normative preference builds a reservoir of support that enables competitive regimes to survive when times are hard. It is a procedural legitimacy that helps democracy withstand periods of weak performance. To the extent that actors value the democratic process, they derive "procedural utility" that potentially compensates for other losses (Frey et al. 2004).[12]

---

[12] The idea of procedural utility implies noninstrumental preferences. On noninstrumental preferences and motivations, see Bowles (2004: 109–19); Camerer and Fehr (2004); Sánchez Cuenca (2008); Wood (2003), as well as the already cited literatures on procedural utility and procedural

Many scholars have asserted that democracy has intrinsic (i.e., independent of policy outcomes) value (Coutinho 1980; Dahl 1971: 17–32; Dahl 1989; Lamounier 1981; Mackie 2003; Przeworski 1999; O'Donnell 2010; Weffort 1984, 1989). If scholars can believe that democracy has intrinsic value, political leaders and other actors can share that belief.[13] Yet the idea that a value commitment to democracy could be a major asset for the durability of democracy is far from consensual. Most theoretical traditions downplay or neglect the impact of actors' normative preferences on regime outcomes.

In Latin America, many human rights organizations have strong value preferences about the political regime. Leaders of these organizations took huge risks and often incurred tremendous costs to fight for human rights and democracy. Many did so not to enhance their own personal interests (unless we adopt a tautological conception of interests) or their preferred outcomes regarding the economy, education, or social policy. They fought to defend basic human rights, which by definition are a core part of a democratic regime.

The Catholic Church's fight on behalf of human rights and democracy in some Latin American countries expressed a value commitment above and beyond any particular policy interests. In Brazil, from the late 1960s until 1985, Catholic bishops and activists criticized human rights abuses and called for a return to democracy (Mainwaring 1986). The core message about human rights and democracy sprang from a commitment to the dignity of the human individual, not from a conviction that democracy would be more favorable to the Church in narrow institutional terms or to other policy preferences of the bishops.

The idea that actors can value a political regime independently of its policy results draws on social science research that has demonstrated that individuals value procedures in addition to outcomes (Frey et al. 2001; Frey et al. 2004; Frey and Stutzer 2005; Gangl 2003; Hibbing and Theiss-Morse 2001; Levi et al. 2009; Lind et al. 1993; Stutzer and Frey 2006). Hofferbert and Klingemann

---

justice. Our distinction between policy and normative preferences resembles Harsanyi's (1982) distinction between personal and moral preferences, but with some differences. Like Harsanyi's definition of moral preferences, our understanding of normative preferences refers to support for general rules, independent of the material benefits expected by individuals under such rules. But by contrast to Harsanyi, we do not claim that normative preferences reflect an impersonal idea of social welfare according to which all members of society are weighted equally. Moreover, highly inconsistent policy and normative preferences are hard to sustain for long periods because of psychological and practical political reasons.

[13] Some classic works on democracy made related arguments. Lipset (1960) and Linz (1978b: 16–23; 1988) understood democratic legitimacy as creating a reservoir of support for democracy that would enable it to withstand poor performance in hard times. Linz's distinction (1978b: 27–38; 1978a) between loyal, semi-loyal, and disloyal opposition also presupposes differences in a normative commitment to democracy. See also Barros (1986); Berman (1998); Bermeo (1990: 371–73); Dahl (1971: 124–88); Lamounier (1981); Levine (1973); Magaloni (2006); O'Donnell (1986: 15–18); Ollier (2009); Packenham (1986); Walker (1990); Weffort (1984, 1989). In some game theoretic approaches to democratization, some actors have deep value commitments to regime change (Kuran 1991; Lohmann 1994; Magaloni 2006).

(1999) and Rose and Mishler (1996) showed that citizens in Central and Eastern Europe independently valued democracy above and beyond any policy outcomes. Hofferbert and Klingemann (1999) compared the impact of individuals' assessments of state performance in protecting human rights with their assessments of their household' financial situations on democratic satisfaction in eighteen postcommunist countries of Central and Eastern Europe. In seventeen of the eighteen countries, individuals' assessments of the human rights situation, not household financial situation, were the better predictor of satisfaction with democracy. Rose and Mishler (1996) found that in seven postcommunist countries, citizens' perceptions about whether there was more freedom since the fall of communism had far greater impact than their assessment of their families' economic situations on their support for authoritarianism. Magaloni (2006: 225) showed that in the 2000 Mexican presidential elections, "political change and democratization were more salient than the economic policy issues that divided the opposition." Rephrased in the terms of our theory, voters' positions on democracy as a political regime were more important than their policy preferences in determining their vote choice. Moreno (1999) provided evidence that many voters valued democracy intrinsically in a wide range of new democracies; a cleavage over preference for democracy was an important electoral divide. Torcal and Mainwaring (2003) made a converging argument for Chile. Other scholars have shown that individuals accept outcomes if they perceive the process to be fair, just, or legitimate more readily than they accept the same or even better outcomes if they perceive the process as unfair, unjust, or illegitimate (Gangl 2003; Levi et al. 2009; Tyler 1990).

The quantitative evidence about procedural utility, procedural justice, and voters who intrinsically value democracy as the best form of government comes from individual-level data. We claim that some collective actors also value democracy. Many political parties and politicians, churches, workers' and peasants' organizations, human rights groups, and some business organizations (C. Acuña 1995) might have strong reasons to intrinsically value democracy. They might value the freedoms that are a defining feature of democracy; the opportunities for individual and group political participation, expression, and debate; the potential to influence decision making; the relative transparency that democracy should offer; the cultural expression that democracy affords; and the institutionalized opportunities to replace leaders. Even if their own members are not directly threatened, churches, human rights groups, and convinced democrats might value democracy on moral grounds, because other people will suffer the consequences of dictatorship.

Some actors believe that a form of dictatorship is intrinsically superior to other political regimes. In the contemporary West, outside of Cuba, few actors have a normative preference for dictatorship, although Venezuela's Hugo Chávez articulated that a participatory, plebiscitarian regime without strong checks and balances is the normative ideal. But until the 1990s, some leftist actors had a normative commitment to socialist dictatorship, and in the 1920s and 1930s, some right wing organizations had a normative preference for fascist dictatorship. Throughout the twentieth century, many groups in Latin America advocated forms of government dominated by a strong leader without effective checks and balances. Outside of the West, some still have a normative preference for dictatorship (e.g., some actors prefer Islamic theocracy on value grounds).

In some dictatorships – particularly in neo-patrimonial regimes – political actors made personal loyalty to the leader the foundation of the regime (Chehabi and Linz 1998). Commitment to a form of government based on a given leader is often expressed in the idea that the ruler is an extraordinary man chosen to perform a historical mission.[14] Political actors also exercise the cult of personality out of fear and in pursuit of rewards, but personal loyalty to the leader is sometimes a source of normative commitment to certain forms of dictatorship.

Strong value preferences for democracy limit how actors pursue their policy goals. If actors value the regime, they may be willing to endure policies that hurt their interests because they perceive them as legitimate binding decisions. Conversely, they may be willing to reject beneficial policies because they are not adopted by a legitimate regime.

Our emphasis on actors' normative attitudes toward democracy and authoritarianism draws on multiple traditions in political science, psychology, economics, and sociology in addition to the work on procedural utility and procedural justice. Linz's (1978a, 1978b) distinctions between the loyal, semi-loyal, and disloyal oppositions revolve around differences in attitudes toward the regime. The loyal opposition has a normative preference for democracy; it values democracy as a regime above and beyond any particular policy outcomes. These differences in attitudes toward the regime have an important impact on actors' behavior and therefore on regime dynamics and outcomes. Linz's distinctions capture what we are striving to convey, but we characterize the regime and its supporters (not only the opposition) and characterize the actors under authoritarian as well as democratic regimes. Several other works have underscored the effect of actors' attitudes toward democracy and dictatorship on regime outcomes (Berman 1998; Capoccia 2005; Dahl 1971: 124–88; O'Donnell 1986: 15–18; Stepan 1971: 153–87; Walker 1990).

Our thinking also draws on literature that has underscored the impact of beliefs on political outcomes (Blyth 2002; Finnemore 1998; Goldstein 1993; Goldstein and Keohane 1993; Hall 1989; Lynch 1999; Philpott 2001; Sikkink 1991; Wendt 1999). In our theory, actors' beliefs about the intrinsic normative value of a political regime affect their decisions, which in turn influence the regime coalitions and the outcome. Work on social movements has highlighted the importance of framing processes. Framing involves actors' beliefs and

---

[14] This idea is reflected in the usage of honorary tiles such as "meritorious" (*benemérito*) in the case of Juan Vicente Gómez in Venezuela or "benefactor of the motherland and father of the new nation" in the case of Rafael Trujillo in the Dominican Republic. On the cult of Trujillo, see Derby (2009).

therefore is relevant to our concern about actors' normative preferences regarding the political regime (Benford and Snow 2000). A value preference for democracy frames how an actor perceives a situation and hence how the actor behaves. Finally, work that indicates that individuals have noninstrumental motivations for political behavior (Brockett 2005; Camerer and Fehr 2004; Elster 1989a, 1989b: 32–35; Hirschman 1982: 84–91; Sánchez Cuenca 2008; Wood 2003) is consistent with our argument that normative preferences are part of some actors' calculations.

In seeing battles about political regimes as hinging critically on actors' policy preferences, we draw on a tradition that includes Acemoglu and Robinson (2006), Boix (2003), and Rueschemeyer et al. (1992). Our claim that some actors have independent value preferences about the political regime, however, leans on a different tradition that views actors' value preferences or beliefs as potentially important in explaining political outcomes (Berman 1998; Blyth 2002; Dahl 1971: 124–88; Finnemore 1998; Goldstein 1993; Goldstein and Keohane 1993; Hall 1989; Sikkink 1991, 1993; Stepan 1971: 153–87; Wendt 1999).

Our focus regarding normative preferences is on organized actors, movements, and presidents, not on mass political culture. Some works see a mass democratic political culture as a key to democracy (Almond and Verba 1963; Eckstein 1966; Inglehart 1990, 1997; Inglehart and Welzel 2005). This is a different emphasis than ours. A mass commitment to democracy is a valuable resource for democratic leaders, but our theory does not hinge on mass beliefs and values.

Tradeoffs between Policy Goals and Normative Preferences

When actors have a value preference about the regime, both policy goals and normative principles motivate their behavior in battles over political regimes. Certain policy preferences may ultimately constrain regime choices (and conversely, certain value preferences constrain actors' policy options), but consistency between actors' policy goals and their value preferences about the regime is not guaranteed. Actors often confront difficult trade offs.

In some historical circumstances, actors' policy preferences are aligned with value preferences (if they have them) about the regime. In the late 1980s, toward the end of the Pinochet dictatorship, the Chilean Socialists had a value preference for democracy as well as preferences for economic and social policies different from those the Pinochet government pursued. A change to their preferred regime – democracy – was compatible with, and indeed a sine qua non for, a change toward their preferred policies.

In many circumstances, however, policy preferences and value preferences about the regime collide, either because the normatively desirable regime is unwilling or unable to alter the policy status quo in the desired direction at the desired speed, or because the preferred regime is likely to alter the desired status quo at a threatening pace. In these cases, political actors have to choose between their policy goals and the political regime that they prefer on normative grounds.[15] For example, between 1970 and 1973, minority factions of the governing Chilean Socialist Party fought to preserve democracy even as they hoped to implement a radical policy agenda. President Salvador Allende himself was in this minority faction. These factions faced a difficult trade-off between their policy preferences and their normative preference for democracy. Fastidiously working to preserve liberal democracy would have required major compromise on the policy agenda. Advancing a radical policy agenda within the institutional constraints of liberal democracy was extremely difficult.

Prior to the third wave, many actors were willing to sacrifice democracy if they believed that doing so would enhance their chances of a good policy outcome. Reflecting on Bolivia's failed transitions from 1977–80, Whitehead (1986a: 67–68) wrote:

Formal democracy may not be an entirely convincing end in itself for popular movements that have urgent material needs to satisfy. . . . Important groups within such movements inevitably demand that social redistribution accompany formal democracy. And in due course, if it is necessary to preserve the new pattern of distribution by sacrificing some of the formal liberties which accompanied democratization, Latin American history suggests that some popular movements . . . may . . . make that sacrifice to 'save the revolution.'

This quote poignantly captures the tension between democracy and radical policy preferences (see also Figueiredo 1993; Mayorga 1991).

When policy preferences and value preferences about the regime enter into tension, this situation offers a unique window of opportunity to explore the weight of the latter. If actors' policy and value preferences align, the relative weight of value preferences is indeterminate, and explanations based on values appear as mere justifications (when invoked by elites themselves) or as tautologies (when invoked by external observers). But when policy and value preferences about the regime collide, the actors' behavior reveals how much they weight normative preferences vis-à-vis policy preferences.

Although for analytical purposes we treat radicalism as distinct from normative regime preferences, the two factors are empirically related. The urgency displayed by radical actors to achieve their policy preferences typically correlates with a low normative commitment to democracy. The compromise required in democratic politics is often incompatible with the rapid change (or the recalcitrant status quo) that radical actors seek. Radical actors prioritize policy outcomes over the democratic process. Thus, normative preferences for democracy and radicalism are hard to reconcile. When pressed to make choices, cognitive dissonance and political strategy may lead radical actors to abandon normative

[15] The title of Figueiredo's book (1993) on the breakdown of democracy in Brazil in 1964, *Democracia ou Reformas?* (Democracy *or* Reforms?), captures this dilemma well.

commitments to democracy over time. Ultimately, they are likely to become a subset of those with a low normative commitment to democracy, but without necessarily developing a normative preference for authoritarian rule.

INTERNATIONAL INFLUENCES ON REGIME OUTCOMES

Political actors are always embedded in a historical context shaped by domestic as well as international conditions. Philosophical debates about the desirability of certain types of political regimes emerge in the context of transnational flows of ideas. Principled positions about public policy are frequently promoted by international forums (e.g., party internationals) and organizations (e.g., international financial institutions). Moreover, the resources that domestic regime coalitions need to prevail are often dependent on external allies.

Our remaining hypotheses address such external conditions. We claim that (H4) *strong international support for democracy increases the probability of democratic transitions.* Conversely (H5), *strong international support for democracy reduces the risk of breakdowns.* It follows that weak international support for democracy undermines the possibility of a transition and increases the odds of breakdowns.

International actors have considerable influence over regime outcomes in Latin America. They affect domestic regime outcomes in six ways, all of which can work for or against democracy.

1. Through a transnational diffusion of beliefs, international actors affect domestic actors' attitudes to democracy and dictatorship and their moderation or radicalism. For example, intellectual and political leaders of the left in Brazil, the southern cone countries, and some European countries (especially Italy, France, and Spain) interacted and influenced each other, creating a shift toward more positive attitudes toward liberal democracy in the aftermath of the coups in Brazil (1964), Chile (1973), Uruguay (1973), and Argentina (1976). Similarly, the expansion of a global human rights movement in the 1970s and the 1980s illustrates the diffusion of beliefs that strengthen democratic regimes domestically. Conversely, the Cuban revolution illustrates the transnational diffusion of beliefs that increased the odds of breakdowns. The Cuban revolution enhanced the appeal of socialist dictatorship for the left throughout the region and fostered the conviction that such regimes could be established in the short term, triggering a strong counterreaction from conservative forces.

2. External events and actors can influence domestic actors through demonstration effects, that is, by showing the feasibility of regime change. An example of this mechanism was the Arab Spring of 2011. Successful efforts to mobilize against long-standing dictatorships in Tunisia and Egypt inspired similar mobilizations in other Arab countries including Libya and Syria.

3. International actors provide incentives or impose sanctions that affect domestic actors' benefits and losses under the two competing regime coalitions. Since around 1990, international actors have provided incentives or imposed sanctions in order to prevent breakdowns in the Americas. As an example of sanctions that attempted to alter the balance of resources between the two coalitions, the Organization of American States, the United States, and the European Union imposed sanctions against Honduras after the coup that overthrew President Manuel Zelaya in June 2009 (Ruhl 2010). Sanctions create economic costs for many domestic actors, so actors' calculations about policy benefits under a future dictatorship may change.

4. International actors can allocate resources to empower particular domestic actors. Foreign countries and international organizations offer material aid, training, technical assistance, and moral support for some domestic groups. In this case, the goal is not to provide incentives for some local actors to change their mind about the best type of regime, but to tip the balance of political resources in favor of the coalition that already embraces the regime preferences supported by the external allies. Foreign players may distribute resources to empower particular domestic actors in order to facilitate the overthrow of a competitive regime (as in the case of U.S. support for Chilean conspirators in 1973) or in order to prevent breakdowns (as in the case of U.S. opposition against Ecuadorian conspirators in 2000).

5. Some international actors such as the Catholic Church are simultaneously domestic actors. The Catholic Church has a reach that spans much of the world and a global mission, and the Vatican has considerable sway throughout the entire Church. But the Church is also a domestic actor. It sometimes supported breakdowns (e.g., the Catholic Church in Colombia in the late 1940s, in Spain in the 1930s, and in Venezuela in 1948) or resisted them (e.g., the Catholic Church in Guatemala in 1993), and sometimes supported authoritarian regimes. In other cases (e.g., Brazil from the 1970s until 1985), it supported transitions to democracy.

6. International actors – almost always the U.S. government in the case of Latin America – sometimes overthrow a regime and replace it. In the first three decades of the twentieth century, U.S. direct military intervention and occupation in the Caribbean and Central America was frequent. In the post-1945 period, the only examples are Panama in 1989, where the U.S. military overthrew a dictator and began the process of restoring democracy, and the Dominican Republic in 1965, when the United States invaded to *prevent* a transition to democracy. Although the United States did not directly topple the freely and fairly elected government of Guatemala in 1954, it sponsored an invasion to depose the left-leaning semi-democratic regime. The Central Intelligence Agency (CIA) recruited an ex-Guatemalan army leader to organize a militia, and then fully funded the militia when it invaded Guatemala from neighboring Honduras.

LEVELS OF ANALYSIS AND STRATEGIC INTERACTIONS

Our theory articulates how different levels of analysis (the international system, countries, actors within countries) and different variables are interrelated. Figure 2.1 visually summarizes the core of this theoretical framework, situating our theory between structural approaches (which appear as background conditions in Figure 2.1) and contingent-action approaches (which begin with the regime coalitions). Boxes in the graphic reflect broad analytical categories, not operational variables.

Figure 2.1 presents a heuristic representation of the causal sequence approaching the time (labeled t_0) at which regime outcomes are realized. The dependent variable, whether a regime survives or changes in a given year, is located temporally at time o on the horizontal axis. The strength of the competing regime coalitions (which is not directly observed) directly determines regime outcomes. Actors' policy preferences and their normative preferences about political regimes shape their decisions about joining particular regime coalitions. The competing goals of those coalitions ultimately determine the direction of the political regime.

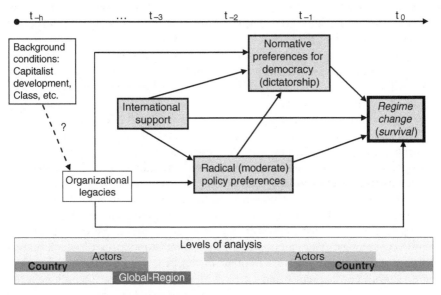

FIGURE 2.1 Causes of Regime Survival and Change
Key: *t* indicates historical proximity to regime outcomes (change or stability).
  The lower panel reflects the level of analysis characteristic of studies focusing on each type of variable: actors (individuals and their organizations), country (historical trajectories, national conditions, and national outcomes), and the global international system (the regional and worldwide contexts).

The three explanatory categories that are at the core of our theory (policy preferences, normative regime preferences, and international conditions) appear in the shaded boxes. These three factors are theoretically and empirically interrelated but not to such a degree that they create serious problems of multicollinearity or limited diversity, as we shall see in Chapters 4 to 6. For instance, actors with radical policy preferences tend to lack strong preferences for democracy, but not every actor that rejects radical preferences is committed to democracy. The figure depicts a causal connection between policy and regime preferences, to reflect those linkages.

International actors and influences enter our theory primarily as more distant causal factors that affect domestic actors' attitudes toward democracy and dictatorship, their policy preferences, and their resources. Because the impact of external actors is often mediated by those proximate variables, we have placed international factors temporally prior to domestic actors' attitudes toward dictatorship and democracy and to their policy preferences. Strong democratic currents at the international level affect actors' political beliefs (including their commitment to democracy) and policy preferences. International forces also affect the internal distribution of resources (both moral and material) among the domestic players. Foreign governments sometimes have a direct impact on regime change through military invasion or withdrawal.

Although our theory focuses on relatively proximate causal variables, these proximate causal variables are shaped by organizational legacies. Parties and other organizations have considerable autonomy with respect to the structural and cultural variables that are at the core of competing theories. For this reason, in Figure 2.1 we represent the linkage between background conditions and organizational legacies tenuously, with a broken arrow and a question mark. Parties filter those influences in different ways, shaping constituencies' understanding of their interests (Chhibber 1999; Chhibber and Torcal 1997; Przeworski and Sprague 1986; Sartori 1969; Torcal and Mainwaring 2003).

The lower panel in Figure 2.1 depicts the level of analysis implied in each theoretical component. Regime outcomes are conceptualized and measured at the national level. The analysis of coalitions based on regime and policy preferences pushes us to a level of greater specificity (particular actors within the national context), and the analysis of international factors moves our focus into a level of greater generality (the broader Latin American and global contexts).

Figure 2.1 does not represent the strategic interactions among players. However, strategic interactions are an important component of our argument because actors' regime choices respond to the behavior and regime choices of other actors (see Chapters 5 and 6). Radicalism and normative commitment to a regime type tend to trigger strategic responses from other actors in the system. Where some powerful actors are radical, the likelihood that other powerful actors will be strongly committed to democracy tends to decline. Consider, for example, a competitive regime in which actor A has a moderate preference for democracy and for a left-wing policy to be achieved over the long term, whereas actor B is indifferent toward the nature of the regime but prefers an extreme right-wing policy. Imagine that under the rules of the competitive regime the two players exercise a reciprocal veto and never achieve their preferred policy goals. If actor B embraces a radical strategy and seeks to impose its preferred policy through intimidation and violence, A may conclude that democracy is not worth the policy cost. Any accommodation with intransigent actor B will drive policies toward the extreme right. Rather than accepting B's demands, A may seek the preemptive imposition of left-wing policies and the exclusion of B from the policy process altogether (trading normative regime preferences for policy insurance). In this simplified example, the two competing coalitions ultimately adopt strategies that undermine democracy even if the players did not prefer a dictatorship at the outset.

Value preferences about the regime by one actor also affect others. If candidate A willingly conceded the election to B at time $t - 1$, politician B may be willing to accept her own defeat at time t, anticipating that A will in turn acknowledge the result of the next election at $t + 1$. If instead A tried to rig the election at time $t - 1$, B may wonder whether she should transfer power to A at time t given that, although A has won the election, as an incumbent he will be reluctant to admit defeat and to relinquish power in the future. Historical cycles of populist rule and military intervention in Argentina, Brazil, Ecuador, and Panama during the twentieth century partly reflect a similar inability of the competing coalitions in those countries to offer mutual reassurances.

THREE CAUSES OF REGIME CHANGE

Regime changes result from a shift in the balance of power among actors, a transformation in the relative leverage of regime coalitions that tips the balance in favor of a different kind of regime. These transformations may occur because (1) new actors emerge and join the opposing coalition; (2) the relative distribution of political resources among existing actors changes in favor of the opposition; or (3) enough political actors switch sides and tip the balance of forces against the current regime.[16]

The emergence of new political actors (e.g., the organization of the emerging industrial working class in labor unions and labor parties; the emergence of a human rights network) often involves a redistribution of power. If the emerging actors prefer regime change, a new adversarial coalition may emerge, or a previously existing one might grow stronger.

New actors sometimes emerge as the result of structural change such as industrialization, urbanization, and other forms of modernization. In Latin America, a more common and immediate source of the emergence of new actors has been political. In most Latin American countries, politics has not been a static landscape in which the same actors competed for power over generations. High electoral volatility in many Latin American countries, the vanquishing of old parties, and the emergence of important new ones mean that new actors

---

[16] We discuss externally (i.e., foreign) induced regime change in Chapter 7.

appear. Often, these new parties bring different regime and policy preferences than the actors that have disappeared or receded in importance.

Just as new actors can emerge and tilt the balance of power between the incumbent regime and the opposition, existing actors can lose power or disband. The disappearance of these actors can also cause regime change or can help explain changes in regime dynamics. The case studies of Argentina (Chapter 5) and El Salvador (Chapter 6) underscore how frequent and important the emergence of new actors and the displacement of old ones have been in the dynamics of Latin American political regimes.

A second potential cause of regime change is that the relative power of actors changes over time. This can occur as a result of the structural and cultural changes associated with modernization or as a consequence of the efforts of the state or international actors to bolster some actors. Modernization produces change in actors' relative power over time. In the twentieth century, Latin American societies urbanized at a rapid pace. Over time, urbanization changed the relative power of different actors. Urban actors gained resources at the expense of the countryside. Mayors of large cities gained power because of urbanization and (in many cases) decentralization; hinterland landowners lost some of their relative power. Organized labor was a more powerful actor in Latin America in the 1960s and 1970s than it had been at the turn of the twentieth century. Over time, the changing balance of resources tends to empower one regime coalition vis-à-vis the other, sometimes allowing it to challenge the existing political regime.

In Chapter 6, we highlight another source of change in actors' resources. Right-wing death squads were important actors in El Salvador in the late 1970s and early 1980s. Because of U.S. pressures to reduce the most egregious human rights abuses and great U.S. leverage arising from the fact that the Salvadoran government and armed forces desperately needed U.S. military aid, and also because the growing electoral success of a new conservative party gave the right a prospect of protecting its interests through the ballot box, death squads became less important over the course of the 1980s. Their weakening reduced the power of the right-wing authoritarian coalition and helped pave the wave for peace negotiations and democracy. In the 1980s, the United States insisted that El Salvador hold competitive elections with a valid vote count, financially and symbolically supported the centrist Christian Democratic Party (PDC), sometimes applied pressure against the most extremist elements of the Salvadoran armed forces and against death squads, and dramatically increased military aid. The net effect was to strengthen the military and to bolster less extremist elements within the armed forces and within the conservative party, ARENA.

If enough powerful actors embrace the goal of establishing a different regime, the balance of forces may tip in favor of regime change even if the relative distribution of political resources across individual groups remains unaltered. There are two general reasons why some actors change their regime coalition. First, some previously neutral actors conclude that regime change will be beneficial (or detrimental) to their policy preferences, or some previous regime supporters (or opponents) defect to a neutral position. Second, some actors change their normative regime preference – for example, they become normatively committed to democracy and hence become staunch defenders of a competitive regime.

Political actors, especially those without normative preferences about the regime, sometimes switch coalitions to protect their policy goals. Even if actors have stable policy preferences,[17] they can change their regime coalition either because the incumbent regime fails to satisfy their policy interests, leading them to turn against the regime, or because it satisfies their interests more than they expected, leading them to join the regime coalition. Actors may conclude that regime change would be beneficial to their policy interests because of disappointment with the current regime's policy outcomes. The regime's policies may hurt some actors' interests deeply or irreversibly. If, for example, the government expropriates landowners' property without compensation, the landowners might conclude that the regime (and not merely the government) is so damaging to their policy interests that they will mobilize against it. Business might shift to the coup coalition if the government is moving in a direction that could lock in antibusiness policies (as many business organizations did in response to the statist, leftist policies of President Juan Perón in Argentina during his first term, 1946–51, or President Hugo Chávez in Venezuela, 1999–2013). The first example involves the *intensity* of losses, whereas the second one involves the *duration* and potential irreversibility of policy losses. The most damaging losses to actors combine intensity and duration. Many democratic breakdowns were triggered in part by the opposition's fear that the incumbent president would violate the constitution to remain in power, making the losses irreversible and thus violating the intertemporal bargain that characterizes stable democracy (Przeworski 1991: 10–50).[18] Likewise, transitions to democracy can be triggered when actors abandon the authoritarian coalition because its policies fail to meet their interests. Just as some actors can turn against the incumbent regime, over time some initially hostile actors can conclude that the incumbent regime meets their policy preferences better than they expected. In that case, shifts toward the regime coalition occur, making it more likely that the incumbent regime will endure.

These first examples involved actors that change regime coalitions because of the policy performance of the incumbent regime. Actors can also shift their regime coalition because their perception of the probable costs and benefits of

---

[17] Actors do not always have stable policy preferences (Bowles 1998; 2004: 103–09). Our point is that even under the restrictive assumption that they do, they can still change their regime coalition.

[18] See Figueiredo (1993: 177–82) on the opposition's suspicions about Brazilian President João Goulart's willingness to violate the constitution in 1963–64, shortly before the April 1, 1964 coup. See Yashar (1997: 136) on similar suspicions harbored by the right that Guatemalan President Jacobo Arbenz (1951–54) would disregard Supreme Court decisions. The 2009 breakdown in Honduras followed a similar pattern. The Supreme Court, the legislature, and the army supported the overthrow of President Manuel Zelaya, fearing that he would violate the constitution and seek to find a way to remain in power.

a new regime changes. Chapter 6 on El Salvador provides an example. During a devastating civil war in the 1980s, the military and big business, on the one side, and a revolutionary guerrilla front, on the other, were mortal enemies. As the 1980s drew to a close, both sides exhibited a willingness to compromise and enter into peace negotiations. Because of this mutual de-radicalization, both sides concluded that the costs of peace and democracy were likely to be tolerable.

In addition, political actors may switch coalitions in response to changing normative preferences about the regime.[19] Political learning can induce actors to change their attitudes about democracy and dictatorship, and this shift can lead them to migrate to another regime coalition. This point raises two important questions: Is an explanation of regime change based on the evolution of normative preferences merely obvious or tautological? And if neither, what mechanisms can account for the endurance or transformation of normative regime preferences over time? We address these issues next.

CHALLENGES TO THEORIES ABOUT NORMATIVE
PREFERENCES

In discussions about this book with scores of colleagues, the claim that normative preferences help explain regime outcomes has generated the most controversy. Notwithstanding important direct antecedents to this claim (Berman 1998; Dahl 1971; Linz 1978a, 1978b; Rouquié 1982; Viola 1982; Walker 1990) and substantial literatures on procedural utility, procedural fairness, and individual-level commitment to democracy that provide microfoundations to our theory, many political scientists are skeptical of arguments that invoke actors' beliefs as an explanatory variable. Therefore, we anticipate six possible concerns in this section.

The first is that it might seem patently obvious and hence trivial that if actors have a normative preference for democracy, transitions to competitive regimes will be more likely and breakdowns of competitive regimes will be less likely. However, most work on regime survival and fall does *not* invoke actors' normative preferences but rather focuses on factors that are either more distant (e.g., structural explanations, mass political culture) or more proximate (contingent action and agency approaches) in the causal chain. Arguments about the impact of actors' normative preferences are not the standard fare in work on political regimes. Modernization theory, class theories, and Inglehart's cultural theory based on mass values and attitudes, for example, highlight explanatory variables that are more distant in the causal chain. Many theoretical approaches assume

---

[19] Conventionally, most work in the social sciences assumed that individuals and actors have fixed preferences. In recent decades, scholars have explored endogenous preferences. See Bowles (1998; 2004: 103–09).

that actors have only instrumental preferences about outcomes, not normative preferences about the regime as well.

Also, somewhat at odds with our theory, Karl (1990) and Rustow (1970) argued that democracy is often the second-best alternative for actors; they spoke of democracy without democrats. This perspective explicitly questions whether actors' normative preferences are important. From our perspective, democracy without democrats is possible, but it is likely to be a very fragile equilibrium.

An explanation based on normative preferences could be treated as obvious only if we claimed that these preferences always explained outcomes. This is not at all our argument. In our theory, actors' instrumental logic (their policy preferences) is always important. Some actors do not have normative preferences;[20] their policy preferences and strategic calculations about what outcomes are possible determine their choice of regime coalition. Under these circumstances, the impact of normative commitments on the regime outcome can be determined only through empirical research.

Second, arguments that attribute causation to actors' normative preferences must address the concern that these preferences are too close in the chain of causation to the dependent variable (whether a regime survives or falls). Our response is that (1) causally distant explanations such as structural and mass cultural theories fail to explain regime outcomes for Latin America; (2) these causally distant approaches do not go very far toward explaining actors' policy or normative preferences (see Chapter 3); (3) explanations of regime outcomes *must* work through actors' behavior; and (4) normative preferences strongly inform some actors' behavior. If all four parts of this response are correct, then to understand regime change and survival, we *must* consider actors' normative preferences. Far from being too close in the chain of causality to be a useful explanation, then, they are a necessary part of the explanation. Yet they are not sufficient. Actors with an initial moderate normative preference for democracy for instance, may fail to defend a democratic regime if it imposes catastrophic policy losses while an alternative authoritarian coalition offers better policy terms.

Let us briefly anticipate how we develop these four points throughout the book.

1. We provide the primary empirical evidence that causally distant explanations are not very helpful for explaining regime outcomes in Latin America in Chapters 4 and 9, with additional evidence in the qualitative case studies (Chapters 5 and 6).

2. A theory that invokes actors' normative preferences must verify that these preferences are not reducible to broader cultural or structural variables. If, for example, class position determined actors' normative preferences, we should focus on the more temporally distant causal variable (class

---

[20] We coded 563 out of 1,460 actors (38.6%) as having no normative preference for democracy or dictatorship.

position) rather than on normative preferences. Class would then have the true explanatory power; normative preferences would be at best an intermediary variable. In Chapter 3, we show that conventional structural variables help explain normative preferences and radicalism, but that the impact is modest. We examine this issue quantitatively by looking at the impact of structural variables on normative preferences. The quantitative evidence in Chapter 3 shows that normative preferences are not reducible to structural variables often used to help explain regime outcomes. Likewise, in the qualitative analysis in Chapters 5 and 6, structural variables do not adequately explain actors' normative preferences.

3. The claim that explanations must work through actors' behavior is generally accepted in theory, but approaches that focus on causally distant explanations usually do not recognize it in practice. Even if structural or broader cultural variables help explain regime outcomes, they necessarily work through political actors. For example, the explanation for why a higher level of development reduces the probability of a democratic breakdown in a broader sample than the Latin American cases *must* be that the constellation of actors and/or their preferences are more favorable to democracy than at lower levels of development – exactly what Lipset (1959) and Diamond (1992) argued.

4. We intend to demonstrate throughout the book that normative preferences strongly inform some actors' behavior and as a result influence regime outcomes. Chapter 4 provides quantitative evidence; Chapters 5 and 6 offer qualitative evidence.

Third, normative preferences should not be a *deus ex machina* that springs from nowhere and explains everything. We do not offer a full account of the origins of actors' preferences; this would go beyond our capabilities and the current state of social science. Nevertheless, in the next section of this chapter, we begin to address causes of stability and change in actors' preferences. In Chapter 3, we statistically explore the origins of actors' preferences, and in the qualitative case studies, we offer partial accounts for why actors sometimes change preferences. Finally, in Chapter 7, we argue that international influences affect domestic actors' preferences. The quantitative and qualitative evidence show that actors are more likely to develop normative preferences for democracy under democratic regimes; that early authoritarian legacies make the development of normative preferences for democracy more difficult; that structural variables do not go very far in accounting for normative attitudes toward democracy and dictatorship (though actors in poor countries are less likely to have solid normative preferences for democracy); and that a democratic regional environment is favorable to the emergence of normative preferences for democracy.

Although normative preferences are part of our theoretical account, many regime outcomes can be explained on the basis of instrumental actors pursuing their policy goals. As Figure 2.1 showed, normative preferences are but one of several important components of our theory.

Fourth, arguments about actors' normative preferences must provide evidence that actors do not support regimes merely for instrumental policy outcomes and must avoid tautologies. *Empirically*, a theory that uses normative preferences must distinguish to the extent possible between normative and outcome-based preferences for a regime type. The empirical evidence against the idea that democracy survives only because actors are satisfied with policy outcomes is substantial, as we show in Chapters 4, 5, 6, and 9. To briefly anticipate one part of this evidence here, democracy has survived at a far greater rate during the third wave, despite grave economic crises in most countries, than it did in earlier periods, despite far better economic performance. In Argentina, democracy survived despite terrible economic and social outcomes during the first two decades of democracy (1983–2003).

We explain another part of our strategy for distinguishing between normative preferences and situational support for a regime in Chapter 3. We use clear and explicit coding rules designed to establish a high threshold for concluding that an actor has a normative preference for a regime type. These coding rules provide guidelines for distinguishing between actors' sincere normative preferences and their situational or opportunistic behavior and discourse. The coding rules are intended to minimize this possibility. Some behavioral patterns, such as the leaders' reluctance to tamper with electoral procedures or to perpetrate minor forms of fraud to avoid electoral defeat, and some ideational patterns, such as their rejection of authoritarian ideologies during historical periods when such ideas are in vogue, are empirical indicators of normative commitments.

Conceptually, the idea that actors' normative preferences affect regime outcomes is not tautological. Many actors choose a regime coalition for purely instrumental reasons (i.e., based on policy outcomes). They do not have normative preferences. Others have normative preferences that can be distinguished from instrumental outcome preferences, yet they might not have much influence on regime outcomes.

In addition, to avoid a tautology, the coding rules for normative preferences about the political regime cannot include indicators implicit in the coding of regime types. We would have a tautology if behaviors that directly affected the regime were used to infer regime preferences. To address this problem, the coding rules clearly distinguish between the historical information used to code actors' normative preferences and the nature of the political regime. We also employed different research teams to classify political regimes and to code political actors, in order to minimize coder effects.

Empirically, the relationship between actors' normative preferences and the political regime does *not* appear to be tautological in our dataset (which we describe in Chapter 3). The mean value for actors' normative preference for democracy on a scale that ranges from -1 (all actors normatively prefer dictatorship) to 1 (all actors normatively prefer democracy) is .47 under competitive regimes and –.22 under authoritarian regimes. If the relationship were empirically tautological, the mean score under democracies would be 1 and the mean score under dictatorships would be –1.

Fifth, a theory that emphasizes normative preferences to explain regime outcomes must consider the possibility of reverse causality – that is, that the nature of the political regime explains actors' normative preferences rather than vice versa. For example, if a new democratic regime shows that it is able to promote effective governance, some actors might over time develop a normative preference for democracy. The problem of reverse causality is compounded by the fact that actors' normative preferences are not always static.

Reverse causality is not merely a theoretical possibility, but a reality in many cases. The challenge is to show that reverse causality is not the whole story. To address this issue, to the extent possible, we statistically examine reverse causality for all twenty Latin American countries from 1945 to 2005 in Chapter 4. We also qualitatively examine reverse causality for Argentina (Chapter 5) and El Salvador (Chapter 6). The quantitative and qualitative evidence both support the assertion that actors' normative preferences help explain the survival and fall of both democracies and dictatorships even after controlling for reverse causality.

Finally, a theory that revolves in part around actors' normative preferences must show causal mechanisms. Through what causal mechanisms does a normative preference for democracy affect actors' behavior and ultimately regime outcomes? We have already sketched the core of an answer: actors that believe in the intrinsic merits of democracy are willing to accept policy losses to preserve democracy. They do not turn against the regime in hard times. Actors that do not have a normative preference about the political regime more readily turn against it in hard times. We further develop this point in the qualitative case studies.

Political science has often reacted to these challenges by neglecting actors' preferences in the study of political regimes. But normative preferences are too important in shaping actors' behavior, and therefore ultimately in affecting regime outcomes, to neglect.

STABILITY AND CHANGE IN ACTORS' PREFERENCES

In our dataset of 1,460 actors (described more fully in Chapter 3), stability in actors' preferences is the norm, and change is the exception. The correlation between actors' normative preferences in one presidential administration and the next is .84, and the correlation on the radical policy scale is .75. Although these correlations are high, they register some change.

Once we admit the possibility of reverse causality and endogenous preferences, we must assess the conditions for actors' preference maintenance and change. This is particularly important in order to understand the transformation of actors' preferences in different historical contexts. In this section, we offer some preliminary observations about this issue.

Organizational Legacies and Path Dependence

The history of political organizations helps explain their policy preferences and attitudes toward democracy at a given point in time. Organizations tend to socialize their members into somewhat stable value attitudes toward democracy (and dictatorship) and toward certain policy preferences. Militaries, churches, owners' and workers' associations, and major parties usually survive individual leaders. Usually, they have fairly stable normative preferences toward the political regime and demonstrate fairly stable positions along our radicalism/moderation scale. Political organizations therefore typically generate continuity in regime and policy preferences over the course of long historical periods (Berman 1998; Mahoney 2001; Sartori 1976; Thelen 1999).

In modern representative democracies, parties are usually the most important carriers and shapers of normative attitudes toward democracy. As Sartori (1976) argued, they are also a major determinant of radicalization or moderation in competitive regimes (see also Sani and Sartori 1983; Scully 1992; A. Valenzuela 1978). Parties develop identities, social bases, and activists that make profound subsequent ideological fluctuation unlikely (Downs 1957; Lipset and Rokkan 1967). These identities and parties' efforts to remain faithful to their bases and activists tend to create continuity in value commitments toward the regime and in policy preferences. As Downs (1957: 103–11) noted and many researchers have subsequently confirmed,[21] major parties rarely undertake profound changes in their policy positions – and in their attitudes toward dictatorship and democracy. For parties, undertaking profound change risks alienating activists and voters alike. Therefore, in almost all competitive regimes – and in many authoritarian ones, such as the PRI-led (Partido Revolucionario Institucional) regime in Mexico from 1940 until 2000 – parties maintain stable value preferences in favor of certain regime types and certain policies.

Parties are not the only important historical carriers of regime and policy preferences. Political leaders who shape countries' trajectories over a long period of time (e.g., Juan Vicente Gómez in Venezuela between 1908 and 1935; Rafael Trujillo in the Dominican Republic from 1930 to 1961; Fidel Castro in Cuba since 1959) also usually have stable preferences about the political regime and stable policy preferences. Unions, militaries, business associations, and other organizational actors also create continuity in normative preferences toward democracy and dictatorship and in policy preferences. In this respect, we follow scholarship that has emphasized the path dependence created by organizations (Collier and Collier 1991; Kitschelt 1994; Lipset and Rokkan 1967; Mahoney 2001; Pearson 2003; Przeworski and Sprague 1986; Sartori 1976; Thelen 2004).

---

[21] Kitschelt (1994); Lipset and Rokkan (1967); Przeworski and Sprague (1986); Sartori (1976).

Changes in Preferences

Actors' normative preferences are usually stable, but they can change. If continuity in actors' preferences were the entire story, the history of political regimes in Latin America would reflect greater stability and less change than characterized the first three quarters of the twentieth century. An appreciation of organizational legacies must combine attentiveness to path dependence and awareness of change. In many historical contexts, leaders effectively "convert" organizations in order to pursue new goals (Thelen 2004).

Organizations and political leaders change their attitudes toward democracy and dictatorship and their policy preferences for several reasons. First, traumatic experiences can lead actors to reassess their preferences and beliefs. Many works on the Latin American left have argued that such a learning effect occurred in parts of Latin America in the 1970s and 1980s (Barros 1986; Bermeo 1990: 371–73; Castañeda 1993; O'Donnell 1986: 15–18; Ollier 2009; Packenham 1986; Roberts 1998; Walker 1990; Weffort 1984, 1989). The dictatorships in the southern cone and Brazil from the 1960s through 1990 (when the Chilean military regime relinquished power) provoked a widespread rethinking of the value of democracy. Venezuela's Catholic Church and COPEI, the Christian Democratic Party, became much more wedded to liberal democracy after the experience of the 1948–58 dictatorship (Levine 1973). In Argentina, after years of working to proscribe the Peronists and thereby greatly curtail democracy, the Radical Party in 1969, during the throes of a repressive dictatorship, altered its behavior and embraced free and open elections. In El Salvador, a peasant uprising supported by the Communist Party in 1931 generated deep fear in landowners and deepened a visceral, intransigent reaction against leftist and popular movements. Also in El Salvador, electoral fraud in 1972 convinced some individuals that democratic reform was impossible and moved them toward greater radicalization (Brockett 2005: 75–78).

The trauma caused by repressive dictatorships is a typical example of this mechanism, but other kinds of painful experiences can also prompt organizational change. Hyperinflation produced a major policy reorientation in Argentina's Peronist Party from 1989 to 1999 (Levitsky 2003; Stokes 2001; Weyland 2002) and in the traditional left-of-center parties (the MNR and MIR) in Bolivia in the mid-1980s (Mayorga 1997). Hyperinflation had devastating social and economic consequences, and it pushed these parties to break dramatically with their past nationalistic and statist economic policies and embrace market-oriented policies.

In the Latin American context, scholars must pay more attention to changes in actors' preferences than would be the case in the advanced industrial democracies because since 1945, Latin American countries have experienced more traumatic changes such as repressive dictatorships, internal militarized conflicts, and hyperinflation. These traumas provide the grist for actors' changes in preferences. The qualitative case studies in Chapters 5 and 6 show that in

Argentina and El Salvador, several key actors underwent deep changes in normative and policy preferences because of major traumas.

Second, organizations undergo routine processes of change even when they are not faced with major traumas or positive learning experiences. After an electoral defeat, one leader or faction of a party might successfully challenge another for control of the organization. The emergent faction or leader might have a different normative orientation toward the political regime, or might be more moderate or more radical along our policy dimension.

A prominent party leader dies, paving the way for generational change that ushers in change in attitudes toward democracy and dictatorship and policy preferences. A party might change its orientation to respond to a new electoral contender. In these quotidian processes to reshape organizational preferences and orientations and to win internal control, incremental change occurs, sometimes leading to a significant cumulative reorientation (Thelen 2004).

Militaries can also change their normative and policy preferences because of a change in the leadership. Leaders of a new democracy might dismiss some officers who were most identified with authoritarian rule and appoint a new leadership more supportive of democracy (see Chapter 6 on El Salvador). New military leadership does not automatically change organizational preferences, but the new leadership sometimes has the will and capacity to initiate a process of change. In the cases of Argentina and El Salvador, several turnovers in leadership produced change in organizational preferences.

Third, sometimes actors change normative preferences because of gradual learning attributable to positive or negative experiences under the existing regime. What starts off as an acceptance, sometimes even a begrudging one, of democracy can over time evolve into a normative preference for democracy, especially if it is combined with a change in organizational leadership. Over time, for example, the two main parties in El Salvador since 1994, ARENA and the leftist FMLN (Farabundo Martí National Liberation Front), both of which began as extremist organizations with a normative preference for dictatorship, have developed a fairly solid though not fully consistent normative preference for democracy. A devastating civil war, a military stalemate, and leadership change led to the initial transformations in normative preferences away from right-wing and socialist dictatorship, but it took the decent functioning of democracy over time for both parties to develop a normative preference for democracy.

Conversely, where democracy malfunctions in countries with widespread poverty or high inequalities, it is less likely that initially uncommitted actors will develop a normative preference for democracy and easier for actors indifferent or hostile to democracy to gain power. In many Latin American countries, weak states have hindered the decent functioning of democracy (O'Donnell 1993, 2010) and created space for such indifferent or hostile actors. Normative preferences do not emerge ex nihilo but rather in response to domestic politics and international influences.

External Sources of Policy Preferences and Norms

Fourth, the international diffusion of normative principles about political regimes and policy models can encourage actors to reorient their preferences and socialize new generations into different ideals. The Cuban revolution inspired a new model for much of the left throughout Latin America. Political learning on the Chilean left after the military coup of 1973 was significantly influenced by experiences in other countries. Most of the Chilean left gradually came to embrace liberal democracy, in part because of international (mainly, southern cone and Western European) debates about socialism and democracy. In the post-1999 period, for some political actors in a handful of countries in Latin America, Hugo Chávez served as a new model. International diffusion helps explain concurrent shifts in similar organizations operating in different countries during the same historical period.

Changes in the normative value assigned to different regimes can also result from new intellectual trends and philosophical perspectives. In the eighteenth century, the political ideas of the Enlightenment undermined the legitimacy of absolutist monarchies and created preferences among actors for written constitutions, explicit declarations of human rights, and republican rule. Referring to constitutional organization of the newly independent Latin American countries, Weyland (2009: 47) noted that, "In addition to Spanish liberalism, which found a particularly prominent expression in the Constitution of Cádiz (1812) and the liberal 'revolution' of 1820, French, North American, as well as British ideas had a significant impact on the new-born nations of the Western hemisphere." Similarly, in the twentieth century, the ascent of Marxism created preferences for a "dictatorship of the proletariat" among influential players. In these cases, political actors did not modify their normative regime preferences as a result of their own experiences; rather, the dissemination of utopian ideals inspired their desires for change.

Explanations of actors' changing orientations based on domestic processes may account for the transformation of political regimes in particular countries. But as we pointed out in Chapter 1, they cannot easily explain *convergent* regime change. Convergence takes place when multiple changes of a similar nature take place in different countries over a relatively short span. In order to understand waves of regime change, we must conceptualize the external mechanisms that help synchronize the transformation of normative values and policy preferences of domestic actors in multiple locations during the same historical period.

A detailed identification of those external mechanisms will be the focus of Chapter 7. In this section, we simply emphasize that foreign actors and international processes are a necessary component of our theoretical framework. International factors exercise influence over the policy preferences of domestic actors as well as over their normative commitments to democracy or authoritarianism.

The diffusion of new policy models is often propelled by international forces (Weyland 2005). Transnational dissemination of policy models may alter the policy preferences of domestic actors. Or they may induce the replication of policies that hurt traditional elites (and thus drive those elites to conspire against the regime in multiple countries simultaneously), and the diffusion of radical policy goals that are hard to achieve within the constraints of the existing regime (and thus encourage radical actors to attempt to topple the existing regime in several locations concurrently).

Changes in normative preferences about the regime can also occur as a result of the international dissemination of new ideas, institutional models, and philosophical principles.[22] Markoff (1999) documented that many institutional innovations that define modern democracy (e.g., written constitutions, female suffrage, stable political parties) were initially adopted in peripheral countries and later disseminated into the major powers, which then relayed the example to other recipients. In his search for exogenous sources of institutional change, Weyland similarly concluded that, "Throughout history, yet at an increasing rate with the advance of globalization, political actors have been attracted to and impressed by ideas designed in other political units. ... As decision-makers commonly take inspiration from external ideas and models, institutional change often proceeds in waves" (Weyland 2009: 42).

CONCLUSION

Our theoretical framework emphasizes the role of political factors that affect regime stability and change by operating in the medium and short run. First, we hypothesize that policy radicalism is damaging to the prospects of competitive regimes. Conversely, policy moderation facilitates the survival of competitive regime (H1).

Second, building on the concept of procedural utility and on work that has emphasized the impact of actors' beliefs on political outcomes, we hypothesize that actors' normative support for authoritarian regimes or leaders hinders democratization and stabilizes nondemocratic regimes (H2), while a normative commitment to democracy increases the durability of competitive regimes (H3). In general, actors' beliefs frame the way they perceive the political world and their own interests. More specifically, actors' belief in the normative desirability of democracy and dictatorship influences their willingness to accept policy sacrifices and their choice to join the democratic or authoritarian coalitions.

Third, building on an extensive literature on the diffusion of political regimes and international influences on political regimes, we hypothesize that a regional environment of many democracies enhances the survival rate of competitive regimes (H4) and increases the transition rate from dictatorship to competitive regimes (H5).

---

[22] For example, in recent years, a literature has emerged on the international diffusion of norms about human rights (Keck and Sikkink 1998).

These five hypotheses are more interesting as a system (i.e., as an integrated theory) than individually (as separate predictions). Our second and third hypotheses are not surprising at all, although it is far from consensual that actors' attitudes toward democracy and dictatorship actually affect regime outcomes. The interesting point is that the hypotheses may combine to produce different outcomes. An initial commitment to democracy among some actors may be cancelled by emerging radicalism among other actors, for example. Or potentially radical players may, by contrast, behave moderately if other actors are committed to competitive politics and they believe that competitive politics will serve their policy goals. That is, the rooting of the hypotheses in assumptions about actors' motivations, the possible configurations anticipated by the hypotheses, and interactions among the actors are more interesting than the *ceteris paribus* individual predictions.

3

Competitive Regimes and Authoritarianism in Latin America

This chapter presents key pillars of the research strategy for this book – in particular, how we measure and track the dependent variable (political regimes in Latin America) and the independent variables that are at the core of our theory. The chapter has four primary purposes. First, we present an abbreviated version of our rules for coding political regimes. When we first thought of writing this book, we decided that the first step needed to be developing a theoretically and conceptually grounded and empirically valid coding of political regimes for Latin America. The only existing measures or classifications of political regimes for the great bulk of the period we initially coded, from 1945 to 1999, were the Polity scores, which range from –10 (highly repressive) to 10 (highly democratic) and Przeworski et al.'s (2000) dichotomous classification (democracy versus dictatorship).

As we argued in our earlier work (Mainwaring et al. 2001, 2007), the Polity scores had theoretical and conceptual shortcomings and were empirically questionable for many Latin American cases. Other scholars subsequently made converging arguments (Bowman et al. 2005; Munck 2009; Munck and Verkuilen 2002). Przeworski et al. (2000) made fundamental contributions to thinking about how to classify political regimes, but for much of the world, their democracy/dictatorship dichotomy is too blunt. Freedom House scores began in 1972, and for the first two decades they had significant conceptual and empirical shortcomings. Our conviction that existing measures and classifications had these flaws led us to develop a simple trichotomous classification of political regimes for Latin America. Based on historical research, we coded regimes for the twenty Latin American countries as democratic, semi-democratic, and authoritarian from 1900 to 2010.[1]

---

[1] Daniel Brinks coauthored this work and two earlier articles on this issue (Mainwaring et al. 2001, 2007). The version presented here extends our earlier regime classification back to 1900 (from

Second, we show the evolution of political regimes in these Latin American countries over these 111 years, with particular attention to regional (as opposed to country-specific) patterns. We offer an operational definition of waves of democratization and compare the historical waves of democratization globally and in Latin America. Regime change rarely happens in isolation. Although transitions and breakdowns take place in particular countries, these events are often preceded and followed by similar changes in neighboring regimes. A sequence of similar political transformations in a relatively short historical period creates a "wave" of change.

Third, we discuss the measurement of our main explanatory variables. Figuring out a way to measure actors' policy moderation and their normative preferences about political regimes presented daunting challenges. We developed careful coding rules and then coded all of the main political actors' policy preferences and normative preferences about the political regime in all twenty countries from 1944 to 2010. A team of nineteen research assistants made this endeavor feasible.

We discuss the measurement of international factors, including worldwide trends, U.S. policies toward Latin America, and regional dissemination effects. Previous research on international factors in democratization has not consistently disentangled different international mechanisms. We present our strategy for disentangling the effects of U.S. policy toward Latin America, worldwide diffusion effects on regimes in Latin America, and regionally specific effects. Given the burgeoning emphasis on international factors in democratization, it is important to begin assessing which of these mechanisms is causally important in different contexts.

Finally, we offer empirical evidence to validate our measures of the explanatory variables and to support the causal sequence represented in Figure 2.1 of the previous chapter. In the concluding section we address the endogenous nature of actors' preferences, which are not only proximate causes of regime change but also the consequences of more distant international, institutional, and structural forces. Our analysis shows that actors' preferences are partly predicted by structural variables and by international trends, but they cannot be reduced to structural conditions. Moreover, radicalism emerges as a strong predictor of normative regime preferences even after accounting for potential endogeneity. Our conclusions emphasize the importance of measuring proximate causes in order to explain regional changes in democratization.

POLITICAL REGIMES DEFINED

A political regime is a set of norms that regulate the ways in which individuals access top leadership positions in the state and the prerogatives and limitations

1945) and forward to 2010 (from 2004). See the Web site for this project for further details: http:// kellogg.nd.edu/democracies-materials.shtml.

they have in the policy-making process. More expansively, it is a set of informal and formal rules that define: (1) who selects the top officials in the government (president or prime minister, members of the legislature if there is a legislature); (2) what resources (votes, military power, etc.) and procedures (i.e., elections, inheritance, a coup, etc.) individuals use to access these positions; (3) what institutional and legal constraints rulers face in exercising power and implementing policy (i.e., the rights of their citizens or subjects, the powers of courts and legislatures); and (4) to what extent the authority of the top leaders can be limited by other, informal veto players. As Fishman (1990a: 428) summarizes, "A regime determines who has access to political power, and how those who are in power deal with those who are not." In modern democracies, for example, rulers take office as a result of competitive and inclusive elections, they adopt policies without violating fundamental rights, and they face constraints from legislators, judges, and social movements – but not from army rebels or foreign powers. Regime change takes place when those norms and practices are fundamentally replaced or altered.

CLASSIFYING POLITICAL REGIMES[2]

Our classification of political regimes begins with a definition of democracy that revolves around four dimensions. First, the head of government and the legislature must be chosen through open and fair competitive elections.[3] Such elections are a core ingredient of modern representative democracy. Fraud and coercion may not determine the outcomes for democratic elections. Elections must offer the possibility of alternation in power even if, as occurred for decades in Japan, no actual alternation occurs for an extended time.

Second, the franchise must include the great majority of the adult population. This means something approximating universal adult suffrage for citizens. Many countries have minor exclusions (the insane, convicts) that do not detract from their democratic credentials. If large parts of the population are excluded, the regime may be a competitive oligarchy, but in the past few decades it could not be considered a democracy. For the first half of the twentieth century, we consider some regimes democratic notwithstanding significant exclusions (e.g., women) that were characteristic of those times.

Third, democracies must protect political and civil rights such as freedom of the press, freedom of speech, freedom to organize, the right to habeas corpus, and so forth. Even if the government is chosen in free and fair elections with a broad suffrage, in the absence of an effective guarantee of civil and political

---

[2] The agenda-setting Varieties of Democracy project began as we were finishing this book. See Coppedge et al. (2011, 2012). Because the data collection for this project was still not complete, we were not able to incorporate it.

[3] The election of the head of government is often indirect. This is true in all parliamentary systems and in presidential systems that have electoral colleges.

rights, it is not democratic as that word is understood in the modern world. El Salvador and Guatemala in the 1980s, among other cases in recent decades, illustrate the point. A liberal component – the protection of individual liberties – is a necessary element of contemporary democracy. Because the liberal dimension is a defining characteristic of contemporary democracy, Zakaria (1997), Diamond (1999: 42–51), and Merkel's (2004) concept of "illiberal democracy" is problematic; it suggests that regimes that do not protect civil liberties and political rights might still be democracies (Plattner 1998). Illiberal regimes with competitive elections are semi-democratic at best and in some cases authoritarian. In fact, the extent to which elections can be fair without a significant liberal component is limited. Electoral procedures need liberal components (freedom of association, freedom of movement, freedom of expression, etc.) in order to have democratic content.

Fourth, the elected authorities must exercise real governing power, as opposed to a situation in which elected officials are overshadowed by the military or by a nonelected shadow figure (J. S. Valenzuela 1992). If elections are free and fair but produce a government that cannot control major policy arenas because the military or some other force does, then the government is not a democracy. By our stringent definition, some of the "defective democracies" of which Merkel (2004) speaks are not merely defective; they are not democracies.

Based on these four dimensions, we classify governments as competitive (democratic or semi-democratic) or authoritarian using a simple aggregation rule. When governments commit no significant violations of any of the four criteria, we code them as democratic. If they incur in partial but not flagrant violations to any of those principles we treat them as semi-democratic. They rank as authoritarian if they present one or more flagrant violations of those principles. In other terms, we employ the minimum score of the four dimensions to determine the overall level of democracy (full, partial, or none).[4] We list the coding rules employed to identify such violations in Appendix 3.1.

Table 3.1 shows our classification for the twenty Latin American countries for the 1900–2010 period.[5] Because our coding reflects the situation of each country on December 31 of every year, regimes that lasted only a few months (such as the democratic regime in the Dominican Republic between February and September 1963) do not appear in the table. For most historical cases the coding rules presented in Appendix 3.1 offered clear guidance to determine if (and to what extent) democratic principles had been violated in the country, but some controversial regimes defied easy classification, and some degree of historical judgment was always required to classify the cases.

---

[4] Therefore, we allow for no compensation across dimensions. See Mainwaring, Brinks, and Pérez-Liñán (2007), Munck (2009: chapter 4), and the Web site for this project for a more extensive discussion.

[5] On the Web site for this project we report the empirical coding of the four dimensions for the twenty Latin American countries.

TABLE 3.1. *Political Regimes in Latin America, 1900–2010*

Country	From	To	Regime
Argentina	1900	1915	A
	1916	1918	D
	1919	1919	SD
	1920	1920	D
	1921	1921	SD
	1922	1929	D
	1930	1945	A
	1946	1950	SD
	1951	1957	A
	1958	1961	SD
	1962	1962	A
	1963	1965	SD
	1966	1972	A
	1973	1974	D
	1975	1975	SD
	1976	1982	A
	1983	2010	D
Bolivia	1900	1955	A
	1956	1963	SD
	1964	1978	A
	1979	1979	SD
	1980	1981	A
	1982	2006	D
	2007	2010	SD
Brazil	1900	1945	A
	1946	1953	D
	1954	1955	SD
	1956	1963	D
	1964	1984	A
	1985	2010	D
Chile	1900	1923	SD
	1924	1924	A
	1925	1926	SD
	1927	1931	A
	1932	1972	D
	1973	1989	A
	1990	2010	D
Colombia	1900	1909	A
	1910	1948	SD
	1949	1957	A
	1958	2010	SD
Costa Rica	1900	1901	A
	1902	1905	SD
	1906	1909	A
	1910	1916	SD
	1917	1919	A
	1920	1927	SD
	1928	1947	D
	1948	1948	A
	1949	1952	SD
	1953	2010	D
Cuba	1900	1939	A
	1940	1951	SD
	1952	2010	A
Dominican Republic	1900	1923	A
	1924	1927	SD
	1928	1977	A
	1978	1993	D
	1994	1995	SD
	1996	2010	D
Ecuador	1900	1933	A
	1934	1934	SD
	1935	1943	A
	1944	1945	SD
	1946	1947	A
	1948	1960	D
	1961	1962	SD
	1963	1967	A
	1968	1969	SD
	1970	1978	A
	1979	1999	D
	2000	2000	SD
	2001	2003	D
	2004	2010	SD
El Salvador	1900	1983	A
	1984	1993	SD
	1994	2010	D
Guatemala	1900	1925	A
	1926	1930	SD
	1931	1944	A
	1945	1953	SD
	1954	1985	A
	1986	1999	SD
	2000	2001	D
	2002	2010	SD
Haiti	1900	1994	A
	1995	1998	SD
	1999	2005	A
	2006	2010	SD

TABLE 3.1. (*cont.*)

Country	From	To	Regime	Country	From	To	Regime	Country	From	To	Regime
Honduras	1900	1928	A	Panama	1945	1947	SD	Uruguay	1900	1915	A
	1929	1934	SD		1948	1955	A		1916	1918	SD
	1935	1956	A		1956	1963	D		1919	1932	D
	1957	1962	SD		1964	1967	SD		1933	1934	A
	1963	1970	A		1968	1989	A		1935	1941	SD
	1971	1971	SD		1990	1993	SD		1942	1942	A
	1972	1981	A		1994	2010	D		1943	1972	D
	1982	1998	SD	Paraguay	1900	1988	A		1973	1984	A
	1999	2008	D		1989	2007	SD		1985	2010	D
	2009	2009	A		2008	2010	D	Venezuela	1900	1945	A
	2010	2010	SD	Peru	1900	1911	A		1946	1947	SD
Mexico	1900	1910	A		1912	1913	SD		1948	1958	A
	1911	1912	SD		1914	1914	A		1959	1998	D
	1913	1987	A		1915	1918	SD		1999	1999	SD
	1988	1999	SD		1919	1938	A		2000	2001	D
	2000	2010	D		1939	1947	SD		2002	2008	SD
Nicaragua	1900	1928	A		1948	1955	A		2009	2010	A
	1929	1935	SD		1956	1961	SD				
	1936	1983	A		1962	1962	A				
	1984	1989	SD		1963	1967	D				
	1990	1996	D		1968	1979	A				
	1997	2010	SD		1980	1982	D				
Panama	1904	1915	SD		1983	1984	SD				
	1916	1917	A		1985	1987	D				
	1918	1927	SD		1988	1991	SD				
	1928	1931	A		1992	1994	A				
	1932	1935	SD		1995	2000	SD				
	1936	1944	A		2001	2010	D				

This trichotomous classification is ordinal; it moves from more to less democratic. At the top of the scale, democratic regimes meet the four conditions of the definition. The semi-democratic category includes a variety of regimes that sponsor competitive elections but still fail to measure up to democracy. We discuss these two forms of government under the general label of "competitive regimes." For the purposes of this book, the most important distinction among regimes is between competitive (democratic or semi-democratic) systems and authoritarian systems.

We use the term "authoritarian" to embrace many kinds of authoritarian regimes, from highly repressive to rather lenient forms of nondemocratic rule. Although our classification does not distinguish subtypes of authoritarianism, such distinctions are relevant for other purposes (Linz 2000; Linz and Stepan 1996: 38–54; Levitsky and Way 2002, 2010). In later chapters we occasionally use "competitive authoritarianism" to refer to authoritarian regimes that have electoral competition but clearly unfair elections (Levitsky and Way 2010). This label underscores that although they are not a subset of our category of competitive regimes, such regimes are closer to – and sometimes hard to distinguish from – semi-democracies.

Our category of competitive regimes (democracies and semi-democracies) roughly overlaps with the type of regime that Przeworski et al. (2000) identified as democratic. A comparison of our trichotomous scale with the Przeworski and colleagues' dichotomous classification, extended by Cheibub and Gandhi for the 1946–2002 period, indicates that more than 99 percent of the regime-years we coded as democratic and 79 percent of the regime-years we coded as semi-democratic were treated by Przeworski and his collaborators as democracies (Przeworski et al. 2000; Cheibub and Gandhi 2004).

Our classification is more stringent than other trichotomous classifications based on the Polity IV scale (Gurr, Jaggers, and Moore 1990; Jaggers and Gurr 1995; Polity IV Project 2012).[6] Researchers in the Polity project have distinguished between autocracies (with scores ranging between –10 and –6 in the Polity scale) from "anocracies" (–5 through 5), and democracies (6 to 10). Between 1900 and 2008, more than 65 percent of Polity's "anocracies" were authoritarian systems according to our rules, and only 24 percent were semi-democracies. Somewhat closer to our classification is the distinction made by Epstein et al. (2006) between autocracies (ranging between –10 and 0 in the Polity scale), partial democracies (1 through 7), and full democracies (8 to 10). About 32 percent of the cases that qualified as "partial democracies" for the 1900–2008 period were authoritarian according to our rules, while 37 percent were semi-democracies and 31 percent were democracies. A majority of countries with Polity scores of 1 or 2 are authoritarian according to our coding rules.

---

[6] The Polity scale ranges between –10 (authoritarian) and 10 (democratic). The threshold of 5 is conventionally employed to distinguish full democracies from other types of regimes.

Thus, our category of semi-democracy is best *approximated* by Polity scores between 3 and 7, and our category of democracy by scores between 8 and 10.

In this book we focus on two major patterns of regime change: the breakdown of competitive regimes into authoritarianism, and transitions from authoritarianism into competitive politics. More than the development of semi-democracies into full democracies (or the erosion of the latter into the former), these two patterns of regime change determine the flow of historical waves of democratization and counterwaves of dictatorship.

WAVES OF DEMOCRATIZATION AND AUTHORITARIANISM

The post-1977 wave of democratization has been far more extensive, involving far more countries, and has lasted for longer than any previous wave of democracy in Latin America. But what is a "wave" of democratization? And how can we assess the magnitude of this change?

According to Huntington's (1991: 15) classic work, "a wave of democratization is a group of transitions from non-democratic to democratic regimes that occur within a specified period of time and that significantly outnumber transitions in the opposite direction." Because Huntington did not provide any concrete operational rules, the number and duration of such "specified periods" of democratic expansion requires further clarification (Doorenspleet 2000). Huntington identified three global waves of democratization: from 1828 to 1926, from 1943 to 1962, and from 1974 to 1991 (when his book was published).

Huntington's definition is not precise enough to identify waves of democratization. If during any given period the number of transitions outnumbers breakdowns, the proportion of democracies increases.[7] For Huntington, any period during which the proportion of democracies expands significantly could be a wave of democratization. However, many historical periods that fulfill this requirement would not be normally labeled as such. For example, using our classification of political regimes, 10 percent of the countries in Latin America had competitive regimes in 1906 and 95 percent of them had competitive regimes by 2006. The proportion of competitive regimes increased over this century, but no analyst would argue that a century-long wave of democratization took place in Latin America. Too much fluctuation occurred over the course of a hundred years, as democracy expanded and receded several times during the twentieth century.

We define as a wave of democratization any historical period during which there is a sustained and significant increase in the proportion of competitive regimes (democracies and semi-democracies). By sustained we mean that no counterwave or no extensive period of stagnation interrupts the expansive trend. By significant

---

[7] This claim assumes a fixed number of countries. Otherwise, the creation of new authoritarian states may overcome the greater frequency of transitions to democracy. For this reason, we interpret the definition in terms of the relative proportion of democratic regimes.

we mean that the proportion of competitive regimes at the end of the period is greater than the proportion of regimes at the beginning, and that the difference between the two proportions is statistically significant at $p < .10$ level.[8]

A wave must begin in a year in which the number of competitive regimes increases and ends when 1) the number of competitive regimes decreases to mark the start of a counterwave or of a period of stagnation; or 2) a period of stagnation begins. For consistency, a counterwave is operationalized as a statistically significant decline in the proportion of competitive regimes. A wave of democratization stagnates if the number of competitive regimes declines slightly or remains the same continuously for ten or more years.[9] A wave can temporarily crest and then resume, but for our operational purposes, any period of stagnation lasting a decade or longer terminates the cycle. It is possible to evaluate the impact of a wave in terms of its *magnitude* (the difference between the proportion of democracies and semi-democracies in the initial and in the final year) and its *duration* (the length of the time spell until its termination, or alternatively until the point of stagnation).

To illustrate this definition, Figure 3.1 displays the proportion of countries worldwide that received a score of 3 or greater in the Polity scale between 1800 and 2008. The Polity index is lenient with countries in the early twentieth

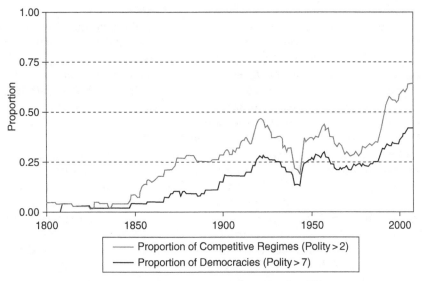

FIGURE 3.1 Proportion of Competitive Regimes Worldwide (Polity IV), 1800–2010
Source: Polity IV 2012.

---

[8] To assess this requirement, we employ a one-tailed z test of the difference between proportions with a correction for continuity.
[9] The specific number of years is somewhat arbitrary, but it does not make sense conceptually to discuss a lengthy period of stasis as part of a surge in democratization.

century, so we have selected a threshold to approximate our definition of competitive regimes above the value of 1 adopted by Epstein et al. (2006) to identify "partial democracies." The proportion of "full democracies" with scores above 7 is also reported for reference.

Using our definition of waves and Polity's classification of political regimes, there was one cycle of democratization in the nineteenth century and three in the twentieth century. The first wave started in 1847 and ended, according to the stagnation rule, in 1883. This wave lasted for thirty-seven years and expanded the share of competitive regimes by 24 percent. The first wave of the twentieth century started in 1901 and ended in 1922, raising the proportion of competitive regimes by 19 percent over twenty-two years. Huntington referred to these two cycles jointly as a single wave of democratization. Starting in 1923, a surge of reactionary regimes reduced the proportion of competitive systems to a nadir of 19 percent in 1943.

The so-called second wave was short in duration but faster in regime change. It started in 1944 and lasted until 1957, producing twenty-five new competitive regimes (at a pace of almost two per year). Even though the absolute number of countries with competitive politics was greater in 1957 than in 1922, the creation of new states meant that the relative share of competitive regimes stayed at 44 percent in 1957. The challenges of decolonization and the Cold War ignited a new authoritarian wave between 1958 and 1977.

The percentage of competitive regimes had declined significantly by 1964 and remained stagnant at about 29 percent throughout most of the 1970s. If we accept Polity's coding, the third wave started in 1978 and was still ongoing by 2008 (the last year in the figure). During this era, the share of competitive regimes grew from 28 percent to 65 percent, at a rate of 2.2 transitions per year. Although the exact dates of initiation and termination vary with regards to Huntington's periodization, the three waves are clearly identified in Figure 3.1 (with the first, long cycle divided in two periods, according to our operational rules).

How did the global waves mesh with developments in Latin America? To address this question, Figure 3.2 plots the evolution of competitive regimes in the region using our classification. This figure for Latin America shows a similar pattern. The first wave started in 1902 and stagnated after 1912, significantly expanding the regional share of competitive regimes from 5 percent (just Chile) in 1901 to 30 percent eleven years later. The proportion of competitive regimes increased to 40 percent by 1926 and dropped to 20 percent by 1936 during the Great Depression, but no statistically significant change in the share of competitive regimes occurred during this period. A new wave of democratization began in 1939 and was later fueled by the pro-democracy spirit toward the end of World War II. It raised the proportion of competitive regimes from 20 percent in 1938 to 55 percent in 1947. But the gains of this period were quickly lost with the onset of the Cold War. By 1954, only five countries (25 percent) were democratic or semi-democratic, reversing the situation to the late 1920s.

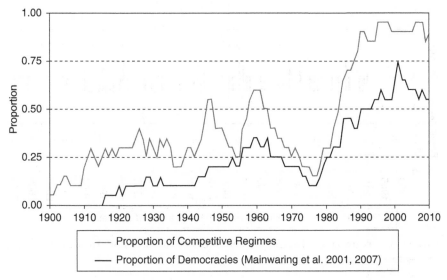

FIGURE 3.2 Proportion of Competitive Regimes in Latin America, 1900–2010
Source: Table 3.1.

Within few years, the counterwave was reversed, and the percentage of competitive regimes bounced back from 25 percent in 1955 to 60 percent in 1961. This period was marked by the pacts to reestablish competitive rule in Colombia and Venezuela and by the attempt to establish a semi-democratic regime excluding Peronism in Argentina. According to our operational rules, the 1939–1947 and 1956–1961 periods represent two historical cycles of democratization. We refer to them broadly as the second wave of democratization to preserve a consistent periodization at the global and regional levels, but the 1940s and the 1950s actually involved two different moments of democratization in Latin America.

This new cycle of democratization, however, was short-lived. In the context of the Cold War, and with the pressure added by the immediacy of the Cuban revolution, many competitive regimes crumbled and bureaucratic-authoritarian regimes multiplied (O'Donnell 1973). By 1977, only three countries had democracies (Costa Rica and Venezuela) or a semi-democracy (Colombia). The region had not seen such unfavorable conditions for democracy in more than seven decades. Starting in 1978, however, a fast and sustained expansion in competitive regimes raised the total number to nineteen by 1995. By contrast to prior waves, the proportion of competitive regimes has not statistically receded. Arguably, this was the most important political transformation in Latin America since the wars of independence.

Figure 3.3 compares the number of transitions (depicted as positive numbers) and breakdowns (as negative numbers) for every year between 1900 and 2010. This graphic depicts the two types of outcomes that we need to

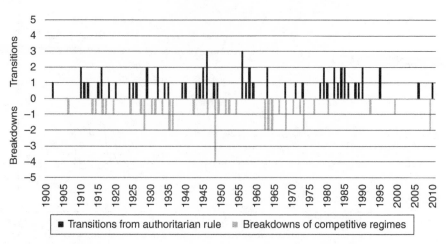

FIGURE 3.3 Number of Transitions and Breakdowns in Latin America, by Year, 1900–2010
Source: Table 3.1.

explain: the establishment of competitive regimes and of authoritarian systems.

Between 1902 and 1912, the ratio of transitions to breakdowns was 5 to 1. In the period of stagnation that followed, from 1913 to 1938, the ratio was 0.88, indicating a slight disadvantage for competitive regimes. During the next surge in competitive regimes, between 1939 and 1947, the ratio was 4.5 to 1 in favor of the establishment of competitive regimes, but the onset of the Cold War depressed the ratio to 0.25 (i.e., one transition for every four breakdowns) from 1948 to 1955. In a new swing of the pendulum, the second wave of democratization witnessed seven transitions and no breakdowns between 1956 and 1961, but an authoritarian wave lowered the ratio to 0.36 between 1962 and 1977. The most impressive swing in democratization took place between 1978 and 1998, when the ratio became 9 to 1 in favor of competitive regimes. Since then and until 2010, the ratio has been 0.67, indicating a potential for limited reversal that we explore in Chapter 8.

Spatial constraints prevent us from discussing each wave in more detail. Other studies have provided historical overviews of political regimes in Latin America (Collier and Collier 1991; Drake 2009; Hartlyn and Valenzuela 1994; Rueschemeyer, Stephens, and Stephens 1992; P. Smith 2005).

The magnitude and durability of the third wave of democratization took scholars and policy analysts completely by surprise. When these transitions to democracy or semi-democracy took place, many analysts saw little chance that democracy would endure. In the early 1980s, a Chilean observer concluded that "the characterization of contemporary Latin America as a region undergoing a change toward increased democratization – liberal, populist, or socialist – is an intellectual hallucination" (Nef 1983: 162). Three years later, Wiarda (1986: 341) argued that

[T]he prospects for democracy [in Latin America] are hardly encouraging. . . . None of these economic conditions is encouraging to the cause of democracy in Latin America, nor do they help established democracies in the region to survive. . . . Given rising expectations, competition for control of the fewer resources that do exist becomes intense, polarized, and violent. . . . Liberal-pluralist democracy is difficult to sustain under such conditions.

Late in the decade, Diamond and Linz (1989: 51–52) concluded: "At this juncture, democracy in Latin America is everywhere in pain. . . . Even as the world awaits with renewed hope the end of authoritarian rule in Chile, the prospect of new democratic breakdowns in Latin America during the 1990s cannot be dismissed."

Analysts from diverse political and theoretical orientations concurred. Most competitively elected governments faced daunting challenges: weak democratic traditions and institutions, egregious social disparities, widespread poverty, and parlous economic conditions. Gurr et al. (1990: 90) expressed this fear: "The beginning of the much celebrated contemporary trend toward democratization in Latin America since the mid-1970s [sic] is evident, but in view of the historical pattern of political swings back toward autocracy, impelled as much by international as domestic factors, the 'trend' should be regarded as a fragile one."

In most countries, democratic and semi-democratic regimes survived despite poor social and economic performances and despite lengthy authoritarian traditions. In Argentina, Bolivia, and Brazil, democratic governments withstood annual inflation rates that went far into quadruple or quintuple digits, peaking at 3,080 percent in Argentina (1989), 11,750 percent in Bolivia (1985), and 2,948 percent in Brazil (1990). In El Salvador and Guatemala, countries with histories of ruthless dictatorships, consistent repression of the indigenous populations, and horrendous civil wars, warring factions established competitive regimes in the 1980s and signed peace treaties in 1992 and 1996, respectively.

The capacity of elected governments to survive in the face of daunting challenges and poor social and economic performance confounded most observers' expectations as well as considerable comparative and theoretical literature on democratization. Today, the scholarly community takes for granted that competitive regimes have survived, but when these transitions to elected governments took place, few observers expected that these regimes would be able to withstand withering economic crises, widespread poverty, egregious income inequalities, and other nettlesome challenges. The near-disappearance of authoritarian regimes represents a positive contrast to what has occurred in some other regions in the third wave of democratization, where many competitive authoritarian regimes have flourished (Diamond 2002; Levitsky and Way 2010; Schedler 2002, 2007).

This is not to say that democracy has achieved its full potential in Latin America. Figure 3.2 shows that this extraordinary wave of democratization ended when the proportion of competitive regimes stagnated after 1998. Most democratic and semi-democratic regimes in the region have notable shortcomings, and the proportion of full democracies declined between 2001 and 2009, indicating a pattern of limited erosion during the first decade of the twenty-first century, which we address in Chapter 8. We intend our theory of regime change to explain not only particular transitions and breakdowns observed in the past, but also the region-wide patterns of transformation documented in this section.

THE ROLE OF POLITICAL ACTORS: MEASURING NORMATIVE AND POLICY PREFERENCES

According to our theory, policy preferences and normative beliefs about regimes are the immediate factors driving political actors to support or undermine competitive regimes. Therefore, historical patterns of radicalization and normative orientations toward democracy and dictatorship among Latin American actors may be critical to explain the region-wide political transformations of the twentieth century.

Tracing the empirical connection between individual actors and the historical changes observed at the regional level demands five tasks. First, we need to identify the main political actors in each country during each historical period. Second, we must code policy radicalism and normative preferences for democracy (or dictatorship) for each actor. Third, information about these preferences must be aggregated to approximate the relative strength of possible coalitions at the national level. Fourth, this aggregate assessment of the distribution of preferences must help predict the timing of regime change in each country. Last, the predicted patterns of regime change at the national level for each of the twenty countries must combine to create cumulative cycles consistent with the regional waves of democratization documented in Figure 3.2.

We discuss the first two tasks in this section and address the remaining tasks in the following chapters. We coded actors' value preferences about political regimes and their policy moderation or radicalism based on secondary sources: history and political science books and articles on the politics of the twenty countries under study. Under our supervision, guided by a twenty-page coding document, nineteen research assistants segmented the history of each country according to presidential administrations and read multiple sources in English, Spanish, or Portuguese for each period. They identified the relevant actors based on explicit but simple rules. Leaders or organizations identified by multiple historical sources as major political actors – that is, those controlling important political resources – during each presidential era are the primary actors.[10]

---

[10] Because of spatial constraints, we do not report full details of the coding rules to identify political actors. These rules and the complete coding criteria are available on the Web site for the book.

Every analysis of political regimes makes decisions – usually implicit about which actors are most important. Obviously, there is no uncontested list of relevant actors for each administration. In order to avoid historiographic "selection bias" – that is, a focus on historical interpretations that reinforce our theoretical perspective (Lustick 1996) – we asked members of the research team to read a wide range of sources on the politics of each administration and to identify actors that were relevant across many of the narratives.

We worked to achieve high-quality coding through a combination of careful and detailed coding rules and extensive historical research. On average, the research assistants cited 50 references per country, and the average country report that explains the coding of actors is 83 single-spaced pages.

Because information for many control variables for our quantitative analysis was available only after World War II, for eighteen of the twenty countries, we limited the coding of political actors to the period from 1944 until 2010. For Argentina and El Salvador, the countries that are covered as qualitative case studies in Chapters 5 and 6, we created a more extensive record of historical actors going back to 1916 and 1927, respectively.

For most administrations, a limited number of actors – typically more than two and fewer than ten – were the decisive political players. The list always included the president (except for a few puppet presidents). For 290 presidential administrations, our dataset has 1,460 actors including 573 parties, party coalitions, and party factions; 327 presidents and the organizations that are relatively subordinate to them (such as their parties under democracies and usually the military under military dictatorships); 175 militaries, military factions, and military organizations; 82 business organizations; 56 guerrilla organizations; 53 popular and civil society organizations; 52 labor unions and federations; 52 powerful individuals who were not the president; 27 churches; 22 social movements; 16 paramilitary groups; and a smaller number of other kinds of actors. We identified their political alignments vis-à-vis the incumbent president by coding whether the actors were (1) the government or government allies; (2) members of the opposition; or (3) neutral or divided with regards to the administration. A complete list of actors for each country and period is available on the Web site for this book.

Radical Policy Preferences

We defined radicalism as the combination of policy preferences toward one pole of the policy spectrum in conjunction with an urgency to achieve these preferences where they do not represent the status quo or with an intransigent defense of these positions where these positions represent the status quo. Radical policy preferences need not be on the extreme left or extreme right, but they must be far enough from the policy preferences of other relevant actors to create some polarization. Although we define radicalism in the realm of preferences rather than behaviors, some behaviors typically are expressions of underlying radical preferences. Therefore, we coded both direct expressions of radical preferences and behaviors that reflect radical preferences.

Radical actors must meet two separate criteria: they must have policy preferences toward a pole of the policy spectrum, and they must exhibit impatience or intransigence to achieve their policy goals. If a party is fairly consistently centrist or amorphous on policy issues, policy radicalism *must* equal o. It does not matter where the party scores on the impatience/intransigence scale. Likewise, if an actor embraces leftist or rightist positions but does not evince policy impatience or intransigence, policy radicalism is o.

The researchers coded political actors as radical when historical evidence indicated that they met any of the following conditions: (1) the actor expressed an uncompromising preference or engaged in uncompromising behavior to achieve leftist or rightist policy positions in the short run or to preserve extreme positions where they were already in place; or (2) expressed willingness to subvert the law in order to achieve some policy goals. The government was also coded as radical if (3) it implemented polarizing policies that deliberately imposed substantial costs to other actors (e.g., expropriations without compensation; labor-repressive regulations to increase labor supply). Nongovernmental actors were coded as radical if (4) they undertook violent acts aimed at imposing or preventing significant policy change. For example, labor unions or other popular organizations might use violent protests to achieve some policy gains. In Colombia, since the 1980s, organized right-wing landowners have used violence to protect their property and increase their political power.[11] If actors were divided or ambiguous about those positions, they were coded as "somewhat" radical. If historical sources did not emphasize any of those traits, we coded the actor as not radical. For measurement purposes, individual actors were given a score of 1 if they were coded as radical, 0.5 if they were somewhat radical, and 0 if they had moderate policy preferences.

We aggregated radicalism scores at the country-year level in three ways: (1) by taking the mean value for all actors; (2) by taking the mean value for the president and other pro-government forces; and (3) by taking the mean value for opposition actors. In Chapter 2 we discussed the possibility that radical positions have opposite effects when they are adopted by members of the government and by members of the opposition. Under an authoritarian regime, radical government officials naturally resist a transition to competitive politics, but the consequences of radical opposition movements are less evident. On the one hand, radical opponents may destabilize the incumbent authoritarian regime, facilitating a transition. On the other, they may trigger a stronger reaction on the part of the government, delaying

---

[11] There is an asymmetry in the coding rules between the government and nongovernmental actors: we did not count governmental violence intended to impose policy change as an indicator of radical policy preferences. The reason is that the coding rules must clearly separate radicalism (as an independent variable) from the political regime (the dependent variable). Barring exceptional circumstances such as an armed insurrection or a riot that the government combats while fully respecting the constitution, governmental violence intrinsically affects the dependent variable.

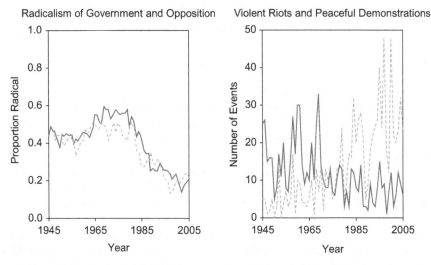

FIGURE 3.4 Radicalism and Mass Protests in Latin America, 1945–2005
Note: In the left panel, the solid line reflects the average level of radicalism for governments in the region, and the dotted line reflects the average for opposition groups. In the right panel, the solid line reflects the regional frequency of violent riots, and the dotted line reflects the frequency of antigovernment demonstrations.
Sources: Research for this book and Banks (2004).

regime change; or they may succeed in overthrowing the rulers and impose an authoritarian regime of opposite ideological sign. To explore these alternative causal mechanisms, we computed separate levels of radicalism for the government (and its allies) and for opposition actors for each regime-year.[12]

The right panel in Figure 3.4 displays the evolution of radicalism for the government and the opposition in the average Latin American country between 1945 and 2005. Levels of radicalism remained consistently high among government and opposition forces until the mid-1980s, when they declined considerably. On average, three-fifths of the governments and half of the opposition actors had radical policy preferences in 1969, but only a fifth of them were radical by 2005.

The behavioral consequences of radical policy preferences can be assessed by looking at the right panel in Figure 3.4, which shows the yearly number of violent riots and peaceful demonstrations reported by Banks' Cross-National Time-Series Data Archive in Latin America. Riots are defined as "any violent demonstration or clash of more than 100 citizens involving the use of physical force." By contrast, antigovernment demonstrations are "any peaceful public gathering of at least 100 people for the primary purpose of displaying or voicing their opposition to government policies or authority" (Banks 2006). The decline in radicalism did not mean a

---

[12] When actors were neutral or divided, they were treated as "half" case contributing to the average of the government *and* the opposition in the country.

demobilization of Latin American citizens, but it led to the substitution of violent protests for nonviolent demonstrations among groups demanding social change.

Normative Regime Preferences

A normative preference for democracy means that an actor values democracy intrinsically, that is, above any policy outcomes. The actor has an ideological commitment to democracy as the best kind of political regime. Likewise, a normative preference for dictatorship signals that an actor actually embraces a nondemocratic regime as its first choice *in principle*. A normative preference for a regime type (democracy or dictatorship) is the opposite of strategic, instrumental, or opportunistic support for a regime. It means that an actor is willing to accept policy sacrifices in order to achieve or preserve the regime type.

A normative preference for dictatorship is not the same as a situational preference in which an actor supports a dictatorship at a given historical moment because the dictatorship will yield some policy benefits. The fact that an actor supported a dictatorship at a particular moment in time does not mean that the actor has a principled preference for dictatorship. Likewise, the mere fact that a government engages in repression does not demonstrate a normative preference for dictatorship. Nor does conspiring against a democracy necessarily show a normative preference for dictatorship. If an actor believes that some kind of dictatorship is *generally* superior to democracy because it offers the opportunity for efficient, technocratic decision making without interference by politicized nonrational actors (legislatures, parties), this is one example of a normative preference for dictatorship.

As we noted in Chapter 2, the coding rules must distinguish between actors' normative preferences and their situational, insincere, or opportunistic decision to support a given regime. Otherwise, we would run a grave risk of inferring that actors' support for a given regime implies a normative preference for that regime type. This would debase the notion that normative preferences are important in understanding regime outcomes. Our coding rules are therefore designed to distinguish between actors' normative preferences and situational support for a regime.

Because political actors often pay lip service to democracy, we looked for discursive or behavioral indicators of support for dictatorships and for explicit indicators of *low* preferences for democratic norms, and accepted statements in support for democracy as valid if those negative indicators were absent. Indicators of a normative preference for dictatorship signal that actors actually embraced a nondemocratic regime as their first choice, not that they were just uncommitted to democracy. In the absence of an explicit preference for dictatorship, we recorded no normative preference for democracy when actors signaled their willingness to accept violations of any of the four democratic principles discussed in earlier sections (free and fair elections, universal suffrage, civil liberties, and civilian rule) for political gain.

Our measure of normative regime preferences ranges from -1, when actors are explicitly committed to some form of dictatorship, to 1, when actors show a consistent and strong normative preference for democracy. Our scale also allows for three intermediate values: −0.5 (a fairly strong but not entirely consistent normative preference for some form of authoritarian regime), 0 (no clear and consistent normative preference), and 0.5 (a fairly strong but not entirely consistent preference for democracy).

We coded actors as normatively preferring dictatorships, or −1, if they displayed at least one of the following characteristics: (1) expressed overt hostility toward democracy or advocated a new form of government to transcend modern democracy; (2) praised authoritarian rulers or regimes (not just their policies) as models to be emulated; (3) expressed loyalty to an individual presented as the only person deserving to rule the country, and treated any leader who challenged this (current or potential) ruler as illegitimate; (4) expressed loyalty to a single party, presented as the only organization with a legitimate right to rule the country in the foreseeable future, and treated any organization that challenged this (current or potential) ruling party as illegitimate. In the case of public officials, we also coded them as holding a preference for dictatorship when they (5) made a sustained argument in defense of concentrating power beyond constitutional rules, or in defense of extending their hold of power into an indefinite future. We coded presidents as normatively preferring nondemocratic regimes if they (6) advocated permanent restrictions to the four dimensions of democracy introduced earlier, such as the elimination of an elected Congress, restrictions in voter rights, the indefinite suspension of constitutional rights, or an active role of the military in politics. Actors displaying any of those six traits were coded as showing a preference for dictatorship. We coded their preference for dictatorship as "limited," or −0.5, when individual leaders had ambiguous or fluctuating positions, or when collective actors showed internal divisions on these issues.

In the absence of explicit support for dictatorships, we looked for indicators of a weak normative preference for democracy. Actors were coded as *not* holding a preference for democracy (i.e., given a score of 0 on our scale) if they displayed at least one of the following characteristics: (1) expressed ambivalence or indifference about democracy (e.g., by criticizing "bourgeois," "liberal," or "formal" democracy) or indicated that they valued some policy outcomes above democratic rules of the game; (2) expressed hostility toward democratic institutions (parties, legislatures, courts, electoral bodies) beyond challenging specific decisions; (3) questioned the validity of democratic procedures when they produced unfavorable results; (4) claimed to be the sole representatives of the people; (5) questioned the legitimacy of any opposition outside an encompassing national movement; or (6) consistently dismissed peaceful opponents as enemies of the people or the country. Government officials were also coded as lacking a normative preference for democracy when they (7) introduced programs of partisan indoctrination into the public school system or the military, and when they (8) manipulated institutional rules frequently in order to gain political advantage. Nongovernmental actors were treated as lacking strong preferences for democracy when they (9) expressed willingness to subvert the constitution or

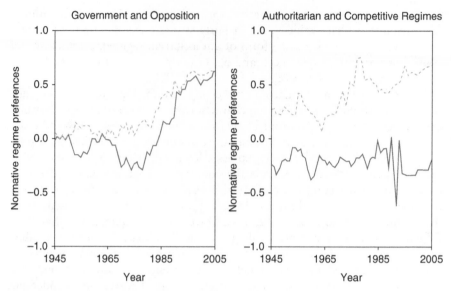

FIGURE 3.5 Normative Regime Preferences in Latin America, 1945–2005
Note: Positive values indicate support for democracy and negative values indicate support for dictatorship. In the left panel, the solid line reflects the average preferences for governments, and the dotted line is the average for opposition groups. In the right panel, the solid line reflects the average preferences in authoritarian regimes (all actors); the dotted line shows the average preferences in competitive regimes.

(10) accepted the use of fraud, political exclusions, or violence for political purposes. Actors were coded as lacking a normative preference for democracy (a score of 0 on our scale) if they decisively met any of the ten criteria; as having a "fairly strong but not entirely consistent" preference (0.5) if they exhibited ambiguity in any of the ten indicators, and as having a strong normative preference for democracy (1 on our scale) if they did not manifest any hostile orientations and accepted outcomes as legitimate because of the democratic process regardless of the specific outcome.

As in the case of radicalism, we aggregated scores for normative preferences by taking the mean for all actors in every country-year. We again computed separate values for government and opposition forces, although the distinction is less relevant in the case of normative orientations – support for democracy should favor transitions and prevent breakdowns among all groups. Figure 3.5 displays the evolution of regime preferences between 1945 and 2005. The left panel compares the mean values for the government and the opposition, while the right panel compares the values for all actors under competitive (democratic and semi-democratic) and noncompetitive regimes.

The left panel suggests some important conclusions. The typical political actor in Latin America has become increasingly committed to democracy since the 1980s. Even at the present, however, this normative commitment is far from universal. During the second half of the twentieth century, governments typically trailed the opposition in terms of their normative preferences for democracy, with a greater gap during the era of bureaucratic-authoritarian regimes in the late 1960s and the 1970s. Not surprisingly, opposition forces began to value liberal democracy earlier and led the transformation of normative preferences that altered the regional political landscape after 1977. Until the 1980s, however, the average values for the opposition forces remained close to zero, indicating at best indifference toward democratic principles, and potentially explaining a volatile regime environment in the region.

The right-hand panel of Figure 3.5 underscores a consistent gap between the normative regime preferences of political actors under authoritarian and competitive regimes. This gap is consistent with our claim that actors with a normative preference for democracy tend to create and sustain competitive regimes, but it also hints at the possibility of reverse causation. Because government officials usually deploy state power in order to protect the incumbent regime, actors with democratic ideals proliferate under competitive politics and actors with authoritarian principles thrive under authoritarianism. This is perhaps most obvious under authoritarian systems, where organizations and individuals with democratic preferences may be simply repressed, dismantled, or exiled. Democratic regimes also promote the propagation of like-minded actors through public education and the selective repression of violent illegal movements. This form of reverse causation complicates the empirical testing of our hypotheses about normative preferences. We address this issue more systematically in the last section of this chapter and when we discuss problems of endogeneity in the next chapter.

MEASURING INTERNATIONAL FACTORS

In Chapter 2 we argued that international factors have direct and indirect effects on regime change. International actors may pressure incumbents to step down or provide resources to particular domestic actors to support regime change. They may also influence the policy preferences and normative beliefs of domestic actors and thus affect the political process in more subtle ways.

Intuitively, waves of democratization should be driven by causal mechanisms that operate simultaneously in multiple countries, reducing the average risk of breakdown or increasing the average probability of a transition in the region. Convergent regime change (or convergent regime stability) could be explained by a set of mechanisms discussed in the literature under the comprehensive label of "diffusion." As we discuss at length in Chapter 7, convergent regime change may be stimulated by transnational actors, by regional powers, by diplomatic support or foreign assistance, and by the dissemination of norms, beliefs, and organizational models. Democratic or authoritarian forces may be inspired by events elsewhere and emulate their tactics, or they may be discouraged by the failure of similar groups abroad and learn from their mistakes.[13]

Previous research has not gone far enough to disentangle these various mechanisms. If an increase in the number of democracies worldwide at time t is correlated with a greater probability of any existing authoritarian country becoming democratic at time $t + 1$, this could in principle mean that that the world is being swept by democratic ideals (Fukuyama 1992), that democratic nations are gaining control of international organizations and pressuring other countries for democratization (Pevehouse 2005), that policy makers in authoritarian countries are reading the signs of the times and emulating their neighbors (Gleditsch 2002), or any combination of the those explanations. To disentangle some of these causal mechanisms, we created separate variables for three effects that are often lumped together: the impact of the global political environment, the effects of U.S. policy toward democracy and authoritarianism in the region, and regional diffusion effects in the strict sense.

Trends outside Latin America

Convergent regime change within a region could be explained by powerful historical phenomena originating outside of the region. At least four types of phenomena could drive such effects. First, secular ideational transformations such as the rise of the Enlightenment in the eighteenth century and the expanding influence of Marxism in the twentieth may progressively acquire transregional reach and affect regimes across different regions. Second, dramatic regime changes outside of the region can make new forms of government available to domestic political actors, who rely on the "heuristics of availability" to pursue similar changes in their own countries (Weyland 2005, 2006). The American, French, and Russian revolutions were extraordinary episodes of this kind. Third, systemic changes in the relative strength of world powers – typically determined by wars – may empower some domestic actors and facilitate the adoption of certain forms of government. For example, Figures 3.1 and 3.2 showed a surge in democratization (worldwide as well as in Latin America) toward the end of World War II. Last, global economic processes such as the crisis of the 1930s may undermine or boost incumbent regimes across the world.

These processes operate transregionally. When such mechanisms are in operation, convergent regime change will manifest itself in multiple regions simultaneously. Thus, some of these mechanisms can explain global waves of democratization, decolonization, policy reforms, and other convergent trends.

Figure 3.6 shows the proportion of competitive regimes for all countries in the world, excluding Latin America, using the Polity IV dataset. The figure indicates

---

[13] Convergent regime change may also be caused by external military imposition in multiple countries at the same time, but this mechanism is less relevant for the region and period under study.

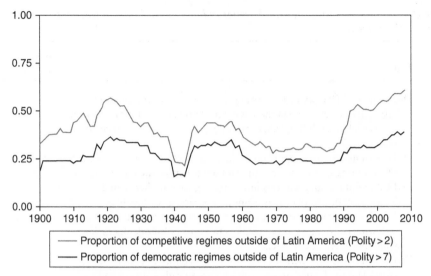

FIGURE 3.6 Proportion of Competitive Regimes outside Latin America, 1900–2010
Source: Polity IV 2012.

some correspondence, but also important differences with the patterns in Figure 3.2. The democratizing trend until the 1920s was much stronger among the non-Latin American independent nations (Polity excludes colonial territories, so a vast proportion of the world is unaccounted for in the early twentieth century). Likewise, the decline between 1923 and 1943 was much steeper outside of Latin America. Paradoxically – given that the third wave of democratization was ignited in Southern Europe – it becomes manifest only in the 1990s if we exclude the Latin American cases.

The correlation between the proportion of competitive regimes reported in Figures 3.2 (for Latin America) and 3.6 (for other regions) is just .46, indicating a positive but mild correlation between trends in Latin America and global trends outside of the region. Thus, it is possible that some extra-regional mechanisms played a role in Latin American transformations, but their effects were limited and mediated by more proximate regional conditions. We assess the effect of extra-regional trends by including the average Polity score for non-Latin American countries (lagged by one year) in our empirical models. In our primary models, we weight all countries in the world equally.

U.S. Policy toward Latin America

Conventional wisdom holds that U.S. policies toward Latin America have had a fundamental impact on the prospects of democratization throughout the region. It is widely believed that U.S. intervention in the Caribbean in the early twentieth century, as well as its focus on containing communism in the 1960s, hindered

TABLE 3.2. *Rules to Code U.S. Foreign Policy toward Political Regimes in Latin America*

Item	Score (if Yes)
1　Did influential U.S. policy leaders express a preference for democracy in Latin America even when there were trade-offs with other important values such as stability, U.S. economic interests, and U.S. security interests?	+1
2　Did the United States support coups, armed rebellions, or U.S. military interventions against democratic and semi-democratic governments?	−1
3　Did U.S. military interventions limit sovereignty (and hence limit democracy) of democratic or semi-democratic governments?	−1
4　Did the United States actively promote the democratization of authoritarian regimes and/or make efforts to bolster democracies when they were under threat?	+1
5　Did the United States criticize authoritarian regimes that were not leftist? Did the United States criticize human rights abuses and infringements on civil and political rights by regimes that were not leftist?	+1
6　Did U.S. foreign policy leaders clearly support authoritarian regimes?	−1
7　Did U.S. leaders express the view that Latin American countries could not be democracies because of cultural dispositions?	−1
8　Did the United States practice a policy of nonrecognition when a military coup or rebellion overthrew a democratic or semi-democratic government?	+1

Note: if the answer to the question was negative, items received a score of 0. The cumulative score ranging between −4 and 4 was rescaled to range between 0 and 1. (See Appendix 3.2 for more detailed information on the coding of sources and aggregation procedures.)

Latin American democratization. Conversely, it is often stated that President Carter's (1977–81) focus on human rights facilitated the emergence of competitive regimes. Although a matter of great contention, the regional impact of U.S. policies on regime change is not easy to trace.

There was no prior reasonably valid measure of U.S. foreign policy toward democracy in Latin America. Therefore, it was difficult to assess the impact of U.S. policy on political regimes beyond case studies. To address this lacuna, we developed a quantitative index ranging between 0 (no U.S. support for democracy in Latin America) and 1 (high U.S. support for democracy).

We coded each presidential administration using multiple secondary sources to assess the eight questions presented in Table 3.2.[14] Questions 2, 3, 6, and 7

---

[14] If U.S. policy regarding political regimes in Latin America changed during a presidential term, we used each year as the time period.

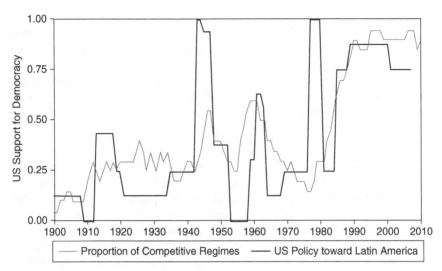

FIGURE 3.7 U.S. Policy toward Democracy in Latin America, 1900–2008
Source: Authors' classification (see Appendixes 3.1 and 3.2).

address U.S. behavior and attitudes that are harmful to democracy in Latin America, while questions 1, 4, 5, and 8 address U.S. behaviors intended to support democracy in Latin America. The first set of questions was coded 0 (when the answer was negative) or −1 (when the answer was affirmative). The second set of questions was coded 0 (when the answer was negative) or +1 (affirmative). We added the scores for the eight questions, producing a scale from −4 to +4, and rescaled the scores to range from 0 (a policy indifferent to regime type) to 1 (a solidly pro-democracy policy). We describe the precise coding rules for the eight questions and the aggregation procedure in Appendix 3.2.

Figure 3.7 shows the aggregate scores for each period. It displays considerable coincidence with Figure 3.2 (the proportion of competitive regimes is overlaid for reference): the correlation between the U.S. policy index and the proportion of competitive regimes is .67. Based on these scores, U.S. policy toward political regimes in Latin America was unfavorable to democracy from 1900 to 1943. To varying degrees, U.S. policy was favorable to democracy in Latin America from 1944 to 1947, 1961 to 1963, 1977 to 1980, and 1985 to 2007 (the last year for which we coded historical sources).

Dissemination within the Region

In addition to global trends and hegemonic powers, changes in neighboring countries may affect the preferences and resources of domestic coalitions. We estimate the presence of a favorable regional environment using the average score in our democracy scale for the whole region (but excluding the country in question) during the previous year. The coding for this indicator is based on our trichotomous measure of democracy. The value of this variable can theoretically range from o, if none of the other nineteen countries in the region were democratic in a given year, to 1 if all nineteen countries were democratic in that year. To compute this average, we gave semi-democratic countries a score of 0.5. We exclude the country in question and lag the variable to minimize problems of endogeneity. Therefore, the variable reflecting the regional environment is defined for any country i at time t as:

$$R_{it} = (D_{t-1} + 0.5S_{t-1} - \gamma_{it-1})(N/(N-1)) \qquad (3.1)$$

where R_{it} is the value of the regional indicator, D_{t-1} is the proportion of democracies in the region during the previous year, S_{t-1} is the proportion of semi-democracies in the region during the previous year, and γ_{it-1} is a correction term that acquires a value of $1/N$ if the country was democratic, and $1/(2N)$ if the country was semi-democratic during the previous year (i.e., excludes the country's score if the regime was competitive during the past year). The second term $(N/(N-1))$ reweights the proportions to reflect the fact that the specific country was excluded from the denominator. In our sample, the number of countries is 19 until Panama's independence in 1903, and $N = 20$ afterward.

Our primary measure of the regional context does not weight countries according to their reciprocal distance, size, or other criteria. We checked the robustness of the results using spatial lags (i.e., weighting cases according to their reciprocal distance) in Chapter 4.

ACTORS' PREFERENCES AS ENDOGENOUS EXPLANATIONS

In this concluding section, we explore the relationship among some independent variables, emphasizing how some of them potentially influence the development of normative regime preferences. We show that normative preferences are not a mere reflection of structural preconditions or other predictors. In order to do so, we address the endogenous origin of actors' normative principles.

Normative regime preferences – discussed under different labels – often emerge as a powerful explanation in historical case studies, but they are treated as an unobserved variable in cross-national quantitative studies. Three reasons explain this omission: (1) normative orientations are difficult to measure for a large number of actors over long historical periods; (2) because they are somewhat proximate to regime outcomes, even if they are properly measured their causal effects on regime change are hard to assess; and (3) most theories have treated normative preferences as epiphenomenal, as by-products of the actors' institutional or structural positions, effectively denying actors agency.

Table 3.3 presents several regression models in which normative regime preferences (ranging between –1 and 1) are the dependent variable. The units of analysis are all country-years in Latin America between 1945 and 2005, making the sample equivalent to the one used for the analysis in Chapter 4. In the first model (3.3.1), regime preferences are modeled as a function of several structural

TABLE 3.3. *Models of Normative Regime Preferences*

	3.3.1 Structural	3.3.2 International	3.3.3 Radicalism	3.3.4 Dynamic	3.3.5 Fixed Effects
Radicalism (all actors)			-0.891*** (0.033)	-0.218*** (0.019)	-0.934*** (0.034)
Region, $t-1$		0.500*** (0.100)	0.065 (0.073)	0.023 (0.035)	0.064 (0.066)
U.S. policy		0.112** (0.045)	0.046 (0.032)	0.030* (0.015)	0.031 (0.026)
Polity outside region, $t-1$		0.047*** (0.011)	0.005 (0.008)	-0.004 (0.004)	0.020*** (0.007)
Per capita GDP, $\ln t-1$	0.321*** (0.024)	0.211*** (0.023)	0.164*** (0.016)	0.020** (0.008)	0.276*** (0.031)
Industrial labor	0.002 (0.002)	0.002 (0.002)	-0.009*** (0.002)	-0.002** (0.001)	-0.005** (0.002)
Oil and minerals	0.053 (0.038)	0.059* (0.034)	0.050** (0.024)	0.014 (0.012)	0.085 (0.068)
Growth, 10 years	-0.535 (0.656)	0.468 (0.614)	-0.806* (0.438)	-0.040 (0.212)	-1.440*** (0.384)
Democracy, 1900–44[a]		0.656*** (0.069)	0.136*** (0.052)	0.017 (0.025)	n.a.
Authoritarian, $t-1$			-0.349*** (0.023)	-0.038*** (0.012)	-0.213*** (0.020)
Regime preferences, $t-1$				0.837*** (0.013)	
Constant	-2.324*** (0.160)	-1.867*** (0.150)	-0.450*** (0.114)	-0.003 (0.055)	-1.383*** (0.213)
N	1,220	1,220	1,220	1,220	1,220
R²	0.184	0.341	0.672	0.923	0.633

Note: Entries are regression coefficients (standard errors). Dependent variable is normative regime preferences for the average actor in each country-year (higher values indicate greater support for democracy).
[a] Regime legacies are excluded from the fixed-effects model because this predictor has no within-country variance.
*** $p < 0.01$, ** $p < 0.05$, * $p < 0.1$.

variables conventionally invoked in the quantitative democratization literature: the level of development, measured as the natural logarithm of per capita GDP in 2000 U.S. dollars; the percentage of the labor force working in manufacturing and mining; a dichotomous indicator measuring whether oil and minerals represent more than 10 percent of national income (intended to assess the consequences of the "resource curse"); and the levels of economic growth under the incumbent regime, measured as the average rate of change in GDP over the past decade.

We discuss structural variables and their theoretical underpinnings in greater detail in the next chapter. For the purposes of this section, note that only per capita GDP has a significant effect on the normative support for democracy expressed by political actors. The direction of the effect is consistent with modernization theory (Lipset 1959); in wealthier countries, actors are more likely to have a normative preference for democracy. However, the overall predictive power of structural variables is low: 82 percent of the variance in normative orientations toward the political regime remains unexplained if we focus only on structural explanations. For Latin America, structural variables are weak proxies for the more proximate factors that drive regime change.[15]

The second model in Table 3.3 includes some contextual explanations for the development of normative commitments. We include our three measures of the international environment discussed earlier: the level of democracy in the region, U.S. policy toward Latin America, and the average Polity score outside of Latin America. In order to capture historical legacies of prior democratic experiences, the model also includes a country-level variable reflecting the average level of democracy in the country between 1900 and 1944. This variable summarizes our coding of the political regime during those forty-five years, with democratic years receiving a value of 1, semi-democratic ones a value of 0.5, and authoritarian ones a value of 0. The results show that historical legacies have a strong influence on the normative orientations of actors (Pérez-Liñán and Mainwaring 2013). In countries with stronger democratic legacies in the first forty-five years of the twentieth century, actors were more likely to develop normative preferences for democracy. In Model 3.3.2, all three international factors influence domestic actors' orientation: U.S. policy favorable to democracy, a democratic environment in the other Latin American countries, and a democratic environment in the world encourage the development of normative preferences for democracy. These findings are consistent with our claim in Chapter 2 that domestic politics and international influences shape actors' normative preferences. Their effects become statistically insignificant once we control for radical preferences and the nature of the regime in Model 3.3.3, indicating that international influences may operate in indirect ways.

The remaining models include two more proximate factors driving normative orientations toward democracy: the radicalization of policy preferences and the

---

[15] We also computed an equivalent model (not shown to save space) including the Gini index of income inequality as an additional predictor. Because data on income inequality is scant, the number of observations dropped by about 40% ($N = 665$) even after we interpolated scores for this variable. The R^2 remained low (.15), confirming our general point about the limited usefulness of structural proxies. Against theoretical expectations, the coefficient for the Gini index was positive, meaning that in country years with higher income inequality, actors had stronger normative preferences for democracy. With the reduced sample, a cautious interpretation of this finding is in order. Latin American countries faced crippling economic problems in the 1980s and first half of the 1990s. The response to economic crisis exacerbated income inequalities. Concomitantly, but not causally related, normative preferences for democracy were becoming more widespread.

nature of the incumbent regime. As explained in Chapter 2, radicalism may encourage intransigent actors to embrace authoritarian principles in order to advance (or protect) extreme policy goals. At the same time, Figure 3.6 indicated that actors in authoritarian systems consistently display lower levels of support for democracy than actors in competitive regimes. This may be explained by the fact that democratic actors "select out" from the authoritarian pool (producing a transition to democracy, a possibility that we explore in the next chapter) or by the fact that authoritarian regimes "weed out" democratic actors through coercion or exile. The dichotomous indicator for authoritarian regimes in 3.3 is intended to capture the latter possibility.

The results in model 3.3.3 indicate that radicalism is a very powerful predictor of normative regime preferences, and that actors display lower levels of support for democracy under authoritarianism even after controlling for structural and international conditions. Those results are robust and hold in a dynamic model including the lagged values of the dependent variable (3.3.4), and in a fixed-effects model (3.3.5). This finding is also supported by a model – not shown to save space – treating radicalism of the government and the opposition as separate variables (both coefficients are negative and significant). Such results are not surprising or counterintuitive, but they suggest two final questions to validate our measurement of the main independent variables.

First, if radicalism is an important predictor of (low) normative support for democracy, to what extent is radicalism itself endogenous to regime preferences? Is the relationship simply showing, for example, that some unobserved historical trend or factor drives both variables? To address this issue, we estimated a simultaneous equation model, presented in Table 3.4, in which levels of radicalism and support for democracy are estimated as a system, and the error terms for the two equations are allowed to be correlated. In this system of two equations, international factors and structural conditions are treated as common explanations for radicalism and normative regime preferences. We identified the equations by including a dichotomous indicator of internal armed conflict (from the UCDP/PRIO Armed Conflict Dataset) as a predictor of radicalism, and regime legacies and authoritarianism as predictors of normative regime preferences. Radicalism in turn is included in the second equation as an endogenous predictor of normative regime preferences. To account for the possibilities of reverse causality (that is, normative preferences driving radicalism) or of unobserved factors driving both variables, we allowed residuals in the two equations to be correlated. The results show that radical policy preferences are driven in part by structural and international forces, yet the negative influence of radicalism on democratic values does not vanish when we allow for an endogenous relation.[16]

---

[16] The SEM model was estimated using M*plus* software. The R^2 for an OLS model of radical policy preferences using an equivalent specification is 0.25, indicating that structural conditions, international forces, and armed conflict are just partial explanations for policy preferences.

TABLE 3.4. *Simultaneous Equations of Policy Radicalism and Regime Preferences*

Outcome	Radicalism		Regime preferences	
Predictor	Coef.	(s.e.)	Coef.	(s.e.)
Radicalism (all actors)			−1.046 ***	(0.143)
Region, $t-1$	−0.217 ***	(0.063)	0.036	(0.078)
U.S. policy	−0.040	(0.028)	0.041	(0.032)
Polity outside region, $t-1$	−0.024 ***	(0.007)	0.000	(0.009)
Per capita GDP, ln $t-1$	−0.084 ***	(0.014)	0.149 ***	(0.021)
Industrial labor	−0.009 ***	(0.001)	−0.010 ***	(0.002)
Oil and minerals	0.073 ***	(0.022)	0.057 **	(0.025)
Growth, 10 years	−1.294 ***	(0.390)	−1.076 **	(0.502)
Internal armed conflict	0.203 ***	(0.026)		
Democracy, 1900–44			0.140 ***	(0.052)
Authoritarianism, $t-1$			−0.352 ***	(0.023)
Constant	1.308 ***	(0.091)	−0.233	(0.225)
Residual correlation			0.013	(0.011)
N			1,220	

Note: Entries are regression coefficients in SEM (standard errors). Dependent variable is normative regime preferences for the average actor (higher values indicate greater support for democracy). *** $p < 0.01$, ** $p < 0.05$, * $p < 0.1$.

Second, and more important, to the extent that normative regime orientations are influenced by past regime legacies and by the nature of the incumbent regime, there is an important inkling of reciprocal causation between regime types and regime preferences. Past experiences with democracy increase levels of support for democracy among political actors at the present, which in turn may affect the likelihood of democratic transitions or breakdowns in the near future. In order to test the causal impact of normative orientations, we need to account for these potential confounding effects in later chapters.

We have created original measures of policy and regime preferences for 1,460 political actors under 290 Latin American administrations. The preliminary evidence presented in this chapter shows that actors' orientations and preferences cannot be reduced to prevailing structural forces, even though some structural conditions and international factors affect their development. This evidence provides a unique opportunity to test actor-centered explanations of regime change, a task we undertake in the rest of the book.

4

Regime Survival and Fall

A Quantitative Test

This chapter presents most of the quantitative evidence related to three primary research questions in this book. First, what factors help explain democratic transitions in Latin America? Second, what factors explain the breakdown of competitive regimes once established? And third, to what extent do those explanations account for the dramatic wave of democratization that began in 1978?

The chapter is structured in five sections. The first provides an operational definition of our two dependent variables (transitions and breakdowns), summarizes the strategy for statistical analysis, and uses our classification of political regimes in Latin America to document the decline in the risk of democratic breakdowns and the surprising expansion of democratic transitions that took place after 1977. The second part of the chapter introduces our control variables, which reflect alternative explanations dealing with structural preconditions, regime economic performance, and institutional factors. We discussed the operationalization of the indicators of regional diffusion effects, U.S. support for democracy, and actors' normative regime preferences and radicalization in the previous chapter.

Section three presents the results of the statistical analysis for democratic transitions and breakdowns. Transitions are more likely to occur after other transitions have taken place in neighboring countries and when domestic political actors have a normative preference for competitive politics. We document possible indirect effects of radicalism in preventing democratic transitions. Radical opposition actors undermine dictatorships, facilitating the establishment of competitive regimes. Competitive regimes are less likely to break down when more countries in the region are democratic and when elites are committed to democratic ideals. Radicalism undermines competitive regimes indirectly through the erosion of normative preferences for democracy.

The fourth section shows how the results of survival models estimated at the country-year level translate into an aggregate distribution of political regimes at the regional level. We test the validity of our explanation for the third wave of

democratization by proving that the aggregate level of democratization predicted by our statistical models over the long run is similar to the historical
outcomes observed in the region after 1977. The concluding section summarizes
the implications of these findings for our theory.

EXPLAINING REGIME CHANGE THROUGH QUANTITATIVE ANALYSIS

The events of interest for our theory (regime transitions or breakdowns) take
place in particular countries in specific years. Thus, each political regime in each
year counts as one observation for our analysis; we call this unit a regime-year
(or country-year). Given the difficulty of finding valid indicators for the decades
before 1945, the analysis focuses on 20 countries between 1945 and 2005, for a
total of 1,220 regime-years.

For any country during two consecutive regime-years, the trichotomous
classification of regimes introduced in the previous chapter yields nine possible
situations (presented in Figure 4.1). When a certain type of regime (democratic,
semi-democratic, or authoritarian) existing in the prior year, $t-1$, remains in
place by the end of next year (t), this indicates a situation of regime *stability*,
captured by cells I, V, and IX in the downward diagonal. (An authoritarian
regime may be overthrown and replaced by a different authoritarian regime, but
we are tracking regime *types* in this book.)

The four shaded cells in Figure 4.1 reflect four possible patterns of regime
change from competitive regimes to dictatorships or vice versa. The term *transition* refers to the change from authoritarianism into competitive politics.
A transition may yield two different outcomes: democracy (cell III) or semi-
democracy (cell II). In most historical cases, change from authoritarianism

Regime at time t–1	Regime at time t		
	Authoritarian	Semi-Democracy	Democracy
Authoritarian	I Regime stability $1-(p^S_t + p^D_t)$	II Transition to SD p^S_t	III Transition to D p^D_t
Semi-Democracy	IV Breakdown of SD b^S_t	V Regime stability $1-(b^S_t + q^D_t)$	VI Deepening q^D_t
Democracy	VII Breakdown of D b^D_t	VIII Erosion q^S_t	IX Regime stability $1-(b^D_t + q^S_t)$

FIGURE 4.1 Transition Matrix for a Trichotomous Regime Classification
Key: p^S_t, probability of transition to semi-democracy; p^D_t, probability of transition to
democracy; b^S_t, risk of breakdown for a semi-democracy; q^D_t, probability of deepening
for a semi-democracy; b^D_t, risk of breakdown for a democracy; q^S_t, risk of erosion for a
democracy.

into a competitive regime has meant a major qualitative transformation in politics – usually a change from no elections, or elections whose outcome is known ex ante, to truly competitive elections.[1]

Similarly, the term *breakdown* refers to situations in which competitive regimes become dictatorships. This takes place because either democracies (cell VII) or semi-democracies (cell IV) collapse. Most breakdowns involve dramatic events (such as military coups) that unequivocally mark the end of a competitive regime, but occasionally semi-democracies have degraded into authoritarian politics because incumbents progressively constrained the possibility of political competition. In such cases, we identified a single year as the crossover point (e.g., Argentina in 1951, Venezuela in 2009), even though the process is usually gradual, contested, and hard to date with precision.

The figure helps identify two additional patterns of regime transformation. *Democratic deepening* (cell VI) refers to the transformation of semi-democracies into full democracies, and *democratic erosion* (cell VIII) refers to the transformation of democracies into semi-democracies. Processes of erosion and deepening have been important in the early twenty-first century, and we discuss such changes briefly in Chapter 8. However, they represent transformations *within* the family of competitive regimes, and as such they are not responsible for waves of democratization.

The notation in the cells of Figure 4.1 represents the probability of regime change (or stability), conditional on the initial form of government. For instance, in cell II we locate the hypothetical probability p^S_t that a regime that was authoritarian at $t-1$ becomes semi-democratic at time t. In cell III we locate the probability p^D_t that a regime that was authoritarian at time $t-1$ becomes fully democratic at time t, and so on. This matrix of hypothetical probabilities defines a Markov chain driving the distribution of political regimes in any given historical situation. Waves of democratization are driven by the values corresponding to cells II and III (i.e., the overall probability of a transition) and to cells IV and VII (i.e., the overall risk of breakdown).

The first three columns in Table 4.1 identify the patterns of regime change according to Figure 4.1. The final column presents the number of regime-years corresponding to each cell between 1945 and 2005. Of 576 country-years under authoritarian rule in the sample, 539 survived into the next year, and there were 37 transitions, 14 to democracy and 23 to semi-democracy. Out of 644 country years of competitive regimes, there were 26 breakdowns. The bold-faced rows represent change from competitive regimes to dictatorship or vice versa.

The table also shows the percentage of observations in each regime category (at $t-1$) that remained stable or changed to a different category by the following

---

[1] The exceptions to this rule are generally cases of hegemonic party systems in transition, for which increasing competition may mean a progressive change from authoritarianism into semi-democracy without a clear disruption of the old regime in the short run. However, the regime may be deeply transformed if as a result of this opening full democracy is established in the medium term (as, for instance, in Mexico between 1988 and 2000).

TABLE 4.1. _Patterns of Regime Change, by Period (1945–2005)_

Regime at			Probability of outcome[a]		N
_t – 1_	_t_	(Cell) Pattern	1945–77	1978–2005	1945–2005
Authoritarian	A	(I) Stability	95.4	89.0	539
	SD	(II) Transition 1	3.2	6.1	23
	D	(III) Transition 2	1.5	4.9	14
Semi-Democratic	A	(IV) Breakdown	18.0	2.1	21
	SD	(V) Stability	80.0	90.2	209
	D	(VI) Deepening	2.0	7.7	13
Democratic	A	(VII) Breakdown	3.4	0.0	5
	SD	(VIII) Erosion	2.7	3.6	13
	D	(IX) Stability	93.9	96.4	383
Total N			660	560	1,220

[a] Probability of outcome at time _t_ (as percentage of regime-years observed at _t_ – 1)
Source: Regime classification by Mainwaring, Brinks, and Pérez-Liñán (see Table 3.1).

year (_t_). We disaggregate the information for two subperiods, 1945–1977 and 1978–2005. Ninety-five percent of the authoritarian country-years survived into the next year between 1945 and 1977, but the survival rate dropped to 89 percent after 1977. This information sheds some light on the mechanisms driving the third wave of democratization. The probability of an authoritarian regime transiting into democracy grew from 1.5 percent in 1945–77 to 4.9 percent in 1978–2005 (expanding by 235 percent), while the probability of transition into semi-democracy increased from 3.2 percent to 6.1 percent (expanding by 93 percent). A far more dramatic change in the breakdown rates of competitive regimes occurred in the third wave. The risk of any semi-democratic regime becoming authoritarian in the next twelve months declined from 18 percent in 1945–77 to 2.1 percent in 1978–2005 (a reduction in risk of 88 percent), and the probability of a democratic regime becoming authoritarian dropped from 3.4 percent to virtually zero. Using a demographic metaphor, both a greater birth rate and a sharply lower mortality rate drove the expansion in the population of competitive regimes after 1977. Can the regional change in the third wave be explained by individual transformations at the country level, as most theories of democratization would argue, or did broader, region-wide or worldwide forces play an important role in empowering democratizing coalitions within each country?

Estimation

In the following pages we develop a statistical analysis of this problem using transition models. We divide the set of regime-years in two subsamples:

authoritarian regimes that could undergo transitions and competitive regimes exposed to the risk of breakdown.[2] For each subsample we estimate discrete-time event-history models in which a change of regime type is the outcome of interest.

The dependent variable for authoritarian regime-years has three possible outcomes: authoritarian "stability" (the authoritarian regime survived from one year to the next), transition to semi-democracy, or transition to democracy. The dependent variable for competitive regimes (democratic or semi-democratic) focuses on two outcomes: whether competitive systems survive or break down into authoritarianism in a given year.[3]

Given the nature of the dependent variables for each subsample, we employ a logistic estimator for ordered outcomes to predict the probability of transitions from authoritarian rule into democracy or semi-democracy, and a binary logit estimator to assess the probability of breakdowns into authoritarianism. The ordered logit accommodates the possibility that establishing a semi-democracy may be easier than establishing a full democracy. The estimator for the set of competitive regimes accounts for the possibility that a semi-democracy may be more fragile than a full democracy by including a dichotomous indicator for semi-democratic cases in the right-hand side of the equation.[4] The survival of political regimes may also vary with unobserved, country-level characteristics. To anticipate this potential source of heterogeneity, we estimate frailty models (i.e., with a country-specific baseline hazard) using random effects in our main models.

Following Carter and Signorino (2010), we control for duration-dependence in the survival models using a cubic transformation of the regime's age.[5] This simple procedure is more flexible than the one employed by most event-history estimators. Such flexibility is important because the inauguration of a new regime does not always coincide with a transition or breakdown, and conversely

[2] Equivalent results could be obtained using a dynamic transition model with a pooled sample (e.g., Boix and Stokes 2003; Epstein et al. 2006; Przeworski et al. 2000). Splitting the dataset simplifies the presentation of the results and provides greater flexibility for the treatment of frailty parameters.

[3] Because we focus on regime changes affecting waves and counterwaves of democratization, we subsume partial transformations within the family of competitive regimes (the erosion or deepening of democracy) into the broader category of "survival." This restriction is also necessary because of the small number of cases for some categories.

[4] Given the small number of breakdowns in our sample (n = 26), our analysis operates under the assumption that independent variables will have a similar impact on all competitive regimes. Epstein et al. (2006) claimed that treating partial and full democracies as part of the same pool potentially introduces problems of causal heterogeneity. Their data suggested that some variables such as GDP per capita, urbanization, and trade openness have different effects on the two types of regimes. However, the small number of breakdowns precludes a careful analysis of this issue here.

[5] This parameter is relevant for substantive reasons as well. Rustow (1970) argued that following a regime transition, the "habituation" phase is critical to establish the long-term survival of the regime. If a regime "consolidates," the hazard rate should decline monotonically as times goes by.

the occurrence of a transition or breakdown does not always coincide with the inauguration of a new regime. Such temporal inconsistencies occur for two reasons. First, several distinctive authoritarian regimes may emerge and collapse during a continuous spell of authoritarianism. For instance, the Batista dictatorship in Cuba (1952–59) was overthrown by the Castro regime in 1959. To avoid treating any sequence of different autocratic regimes as a single spell, we reset the regime age to zero when the ruler changed *and* comparative studies of dictatorship (Geddes 2003; J. Wright 2008) reported a transformation in the patterns of authoritarian rule. Second, in a few cases, a revolutionary party imposed non-democratic rule for a transitional period and some years later allowed for competitive elections that established a competitive regime. For example, the Bolivian National Revolutionary Movement took power in 1952 but did not hold elections until 1956, and the Nicaraguan Sandinistas took power in 1979 but did not hold elections until 1984. In those rare cases, the age of the regime was not reset to zero when semi-democracy was established.

ALTERNATIVE EXPLANATIONS

Our quantitative analysis seeks to test the plausibility of theoretical understandings of regime change and stability presented in Chapter 2. In Chapter 3, we described how we conceptualize and measure actors' policy radicalism, their normative preferences about the political regime, the regional political environment, U.S. policy regarding democracy and authoritarianism in Latin America, and the world political environment. This section describes the control variables employed in our models to test alternative theoretical explanations.

Our empirical analysis includes several other factors intended to capture structural preconditions, the economic performance of the incumbent regime, human capital, and the nature of institutional design. Our theoretical perspective on regime stability and change makes us wary of simple socioeconomic explanations of democratization. At the levels of development observed in most Latin American countries in the twentieth century, the effects of development on the political regime are mediated by many currently unknown and undertheorized conditions. However, many influential arguments in comparative politics have emphasized the impact of domestic structural variables on political regimes, and therefore we try to control – to the extent that data are available – for most of the prominent explanations.

Modernization
The most common and long-standing structural theory of democratization is modernization theory. One of the most consistent findings in the democratization literature has been that the level of modernization has a major impact on the likelihood of democracy (Bollen 1980; Bollen and Jackman 1985a, 1985b;

Burkhart and Lewis-Beck 1994; Coppedge 1997; Dahl 1971: 62–80; Diamond 1992; Epstein et al. 2006; Huntington 1984, 1991; Jackman 1973; Lipset 1959; Lipset, Seong, and Torres 1993; Londregan and Poole 1996; Przeworski et al. 2000; Rueschemeyer, Stephens, and Stephens 1992).[6] If some variant of modernization theory holds up for Latin America, democracies would be less likely to break down at higher levels of development, or transitions to competitive regimes would also be more likely at higher levels of development. We measure the level of development using per capita GDP in 2000 U.S. dollars, following the World Development Indicators (World Bank 2007).[7] We supplemented the data using information from Maddison (2003), the Oxford Latin American Economic History Database (Bergés et al. 2007), and the Penn World Tables (Heston and Aten 2006).[8] Because the effect of wealth on democracy is nonlinear (Jackman 1973; Lipset 1959; Lipset, Seong, and Torres 1993), we used a one-year lag of the natural logarithm of per capita GDP.

Our additional tests also include an indicator of literacy as an alternative to per capita income. Several scholars (Darden and Grzymala-Busse 2006; Diamond 1992; Inglehart 1997; Lipset 1960) have argued that higher literacy rates are favorable to the emergence or stabilization of democracy. Inglehart (1997: 168–71), for example, argues that increasing education enables people to participate more in democratic politics and gives them more desire to do so. Although literacy measures a cultural approach to democracy and per capita GDP measures a structural variable, the two are linked theoretically: wealthier countries provide their citizens with more educational opportunities, and in turn, greater education seems to boost productivity and thereby support economic growth (Birdsall 1999; Glaeser et al. 2004). We measured literacy as the percentage of people ages fifteen and older able to read and write, using figures from the Cross-National Time-Series Data Archive (Banks 2006).[9] The correlation between literacy and logged per capita GDP in our sample is .69 (N = 1,220).

---

[6] This finding has been challenged in the Latin American context (Landman 1999; Mainwaring and Pérez-Liñán 2003; O'Donnell 1973).

[7] In principle, a positive correlation between per capita income and the likelihood of democracy could occur because democracies promoted more rapid economic growth than non-democracies (i.e., there could be a problem of endogeneity). If this were the case, even if the two kinds of regimes started out at the same per capita level, the democracies would end up with a higher per capita income, accounting for the positive correlation. This type of bicausality or reverse causality is not a problem with our sample because democracies did not grow at a statistically significant faster pace than non-democracies. The average annual per capita growth rate for democracies was 1.51%; for semi-democracies it was .94%; and for authoritarian regimes it was 1.41% (means for dictatorships and democracies are not statistically different at the .1 level).

[8] We used the alternative sources to compute yearly growth rates for country-years with missing data in the WDI database. Growth rates were used in turn to project WDI figures. For Latin American countries without national accounts in the early twentieth century, we employed available data on exports and imports to predict growth rates, and then followed the same procedure.

[9] We employed linear interpolation to impute missing values in the dataset.

Class Structures

A second group of structural arguments about political regimes emphasized class structures. Diamond (1992), Lipset (1959), Moore (1966), and Rueschemeyer et al. (1992), among others, see the prospects for democracy as resting significantly on the nature of the class structure. We use the percentage of labor force in manufacturing as a gross indicator of the numerical leverage of the working class. The size of different classes is a partial test of Rueschemeyer and colleagues' arguments; they explicitly argued that class size is an important determinant of democracy (p. 59). Per capita GDP is correlated at .44 with the percentage of the labor force working in manufacturing ($p < .001$), but this correlation does not cause serious problems of multicollinearity.

One regression also includes a measure of income inequality. Acemoglu and Robinson (2006) and Boix (2003) claim that the emergence and survival of democracy depend heavily on income distribution (see also Dahl 1971: 81–104). Income inequality data is sparse for a few Latin American countries, and it is unreliable for a few others before the 1990s. We measured income distribution using the Gini index (in a 0–100 scale, where higher values indicate greater inequality). We gathered data from three main sources: Deininger and Squire (1996), the World Bank's *World Development Indicators* (2007), and the World Income Inequality Database (United Nations University 2007). To maximize the comparability of the data points, we employed observations that satisfied three criteria: (1) they were based on nationally representative surveys; (2) they covered the entire population rather than subsets such as urban or rural areas; and (3) they included all types of income. We did not include observations that were grossly inconsistent with other estimates of income inequality for the same country during the same historical period. Specifically, we eliminated any figures that reflected a change of fifteen or more points in income inequality relative to the immediately antecedent or subsequent estimate within a five-year period. Using the remaining data points, we interpolated the missing values in the dataset. This procedure created a time-series with 665 observations for 18 countries in the period between 1961 and 2004. No information was available for Cuba or Haiti, or prior to the 1960s. Because the inclusion of this variable reduces the sample size and the historical coverage of our sample considerably, we computed separate models to test the effects of inequality.

Resource Dependence

A third structural explanation of democratization emphasizes the state's dependence on oil and mineral exports. Several scholars have argued that countries that depend on natural resources such as oil are likely to experience vicious cycles detrimental to democracy (Karl 1997; Ross 2001; but see Haber and Menaldo 2011). Accordingly, we include a dichotomous measure of natural resource dependence, coded 1 if exports of oil and minerals typically represented more than 10 percent of the gross national income (in Bolivia, Chile, and Venezuela between 1945 and 2005, and in Ecuador since 1973).[10]

Regime Economic Performance

Economic performance is relevant for our theoretical perspective because if political actors conclude that the regime is failing to deliver acceptable policy outcomes, they may support a regime change. Several scholars (Diamond 1999: 77–93; Diamond and Linz 1989: 44–46; Gasiorowski 1995; Geddes 1999; Haggard and Kaufman 1995; Lipset et al. 1993; Przeworski et al. 2000) have argued that competitively elected or authoritarian regimes are more likely to break down if their economic performance is poor. We use the rate of change in per capita GDP as the main indicator of performance.

We do not expect short-term changes in economic performance to have dramatic effects on the stability of the regime because political actors may interpret those changes as the result of exogenous shocks or blame the incumbent government rather than the regime. But we hypothesize that sustained positive performance will make actors more willing to support (or tolerate) the regime, while sustained negative performance will encourage more actors to join an adversarial coalition. For this reason, the main variable capturing regime performance in our models is medium-term economic growth. This indicator captures the average rate of change in per capita income over the past decade (when the regime is at least ten years old) or the average rate since the establishment of the regime (if it is younger).[11]

One analysis also includes a measure of inflation, reflecting the evolution of the consumer price index.[12] Data on inflation was missing for some periods (e.g., Haiti between 1945 and 1952) and for Cuba altogether, so we present models including inflation as separate regressions. We assumed that the impact of inflation on regime change is nonlinear: an increase in inflation from 0 to 100 percent should have a greater impact on regime stability than an increase from 900 to 1,000 percent. For this reason, we calculated the natural logarithm of the inflation rate.[13] As in the case of growth, our indicator captures medium-term performance by taking the average value for this indicator over the past decade or since the inception of the regime.

---

[10] As an alternative, continuous measure, we used the average proportion of the gross national income represented by exports of fuel and minerals during the past five years (computed from the World Development Indicators). Information for this variable was not available before 1967 (1972 in most cases), but the results remained consistent. Because of the missing values before 1972, we employed the dichotomous indicator in our models.

[11] We also tested alternative models with short-term (previous year) effects of growth and inflation (not shown). These variables do not alter the main conclusions.

[12] Inflation was obtained from the World Development Indicators database for the 1961–2005 period and from the Global Financial Database and from ECLAC (the Economic Commission for Latin America and the Caribbean) reports for the 1945–60 period (ECLAC 2001).

[13] The actual formula employed was $ln[1 + i_{t-1}]$ for any case of $i \geq 0$ and $-ln[1 + |i_{t-1}|]$ for $i < 0$ (i.e., deflation), where i is the annual percent change in the consumer price index (Gasiorowski 2000: 326).

Formal Institutions

An extensive literature has emphasized the role of institutional design in creating stable democracy. This literature is relevant for analyzing the survival of competitive regimes, but not for the analysis of transitions from authoritarianism. One such argument refers to the power of the executive branch vis-à-vis congress. Shugart and Carey (1992) argued that presidentialism functions more effectively with weaker constitutional presidential powers. A high concentration of power in presidential hands encourages the executive branch to bypass congress and promotes institutional tensions in the regime. To assess this argument, we used Shugart and Carey's (1992) measure of presidential powers for the competitive regimes in our sample.[14]

A second institutional debate has centered on the nature of party systems in presidential regimes. Kenney (2004), Linz (1994), Mainwaring (1993), and Stepan and Skach (1994) argued that presidential regimes with fragmented party systems are more prone to breakdown. They claimed that when presidents had minority support in congress, impasses between the president and congress were more common, sometimes leading to democratic breakdown. Cheibub (2002, 2007) challenged this analysis, arguing that there is no relationship between party system fragmentation and democratic survival in presidential systems. To assess this factor, we created a dichotomous variable coded as 1 if the effective number of parties in the lower (or only) chamber was equal or greater than 3.0 in a given year. The effective number of parties (ENP) is a mathematical calculation that weights parties according to their size and indicates the level of party system fragmentation; an effective number of 3.0 or more parties clearly indicates multipartism.[15] We employ a dichotomous indicator for theoretical reasons and because of missing information on the precise number of parties for Ecuador in the 1950s and Peru in the mid-1940s. The debate about the impact of party system fragmentation and presidential powers on democratic stability in presidential regimes is not relevant for explaining transitions from authoritarianism, but it might help explain the *stability* of democratic and semi-democratic regimes once established.

STATISTICAL ANALYSIS

This section presents the results of the statistical models for transitions and breakdowns. Both transitions and breakdowns are rare events that are

---

[14] The index of presidential powers reflects the sum of two point-score measures, an index of legislative powers, reflecting proactive and reactive powers in the constitution, and an index of nonlegislative powers, reflecting control over appointments and dissolution of congress (Shugart and Carey 1992). In our sample of competitive regimes, the scores for the index ranged between 5 and 22.

[15] The formula for the effective number of parties (ENP) is $1/\Sigma p^2$, where sigma indicates the sum of p^2, the proportion of seats (squared) obtained by each party (Laakso and Taagepera 1979).

difficult to predict. Between 1945 and 2005, thirty-seven transitions from authoritarianism took place in the region (nineteen before 1978 and the remaining eighteen afterward). The units for the analysis of this outcome are authoritarian regime-years ($N = 576$). During the same period, twenty-six competitive systems broke down into authoritarian rule. The units of analysis for this outcome are competitive regime-years ($N = 644$). For both outcomes, we present general results first, followed by a discussion of endogeneity and by a series of robustness tests.

Transitions to Competitive Regimes

Table 4.2 presents the results of six discrete-time survival models in which the outcome of interest is a transition to competitive politics. The dependent variable is coded trichotomously: 0 indicates the persistence of authoritarian rule by December 31 of each year, 1 indicates a transition to semi-democracy, and 2 indicates a transition to democracy. We employ ordered logistic regression as the estimating technique, including random effects to account for unobserved frailties in models 4.2.1 through 4.2.5.

Model 4.2.1 considers only "distant" explanations of regime change: economic development, the size of the labor force in industry, dependence on oil and mineral exports, and medium-term economic growth. None of the structural variables are significant for democratic transitions, and the negative findings are generally consistent across specifications. The exception is that a larger working class seems to support democratization in the fully specified models.

Structural factors, and in particular the level of economic development, did not explain transitions to democracy in Latin America in the second half of the twentieth century. The absence of significant effects in model 4.2.1 suggests that scholars seeking to understand transitions to democracy (Di Palma 1990; Levine 1973; Linz and Stepan 1996; O'Donnell and Schmitter 1986; Przeworski 1986, 1991) were right to emphasize the role of contingency and agency rather than structural factors in regime transitions. The results support the claim that transitions in Latin America were not very much determined by structural and regime performance factors, although a larger working class may have encouraged democratization during the second half of the twentieth century (Rueschemeyer et al. 1992).[16]

---

[16] Our negative findings contrast with the results of a worldwide analysis of Epstein et al. (2006), who found a greater likelihood of transitions at higher levels of development. The Latin American pattern thus differs from the global one – unless there is specificity to the countries in Latin America's income range, which seems unlikely based on our previous work (Mainwaring and Pérez-Liñán 2003; 2007).

TABLE 4.2. *Survival Models for Authoritarian Regimes (Transitions), 1945–2005*

	4.2.1	4.2.2	4.2.3	4.2.4	4.2.5	4.2.6[a]
Actors' Preferences						
Radicalism (all)		−1.452		1.012		
		(1.633)		(0.893)		
Radicalism (ruler and allies)			−2.405***		−1.150*	0.663
			(0.913)		(0.588)	(0.639)
Radicalism (opposition)			1.158		2.284***	2.274***
			(0.959)		(0.817)	(0.693)
Normative preferences (all)				2.680***	3.228***	
				(0.564)	(0.635)	
Instrumented						3.921***
						(0.722)
International Factors						
Region, $t-1$		2.891*	5.131*	2.243**	3.985**	2.677*
		(1.597)	(3.051)	(0.951)	(1.736)	(1.597)
U.S. policy, t		0.980**	1.403*	0.878	1.054*	0.710
		(0.476)	(0.756)	(0.545)	(0.583)	(0.686)
Polity outside the region, $t-1$		0.003	−0.072	0.011	−0.070	−0.165
		(0.223)	(0.196)	(0.144)	(0.163)	(0.202)
Alternative Explanations						
Per capita GDP, ln $t-1$	−0.348	−0.692	−0.443	−0.359	−0.379	−0.460
	(0.784)	(1.667)	(0.513)	(0.423)	(0.575)	(0.466)
Industrial labor, $t-1$	0.093	0.103	0.095	0.094**	0.117**	0.089*
	(0.076)	(0.108)	(0.077)	(0.044)	(0.056)	(0.047)
Oil and mineral exports	0.767	0.911*	0.890	0.605	0.634	0.311
	(0.746)	(0.542)	(0.667)	(0.496)	(0.656)	(0.342)
Growth, 10 years	−20.624	−16.031	−22.762	−10.006	−14.482	−9.409
	(15.845)	(16.472)	(17.995)	(12.965)	(14.700)	(12.385)
Age of the regime	0.239	0.165	0.227	0.125	0.133	0.124
	(0.191)	(0.162)	(0.215)	(0.116)	(0.127)	(0.117)
Age of the regime^2	−0.010	−0.007	−0.009	−0.006	−0.005	−0.005
	(0.007)	(0.005)	(0.008)	(0.005)	(0.006)	(0.006)
Age of the regime^3	0.000	0.000	0.000	0.000	0.000	0.000
	(0.000)	(0.000)	(0.000)	(0.000)	(0.000)	(0.000)
Intercepts (thresholds)						
Semi-democracy	3.171	1.331	4.701	3.902	5.043	4.871
	(4.126)	(10.111)	(3.074)	(2.933)	(3.635)	(3.334)
Democracy	4.241	2.447	5.885*	5.014*	6.229*	6.019*
	(4.121)	(10.054)	(3.106)	(2.974)	(3.641)	(3.359)

TABLE 4.2. (*cont.*)

	4.2.1	4.2.2	4.2.3	4.2.4	4.2.5	4.2.6^a
Intercept variance	0.741	1.303	2.906	0.000	0.361	
	(0.814)	(2.172)	(3.223)	(0.001)	(0.656)	
Number of observations	576	576	576	576	576	576

Note: Entries are random-effects ordered logistic coefficients (standard errors).
^{a} Standard errors were bootstrapped for 5,000 replications.
$^*p < 0.1$, $^{**}p < 0.05$ $^{***}p < 0.01$.

In model 4.2.2 we move one step further in the causal path depicted in Figure 2.1, taking into account international conditions and the average level of radicalism in the regime. Regional influences have a powerful effect on the likelihood of transitions: a more democratic environment facilitates the demise of authoritarianism in neighboring countries. There is also some evidence indicating that transitions are more likely when U.S. policy makers are committed to democracy, although this result is less consistent across models. Global trends beyond the region do not affect regional regime outcomes.

Model 4.2.2 suggests that the level of radicalism for the average political actor has no significant impact on the timing of democratic transitions. This finding could reflect that radical policy preferences are irrelevant or, as discussed in Chapters 2 and 3, that radical governments and radical oppositions have different consequences for authoritarian survival. If the latter is true, opposite causal effects for different groups could cancel reciprocally. To test this possibility, model 4.2.3 includes separate measures of radicalism for the government and its allies and for opposition groups. Radical governments lower the probability of a transition, but radical oppositions seem to accelerate the downfall of authoritarian rule. The positive coefficient for opposition radicalism fails to achieve conventional levels of significance in 4.2.3 but does so in the fully specified models.

Equations 4.2.4 and 4.2.5 incorporate the proximate cause hypothesized to trigger regime change: actors' normative preferences for democracy. The impact of this variable is substantively powerful and statistically significant. An increase in normative preferences for democracy among domestic actors is likely to accelerate the transition to competitive politics. Controlling for this variable, the negative effect of government radicalism becomes only marginally significant and the positive effect of opposition radicalism is augmented.

Changes in the significance of radicalism variables in models 4.2.3 and 4.2.5 are consistent with prior results (Tables 3.3 and 3.4 of the previous chapter) showing that levels of radicalism affect normative support for democracy. To the extent that government radicalism reduces support for democracy among incumbent officials and their allies, the negative effect of this variable is depressed once we control directly for normative preferences. In turn, the presence of a radical opposition has a dual effect: it undermines the possibility of a transition indirectly, by reducing support for democracy among opposition groups, but it also facilitates the transition directly, by weakening the authoritarian regime. The direct and indirect effects are confounded in model 4.2.3, but the direct positive effect becomes salient once we control for normative regime preferences in 4.2.5.[17]

Endogeneity Issues

The evidence presented in Table 4.2 indicates that normative regime preferences have a profound impact on the prospects of democratization. However, we need to consider more thoroughly the possibility of reverse causality by which the political regime shapes actors' normative preferences. In Chapter 3 we documented some indications of reverse causality: political actors that embrace democratic ideals are more likely to be prevalent when their countries had prior histories of democracy between 1900 and 1944, and authoritarian regimes regularly suppress actors with normative orientations toward democracy. This reverse causality poses important challenges for causal inference. If a past history of competitive politics produces greater normative support for democracy at the present, it is possible that some long-standing conditions or unobserved episodes in the history of particular countries drive both the probability of transitions and the distribution of actors' preferences over the long run. Moreover, if competitive regimes promote democratic ideals and authoritarian regimes suppress democratic actors, the correlation between normative preferences and regime outcomes may simply reflect that certain kinds of actors are "selected" into (or excluded from) some types of regimes.

To address this problem, we "purged" our indicator of normative support for democracy from the confounding effects of reverse causality. We regressed

[17] Unfortunately, the precise magnitude of indirect effects is difficult to establish unless we make very strong assumptions (Glynn 2012). To verify our interpretation, we estimated the effects of government and opposition radicalism for two subsets of authoritarian regimes: those with prevailing patterns of normative support for democracy ($x > 0$) and those with prevailing patterns of normative support for dictatorship ($x < 0$). (The model was otherwise equivalent to 4.2.5.) Under support for democracy, the negative coefficient for government radicalism became larger and the positive coefficient for the opposition remained similar in size. Under support for dictatorship, by contrast, both coefficients became insignificant, suggesting that radicalization is inconsequential for the possibility of transitions when political actors are already committed to authoritarian rule. In the latter case, radical oppositions may still destabilize the incumbent authoritarian regime, but their actions will not lead to democratization.

our measure of normative regime preferences against the average level of democracy between 1900 and 1944 and a dichotomous indicator for authoritarian rule at $(t-1)$, using all regime-years in our sample ($N = 1,220$).[18] We retrieved the error term for this equation (a variable rid of the influence of past regime histories) and estimated predicted levels of support for democracy using this instrument plus the exogenous variables in model 4.2.5. Finally, we substituted these predicted values for the observed values of normative regime preferences in an instrumental-variable model of transitions replicating the specification of 4.2.5 ($N = 576$). The set of equations was reestimated 5,000 times using sampling with replacement in order to bootstrap the standard errors.[19] The results of this exercise, presented in the last column of Table 4.2, indicate that normative regime preferences remain a powerful predictor of transitions to competitive politics even after we account for possible problems of endogeneity.

Additional Transition Models

Table 4.3 reports four alternative transition models incorporating additional predictors. The limited variance of the frailty parameter in Table 4.2 suggests that the baseline hazard does not vary from country to country; thus we eliminated the random effects specification to estimate these complementary models. In model 4.3.1 the indicators of regional and extra-regional diffusion are replaced by a spatial lag that weights the influence of Polity scores in all other countries in the world (including the Latin American neighbors), with similar results. This spatial lags index was measured as $Z_{it} = \Sigma(d_{ij}^{-1} / \Sigma d_{ij}^{-1}) * P_{jt-1}$ where Z_{it} is the value of the index for country i at time t, d_{ij} is the distance between the capital of country i and any other country j, and P_{jt-1} is the Polity score for country j during the previous year. The expression $(d_{ij}^{-1} / \Sigma d_{ij}^{-1})$ weights Polity scores according to the inverse of the distance between the two countries.

The results of this model confirm the importance of international diffusion mechanisms, irrespective of the measure employed. The fact that the global political environment variable almost never has an impact on transitions when we separately include the regional political environment variable suggests that for Latin America, regional rather than global influences are decisive for political regimes.[20]

The remaining models augment the set of measures for structural and performance explanations. Model 4.3.2 includes literacy, model 4.3.3 includes

---

[18] The resulting equation is Y = .28 + .56 (Democracy, 1900–44) – .55 (Authoritarian), where Y is the predicted value for normative preferences. All estimates are significant at $p < .01$; $R^2 = .41$

[19] Given the limited variance of the frailty term in Table 4.2, and for ease of estimation, we removed the random effects in model 4.2.6.

[20] Gleditsch (2002) argues that this is generally true. The only model in which the global Polity score affects the probability of transitions is Model 4.3.3, in which, against expectations, a higher global Polity scores lowers the probability of a transition.

TABLE 4.3. *Additional Transition Models*

	4.3.1	4.3.2	4.3.3	4.3.4
New variable:	Spatial lag	Literacy	Gini index	Inflation
Actors' Preferences				
Radicalism (ruler and allies)	−0.959*	−0.881	−0.419	−0.784
	(0.573)	(0.570)	(0.903)	(0.615)
Radicalism (opposition)	1.962***	2.304***	2.727**	1.779**
	(0.632)	(0.691)	(1.302)	(0.718)
Normative preferences (all)	3.242***	3.266***	5.020***	2.937***
	(0.670)	(0.670)	(1.455)	(0.713)
International Factors				
Region, $t - 1$		3.044**	10.651***	3.479**
		(1.516)	(2.692)	(1.517)
U.S. policy, t	0.963*	0.931*	2.098**	0.762
	(0.540)	(0.561)	(0.946)	(0.599)
Polity outside the region, $t - 1$		−0.027	−1.485***	0.008
		(0.180)	(0.519)	(0.184)
Polity spatial lag, $t - 1$	0.236**			
	(0.107)			
Alternative Explanations				
Per capita GDP, ln $t - 1$	−0.213	−0.356	−2.133***	−0.084
	(0.353)	(0.444)	(0.810)	(0.382)
Literacy rate		0.011		
		(0.016)		
Industrial labor, $t - 1$	0.099***	0.094**	0.206***	0.133***
	(0.033)	(0.037)	(0.065)	(0.040)
Gini index			−0.062	
			(0.051)	
Oil and mineral exports	0.635	0.487	−1.412	0.672
	(0.509)	(0.512)	(0.902)	(0.531)
Growth, 10 years	−13.895*	−10.066	−25.515	−23.391**
	(8.329)	(8.782)	(16.205)	(10.188)
Inflation, 10 years				−0.676
				(0.742)
Age of the regime	0.143	0.104	0.003	0.143
	(0.102)	(0.102)	(0.165)	(0.112)
Age of the regime^2	−0.006	−0.004	−0.000	−0.005
	(0.005)	(0.005)	(0.008)	(0.005)
Age of the regime^3	0.000	0.000	−0.000	0.000
	(0.000)	(0.000)	(0.000)	(0.000)
Intercepts (thresholds)				
Semi-democracy	4.237*	4.916*	−4.639	6.878**
	(2.461)	(2.860)	(7.192)	(2.758)
Democracy	5.380**	6.069**	−3.550	7.978***
	(2.479)	(2.879)	(7.195)	(2.778)
Number of observations	576	576	222	493

Note: Entries are ordered logistic coefficients (standard errors)
* Significant at $p < 0.1$, ** $p < 0.05$, *** $p < 0.01$.

income inequality, and model 4.3.4 includes inflation. None of these predictors is significant. In all models, a larger industrial labor force increases the probability of a transition. As in Table 4.2, the parameters for regime age show no indication of duration dependence among authoritarian regimes. These additional models confirm the importance of normative preferences for democratic transitions and the direct effect of radical oppositions to destabilize authoritarian regimes.

Breakdowns of Competitive Regimes

Table 4.4 presents the results of the discrete-time survival models for the breakdown of competitive regimes. The dependent variable is coded dichotomously: o indicates the survival of the competitive regime and 1 indicates the establishment of authoritarian rule by December 31 of each year. We estimate the models using binary logistic regression, adding random effects to account for unobserved frailties in 4.4.1 through 4.4.5.

The first model in Table 4.4 includes a limited set of predictors representing structural conditions, economic performance, and institutional explanations. The only variable with a significant impact on the risk of democratic breakdown is the one measuring constitutional powers of the executive branch, but the sign of the coefficient contradicts theoretical expectations in the literature.

TABLE 4.4. *Models for Competitive Regimes (Breakdowns), 1945–2005*

	4.4.1	4.4.2	4.4.3	4.4.4	4.4.5	4.4.6[a]
Actors' Preferences						
Radicalism (all)	3.313***			0.966		
	(1.228)			(1.566)		
Radicalism		1.918**			1.034	0.100
(ruler)		(0.891)			(0.989)	(1.331)
Radicalism		0.844			−0.687	−1.159
(opposition)		(1.053)			(0.691)	(1.495)
Normative				−2.391*	−2.698**	
preferences				(1.226)	(1.100)	
Instrumented						−3.366*
						(1.991)
International Factors						
Region, $t-1$	−4.173*	−3.556*		−4.619**	−4.376**	−4.472
	(2.238)	(2.090)		(1.943)	(1.934)	(2.989)
U.S. policy, t	−1.358**	−1.472**		−0.888	−0.830	−0.569
	(0.559)	(0.598)		(0.570)	(0.641)	(1.138)

TABLE 4.4. (*cont.*)

	4.4.1	4.4.2	4.4.3	4.4.4	4.4.5	4.4.6[a]
Polity outside the region, $t-1$		−0.204 (0.342)	−0.331 (0.261)	−0.249 (0.304)	−0.430* (0.249)	−0.336 (0.412)
Alternative Explanations						
Per capita GDP, ln $t-1$	−0.702 (0.604)	−0.242 (0.868)	−0.243 (0.904)	0.270 (0.572)	0.308 (0.531)	0.774 (0.726)
Industrial labor, $t-1$	0.032 (0.033)	0.043 (0.057)	0.026 (0.059)	0.010 (0.051)	−0.001 (0.048)	0.006 (0.066)
Oil and mineral exports	−0.270 (0.502)	−0.963 (0.824)	−0.852 (0.868)	−0.883 (0.700)	−0.977 (0.712)	−0.583 (0.885)
Growth, 10 years	16.306 (11.153)	10.646 (17.550)	9.751 (16.583)	4.676 (12.972)	6.955 (12.856)	−1.122 (17.362)
Presidential powers	−0.184*** (0.046)	−0.251*** (0.089)	−0.250*** (0.080)	−0.241*** (0.047)	−0.247*** (0.049)	−0.260* (0.133)
Multipartism, t	0.133 (0.364)	0.014 (0.672)	0.250 (0.637)	0.255 (0.622)	0.445 (0.643)	0.893 (0.837)
Semi-democracy, $t-1$		2.052*** (0.650)	2.150*** (0.607)	2.086*** (0.648)	2.305*** (0.622)	3.178*** (0.881)
Age of the regime	−0.039 (0.127)	0.230 (0.210)	0.172 (0.220)	0.201 (0.153)	0.214 (0.158)	0.201 (0.195)
Age of the regime^2	0.002 (0.006)	−0.008 (0.009)	−0.005 (0.010)	−0.008 (0.008)	−0.008 (0.009)	−0.008 (0.010)
Age of the regime^3	−0.000 (0.000)	0.000 (0.000)	0.000 (0.000)	0.000 (0.000)	0.000 (0.000)	0.000 (0.000)
Constant	4.058 (4.577)	−0.586 (6.990)	0.063 (7.175)	−2.102 (5.205)	−2.202 (5.258)	−5.916 (6.523)
Intercept variance	0.000 (0.000)	0.497 (0.594)	0.458 (0.880)	0.000 (0.000)	0.000 (0.000)	
Number of observations	644	644	644	644	644	644

Note: Entries are random-effects logistic coefficients (standard errors).
[a] Standard errors were bootstrapped for 5,000 replications.
* $p < 0.1$, ** $p < 0.05$ *** $p < 0.01$.

Contrary to Shugart and Carey, it seems that competitive regimes last *longer* when their constitutions empower the president. This finding could reflect a casual effect – as constitutionally powerful executives may be able to prevent executive-legislative deadlock (Figueiredo and Limongi 1999) – but it could also reflect historical tendencies in constitutional law manifested during the last wave of democratization. The constitutional powers of the executive branch became more expansive in the third wave, and the average score for the Shugart and Carey index among competitive regimes shifted from 14.9 in 1945 to 16.4 in 2005.

In models 4.4.2 and 4.4.3, we move one step further in the causal chain by adding international factors and radicalism to the equation. We also incorporate a dummy variable for semi-democratic regimes to account for the trichotomous nature of our regime classification. The evidence consistently shows that semi-democratic regimes confront a greater risk of breakdown than full democracies. This finding is not surprising – as semi-democracies are closer to authoritarianism in the trichotomous scale – but the substantive interpretation for this result is not self-evident. Semi-democracies involve partial violations of at least one of the four democratic principles discussed in Chapter 3. Thus, in most cases they may represent an institutional crystallization of the absence of normative commitments to democracy among elites. We address democratic erosions in more detail in Chapter 8. For now, we simply document the frailty of semi-democratic regimes, noting that the inclusion of this control imposes a more demanding test for our measures of actors' preferences.

The results in models 4.4.2 through 4.4.5 show that the regional political context has a powerful effect on the survival of democracies. Competitive regimes are less likely to break down when other countries in the region are democratic. There is also some indication that a U.S. foreign policy supportive of democracy is likely to prevent breakdowns, although this effect becomes statistically insignificant once we control for normative regime orientations among domestic actors. As in Table 4.2, general extra-regional conditions had a feeble influence on Latin American dynamics. However, the aggregate nature of this measure does not allow us to claim that specific extra-regional processes (such as the democratic transitions in Spain and Portugal in the mid-1970s) did not have an important influence in Latin America.

Model 4.4.2 indicates that greater radicalism among political actors in the country tends to destabilize competitive regimes, and model 4.4.3 suggests that this effect is particularly powerful when the government embraces radical policy positions. By contrast to the authoritarian cases analyzed in Table 4.2, radical governments and opposition forces do not have opposite consequences for competitive regimes, although the destabilizing influence of radical opponents is statistically insignificant in model 4.4.3.

Finally, models 4.4.4 and 4.4.5 incorporate the most proximate predictor – normative regime preferences. As expected, this variable has a negative effect, reducing the risk of breakdown in democratic or semi-democratic regimes. The inclusion of this proximate cause erodes the significance of our measures of U.S. policy, but not the significance of the variables capturing the importance of the regional environment, the powers of the president, and the frailty of semi-democratic regimes. Consistent with our prior findings in the case of democratic transitions, the destabilizing effects of radicalism become insignificant once we control for normative preferences for democracy. This is an additional inkling of the indirect causal effects of radical policy preferences and their influence on normative regime orientations documented in Chapter 3. Moreover, the effect of radicalism is significant in models without the control for semi-democracy (Mainwaring and Pérez-Liñán 2013).

Endogeneity Issues
As with the case of transitions, the negative effect of normative support for democracy on the risk of breakdowns is confounded by issues of endogeneity arising from reverse causation. In model 4.4.6 we address these problems using an equivalent strategy to model 4.2.6. We estimated normative regime preferences for the full sample ($N = 1,220$) using the average level of our democracy score between 1900 and 1944 and a dichotomous indicator of authoritarian rule at $t - 1$ as the sole predictors. The residual for this model (i.e., the level of support for democracy purged of reverse causation) represented 59 percent of the variance of the endogenous predictor. We then employed this residual, plus the exogenous variables in model 4.4.5, to predict normative regime preferences for every country-year, and used this prediction in lieu of the observed values for the endogenous variable in an instrumental-variable model of democratic breakdowns (4.4.6). The equation system was replicated 5,000 times, using sampling with replacement in order to adjust the standard errors. Although the significance levels of the endogenous variable are somewhat eroded by this procedure (the number of breakdowns is only twenty-six), the results confirm the importance of normative orientations for the survival of competitive regimes.

Additional Breakdown Models
Table 4.5 includes a series of additional models akin to the ones presented in Table 4.3. Because of the lack of variance of the frailty term in Table 4.4, we assumed a common baseline hazard (omitting random effects) to facilitate the estimation of model 4.4.6 and of the robustness tests in Table 4.5. Model 4.5.1 confirms that a more democratic international context (measured through the spatial lag of Polity scores) reduces the risk of democratic breakdown considerably.

The other models add theoretically important independent variables for which there are some missing data. Models 4.5.2 through 4.5.4 indicate that the inclusion of additional structural and performance variables (literacy, income inequality, and inflation) does not alter the main results. In all equations, normative preferences and an auspicious regional environment emerge as powerful predictors of democratic survival. Moreover, the insignificant duration terms in Tables 4.4 and 4.5 prove that, in the absence of such favorable conditions, democracies do not "consolidate" over the course of the years.

TABLE 4.5. *Additional Breakdown Models*

	4.5.1	4.5.2	4.5.3	4.5.4
New variable	Spatial lag	Literacy	Gini index	Inflation
Actors' Preferences				
Radicalism (ruler and allies)	0.955	0.989	0.164	0.626
	(0.843)	(0.881)	(1.976)	(0.919)
Radicalism (opposition)	0.127	−0.656	−6.238**	−0.679
	(0.866)	(0.982)	(3.153)	(1.055)
Normative preferences (all)	−2.239**	−2.727**	−11.645***	−2.743**
	(1.030)	(1.076)	(3.995)	(1.102)
International Factors				
Region, *t* − 1		−4.737*	−20.786**	−4.756**
		(2.611)	(8.426)	(2.378)
U.S. policy, *t*	−1.233	−0.836	−0.602	−1.009
	(0.870)	(0.934)	(2.982)	(0.966)
Polity outside the region, *t* − 1		−0.398	−0.843	−0.378
		(0.290)	(0.787)	(0.278)
Polity spatial lag, *t* − 1	−0.428***			
	(0.154)			
Alternative Explanations				
Per capita GDP, ln *t* − 1	0.338	0.202	2.561	0.071
	(0.458)	(0.603)	(1.933)	(0.493)
Literacy rate		0.007		
		(0.026)		
Industrial labor, *t* − 1	0.035	−0.005	−0.266	−0.004
	(0.043)	(0.047)	(0.174)	(0.046)
Gini index			0.046	
			(0.106)	
Oil and mineral exports	−0.612	−0.892	−3.549	−0.899
	(0.902)	(0.915)	(2.287)	(0.900)
Growth, 10 years	9.607	5.772	−7.668	21.833
	(12.930)	(14.113)	(39.991)	(18.280)
Inflation, 10 years				1.335
				(0.999)
Presidential powers	−0.235**	−0.255***	−0.451	−0.259***
	(0.095)	(0.098)	(0.284)	(0.100)
Multipartism, *t*	0.259	0.429	4.154**	0.386
	(0.541)	(0.563)	(1.879)	(0.569)
Semi-democracy, *t* − 1	2.128***	2.352***	8.400***	2.419***
	(0.705)	(0.775)	(2.904)	(0.789)
Age of the regime	0.189	0.219	1.572***	0.134
	(0.165)	(0.169)	(0.589)	(0.173)
Age of the regime^2	−0.009	−0.008	−0.072**	−0.003

TABLE 4.5. (*cont.*)

New variable	4.5.1 Spatial lag	4.5.2 Literacy	4.5.3 Gini index	4.5.4 Inflation
Age of the regime^3	(0.010) 0.000	(0.010) 0.000	(0.029) 0.001**	(0.011) 0.000
Constant	(0.000) −4.609	(0.000) −1.548	(0.000) −13.896	(0.000) −0.060
	(3.602)	(4.441)	(19.301)	(4.007)
Number of observations	644	644	443	636

Note: Entries are logistic regression coefficients (standard errors).
$^*p < 0.1$, $^{**}p < 0.05$, $^{***}p < 0.01$.

The quantitative analysis in the previous pages tested the core hypotheses introduced in Chapter 2, showing that regional factors condition the possibility of regime change, that radical policy preferences operate indirectly by making authoritarian models of government more attractive (although radical oppositions also destabilize authoritarian regimes), and that a strong commitment to democracy among political leaders makes authoritarian regimes more likely to democratize and competitive regimes less vulnerable to breakdown.

To illustrate the substantive impact of normative preferences and regional diffusion, we simulated the expected probability of transitions and breakdowns under four ideal-typical scenarios. The results of this exercise, based on the estimates from models 4.2.5 and 4.4.5, are presented in Table 4.6. The first scenario assumes that all domestic actors have a strong normative preference for democracy and that all other countries in the region are democratic. In the second one, all actors remain committed to democracy, but the rest of the region is authoritarian. The third scenario reflects a situation in which all domestic actors prefer some form of authoritarianism but the remaining countries in the region are democratic. In the last case, all actors prefer authoritarianism and the region is also authoritarian. The remaining variables in the statistical models were set at their regional means to represent the typical Latin American country in 1978.

The simulation underscores the importance of the direct effects documented in Tables 4.2 and 4.5. Under a fully favorable scenario, a typical authoritarian regime in 1978 would have confronted a 98 percent probability of transition into competitive politics (with a 95 percent probability of transition into full democracy). By contrast, the probability of a democratic breakdown under the same scenario would be virtually zero. With domestic actors committed to democracy but a very hostile international environment, the expected probability of a transition from authoritarianism declines to 56 percent (and only 30 percent to full democracy). The probability of a democratic breakdown in this

TABLE 4.6. *Predicted Probabilities of Transitions and Breakdowns in Four Scenarios*

Normative Preferences for	Region	Authoritarian regimes Transition to		Competitive regimes
		Democracy	Semi-democracy	Breakdown
Democracy (1)	Democratic (1)	.949	.035	.000
Democracy (1)	Authoritarian (0)	.301	.263	.020
Dictatorship (–1)	Democratic (1)	.039	.075	.053
Dictatorship (–1)	Authoritarian (0)	.001	.002	.817

Note: Predicted probabilities reflect the posterior distribution in models 4.2.5 and 4.4.5. Competitive regimes are assumed to be fully democratic, two-party systems with a score of 15 in the Shugart-Carey (1992) index. All other variables were set at their means for 1978. (Radicalism at .56 for the government and at .42 for the opposition, U.S. Policy at 1, Polity outside the region at –2.56, per capita GDP at $ 2,205, industrial labor force at 22.8%, oil and mineral exports at .20, GDP growth at .026, and the age of the regime at 17 years.)

context remains low, at 2 percent. If all domestic actors are committed to an authoritarian project but the regional environment is very favorable to democracy, the probability of a transition is small (11 percent) but the risk of breakdown is also small (5 percent). This result shows that in the short run, regional influences are more effective at the reactive task of preventing breakdowns than at proactive task of promoting democratization – an issue we discuss further in Chapter 8. Under a fully hostile scenario, the probability of a transition drops to 0.3 percent, and the expected risk of breakdown increases to about 82 percent.

The quantitative evidence presented in this chapter supports our hypotheses vis-à-vis more conventional explanations of democratization based on structural conditions, institutions, and economic performance. Our models, however, only predict the probability of regime change for particular countries in particular years. Can those predictions based on country-level regime-years help explain the region-wide wave of democratization experienced after 1977? Only a positive answer to this question can validate our theoretical explanation for the great political transformation experienced by Latin America. We turn to this problem in the rest of the chapter.

FROM NATIONAL EVENTS TO REGIONAL OUTCOMES

What explains waves of democratization? In this concluding section we analyze the relationship between the likelihood of transitions and breakdowns in particular countries – the focus of our theory and our empirical tests – and the aggregate dynamics of regime "waves" at the regional level. We show that our theory of regime change explains not only short-term shifts in the relative proportion of democracies, but also the proportion of competitive regimes at which any wave of democratization or a counterwave is expected to crest.

Although the connection between transitions, breakdowns, and waves of democratization is immediately intuitive, the relation between patterns of regime change at the national level and cycles of regime change at the regional level deserves more systematic attention. National patterns of regime change shape region-wide waves of democratization in two ways. First, it is evident that in the short run, the proportion of democracies in the region increases during periods when the absolute frequency of transitions is greater than the frequency of breakdowns. Second – although less evident – in the long run, the probability of transitions and breakdowns also determines the level at which a wave of democratization "crests" – that is, the proportion of competitive regimes expected for the region.

The notation previously introduced in Figure 4.1 allows us to trace these specific linkages between country-level patterns of regime *change* and the aggregate *levels* of democracy in the region. Let D_t be the proportion of democratic regimes in the region during year t, and S_t be the proportion of semi-democratic regimes for the same year. It follows that the proportion of authoritarian regimes can be expressed as $(1 - D_t - S_t)$. Thus, the overall proportion of competitive regimes (democratic and semi-democratic) in any given year is determined by the proportion of democracies or semi-democracies already in place the previous year, plus the new democracies or semi-democracies gained from transitions, minus the democracies or semi-democracies lost to breakdowns.[21] If the notation in Figure 4.1 represents the probability of transitions or breakdowns for the average country in the region, then:

$$D_t + S_t = D_{t-1} + S_{t-1} \\ + \left(p^D_t + p^S_t\right)\left(1 - D_{t-1} - S_{t-1}\right) - \left(b^D_t D_{t-1} + b^S_t S_{t-1}\right) \quad (4.1)$$

Equation 4.1 demonstrates the intuitively obvious point made earlier: the overall proportion of competitive regimes increases when the absolute frequency of transitions, given by the expression $(p^D_t + p^S_t)\,(1 - D_{t-1} - S_{t-1})$, is greater than the frequency of breakdowns, given by $(b^D_t\, D_{t-1} + b^S_t\, S_{t-1})$.

However, the likelihood of transitions and breakdowns affects not only the number of competitive regimes in the short run. Although less obvious, the probability of transitions and the risk of breakdowns also determine the level at which a wave (or counterwave) of democratization is expected to stabilize in the long run. To prove this point, we restate Equation 4.1 as

---

[21] Democracies and semi-democracies may also change within the superset of competitive regimes through erosions and deepening, but when we consider the sum of the two categories, these changes cancel out because the gains for semi-democracies (erosions) are losses for democracies, and the gains for democracies (deepening) are losses for semi-democracies. Thus, parameters q^S_t and q^D_t drop out from the equation.

$$D_t + S_t = D_{t-1}\left(1 - p^D_t - p^S_t - b^D_t\right)$$
$$+ S_{t-1}\left(1 - p^D_t - p^S_t - b^S_t\right) + p^D_t + p^S_t. \tag{4.2}$$

In this formulation, the proportion of democracies and semi-democracies in the region is presented as a dynamic function of the lagged values of those variables. If the risk of transitions and breakdowns remains stable, the joint proportion of democracies and semi-democracies converges over time to an equilibrium level given by

$$D^* + S^* = \left(p^D_t b^S_t + p^S_t b^D_t\right)\Big/\left(b^D_t b^S_t + p^D_t b^S_t + p^S_t b^D_t\right) \tag{4.3}$$

where $D^* + S^*$ is the limit for the proportion of competitive regimes in the long run.[22] Note that sudden changes in the transition or breakdown parameters will shift the long-run equilibrium for the distribution of political regimes, and thus trigger waves (or counterwaves) of democratization. We explain the foundations for Equation 4.3 in Appendix 4.1.

Given this conclusion, the surge in the number of competitive regimes in Latin America after 1977 could be explained by a shift in the rate of transitions and breakdowns such as the one documented in Table 4.1. Transition rates from authoritarianism to semi-democracy doubled from .032 for the 1945–77 priod to .061 for the 1978–2005 period, and rates from authoritarianism to full democracy tripled from .015 to .049. In turn, breakdown rates for semi-democracies declined precipitously from .180 in the 1945–77 period to .021 in the 1978–2005 period, and breakdown rates for full democracies dropped from .034 to zero. To validate this explanation, we need to address two important questions: Can our statistical models explain this overall shift in transition and breakdown rates? And if so, is this shift sufficient to account for the level of democratization achieved by the region by the early twenty-first century?

To address those questions, Table 4.7 compares the observed rate of transitions and breakdowns for each period (reported in Table 4.1) with the predicted probability of transition or breakdown for the average country-year in each category, using the coefficients of models 4.2.5 and 4.4.5 to estimate those values. The comparison between observed and expected transition and breakdown rates shows that our statistical models are stunningly accurate for reconstructing the transformation of the region after 1977.

The results also allow us to explain the aggregate level of democratization achieved by the region by the end of the third wave. Given the predicted

---

[22] Equation 4.3 assumes that the transition matrix is regular, i.e., at least one of the expressions in the denominator must be positive.

TABLE 4.7. *Observed and Predicted Rates of Regime Change by Period (1945–2005)*

Regime at			Probability of outcome		
$t-1$	t	(Cell) Pattern	1945–77	1978–2005	Based on model
Authoritarian	SD	(II) Transition 1	.032	.061	(Observed)
			.032	.064	4.2.5
	D	(III) Transition 2	.015	.049	(Observed)
			.017	.042	4.2.5
Semi-Democratic	A	(IV) Breakdown	.180	.021	(Observed)
			.167	.030	4.4.5
Democratic	A	(VII) Breakdown	.034	.000	(Observed)
			.031	.002	4.4.5

Note: Observed values indicate the proportion of cases undergoing transitions or breakdowns (as reported in Table 4.1). Predicted values are the means of the posterior probabilities (including unit effects) estimated by the model for each category of cases during each period.

probabilities for the 1978–2005 period reported in Table 4.7, Equation 4.3 indicates that the proportion of competitive regimes in Latin America should have stabilized at around 96 percent (i.e., about nineteen countries of the twenty should have established competitive regimes by the end of the period). The estimates in Table 4.7 therefore provide a precise depiction of the great transformation in Latin American politics.[23]

THE THIRD WAVE IN LATIN AMERICA

We can now make preliminary sense of the dramatic increase in the number of competitive regimes in Latin America since the beginning of the third wave. This wave of democratization is by far the longest-lasting and the broadest that Latin America has ever experienced. A region that previously had usually been dominated by openly authoritarian regimes in most countries was transformed into one where openly authoritarian regimes were the rare exception. Nobody

[23] Predicted values for the 1978–2010 period in Table 4.7 slightly understate the speed at which the aggregate proportion of competitive regimes converged toward the equilibrium level. If we assume a region with twenty countries, two of them democratic and one semi-democratic at t = 1977, and apply the predicted breakdown and transition rates into Equation 4.2 iteratively for thirty-three years, by 2010, about seventeen regimes should be competitive. Yet, the observed number of competitive regimes in Latin America has fluctuated between eighteen and nineteen since 1995. A faster rate of change in the actual historical sequence may be explained by regional diffusion. Transition and breakdown rates reported in the table reflect the average prediction for all country-years in the period. Our simulations assume that those values are stable, but diffusion effects are likely to alter those rates (and the resulting equilibrium) iteratively from year to year. We return to this issue in Chapter 7.

expected such a transformation (Domínguez 1998: 1–12; Mainwaring 1999). Even in the mid-1980s, when the stunning period of democratization from 1978 to 1992 was half over temporally and had already made most of its advances in terms of the number of countries, many analysts expressed skepticism about the sustainability of competitive regimes in Latin America. Based on the region's past, they had reasons to be skeptical.

Democratic and semi-democratic governments face daunting problems in most of the region. Nevertheless, they have endured in the face of these problems and poor governmental performance in most countries. They have survived without interruption in poor countries (Bolivia since 1982, Guatemala since 1986, Nicaragua since 1984), in countries with among the worst income distributions in the world (Brazil, Guatemala), in countries with profound ethnic divides (Bolivia, Brazil, Ecuador, Guatemala), and in countries that have performed poorly economically (most countries in the region from 1982 through 2002). Competitive regimes have lasted in hard times and inauspicious places.

Three factors help explain this profound transformation in Latin American political regimes. First, in the 1980s, radical actors became less common and less powerful, and moderation became the tone of the day in most of Latin America. The empirical findings suggest that radicalization did not have a *direct* negative effect on democratization (radical oppositions sometimes destabilize dictatorships), but had an *indirect* negative impact by eroding normative support for democracy. Throughout Latin America, the Cold War had a pernicious impact on prospects for democracy. It fueled polarization on the left and right, elevated the stakes of politics, and made the United States suspicious of reformist and leftist democratic governments and willing to support authoritarian rightist governments.

In Brazil and the southern cone, the era of radicalized politics ended in the late 1970s and 1980s, as the revolutionary left was vanquished and the right gradually accepted democratic politics. Decreased radicalism in most countries in the 1980s meant that the political stakes of winning and losing declined. Actors in competitive regimes no longer feared that they might suffer catastrophic losses if the regime survived. Democratic politics ceased being a one-shot game of survival or destruction, and instead became an iterated game of incremental gains and losses. Actors came to understand that they could expand or reverse their gains and losses in the next iteration. In the 1990s, the era of revolutionary socialist struggles and reactionary right-wing responses to them came to an end everywhere but Cuba.

In several countries, the disappointing economic and social performance of the 1990s (among other factors) fostered the reemergence of radical political leaders, social movements, popular organizations, and other actors in the late 1990s and 2000s. But competitive political regimes had already become a norm by then, with some institutionalization of this norm through U.S. foreign policy, international law, the OAS, and Mercosur. Moreover, the radical actors of the late 1990s and the 2000s were much less radical than the revolutionary Marxist left of the 1960s and 1970s.

Second, after 1978, more actors were committed to democracy, and far fewer normatively embraced the ideals of a revolutionary "dictatorship of the proletariat" or of a right-wing dictatorship. A new valuing of political democracy and a rejection of old authoritarian models, whether of the Leninist left, the military nationalistic left, or many right-wing variants helped Latin American countries build and preserve democracy despite the severely adverse economic and social results of the 1980s and 1990s. More political actors are committed to democracy than ever before, and those that are not so committed are now generally reduced to shortcutting rather than openly aborting democracy. Latin American governments have developed sanctions against countries that regress into openly authoritarian rule. Serious problems remain on the agenda, but the establishment and survival of competitive regimes is a meaningful achievement, especially in light of Latin America's past.

When few actors are committed to democracy, competitive regimes are highly vulnerable to breakdown. If they become dissatisfied with policy results under democracy and believe that a coup has a reasonable chance of success, actors that are indifferent to regime type have no reason to refrain from joining the coup coalition. If indifference to democracy prevails, the survival of competitive regimes depends on regime performance and the capacity of international actors to create a meaningful threat of sanctions. Before around 1990, this was a very precarious recipe for long-term survival. Conversely, when most actors are committed to democracy, they abide by the intertemporal bargain that Przeworski (1991: 10–50) described: they accept losses today for the right to compete for office tomorrow.

Third, the hemispheric political environment became more hospitable to democracy. The more favorable regional political environment helped reduce the probability of democratic breakdowns and also increased the likelihood of democratic transitions. Incentives to prevent coups by the OAS, U.S., and Mercosur and the transnational dissemination of prodemocratic beliefs and norms helped drastically reduce the incidence of breakdowns of competitive regimes. U.S. policy changed after 1977, with favorable consequences for democracy in Latin America. The Organization of American States and Mercosur reinforced change in U.S. policy by instituting pro-democracy norms. Open authoritarianism became less viable because of international pressures. These changes helped sustain competitive regimes that came into being, and to a lesser but still important degree they nurtured transitions to competitive regimes.

Political variables have been powerful contributing factors to the third wave of democratization. In Latin America, regime survival has depended far more on political factors than on economic performance and the level of development. Decreased radicalism, a greater appreciation of democracy, and a changed international environment including the specter of sanctions against openly authoritarian regimes contributed to the sea change in Latin American politics.

Policy moderation, attitudes toward democracy and a favorable international political environment – for Latin America, more than the structural variables tapped by modernization theory and class theories of democratization – have made a decisive difference in whether competitive regimes survive or break down. After 1977, when the main actors have been committed to democracy and the international political environment has been favorable, democracy has been able to survive for an extended time despite widespread poverty, glaring inequalities, and bad performance. In the past, when key actors were not committed to democracy and the international political environment was unfavorable, democracy faltered even if economic performance was credible and per capita income was moderately high.

CONCLUSIONS

In this chapter we have addressed three questions through quantitative evidence: What factors explain transitions from authoritarian rule in Latin America in the second half of the twentieth century? What factors explain the survival of competitive regimes during this period? And to what extent do those factors, combined, explain the great transformation of Latin American politics at the regional level in the decades after 1977?

Some variables important to our theory presented relatively stable effects under many model specifications. Consistent with our argument in Chapter 2, normative preferences for democracy among domestic political actors constitute the most important factor to facilitate transitions and to prevent breakdowns. This result holds even after we account for the endogenous nature of the predictor and the possibility of reverse causality anticipated in Chapters 2 and 3.

The effect of radical policy preferences is more complex and multifaceted than we initially hypothesized. Radical policy preferences make political actors more likely to embrace normative preferences for authoritarianism, and thus exercise an indirect effect on the likelihood of transitions and breakdowns. It is difficult to estimate the exact size of these indirect effects without making strong assumptions about causal homogeneity (Glynn 2012). But multiple pieces of evidence point to the conclusion that radicalism undermines democratization through normative regime orientations. Once we control for regime preferences, the presence of a radical opposition seems to destabilize authoritarian regimes and facilitate the transition to competitive politics. No similar effect was found for democratic breakdowns.

Again consistent with our theory, international factors also help explain the vastly greater stability of democratic and semi-democratic regimes after 1977. The contribution to democracy was made not so much by U.S. policies toward Latin America or by global influences as by the dynamic transformation of the regional context. Regional forces have played a key role in the creation of waves and counterwaves of democratization after 1945. As we show in Chapter 7, regional mechanisms have important consequences for regime change or stability not only because they disseminate models of change (stability) across countries (Bunce and Wolchik 2011), but also because they help reinforce those models over time.

Some of the most interesting findings are negative. Structural conditions have not had powerful effects on Latin American political regimes – at least when we analyze political development over the course of decades rather than centuries. Structural transformations empower some actors over others, but the political effects of structural transformations depend on actors' regime choices, which are not predetermined by their structural location. Under authoritarian regimes, a larger industrial working class may have been an asset for democratization in the region during this period, but we found no evidence linking the size of the working class to democratic survival. Against "resource curse" theories, dependence on oil and minerals did not hinder transitions to democracy and did not increase the likelihood of breakdowns of competitive regimes.

Przeworski et al. (2000) showed that on a global level, democratic governments are more likely to endure at a higher per capita income level. Their finding was consistent with a much larger literature that argued that more developed countries were more likely to be democracies. A higher level of development, however, had no immunizing impact for democracy in Latin America (see also Landman 1999; Mainwaring and Pérez-Liñán 2003; O'Donnell 1973). Democratic and semi-democratic regimes were vulnerable to breakdown at even fairly high levels of development. This finding is consistent with O'Donnell's (1973) argument that the more developed countries of South America were especially prone to bureaucratic authoritarianism in the 1960s and 1970s and also with our finding (Mainwaring and Pérez-Liñán 2003) that in a wide income band, Latin American countries with a higher level of development were less likely to be democratic.

A final negative finding is that regime economic performance has had little impact on regime survival and fall in Latin America. Democracies were more able to survive despite a vastly worse economic record after 1977. Many of the conditions for democratic survival were less favorable after 1977 than they were between 1945 and 1977, yet democracies and semi-democracies were far less prone to breakdown. Competitive regimes became far less vulnerable under stressful conditions.

O'Donnell and Schmitter (1986) and Przeworski et al. (2000) argued that there is an asymmetry between transitions and breakdowns. They claimed that transitions did not depend on structural factors, but that structural factors were a better predictor of democratic breakdowns. For Latin America between 1945 and 2005, the evidence instead supports Bermeo's (1990) observation of theoretical symmetry between transitions and breakdowns – that is, the idea that similar kinds of factors explain transitions and breakdowns. Structural variables were weak predictors of both types of outcomes, just as international conditions and actors' normative orientations were strong predictors in most models. Although in principle different factors could explain transitions and break-downs, in practice, normative preferences about the political regime and interna-tional factors are important to explain both kinds of regime change in Latin America from 1945 to 2005. Conversely, economic performance has a weak effect on regime change and stability in Latin America for both competitive regimes and dictatorships.

Our statistical findings produce aggregate results that match the overall increase in the rate of transitions from authoritarianism and the decline in the rate of democratic breakdowns observed after 1977. Moreover, these estimates generate long-run predictions for region-wide trends consistent with the great transformation of Latin American politics during the third wave of democra-tization. Thus, the evidence offered by extensive tests is generally supportive of our theory (Coppedge 2012). In the next two chapters, we turn to intensive qualitative tests in order to further demonstrate the causal mechanisms invoked in Chapter 2.

5

From Multiple Breakdowns to Stabilization of Democracy: Argentina

As we saw in Chapter 4, the breakdown rate of competitive regimes declined dramatically in Latin America in the third wave of democratization. Why did competitive regimes break down so readily before the third wave? And what accounts for the vastly lower breakdown rate in the third wave? In this chapter we rely on a qualitative case study to explore these questions and provide *intensive* testing of our theory. The intensive testing focuses on Argentina, which experienced chronic instability during the first and the second waves of democratization but has enjoyed a stable democratic *regime* since 1983, notwithstanding considerable governmental instability from December 2001 to May 2003 and some signs of democratic erosion since 2011.

The two questions we ask about Argentina mirror the theoretical questions that animate this book. What explains the chronic breakdowns of competitive regimes until 1976 despite some favorable conditions? And what explains the dramatic change to democratic survival in the period since 1983 despite some severe social and economic dislocations that almost surely would have produced a breakdown prior to the third wave?

From 1930 until 1983, Argentina frequently cycled between authoritarian and competitive regimes. The proximate key to understanding the high instability of the five competitive regimes that broke down is that the pro-democracy coalition was chronically weak because of the almost complete absence of actors with a normative preference for democracy. When actors became disappointed with the results of competitive regimes, they defected to the authoritarian coalition for short-term gain. All major actors were indifferent or hostile to democracy. Radical actors had major responsibility for the breakdowns of 1951 and 1976 and secondary responsibility for the other three breakdowns. An unfriendly regional environment contributed to the breakdowns of 1930, 1951, 1966, and 1976. The authoritarian coalitions were also consistently fragile.

The absence of radicalism, a favorable international environment, and, most importantly, a reasonably consistent normative preference for democracy among all key actors supported the survival of democracy in Argentina after 1983.[1] In turn, the trauma of the 1976–83 dictatorship helped reorient the labor movement and the Peronist Party (Partido Justicialista) away from their previous instrumental attitudes and toward a normative preference for democracy. The military's disastrous government from 1976 to 1983 convinced the armed forces that they were not particularly skilled at governing, and hence pushed them away from a long-standing recurrent normative preference for right-wing dictatorship. The vanquishing of the revolutionary left, coupled with a democratic reorientation of many of its surviving members, led to the decline of an extremist left-wing actor. The thorough discrediting of the dictatorship led to the disappearance of the extreme right wing. By the early 1990s, the military accepted democratic civilian control and ceased to be an important political actor. The strong international pro-democracy currents of the 1980s and 1990s reinforced these changes.

The research strategy in this chapter entails three stages. In the first, we identify the key actors during each presidential administration of a competitive regime and provide disciplined narratives that highlight their attitudes toward democracy and radicalism, as well as the impact of international influences. These narratives provide the core of our explanation for the transition from repeated democratic failure until 1976 to stable democracy since 1983. Second, we aggregate the information for all actors to assess the overall conditions for democratic survival for each administration. Finally in the third stage, we employ a within-case comparative design to assess the role of our explanatory variables and to rule out alternative explanations for Argentina's changing patterns of democratic stability during the twentieth century.

The dependent variable in this chapter is whether a competitive regime survives or breaks down during a particular presidential administration. We analyze regime outcomes for thirteen presidential administrations during times of democracy and semi-democracy. Although our main objective is to understand the shift from unstable competitive regimes before 1983 to stable democracy afterward, military coups were targeted against particular administrations – and not against others. Moreover, the values of key independent variables often varied with changes in government.

Although spatial constraints precluded the detailed analyses of actors and their interactions that Figueiredo (1993) and Stepan (1978) offered in their excellent analyses of the breakdown of democracy in Brazil in 1964, the study of political actors and their interactions provides leverage for understanding

---

[1] Our argument builds on Dahl (1971: 129–40), O'Donnell (1973, 1978), Potter (1981), Rouquié (1982a, 1982b), P. Smith (1978), Viola (1982), and Waisman (1987, 1989) on the breakdowns between 1930 and 1976, and on O'Donnell (1986: 15–18) and Ollier (2009) on the importance of reduced radicalization and a greater normative preference for democracy in the post-1983 period.

breakdowns and stability. At certain moments, some actors shift from supporting the regime or from the sidelines to supporting a coup. These moments are
important in understanding regime dynamics and outcomes.

After discarding some possible alternative explanations for Argentina's transformation, we conduct a configurational comparative analysis to verify the
consistency of the qualitative analysis based on actors. Section 6 provides a
structured comparison of all democratic and semi-democratic administrations in
Argentina between 1916 and 2010. The qualitative comparative analysis shows
that the convergence of commitment to democracy and de-radicalization has
prevented the return of authoritarianism in Argentina. We emphasize the distinctive role of normative regime preferences in fostering democratic survival in
the current era.

WHY ARGENTINA?

Our country case selection includes one country (Argentina) that went from
many breakdowns of competitive regimes before the third wave to stable
democracy since 1983 and another (El Salvador) that shifted from chronic
authoritarianism before the third wave to a stable competitive regime since
1984 or 1994, depending on whether one counts 1984 or 1994 as the transition
year. We have five reasons for selecting Argentina for the first of the two within-
country comparisons. First, we wanted a country that experienced the three
waves of democratization in Latin America. Argentina, Chile, Guatemala,
Panama, Peru, and Uruguay are the only countries in the region that meet this
criterion. They illustrate better than other countries all the historical stages in the
development of political regimes observed at the regional level. Argentina had
transitions to competitive regimes in 1916, 1946, 1958, 1963, and 1983 and
experienced breakdowns in 1930, 1951, 1962, 1966, and 1976.

Second, it was important to select a country that reflects one of the regional
patterns we seek to explain: a change from failed competitive regimes before
1978 to stability after the third wave of democratization. This criterion eliminated Peru because of the breakdown in 1992. Among the five remaining
countries that meet the first two criteria, it was advantageous to choose a
country whose competitive regime in the third wave has lasted longer. These
countries meet a more demanding test of the second criterion. This slightly
favors Argentina (democratic since 1983), Guatemala (1985), and Uruguay
(1985) over Chile (1990) and Panama (1990).

Third, even in qualitative studies, understanding causal patterns within a case is
facilitated by having several outcomes of both regime survival and breakdown.
Although the logic of causal inference in qualitative work within cases depends
fundamentally on tracing interactions among actors and examining sequences
rather than a large number of observations, having several episodes of both regime
survival and breakdown makes it easier to disentangle competing explanations.
Countries with a larger number of breakdowns combine the advantages of multiple

breakdowns (any single breakdown could be highly idiosyncratic) with the advantages of within-country observations. The countries that experienced most breakdowns from 1900 to 1977 were Panama, Peru, and Argentina, with five each. Because of the 1992 breakdown, Peru is not an example of persistent survival after the third-wave transition. Argentina thus meets second and third criteria combined better than any other country in Latin America.

Fourth, Argentina conforms well to the statistical results in Chapter 4 in the sense that structural variables do not help explain the transformation from repeated breakdowns to stable democracy. In this important respect, the country is not a deviant case by Latin American standards.

Finally, Argentina has traditionally represented a crucial case to challenge some conventional theories of democratization (Eckstein 1975; Gerring 2007: 120–22). Against modernization theory, the country's relatively high income per capita in the first three quarters of the twentieth century did not preclude the breakdown of democracy (Przeworski et al. 2000: 98). Similarly, a powerful working class and relatively low income inequality in the mid-twentieth century did not lead to sustained democratization. Against some class theories of democratization, democracy stabilized after 1983 in a context marked by recurrent economic crises and by sharp increases in poverty and inequality. In all of these respects, the Argentine case is poignant for illustrating broader (as demonstrated through the statistical analysis in Chapter 4) regional trends.

ARGENTINA IN THE FIRST WAVE: 1916–1930

From 1862 until 1930, Argentina enjoyed stable constitutional rule with constitutional presidential successions and no successful military coups. We code the regime as authoritarian until 1915 because of widespread electoral fraud (Botana 1994: 178–83). In 1912, the governing Conservatives and the opposition Radicals agreed on a new electoral law that enshrined the compulsory secret vote for native male Argentines. These reforms established the conditions to transform a pre-democratic oligarchic regime into a democracy. By our coding, Argentina (1916) and Uruguay (1919) were the first countries in Latin America to establish full democracies. The candidate of the Radical Party (Unión Cívica Radical, UCR), Hipólito Yrigoyen, won the next presidential election in 1916 in a landslide. The Radicals governed until 1930, when a coup brought the democracy to an end.

The discussion of the 1916–30 period focuses on two questions. What accounts for the regime's stability from 1916 to 1928, and what explains the breakdown in 1930? The 1916–30 regime achieved impressive democratic gains including a rapid expansion of voter turnout, a peaceful alternation from the Conservatives to the Radicals in 1916, a peaceful shift to a different faction of the governing party in 1922 and again in 1928, and solid protection for civil and political rights in the country's more-developed provinces (which included a majority of the population) (Potter 1981). An initially low level of threat to dominant traditional actors and low radicalization contributed to the successful (if limited by current standards) democratization of 1916–28 (Waisman 1989: 66).

Argentina's democratization of 1916–30 enjoyed many favorable conditions including a high standard of living and substantial economic growth from 1916 to 1929 (Rock 1985; L. A. Romero 2002; Waisman 1987: 36–77). Argentina was far wealthier than Chile, Uruguay, and Costa Rica, which also enjoyed early processes of democratization, and it was wealthier than many Western European countries. In contrast to Argentina, the three aforementioned Latin American countries built long-lasting democratic regimes before the third wave. Argentina's derailment away from a promising democratization path stemmed from the formation of actors that were indifferent toward democracy. From the 1920s on, some powerful actors also had radical tendencies, and the international context for democracy became less favorable.

A Promising Young Democracy, 1916–1928

From 1916 until 1928, Argentina seemed well positioned to develop a stable democracy. During these years, which covered two presidential administrations, a reasonably solid pro-democracy coalition emerged. This coalition included, most importantly, the two presidents (Hipólito Yrigoyen 1916–22, and Marcelo T. de Alvear, 1922–28), and their party, the UCR. Both presidents won landslide electoral victories, and they commanded wide popular support. The UCR was a well-organized party that fought for the establishment of a democracy from the party's creation in 1890. The pro-democracy coalition also included the Socialist Party and the union movement.

For the most part, Presidents Yrigoyen and Alvear and the UCR had a normative preference for democracy and governed in a mostly democratic fashion. Freedom of speech was guaranteed to everyone, and all parties enjoyed freedom to organize (Luna 1988: 315). Luna's (1988: 279–80) biography praised Yrigoyen's "respect for freedom in all of its manifestations" and his tolerance of criticism and dissent. Between 1916 and 1919, in a break with the past, the government avoided violently repressing strikes and indeed sometimes expressed sympathy for the strikers (Luna 1988: 252; Remmer 1984: 191; Rock 1985: 201).

Nevertheless, Yrigoyen's normative preference for democracy was not steadfast (Mustapic 1984). His passivity during massacres of workers in 1919 and 1921 and his frequent use of federal intervention to undermine the opposition are the most salient negatives in terms of his support for democratic rules of the game. Yrigoyen did not authorize the massacres, but he did nothing to punish the perpetrators (Grosso 1968: 168; Luna 1988: 340; Rock 1975: 202–03). The constitution allowed for the federal interventions, but they had a corrosive effect, and Yrigoyen abused his powers to get rid of opposition governors (Mustapic 1984). L. A. Romero (2004: 78) claims that Yrigoyen had a conviction that his opponents were enemies of the nation (see also O'Donnell 1991). After 1919, under pressure from conservative actors and the military, his behavior and discourse occasionally veered off in a less democratic direction (McGee Deutsch 1993: 41). The Radicals rigged elections in some provinces (Rock 1975: 115).

Marcelo T. de Alvear of the UCR won the 1922 presidential election handily with 48 percent of the vote; the second-place finisher captured only 9 percent. More than Yrigoyen, he had a solid normative preference for democracy. According to M. Acuña (1984: 30) and Luna (1988: 355), Alvear was an exemplary democrat. He "accepted checks on executive power that were institutionally the preserve of congress" (L. A. Romero 2002: 52). He was more sparing than Yrigoyen in using federal interventions in the provinces (Luna 1988: 382; Rapoport 2003: 125), and he presented a bill that helped guarantee democratic elections in the provinces (Rapoport 2003: 125).

In spite of the party's name (which referred to the "radical" fight for democratization in the late nineteenth century), Radical administrations were moderate as defined in Chapter 1. The governments did not effect major policy changes (M. Acuña 1984: 32; Waisman 1987: 82–84); continuity was more pronounced than change (Botana 1994: xlvi). Rock (1985: 199) notes that Yrigoyen's government confirmed the UCR's reputation as "timid reformers, basically dedicated to the established order. The program was mild in character."

In 1924, the UCR split into two organizations, the Personalists, who favored Yrigoyen, and the anti-Personalists, who supported Alvear. The anti-Personalists shared Yrigoyen's democratic ideals, but in social and economic policies they were more conservative and traditional (Calviño 1968: 176; Potash 1983: 69; Rapoport 2003: 125–26; Remmer 1984: 122).

The union movement and the Socialist Party were also part of the democratizing coalition from 1916 through 1928. The Socialists considered socialism "the culmination and perfecting of liberal democracy" (L. A. Romero 2002: 36). Most of the union movement and the Socialist Party were moderate actors. During the 1920s, the labor movement, which during the previous administration had sometimes behaved violently, abandoned its revolutionary stands and instead adopted a different tactic, acting now as a pressure group. The labor movement thus abandoned the streets (Rapoport 2003:139).

This combination of a normative preference for democracy and policy moderation on the part of most of the Radical Party, the Socialists, and the labor movement augured well for democratic stability. Unlike the situation in El Salvador (Chapter 6), the authoritarian coalition was weak, and initially no actors had a normative preference for authoritarianism.

But there were also some gathering storms. Most of the traditional political and economic elite "demonstrated little loyalty toward the recently established institutional system and longed for a time when a select elite governed" (L. A. Romero 2002: 2). Opposition to the right of the UCR included the more traditional Conservatives and the more democratic Progressive Democratic Party (Partido Demócrata Progresista). The traditional Conservatives "displayed little respect for democratic procedures" (L. A. Romero 2002: 51). Party opposition to the Radicals was weak electorally, with no chance of regaining in the presidency on the horizon.

The Radicals' electoral hegemony, at first blush a strength of the democratic coalition, made the conservative opposition more disposed to form an authoritarian coalition to regain power. The Argentine Patriotic League (Liga Patriótica Argentina), a right-wing paramilitary organization close to the Conservatives, was an openly authoritarian actor that espoused xenophobic, anti-Semitic, nationalistic ideals and embraced the use of violence to obtain them (Rock 1985: 202).

L. A. Romero (2002: 53) observes that the Conservatives were perfectly willing to consider antidemocratic options. "If the electoral card failed, another would have to be played, which would, one way or another, put an end to a democracy that did not ensure the election of the better bred." With the election of Alvear, who was a member of the propertied elite, the far right such as the Liga Patriótica was somewhat appeased. The new president "had calmed upper-class apprehensions of democracy. Yet these apprehensions had not disappeared" (McGee Deutsch 1993: 49). As Alvear's administration was coming to an end, the prospect of Yrigoyen's return to power in 1928 revived these apprehensions.

The military became increasingly independent (not controlled by the civilian leadership) and important in the 1920s. It also became increasingly receptive to authoritarian ideologies and to criticisms of democracy (L. A. Romero 2002: 34–35). Its disaffection with representative democracy became apparent. During Alvear's administration, there were growing rumors of a coup (Rapoport 2003: 127) and of the existence of antidemocratic secret societies (Luna 1988: 428; Calviño 1968: 177). Powerful sectors of the military were radical: they combined right-wing postures with policy impatience. Another openly authoritarian and radical actor was the right-wing nationalist sector that included the Argentine Patriotic League.

International influences were generally favorable during Yrigoyen's first presidency, but they became less favorable as the 1920s wore on. Many Latin American countries experienced considerable political turbulence during the early decades of the twentieth century, with growing demands for the incorporation of the middle sectors and the working class into the political system. The immediate regional context was favorable to democratization, as both Uruguay and Chile were democratizing. A less favorable (for democracy) international influence was the Russian revolution. The propertied classes felt the threat of an imminent workers' revolution, which led them to question liberal democracy and to regard other systems as better (L. A. Romero 2002: 30).

International conditions for democracy deteriorated during Alvear's administration. By 1928, when Alvear left office, two countries influential for Argentine public opinion had fallen into authoritarian rule. In October 1922, the Fascist march on Rome toppled the Italian prime minister, and Benito Mussolini became the new ruler. A year later, in September 1923, General Miguel Primo de Rivera overthrew the Spanish government and became prime minister. These southern European dictators "exercised a true fascination" (L. A. Romero 2002: 30) for many Argentines, including sectors of the military (Waisman 1987: 235–45).

The Breakdown of 1930

Yrigoyen regained the presidency in 1928 in a landslide electoral victory, but his second presidency was a failure. In September 1930, a military coup led by General José Félix de Uriburu overthrew him, terminating Argentina's first period of democracy. What explains the 1930 breakdown after fourteen years of a competitive regime?

Under Yrigoyen, an increasingly powerful authoritarian coalition crystallized. It included the armed forces, the Conservative parties, the traditional oligarchy, the anti-Personalist faction of the UCR, and the Independent Socialist Party. With the defection of the anti-Personalists to the authoritarian coalition, the democratic coalition was weakened. The predominance of actors that were indifferent or hostile to democracy made the regime vulnerable to breakdown when the Great Depression took hold.

Yrigoyen's style of governing eroded a democratic spirit even if it did not violate the constitution. The 1853 constitution allowed the president to remove provincial governors in extraordinary circumstances, and Yrigoyen used this provision frequently to replace conservative governors. Between his two terms, he intervened in every province, with corrosive effects on democracy. On several occasions, the government also disallowed electoral victories of opposition members of congress. Widespread use of patronage for partisan benefit further stoked disaffection among the opposition. Yrigoyen's actions were polarizing, and they created a sense in the opposition that the playing field was unfair and would be unfair into the foreseeable future.

When they agreed to the electoral reforms of 1912, conservative politicians and the traditional oligarchy wrongly expected that they would continue to win elections (M. Acuña 1984: 29; Botana 1994; Rock 1985: 190; P. Smith 1974: 9; P. Smith 1978: 11). The UCR presidential candidates won 47 percent in 1916, 49 percent in 1922, and 62 percent in 1928, while the leading opposition candidates won only 13 percent, 8 percent, and 10 percent, respectively (Nohlen 1993: 41–42). Even though the UCR presidents were moderate in policy terms, the electoral landslides created a situation of de facto hegemony with no foreseeable possibility of an alternation in power. Conservative actors viewed a horizon of continuous Radical domination; provincial interventions marginalized the opposition and pushed it toward becoming disloyal (Potter 1981; Viola 1982: 14–18).

In 1930, the congressional representatives of the Conservative Party and of the Independent Socialist Party clamored publicly for a coup (Ciria 1968: 17, 141–44; Potter 1981: 107; Rouquié 1982b: 412). Even the anti-Personalist faction of the UCR defected to the disloyal opposition (Bertoni 1968: 116; Ciria 1968: 16; P. Smith 1978: 19–20).

The traditional landowning elite, represented by the Argentine Rural Society, was hostile to Yrigoyen during his second presidency. Confronted with the Great Depression and a declining economy, because of its indifference to democracy, it shifted to the authoritarian coalition and supported the 1930 coup. Rouquié

(1982a,1982b: 411–15) and Waisman (1989: 68) argue that the antidemocratic attitude of the traditional elite was key to understanding the 1930 breakdown and the subsequent difficulties of establishing a stable competitive regime.

Some right-wing actors openly espoused authoritarian ideologies. Radical policy preferences were mainly a phenomenon of this nationalistic, often Fascist-inspired right. The Argentine Patriotic League and sectors of the military (Luna 1988: 429–50) were its leading expressions. Other civilian organizations such as the Republican League and the Radical Klan were less important radical actors. The Patriotic League manifested a "growing tendency to replace the political debate by violent acts" (Potash 1983: 68), and the Republican League took to the streets and generated confrontations with Radicals and the police (Rapoport 2003: 220). The Klan Radical was the Yrigoyenista reply to these right-wing organizations.

Under the influence of authoritarian ideologies from Europe, the military from the 1920s on developed antidemocratic proclivities. It was divided between an openly authoritarian faction that admired Mussolini, Primo de Rivera, and the French authoritarian nationalistic intellectual, Charles Maurras, and a majority faction that was indifferent to regime type but also largely hostile to Yrigoyen (Potash 1983: 80). Although these two factions diverged in their normative preference for authoritarianism, they collaborated in overthrowing Yrigoyen. The president politicized promotions within the military, favoring his political supporters (P. Smith 1978: 16–18). His undue political interference in military affairs generated discontent in a military previously committed to professionalism (Potash 1983: 56–64; Rapoport 2003: 127; Romero 2004: 81; Rouquié 1982a). The appearance of an openly authoritarian actor on the scene was important for the outcome of 1930. General Uriburu advocated corporatist authoritarian ideals (Ciria 1968: 18–21), espoused the elimination of parties and the popular vote, and openly admired some European dictators (Calviño 1968: 179–80; Potash 1983: 74; Rapoport 2003: 214; P. Smith 1974: 98).

International influences also conspired against democracy in Argentina in 1930. The late 1920s and early 1930s were bleak times for democracy in Europe and Latin America. Competitive regimes broke down in the Dominican Republic and Panama in 1928, in Guatemala in 1931, and in Uruguay in 1933. In most of Latin America and Europe, authoritarian ideologies lived a time of ascendance, with a dissemination of authoritarian ideologies to the Argentine military and nationalistic right-wing authoritarian groups (Rouquié 1982a: 186; Waisman 1987: 235–50).

Table 5.1 shows the main actors during the competitive regime of 1916–30 and their scores for the independent variables for each presidential administration. By the second Yrigoyen period, normative preferences regarding the regime and radicalism had become unfavorable for democratic survival.

In Chapter 2, we noted that there are three potentially complementary sources of regime change: (1) new actors emerge or old ones fade, thus affecting the balance of power between the democratic and authoritarian coalitions; (2) some existing actors become more powerful while others become less powerful, affecting the balance of power between the coalitions; and (3) some actors shift

TABLE 5.1 *Historical Conditions for Argentine Competitive Regimes, 1916–30*

Administration	Normative regime preferences	Radicalism	International context
H. Yrigoyen, 1916–22	Yrigoyen and UCR: 1; Socialists: 1; Trade unions: 1; Conservative parties: 0.5; Argentine Rural Society: 0 Argentine Patriotic League: −0.5	Patriotic League: 1 All others: 0	Favorable: Democratization in Uruguay and Chile, republics in Spain and Italy. Unfavorable: Russian Revolution.
M. T. de Alvear, 1922–28	Alvear and UCR: 1; Anti-Personalist faction of the UCR: 1; Argentine Rural Society: 0; Conservative parties: 0 Military: −0.5; Argentine Patriotic League: −1	Patriotic League: 1; Conservative parties: 0.5; Military: 0.5 All others: 0	Favorable: Competitive regimes in Chile and Uruguay. Unfavorable: dictatorships in Spain and Italy.
H. Yrigoyen, 1928–30	Yrigoyen: 0.5; Anti-Personalist faction: 0.5 Conservative parties: 0; Argentine Rural Society: 0; Military: −1; Argentine Patriotic League: −1	Military: 1; Patriotic League: 1; Conservatives: 1 All others: 0	Unfavorable: dictatorships in Spain and Italy. Impact of the Great Depression.

Note: Values show each actor's score for Normative regime preferences (1 is pro-democracy, −1 is pro-dictatorship) and Radicalism (0 is moderate, 1 is radical) for each administration.

coalitions because of a change in perception about how well the regime in power satisfies their policy preferences or because of changes in normative preferences about the political regime. In Argentina, the 1930 breakdown resulted from a combination of the emergence of one new political actor that was a key part of the authoritarian coalition – the military – and of defections from the democratic (the Socialists and Conservatives) or neutral (big landowners) camps to the authoritarian coalition. The military became an important actor because of its role in quelling popular uprisings, because of the influence of authoritarian nationalistic and militaristic ideologies that diffused across borders, and because other conservative actors increasingly invited military intervention as they became more disillusioned with democracy. The defections of the Socialists and Conservatives from the democratic camp to the pro-coup coalition were triggered by growing policy dissatisfaction more than by changes in normative preferences about the regime. But both had grown disillusioned with democracy on normative grounds as well. The Radicals' electoral hegemony and Yrigoyen's willingness to use provincial interventions to crush the opposition robbed them of any chance of alternation in power. The fact that the Conservatives and landowners became indifferent to democracy made them easily disposed to turn against the regime when they confronted a president whom they did not like on policy grounds and, after 1929, an economic crisis.

THE SECOND WAVE: 1946–1976

During the second wave, Argentina entered into rapid cycles of alternating authoritarian and competitive regimes. From 1946 to 1951, 1958 to 1962, 1963 to 1966, and 1973 to 1976, the country had four short-lived competitive periods, leading to successively more repressive dictatorships. After 1943, the authoritarian regimes were also short-lived. What explains why competitive regimes were not able to last despite Argentina's moderately high level of development and moderately low inequality?

Our analysis of these cycles between authoritarianism and democracy builds on Cavarozzi (1983), O'Donnell (1973, 1978), Rouquié (1982a, 1982b), Viola (1982), and Waisman (1987). A crucial characteristic of the period from 1946 to 1976 was the near absence of actors with a normative preference for democracy. As Rouquié (1982b: 341, 380) noted, "All political forces preferred winning over the adversary in power to safeguarding the institutions."[2] Competitive regimes never enjoyed the steadfast support of powerful actors, so they were highly vulnerable to breakdown.

But few actors had a normative preference for dictatorship, so coalitions in support of authoritarian regimes were also fragile. Although most actors were

---

[2] In a converging opinion, Portantiero (1987a: 281–82) wrote that "[b]oth Radicalism in its Yrigoyen faction and even more so Peronism did not see themselves as *parts* of a system, but rather as a totality that expressed the nation and the people. The learning of loyal competition between government and opposition was never seriously undertaken in Argentina." See also Dahl (1971: 130–40); Gómez and Viola (1984).

willing to support coups as a way of achieving their policy goals, they did not form a stable authoritarian coalition. Most actors quickly opposed dictatorships that did not deliver their preferred policies. Because they did not have normative preferences for any regime type, actors used instrumental, short-term logics (O'Donnell 1973, 1982).

In addition, the actors that did have a normative preference for dictatorship did not share the same view of what kind of dictatorship they wanted. President Juan Perón (1946–55) had a normative preference for a populist authoritarian regime. After being overthrown in 1955, Perón gradually left behind his normative preference for authoritarian populism. In the 1960s, one faction of the military became attached to the view that it was uniquely qualified to develop Argentina and that a right-wing military dictatorship was the best possible form of government. In 1969, a leftist guerrilla group emerged, committed to revolutionary socialism. And in the 1970s, right-wing terrorist groups emerged; they, too, had a normative preference for dictatorship. But these actors had radically opposing preferences regarding the kind of dictatorship and the kind of policies they sought. They all worked to subvert competitive and authoritarian regimes, but they were incapable of forming a stable authoritarian coalition. O'Donnell (1973) famously called this cycle of unstable authoritarian and competitive regimes "an impossible game." Reflecting on this era, Huntington (1968: 82) claimed that Argentina's distinguishing characteristic was "the fragility and fleetness of all forms of authority."

As one attempt after another failed, some actors attempted to impose more radical solutions to Argentina's dual problems of regime instability and economic disappointment (Amaral 2001). In the 1970s, a powerful left-wing guerrilla movement, a military increasingly disposed to use extreme violence to cure Argentina of its "illnesses," and right-wing death squads embodied this extremist radicalism. The abject failure of the military dictatorship of 1976–83 and a deep reorientation of Argentina's key actors brought to an end this long cycle of chronic regime instability.

Juan D. Perón, 1946–51

General Uriburu's dictatorship lasted only until 1932. In 1931, he convoked elections, and from 1932 until 1943, Argentina had three presidents including two elected in fraudulent contests (the second resigned because of ill health, and his vice-president assumed the presidency). A military coup in June 1943 put an end to the notoriously fraudulent regime of 1932–43. The 1943–46 dictatorship anticipated the nationalistic, statist, and antiliberal policies of Juan Perón's government from 1946 to 1955.

As occurred in many Latin American countries, the end of World War II opened the door for some democratizing impulses including – in Argentina – the military government's decision to hold elections in 1946. Perón was elected president by a handsome margin (56 percent to 44 percent) in largely free and fair competitive elections.[3] His arrival to a high-level position in national politics dated back to 1943, when he was one of the leaders of the coup that ended the 1932–43 regime. He served as secretary of labor (1943–45) and vice-president and secretary of war (1944–45). His administration forged a lasting alliance with the labor movement, established numerous welfare programs, and expanded social rights. At the same time, it progressively dismantled independent institutions and civil liberties in order to create a populist authoritarian regime.

The Perón administration is one of relatively few cases in Latin America in which a president elected in free elections oversaw the dismantling of a competitive regime.[4] A precise date for the erosion from semi-democracy to authoritarianism is not clear-cut. Although we take 1951 as the cutoff year, the government attempted to establish a hegemonic position from the outset (R. Alexander 1951; Blanksten 1953; Doyon 2006; Rouquié 1982b: 83–122; Viola 1982). Between May and June 1946, Perón ordered the dissolution of the Labor Party and of other minor parties that had supported his candidacy, and created a Unified Party of the Revolution (later renamed Peronist Party). The government refused to seat two elected opposition senators, leaving the Senate with no opposition (R. Alexander 1951: 61). Congress impeached the Supreme Court justices between September 1946 and May 1947, and the administration took many steps to gain control of lower courts (Blanksten 1953: 122–32). The police increasingly harassed political opponents, imprisoned key opposition figures, and undermined freedom of expression and organization.

In 1949, a Constitutional Assembly promulgated a new constitution that extended social rights but also allowed for the immediate reelection of the president and fortified presidential power (R. Alexander 1951: 68–70; Doyon 2006: 210; Plotkin 1994: 45–47). Perón won reelection in a landslide in 1951, capturing 62 percent of the vote in an election conducted under a state of siege and with massive use of state patronage (Doyon 2006: 325–26; Rapoport 2003: 362). The adoption of a majoritarian electoral system reinforced the president's coattails in the legislative contest. After 1951, the opposition controlled only 14 of 158 seats of the lower chamber (Blanksten 1953: 112–14).

In his second term, Perón's authoritarian turn deepened. The opposition radicalized its strategies; rebel military officers attempted violent coups in September 1951, June 1955, and finally September 1955. Peronist mobs responded by sacking the offices of opposition parties, the Jockey Club

---

[3] Some analysts cast doubts on how level the playing field was in the 1946 elections (Blanksten 1953: 67–68; Luna 1975: 442–43). In contrast, Viola (1982: 46–47) notes that the losing coalition accepted the results as fair.

[4] Of twenty-eight breakdowns between 1945 and 2010, only eight cases were instances in which the chief executive remained in office after the regime lost its competitive nature: Ecuador in 1946 and 1970, Colombia in 1949, Uruguay in 1973, Peru in 1992, Haiti in 1999, and Venezuela in 2009. Before 1945, similar episodes took place in the Dominican Republic in 1928, Honduras in 1935, and Uruguay in 1933.

(a symbol of traditional wealthy Argentina), Catholic churches, and opposition newspapers. The government shut down the major newspaper, *La Prensa*, in 1951, and it repressed and harassed opposition media.

Although Perón incorporated the popular sectors to the political process, his hostility toward liberal democracy was evident from the outset. His discourse stressed collectivity above individual rights (Buchrucker 1987: 335–36; Rapoport 2003: 358–59; Sigal and Verón 1982) and treated the political opposition as enemies and traitors. Perón often voiced the idea that his movement represented the nation or the people, while social and political actors outside Peronism represented illegitimate interests.[5] The government introduced Peronist indoctrination into the military (Rouquié 1982b: 84–98), public administration (Doyon 2006: 330–31), and public schools (R. Alexander 1951: 132, 219–20; Plotkin 1994: 162–64; Rapoport 2003: 376–77), and attempted to control the public universities. It also used propaganda to inculcate a cult of personality (Plotkin 1994: 77–78). Streets, railroad stations, public squares, towns, and even two provinces changed their names to Perón and Eva Perón.

The government's policies were somewhat radical; they were statist, nationalistic, and left of center, and the government exhibited intransigence regarding its preferences. In a deeply polarized context, the administration imposed high costs on a small number of business interests by expropriating them with limited compensation. It nationalized important sectors of the economy, including the railroads in 1947 and the International Telephone and Telegraph Company. State control of key sectors (including exports) and intervention in the economy expanded dramatically. The state created many new regulations in all spheres of the economy, and it aggressively intervened in labor relations, often favoring workers against owners (Doyon 2006: 285; Plotkin 1994: 49–50). Through state intervention in markets, exchange rate policies, and government monopolies, it redistributed income from the rural sector to manufacturing and the public sector and from elites to popular sectors. Perón empowered organized labor and the state at the expense of business. The nationalization of some industries and frequent anti-oligarchy and anticapitalist rhetoric created animus and anxiety among business interests. None of these policies in isolation was deeply radical, but together they represented an attempt – albeit not successful in terms of the initial objectives – to profoundly change Argentine society in the short to medium term. W. Smith (1989: 30) correctly underscored that "Peronism was the most radical of Latin American populisms to have captured state power before the late 1960s."

Redistributive policies and the expansion of social rights created a lasting loyalty of the popular sectors toward Perón, who subordinated the labor movement (Ciria 1971: 48–52; McGuire 1997). The government attacked independent labor unions and leaders (Viola 1982: 48–51) and fostered the creation of a

---

[5] For more details on Perón's ideology and discourse, including attention to its authoritarian aspects, see Ciria (1971); Sigal and Verón (1982).

tightly dependent union structure without a commitment to political democracy (R. Alexander 1951: 85–99; Doyon 2006; McGuire 1997; Viola 1982: 52). The labor movement, which after 1945 became the most powerful in Latin America (McGuire 1997: 265–70), developed some radical characteristics. Few unions had far leftist positions, but many mobilized aggressively, exhibited impatience or urgency in their efforts to achieve their policy goals, and sometimes employed confrontational methods.

Perón's hegemonic aspirations and willingness to undercut civil and political rights, combined with policies that imposed high costs on some actors between 1946 and 1955, inspired in opposition leaders the belief that they could win only by overthrowing his government. Because Perón always commanded an electoral majority or plurality from 1946 until 1976, anti-Peronist actors in turn conspired to block the emergence of a fully democratic regime from 1955 until 1973. The opposition feared that it was permanently out of power and that it would continue to pay a very high price under Perón. It became conspiratorial and exclusionary, willing to resort to coups to get to power and willing to proscribe the Peronists to keep them from competing in elections. Most anti-Peronist actors cultivated pernicious alliances with the armed forces, reinforcing the authoritarian proclivities of the Argentine military.

By the early 1950s, the pro-democracy coalition did not include any important actors. The key question was what kind of authoritarianism would prevail – Perón's populist dictatorship or a conservative authoritarian coalition. The main leaders of the Radical Party (UCR) defected to the disloyal opposition. Jailed several times during Perón's presidency because of his opposition activities, Ricardo Balbín (1904–81) ultimately came to believe that there was no other option but a coup. The authoritarian characteristics of the regime and the opposition's willingness to conspire were mutually reinforcing. Hegemonic authoritarian regimes sometimes abort the possibility of the emergence of democratic opponents, and conspiratorial oppositions tend to reinforce the authoritarian proclivities of presidents hostile to democracy.

The military gradually moved toward forming a coup coalition. Rebel officers unsuccessfully attempted coups in September 1951 and June 1955. More partners joined the coup coalition after the June 1955 failed coup when Perón went on the attack against the Catholic Church (Doyon 2006: 348–50; Halperín Donghi 1995: 170–74). In September 1955, the military launched a new coup, this one successful. The pro-coup coalition included the armed forces, the Church, the UCR, and powerful business organizations including the Sociedad Rural Argentina (Argentine Rural Society) and the Unión Industrial Argentina (Argentine Industrial Union).

The Peronists became convinced that many opposition actors were conspiratorial and would fail to respect democracy. For the most part, they were right; Cavarozzi (1983: 17–18) writes that some actors of the anti-Peronist camp in the aftermath of the 1955 coup were committed to "completely wiping out the Peronist cancer." From 1946 until 1970, Radicals and Peronists were deeply suspicious of each other, and all other actors also harbored deep suspicions and animosities toward the opposing players (O'Donnell 1973: 115–99).

Arturo Frondizi, 1958–62

The 1955 coup that removed Perón began a lengthy period of instability in Argentine politics that lasted until 1983, with nineteen presidents in twenty-eight years. Competitive regimes and dictatorships alike were subject to rapid erosion and breakdown.

After three years of military rule (1955–58), Argentina returned to competitive politics in 1958 when the military government withdrew from power and sponsored elections. Even though the elections represented a fair contest for the candidates allowed to participate, they were marred in terms of democratic principles by the proscription of the Peronists. The *duros* within the armed forces and their civilian allies including a prominent part of the UCR preferred the radical suppression of the Peronists.[6] Moreover, the virulent anti-Peronism of President Pedro Aramburu (1955–58) contributed to Peronist radicalization.

If they had been allowed to run, the Peronists would have won the elections – an outcome that was unacceptable to the actors of the coalition that overthrew Perón in 1955. Because of the proscription of the largest party, the competitive regime established in 1958 was born with a congenital defect (Amaral 2001; O'Donnell 1973, 1978). The conservatives' fear of Peronism was a huge contributing factor to what O'Donnell (1973) called "the impossible game": no government, whether authoritarian or semi-democratic, could create a stable governing coalition from 1955 to 1973.

With backing from Perón, who from exile ordered his followers to support the UCRI's candidate, Arturo Frondizi won the presidency and took office in 1958.[7] From the outset, the democratic coalition was weak, consisting mainly of Frondizi's faction of the Radical Party. It confronted a powerful set of actors ready to join an authoritarian coalition at the drop of a hat. The regime was undermined by powerful semi-loyal and disloyal oppositions. The lack of a normative preference for democracy on the part of Argentina's powerful actors doomed the semi-democratic experiment, and Frondizi fell in a coup in 1962.

Frondizi was not a steadfast democrat. Caught between an increasingly restive labor movement (reinforced by a violent but seldom lethal "Peronist resistance") and the radically anti-Peronist military officers, he occasionally equivocated regarding democratic principles. In 1958, in violation of a constitutional requirement that he win congressional approval to do so, the president

---

[6] Cavarozzi (1983: 14) writes that the opposition perceived Peronism as "inherently and irremediably antagonistic to democratic institutions and values," and that if Peronism were not suppressed, it would "deform and even destroy" democracy.

[7] Before the election, the Radicals split into two parties: the "Intransigent" UCR (UCRI), led by Arturo Frondizi, and the "People's" UCR (UCRP), led by Ricardo Balbín.

decreed a state of siege to confront a strike (Smulovitz 1988: 77–78). In 1959 and 1960, the government arrested many labor leaders to defeat strikes and contain the labor movement (Rapoport 2003: 511). In 1960, Frondizi mobilized the military in a counterinsurgency plan to crush the Peronist resistance. The government eventually allowed Peronist candidates to run in the elections for governors and Congress in March 1962. But when the Peronists won several key gubernatorial contests, he bowed to the pressures of the intransigent anti-Peronists and the military and decreed a state of siege in those provinces. The Peronists also won a large number of congressional seats, but the military toppled Frondizi and dissolved Congress until the next general election in 1963 (Kvaternik 1987).

The Frondizi government exhibited moderate policy radicalism. Despite being politically isolated, the government had a highly ambitious developmentalist policy agenda that was polarizing, and it exhibited some policy intransigence. Policy differences across the political spectrum were profound (Cavarozzi 1983: 18–20). Frondizi betrayed his campaign promises to reincorporate Peronism to the democratic process and to follow some of Perón's economic policies. His policies were detrimental to organized labor, and real wages plummeted in 1959. Organized labor and Perón quickly moved to the opposition and went on the offensive, joining the authoritarian coalition. Ricardo Balbín's UCRP moved into the disloyal opposition in 1962 and supported the coup (O'Donnell 1973: 186; Rapoport 2003: 503; Smulovitz 1988: 58–63, 110–12; Viola 1982: 80). The UCRP had been implacably hostile to Perón and allied with the anti-Peronist factions of the armed forces since at least 1951. Organized business also supported the coup. In 1958, some of the anti-Peronist camp wanted to annul Frondizi's election because Frondizi pledged to legalize the Peronists in exchange for their electoral support (Viola 1982: 75) – an indication of their lack of a normative preference for democracy. They wanted "democracy" only if the biggest party were proscribed – in other words, if the "democracy" was not democratic. The right's fear of Peronism led it to intensify its opposition to Frondizi when the president allowed the Peronists to run in the 1962 elections, and later led it to join the coup coalition.

Perón and the labor movement quickly joined the disloyal opposition. Perón tacitly endorsed violence against the regime, and some small clandestine Peronist groups embraced violence (James 1990: 198–202). Some radical leftist unions – a small minority faction of the labor movement – also mobilized against the government (McGuire 1997: 87).

From the beginning of Frondizi's government, the military contemplated a coup (Rouquié 1982b: 149–91). It corroded Frondizi's authority so much that it became the "permanent censor of the government's actions" (Rouquié 1982b: 179–80; also Rapoport 2003: 503; Torre and De Riz 1993: 278–79). The pro-coup coalition gathered force, and the government ended up being very isolated.

The breakdown of 1962 was the only one in twentieth-century Argentina that occurred in an international context that was somewhat favorable as opposed to downright negative for democracy. From 1956 to 1961, a short wave of democratization occurred in Latin America. Transitions to competitive regimes took place in Peru (1956), Bolivia (1956), Panama (1956), Honduras (1957), Colombia (1958), and Venezuela (1959). The tide turned against democracy in 1962, when the competitive regimes in Argentina and Peru broke down, anticipating the onslaught that would follow in subsequent years. U.S. policy was relatively favorable to democracy in Latin America from 1961 to 1963, as President Kennedy emphasized reformist democracies as an antidote to socialist revolution in the wake of the Cuban revolution. Kennedy, however, did nothing to protest the coup against Frondizi, whereas he publicly voiced objections to coups in Peru (1962) and Honduras (1963). Even though U.S. policy toward Latin America was generally prodemocratic, U.S. policy toward Argentina was less so because of concerns about Perón's return.

International ideological currents had a mixed effect on democracy in Latin America during these years. On the one hand, some democratic actors in Latin America aligned with the Alliance for Progress and the Kennedy administration. In many countries of the region, Christian Democratic parties formed during the late 1950s or early 1960s, representing the impulse to create reformist democracies. On the other hand, the Argentine left drew inspiration from the Cuban revolution. Minority sectors of the labor and Peronist movements began to shift to the left, influenced by Fidel's revolution (Halperín Donghi 1995: 224–26). This early polarizing dynamic influenced important actors, including the Argentine military (Rouquié 1982b: 181–86). The United States and conservative Argentine actors (above all the military) demanded greater anti-left orthodoxy of the Frondizi government (Halperín Donghi 1995: 221; Rapoport 2003: 504).

Arturo Illia, 1963–66

Shortly after the March 1962 coup, deep divisions within the military came to the surface. The factions that favored a quick return to competitive politics won out, leading to new general elections in July 1963. The proscription of the Peronists meant that the new semi-democratic regime had the same congenital defect as the regime of 1958–62. This time Perón ordered his followers to cast a blank vote, and Arturo Illia of the URCP won the presidential election with a meager 25 percent of the popular vote. He assumed office in October 1963.

Illia had a democratic temperament, and he governed with a democratic spirit even when he faced disloyal and semi-loyal oppositions (Torre and De Riz 1993: 290). Against the hopes of conservatives, business interests, and the military, he refused to use repression even in the face of workers' factory takeovers in May 1964 (McGuire 1997: 119). The government avoided radical policies and had a decidedly moderate agenda. According to Viola (1982: 87), the freedom of expression and organization during this period was unprecedented since 1946 (M. Acuña 1984: 172–73). The government even lifted electoral proscriptions against Peronist candidates in 1965. But much as occurred with Frondizi, the actors with a steadfast normative preference for democracy were few and far between – Illia and his party were the sole exception. And once again, a pro-coup coalition gathered momentum quickly. Finally, on June 28, 1966, a military coup deposed President Illia.

The opposition to Illia and the semi-democratic regime grew over time. Perón retained an instrumental and opportunistic attitude toward democracy, working to undermine the regime in order to enhance his chances of returning to power. He endorsed violence against the government (James 1990: 276) and supported the 1966 coup (O'Donnell 1982: 66). Most of his followers had similar practices and attitudes (Viola 1982: 95). Labor unions were indifferent to democracy; their political priorities were bringing Perón back and consolidating their own power (Amaral 2001; De Riz 2000: 19–20; James 1990: 222, 235, 267–71; Rapoport 2003: 516; Torre 1989: 34–35). They mobilized aggressively against the regime. The labor movement de facto declared war on the regime in May 1964 with some factory occupations (Rouquié 1982b: 237). Most labor leaders supported the 1966 coup, and several prominent leaders attended the inauguration of the new president, General Juan Carlos Onganía, anticipating that his government would implement pro-union policies (Cavarozzi 1983: 34).

The radical left factions of the labor movement and of the Peronist movement grew in the aftermath of the Cuban revolution (McGuire 1997: 132–41). Radical working-class mobilization contributed to delegitimating the government and the regime, and ultimately to the breakdown in 1966. Labor mobilization drove fear into business interests, which in response began to operate against the government and the regime (Rouquié 1982b: 241–43; Viola 1982: 89).

According to Rouquié (1982b: 248), all major opposition parties demonstrated little or no loyalty to democracy. "The political class and the press openly, even serenely, discussed the possibility of a coup. Military intervention had become such a part of the institutional system that it was debated naturally, as if it were a cabinet crisis. … The values of liberal democracy had eroded very profoundly" (Rouquié 1982b: 244). No important actor outside of Illia and the UCRP openly opposed the 1966 coup, while many openly embraced it (O'Donnell 1973; Rouquié 1982b: 253; Viola 1982: 101). According to Viola (1982: 103, 194), the largest (the Peronists), the third-largest (the UCRI), and the fourth-largest (Frondizi's Movement for Integration and Development, created in 1963) parties all supported the coup. Business organizations also embraced the coup (Rapoport 2003: 520). Cavarozzi (1983: 24–25) writes that the free market bloc became openly antidemocratic by the mid-1960s.

From the outset, the military acted as a disloyal opposition, ready to join the authoritarian coalition. In antidemocratic fashion, it insisted on the proscription of Peronism in the 1963 elections. After the elections, it immediately overstepped the boundaries of democratic civilian control. The armed forces blocked Perón's return to Argentina in December 1964, baring their antidemocratic proclivities.

Some sectors of the military were merely indifferent to democracy, but the sectors that actively espoused authoritarian ideologies and regimes were in ascendance (M. Acuña 1984: 158ff; Torre and De Riz 1993: 294). These sectors viewed democracy in Argentina as intrinsically inefficient (M. Acuña 1984: 158) and mounted a campaign against democracy through the media between 1965 and 1966.

The international situation for democracy in Latin America turned starkly negative after 1962. U.S. support for democracy in Latin America diminished in 1962, then declined profoundly after Lyndon Johnson became president in 1963. Military coups toppled competitive regimes in Peru in 1962, the Dominican Republic, Ecuador, and Honduras in 1963, and Bolivia and Brazil in 1964. The Brazilian military regime of 1964–85 created a new model of bureaucratic-authoritarian rule, with a commitment to remaining in power for a long time. It influenced the Argentine military, projecting the image of a capable, technocratic, modernizing regime that had displaced the inefficient squabbling of democracy (M. Acuña 1984: 161; Rouquié 1982b: 232). Combined with the failure of the semi-democratic model based on the exclusion of Peronism, this external environment facilitated the justification of a long-term authoritarian solution. In Argentina, 66 percent of respondents expressed support for the 1966 coup in a public opinion survey conducted after President Illia was ousted; only 6 percent disapproved (cited in O'Donnell 1978: 138). These survey results demonstrated a stunning lack of public support for democracy (De Riz 2000: 15).

Héctor Cámpora, Juan Perón, and Isabel Perón, 1973–76

In contrast to previous military regimes, the military dictatorship that took power in 1966 aspired to govern for a long time (O'Donnell 1978, 1982), but by 1969 it fractured and began to collapse. It was initially more ambitious in its design to change Argentina, and it was more repressive than the country's previous military dictatorships. President Juan Carlos Onganía fell in a coup in June 1970. His successor, General Roberto Levingston, lasted only nine months (June 1970 to March 1971) before he was ousted by another coup. Finally, General Alejandro Lanusse (1971–73) from the outset planned to restore power to civilians, and did so by allowing elections in 1973.

Argentina's fifth competitive regime of the twentieth century began in 1973 as its most democratic ever. For the first time since 1951, the Peronists were allowed to field a presidential candidate. Running as Perón's officially designated candidate, Héctor Cámpora won in a landslide in a free and fair presidential election on 1973,[8] and he assumed office on May 25, 1973. On June 20, 1973, Perón returned to Argentina after almost eighteen years in exile. Cámpora

---

[8] Cámpora won 49.5% of the vote. Second-place finisher Ricardo Balbín of the UCR captured 21.3%.

resigned on July 13 and called for new elections to allow Perón to run. Raúl Lastiri, president of the Chamber of Deputies, assumed the presidency for a short interim period between July 13 and October 12. Perón won the election even more decisively than Cámpora had, capturing almost 62 percent of the vote, and he took office on October 12. However, he died less than nine months later, in July 1974, at age seventy-eight. His widow and the vice-president, María Estela (Isabel) Martínez de Perón, took office.

After Perón's death, the regime degenerated quickly. Armed confrontations between the Peronist leftist guerrillas and Peronist rightist paramilitary groups escalated dramatically. On March 24, 1976, a military coup ended Argentina's shortest-lived competitive regime and intensified a reign of terror that had already begun after Perón's death.

What explains the dramatic failure of an attempt that began with so much optimism? Once again, the paucity of actors with a normative preference for democracy created an unstable coalition to support Cámpora, Perón, and Isabel Péron and to defend a democratic regime. Actors that do not have a normative preference for democracy readily defect from the pro-democracy coalition if it is in their policy interests to do so. In addition, the 1973–76 period had three powerful actors with a normative preference for dictatorship: the armed forces, right-wing death squads, and revolutionary guerrilla movements.

Perón shifted from his earlier antidemocratic discourse, attitudes, and behavior of the 1946–70 period to an ambiguous discourse, with a predominance of prodemocratic attitudes and practices (De Riz 2000: 130–37). He governed in a less authoritarian manner than in 1946–55 (Cavarozzi 1983: 53), even though he was still far from being the quintessential democratic statesman (De Riz 1987: 103–06; Sigal and Verón 1982: 192–99; Sigal and Verón 1986: 81–83; Viola 1982: 390–506). On the strongly positive side, in November 1970, Perón endorsed a historic agreement with his traditional opponents in the Radical party to work for democracy (M. Acuña 1984: 198–203; Viola 1982: 241–42). On the somewhat negative side, until Cámpora took office, Perón encouraged violence from the Peronist left as a tool in the fight against the dictatorship (James 1990: 319; Ollier 1989: 146). On the starkly negative side, after he took office, Perón was complicitous as his henchman, José López Rega, set up extermination squads to combat the revolutionary left (De Riz 2000: 148–53).

Most of the powerful labor movement was intensely loyal to Perón but indifferent to democracy (O'Donnell 1982: 482; Viola 1982: 510–11, 516–18). Minority factions were prodemocratic, but they did not win control of the movement (McGuire 1997: 165–66). The unions were somewhat radical, albeit not predominantly on the left, in their policy preferences and mobilization strategies. The main labor organizations confronted the Peronist left (often violently), but a minority faction was close to the revolutionary sector (McGuire 1997: 156–57; Viola 1982: 209). This was the first time since 1946 that the revolutionary left had made substantial inroads in Argentina's labor movement.

Only one important actor, the reunified Radical Party, fully embraced liberal democracy. From 1969 to 1973, the Peronists and the Radicals had worked together against the military dictatorship, and the enmity between the two parties faded. In response to the previous wave of dictatorships, the Radical Party renounced its earlier policy of supporting the proscription of the Peronists, thus signaling a commitment to democratic rules of the game. The Radicals remained generally true to democratic practices and attitudes until the final agony of the regime in March 1976 (M. Acuña 1984: 208; De Riz 1987: 154; De Riz 2000: 179). The UCR, however, had limited popular support. As violence overwhelmed politics, it became a less central player, and its voice was drowned out in the cacophony of violence.

The waning years (1969–73) of the military dictatorship also witnessed the emergence of a highly radical, violent, and antidemocratic actor – the revolutionary left. From 1969 on, with the emergence of the revolutionary left bloc, there were three competing regime coalitions. The revolutionary left coalition was much weaker than the authoritarian right and the pro-democracy coalitions, but in the context of the Cold War, it had a profound impact. One of the most powerful leftist guerrilla movements in the history of Latin America, it embraced violence as a way of life and of effecting political change (Gillespie 1982; James 1990; Moyano 1995; O'Donnell 1982: 446–51, 459–65; Ollier 1986, 1989, 2009; Viola 1982; Waldmann 1982). The movement expanded rapidly among the youth after 1969, and by 1970 the Peronist groups *Montoneros* and Revolutionary Armed Forces, as well as the Trotskyite ERP (Ejército Revolucionario del Pueblo, People's Revolutionary Army), were in full operation. Violent popular protests in 1969 helped bring down President Onganía the following year, inspiring the revolutionary left's belief in the efficacy of violence as a tool to bring about political change. From then until its defeat in 1976–77, the revolutionary left employed violence against the armed forces, the police, business and some labor leaders, and leaders of the political right.

From 1973 to 1976, the revolutionary left contributed to a spiral of violence. Consistent with the argument in Chapter 2, it generated fear among other political actors. Its emergence encouraged the formation of right-wing death squads, most of which also functioned within the Peronist movement (Leis 2012). Whereas public opinion had accepted and even supported the revolutionary left's use of violence to defeat the dictatorship of 1966–73 (Ollier 1989: 101), under the new democracy, society gradually became tolerant of right-wing extremism as a way of restoring order. The military continued to be a profoundly antidemocratic actor (De Riz 1987: 190, 201). The 1976 coup enjoyed significant popular support; the failures of the democratic regime were many and profound.

The regional political environment was hostile to democracy from 1973 to 1976. In intellectual circles throughout most of Latin America, this period was marked by the dominance of dependency theory and Marxism. The ascendance of leftist ideologies in some circles and the national security doctrine in others had profound reverberations in the region, encouraging transformative radicalism on the left and reactionary radicalism on the right. Military coups terminated long-lasting democracies in Chile and Uruguay in 1973, and all of Argentina's neighbors – Bolivia, Brazil, Chile, Paraguay, and Uruguay – had dictatorships by 1973. The hemisphere-wide dissemination of the national security doctrine, U.S. support of military dictatorships under Presidents Nixon and (to a lesser degree) Ford, and the great economic success of Brazil's military dictatorship from 1967 to 1980 helped create a climate favorable to military rule.

Table 5.2 summarizes the main conditions shaping the survival of competitive regimes during the second wave of democratization and its long aftermath. There were many deep changes in Argentine politics between 1946 and 1976. Nevertheless, the entire period was marked by some radicalism and a very low normative preference for democracy. International conditions were also detrimental to democracy during most of the long period from 1946 to 1976.

THE THIRD WAVE: STABLE DEMOCRACY SINCE 1983

The military regime of 1976–83 was among the most violent dictatorships in the recent history of South America. The famous *Nunca Más* (Never Again) report by the National Commission on the Disappeared People (CONADEP, Comisión Nacional sobre la Desaparición de Personas) documented 8,961 deaths – a conservative estimate because it is nearly impossible to have a complete count (CONADEP 1984). The dictatorship was in many respects incompetent, including its economic management and its decision to invade the Falkland Islands (Malvinas) and thereby go to war with the United Kingdom in 1982.

The defeat in the 1982 war severely damaged the military's internal cohesion and undermined its support. The authoritarian coalition collapsed, and a new democratizing coalition formed, leading to elections in October 1983. Raúl Alfonsín of the UCR handily won the presidential election with 52 percent of the vote, partly because he and the Radicals represented a quest for democracy and a repudiation of intolerance, violence, and authoritarianism more clearly than the Peronist candidate (Jaunarena 2011). It was the first time that the Radicals had defeated the Peronists when the latter were allowed to run.

Since 1983, Argentina has enjoyed continuous democracy notwithstanding some tumultuous times, very poor average economic performance until 2003 (though with solid growth and low inflation from 1991 to 1998), a dramatic growth in poverty and inequality until 2003, and two severe economic crises (1988–89 and 2001–02). De-radicalization and the prevalence of actors with strong normative commitments to democracy have been key to the survival of democracy. International support for democracy has helped.

Given the long period of democratic continuity, it would be easy to assume retrospectively that building democracy in Argentina was an easy task – that is,

TABLE 5.2 *Historical Conditions for Argentine Competitive Regimes, 1946–76*

Administration	Normative regime preferences	Radicalism	International context
J. D. Perón, 1946–55[a]	Perón and Partido Justicialista: -0.5 (-1 after 1950); Military: 0 (-0.5 after 1950) UCR: 0.5 (0 after 1950)	Perón and PJ: 0.5 (1 after 1950); Military: 0 (1 after 1950) UCR: 0	Favorable: Postwar context in 1945–48; Italian democratization. Unfavorable: Franco's regime in Spain; post-1948 U.S. policy
A. Frondizi, 1958–62	Frondizi and UCRI: 0.5 Organized business: 0; Perón and peronism: 0; UCRP: 0; Organized labor: 0; Military: -0.5	Military: 1; Perón and peronism: 1; Frondizi & UCRI: 0.5; Organized labor: 0.5; Organized business: 0.5 UCRP: 0	Favorable: Wave of democracy in the late 1950s; Kennedy's Alliance for Progress. Unfavorable: Early effects of the Cuban Revolution.
A. Illia, 1963–66	Illia and UCRP: 1 UCRI: 0; Perón and peronism: 0; Organized labor: 0; Organized business: -0.5; Military: -1	Military: 1; Perón and peronism: 1; Organized business: 1; Organized labor: 0.5 Illia and UCRP: 0; UCRI: 0	Unfavorable: Effects of the Cuban Revolution. Emergence of bureaucratic-authoritarianism in Brazil.
H. Cámpora, R. Lastiri J. D. Perón, I. Perón, 1973–76	J. Perón and PJ: 0.5; UCR: 1 I. Martínez: 0; Organized labor: 0; Organized business: 0; Revolutionary left: -1; Right-wing groups: -1; Military: -1	J. Perón: 1; I. Martínez: 1; Revolutionary left: 1; Right-wing groups: 1; Military: 1; Organized business: 0.5 Organized labor: 0; UCR: 0	Unfavorable: Coups in Chile and Uruguay in 1973. Success of the military regime in Brazil. U.S. support for dictatorships.

Note: Values show each actor's score for Normative regime preferences (1 is pro-democracy, -1 is pro-dictatorship) and Radicalism (0 is moderate, 1 is radical) for each administration.
[a] We date the end of competitive politics circa 1951.

that the risk of regime breakdown was initially low. This interpretation would be an example of what Tanaka (1998) called the fallacy of retrospective determinism – the idea that something that actually occurred was destined (or at least highly likely) to occur (see also Carr 1961: chapter 4).

In fact, the democratic regime faced some formidable challenges, especially during the presidency of Raúl Alfonsín (1983–89), when several military uprisings took place and when hyperinflation exploded, and in 2001–02, when a severe financial and economic crisis could easily have derailed democracy. The inflation rate reached 3,080 percent in 1989 and 2,314 percent in 1990. During the severe financial and economic crisis of 2001–02, the urban poverty rate hit 45.4 percent in 2002, appalling for a country whose urban poverty rate had been only 16.1 percent eight years earlier (ECLAC 2005: 317). Since ECLAC started regularly publishing data on poverty at the beginning of the 1990s, no other country in Latin America has registered such an extraordinary increase in poverty. Scholarly work published in 1983–84 at the dawn of democracy correctly signaled that building an enduring democracy was a formidable task. The new democracy faced profound economic problems including a massive foreign debt incurred by the military dictatorship, an authoritarian political culture, a military that, although defeated, was still profoundly authoritarian and powerful, a history of many failed regimes, and weak democratic institutions.[9]

Democracy has survived despite many daunting challenges and poor economic and social results, especially between 1983 and 2003. What accounts for this great historical shift to stable democracy? All three independent variables in our theory changed in directions remarkably positive for democracy during this period.

Actors' Normative Preferences. For the first time in Argentine history, since 1983, most actors have been normatively committed to democracy and there have been no important authoritarian actors. Normative commitments to democracy enabled the regime to survive economic crises in 1989–90 and 2001–02 that were far more severe than the economic problems faced during earlier breakdowns. Whereas the economic problems of 1929–30, 1966, and 1975–76 solidified support for the authoritarian coalition, the severe economic crises of 1989–90 and 2001–02 "did not bring about the discrediting of the democratic regime" (Novaro and Palermo 2004: 12–13, referring to 2001–02; also see Cheresky 2008: 55).

Because the important actors have evinced a normative preference for competitive politics, the pro-democracy coalition has been solid and has remained intact even in moments of enormous political turmoil and economic crisis. All actors, even those that do not have a clear normative preference, have accepted

---

[9] See Oszlak et al. (1984), which offers essays by leading Argentine political analysts on the obstacles to building democracy. Writing several years after the transition, Waisman (1989: 99–104) still signaled several daunting challenges for democracy.

democracy. No actors have an explicit preference for dictatorship, and none has attempted to form an authoritarian coalition since the failed coups toward the end of the Alfonsín government in 1989. We first document and then explain these changes in normative preferences.

Since 1983, the Radicals and the Peronists have consistently been the core of the democratic coalition. Although the Radicals have declined to the point of decreasing relevance in recent years, they were an influential party well into the 2000s.[10] The Peronists won the presidential elections of 1989, 1995, 2003, 2007, and 2011, and the Radicals won in 1983 and 1999. Peronists also governed from December 2001 until 2003 after Radical President de la Rúa was forced to resign amid a plummeting economy and massive popular protest.

Both times that it governed (1983–89 and 1999–2001), the Radical Party presided over economic disasters. Yet it has been the actor with the most steadfast normative preference for democracy. The UCR's transformation to a normative preference for democracy occurred in 1970, as a result of the trauma of successive dictatorships. President Alfonsín was a committed, indeed almost exemplary, democrat (Norden 1996: 80–82).[11] He accepted congressional decisions that blocked his government from undertaking reforms that he deemed important. The other UCR president, Fernando de la Rúa (1999–2001), also had a clear normative preference for competitive politics. He supported freedom of speech, freedom of the press, political tolerance, and public sector transparency (Bonvecchi 2002: 125; Charosky 2002: 210–13; Freedom House 2002; Novaro 2002: 85–91; U.S. Department of State 2002). The UCR has also behaved as a loyal opposition. The party showed an unyielding support for democracy when it institutionally backed President Duhalde (2002–03) in order to guarantee the stability of the regime (Jaunarena 2011). Moved by "a fundamental commitment to democracy," Radical deputies and senators supported Duhalde's policies (Godio 2006: 190).

The Peronists also switched to a reasonably solid normative preference for democracy until the second Fernández de Kirchner administration (2011–present). They largely renounced their previous (1946–55) normative preference for a populist authoritarian regime, although this side of Peronism has strengthened again after 2003. They have not embraced a normative preference for democracy as fully as the Radicals; they still have strong tinges of antiliberal discourse and behavior. We coded the Peronist party as committed to democracy through 2010, although this normative preference had weakened as of this writing in 2012.

---

[10] The FREPASO (Frente por un País Solidario) was a major party/coalition from 1994 to 2001. Formed largely by dissident Peronists, it was part of the coalition that elected de la Rúa in 1999. It disintegrated after the 2001 elections. The FREPASO exhibited a strong normative preference for democracy and policy moderation.

[11] For some caveats, see O'Donnell (1991: 7–11) on Alfonsín's *movimentista* tendencies during the height of his popularity.

Sectors within Peronism have been willing to sacrifice some democratic practices in order to achieve their policy preferences (de Ipola 1987), but the movement distanced itself from the authoritarian proclivities of its past. This transformation is evident in the fact that the PJ accepted its role as a loyal opposition (in Linz's [1978b] sense) under democracy from 1983 to 1989 and from 1999 to 2001 – something it never did between 1955 and 1973.

A military revolt in April 1987 showed the profound transformation among PJ leaders, who offered unwavering support to the Radical administration. Massive demonstrations in support of democracy signaled the citizens' commitment to the regime (Jaunarena 2011). Even after gaining control of Congress in the midterm elections of 1987, and notwithstanding the tremendous failures of Alfonsín's economic policies in 1988–89, the PJ did not attempt to destabilize the regime.

The four Peronist presidents who lasted more than a few weeks (Carlos Menem, 1989–99; Eduardo Duhalde, 2002–03; Néstor Kirchner, 2003–07; Cristina Fernández de Kirchner, 2007–present) have largely demonstrated a normative preference for democracy, but with some willingness to run roughshod over mechanisms of intrastate accountability. Menem generally embraced liberal democracy (Palermo and Novaro 1996: 202–03). The administration was reasonably open toward the opposition, generally tolerant of public criticism, and somewhat accepting of congressional checks (Cheresky 2008: 122–24; Levitsky and Murillo 2005; Llanos 1998; Palermo and Novaro 1996: 256–66). On the negative side, Menem often undercut mechanisms of intrastate accountability, indicating some ambivalence in his day-to-day commitment to democratic principles (Cheresky 1999: 93; Levitsky 2003: 219–21; O'Donnell 1994; Palermo and Novaro 1996: 475–524). He packed the Supreme Court in 1990 (Helmke 2005), made extensive use of presidential decrees to partially circumvent Congress, and dismantled some traditional mechanisms of intrastate accountability such as the Tribunal de Cuentas de la Nación (National Accounting Court) and the Fiscalía Nacional de Investigaciones Administrativas (National Oversight Agency for Administrative Investigations).

More ambiguously, the PJ encouraged the popular mobilizations that led to de la Rúa's fall in 2001 (Auyero 2007; Novaro 2006: 297). However, in contrast to its actions in 1962 and 1966, it did not become an antidemocratic actor (Novaro 2002: 83). The PJ's commitment to preserve a democratic framework enabled the regime to survive in the face of a bruising social and economic crisis.

President Duhalde (2002–03) was committed to democracy and sought to handle the massive social outbursts of 2002 peacefully. The government generally tolerated protest movements (Novaro 2006: 295) and always had "channels open for negotiation with the *piqueteros*" (the protestors) (Godio 2006: 47). The administration preserved a fluid communication with the opposition and avoided radical discourse.

President Kirchner (2003–07) and his government generally exhibited a normative preference for democracy, but with the traditional Peronist antipathy toward mechanisms of intrastate accountability. The administration tolerated public protest and demonstrations and avoided indiscriminate repression of the *piqueteros*. Kirchner allowed peaceful protests while indicating that the government would not tolerate violence and illegal actions (Godio 2006: 119–23). The administration also embraced a proactive human rights policy: in 2003, Congress declared the Due Obedience and *Punto Final* laws void, removing the last legal barriers against trials for the state's human rights violations during the military dictatorship.[12]

At the same time, the Kirchner administration was not unconditionally supportive of freedom of speech (Botana 2006: 84). The president confronted his critics angrily and often penalized the critical press by withdrawing public-sector advertising (U.S. Department of State 2006: para. 2.a.; U.S. Department of State 2007: para. 2.a.). He also concentrated power in ways detrimental to Congress (Cheresky 2008: 56).

With the election of Kirchner's wife, Cristina Fernández de Kirchner, as president in 2007 – which in practice represented a second term for the incumbent administration – the great crisis of 2001–02 was closed. The threat of regime instability that besieged Argentine democracy in the early twenty-first century had been met with re-equilibration (Bosoer 2006; Mustapic 2005; Pérez-Liñán 2007). Fernández de Kirchner carried on the tradition of running roughshod over some mechanisms of accountability. During Fernández de Kirchner's second term (inaugurated in 2011), the Argentine press expressed increasing concern about the antiliberal attitudes of her administration, including the use of tax and criminal investigations to undermine critics and media outlets.[13]

Organized labor developed a reasonably solid normative preference for democracy in the post-1983 period. It vigorously mobilized against the Alfonsín government. However, in contrast to labor's previous indifference and occasional overt hostility to democracy, during the Alfonsín government, labor became committed to the regime. Just one month after Alfonsín's inauguration, in January 1984, the unified CGT issued a document that captured labor's new position on representative democracy: "The rule of law, liberty guaranteed by the legal system, responsible pluralism, and institutionalized participation constitute the only path by which economic development is viable, social justice is possible, and the realization of the human person is guaranteed. For this reason, the labor movement must be a zealous guardian of democratic stability for all Argentines" (quoted in García Lerena 2007: 240–41). McGuire (1997: 21) writes that by the end of the Alfonsín period, the main contending factions within the labor movement "acquired an instrumental stake in the survival of elections and legislative activity," and that the leader of the CGT, Saúl Ubaldini, was committed "to democracy was beyond any serious dispute."

---

[12] Critics note that the Kirchner/Fernández governments have done nothing about human rights abuses committed by the revolutionary left.

[13] *La Nación*, July 29, 2012, p. 28.

The National Confederation of Labor conducted thirteen general strikes between 1983 and 1989, but the Peronist unions did not embrace radical policy positions.

The military has gone from being an antidemocratic actor to supporting democratic regimes. The armed forces have moved far from the antidemocratic ideologies that guided many officers during most of the twentieth century. The military changed from an actor that was consistently willing to lead coup coalitions from 1930 to 1983 into one whose leadership adheres to the idea of civilian democratic control of the armed forces.[14]

During the early years of the democratic regime, the military was divided between factions that accepted civilian control and democracy and minority sectors that remained wedded to the authoritarian tradition and engaged in uprisings in April 1987 and January and December 1988 (Jaunarena 2011; Norden 1996). The revolts failed to garner political support. This is telling of the shift in Argentine public opinion regarding military rule. After 1976–83, the military's confidence that it could solve Argentina's problems and govern more effectively than civilians had dissipated. The confidence of other actors in the military's capacity to govern likewise dissolved. A new army revolt took place in late 1990, but loyal army units repressed the insurgents. By the early 1990s, the military was under civilian control and began to acknowledge excesses during the "dirty war." Military extremism was buried. The military declined in relevance after 1990 and ceased to be an important player in regime politics (Diamint 2006; Norden 1996; Palermo and Novaro 1996: 252).

What explains this transformation in normative preferences? In Chapter 2, we mentioned four sources of change in actors' preferences:

1. Traumatic experiences push actors to reconceptualize their preferences.
2. New leaders and quotidian processes of intraorganizational competition induce a change in organizational preferences.
3. Actors gradually change normative preferences because the incumbent regime has been a positive surprise, and they eventually come to value its *intrinsic* merits, not just its instrumental benefits.
4. External influences cause a change in domestic actors' preferences.

In Argentina, the first two sources of changing preferences were very important, as were external influences. The brutality of the 1976–83 dictatorship reinforced the UCR's democratic commitment and strengthened the sectors of the PJ and of labor that were normatively committed to democracy.[15] Labor and the PJ

---

[14] A few prominent military leaders published memoirs or gave interviews that strongly endorsed the intrinsic value of democracy. See Horacio's Ballester's memoir (1996: 14) and the interview with former president (1971–73) Alejandro Lanusse (1988: 59–63).

[15] C. Acuña (1995) argues that business also changed its normative preferences regarding the political regime, and not only its instrumental policy preferences, after 1983 in response to the disastrous failures, closed nature, and erratic nature of the 1976–83 regime.

suffered terribly from the dictatorship's repression. Thousands of PJ and labor leaders were killed during the military regime; thousands more were tortured, and countless left Argentina. Labor union activity was severely curtailed. The *Nunca Más* report (CONADEP 1984: 289) stated that 30.2 percent of those officially accounted for as murdered by the dictatorship were workers.

Workers suffered large economic losses under the dictatorship. Real wages plummeted by more than 30 percent between 1975 (the last year before the dictatorship) and 1982 (the last full year of the dictatorship) (Rapoport 2003: 845). The combination of an ineptly run war that cost 649 Argentine lives and billions of dollars, severe economic hardships for working-class families, brutal repression, and high organizational costs for labor unions reoriented the PJ and labor toward a normative preference for democracy.[16] Once labor and the PJ became committed to democracy as a value, even subsequent withering economic crises under democracy (1988–90 and 2001–02) did not cause them to defect to the authoritarian coalition. In the midst of the 2001–02 financial meltdown, the Peronist members of the Chamber of Deputies voted to approve March 24 (the anniversary of the 1976 coup) a day of memory of truth and justice. They declared,

The Peronist deputies support this measure not only as Peronists but also as democrats. . . . We have a commitment to democracy. Having suffered through the infamous dictatorship, we must always celebrate the memory of those who were disappeared, persecuted and jailed, of our colleagues who needed to leave the country, and of all those who fought to restore democracy and to ensure that we would never again have a dictatorship in our beloved country. (quoted in García Lerena 2007: 613)[17]

The sequence of events – the change in labor's and the PJ's normative preferences began and occurred largely during the dictatorship –underscores the causal impact of military rule. Alfonsín's electoral victory over an old-style Peronist machine candidate in 1983 was widely interpreted as stemming partly from the former's more steadfast normative commitment to democracy, and it further encouraged change in the PJ. From 1983 to around 1986, public opinion expressed indignation and outrage regarding the human rights atrocities committed by the dictatorship, strengthening voices within the UCR, the PJ, labor, and the military that had a normative preference for democracy. Chastened by the humiliation of defeat in a foolish war and of incompetent governance failures, the military ceased to be a clearly authoritarian actor.

[16] Writing at a time of severe economic problems that had terrible consequences for many workers, Ranis (1992: 6) stated that "Argentine workers' commitment to and support for democracy seemed to reach a new plane in the light of the contrast between the military *proceso* and the new democracy."

[17] Along similar lines, Tcach and Quiroga (2006:13) wrote that "[t]he dictatorship taught the society; it taught it to value the preservation of democracy. ... Argentine society learned the lesson well: the rejection of political violence that undermines and annuls institutional legitimacy and the rule of law."

A new generation of leaders in the UCR, PJ, labor movement, and military replaced those who had always been willing to flirt with coups. In an interview just months after the transition to democracy, labor leader Víctor De Gennaro stated that the consciousness of grassroots labor activists (*delegados de base*) had undergone a profound transformation as a result of the military dictatorship. "These new leaders are completely unlike those who trafficked with the military dictatorship. . . . The March 24 military coup clearly demonstrated that we need our own power to pursue policies that truly promote workers' interests" (quoted in Calello and Percero 1984: 254–55).

External influences reinforced these domestic sources of changing normative preferences and policy preferences. Traumatic events do not automatically produce changes in actors' preferences; the interaction between the trauma of the last military dictatorship and a changing regional political environment was key. The transitions to democracy in Uruguay (1985), Brazil (1985), Chile (1990), and other Latin American countries, a fairly consistent U.S. pro-democracy message from 1985 on, the end of the Cold War and the fall of the Soviet empire, and a reorientation of leftist politics away from revolutionary socialism and toward social democracy in neighboring countries made for a more prodemocratic regional environment.

In addition to these causes of changes in preferences in individual actors, when some old actors are displaced and new ones emerge, the systemic balance in normative preferences can change. This is also an important part of the story in Argentina. The revolutionary left was annihilated during the dirty war. Most individuals who came from the revolutionary left and survived the dictatorship underwent profound political and personal conversions. Most became staunch supporters of democracy (Ollier 2009).

The extreme right wing also disappeared, discredited by its association with a disgraced regime. After Menem quelled the last major military rebellion in 1990, the armed forces became a less relevant political actor (Norden 1996). The causal sequence in Argentina is clear: most actors changed normative preferences even before the regime transition in 1983. In contrast, the gradual disappearance of the armed forces as a powerful political actor shows a reverse causal effect: the regime change prompted the weakening of a formerly extremely powerful authoritarian actor.

Policy Radicalism. In Chapter 2, we noted that traumatic experiences and international ideological currents often help account for changes in attitudes toward democracy and radicalization. In the Argentine case, they help explain the collapse of radical politics. For the revolutionary left, the brutal repression of the 1974–79 period was profoundly traumatic. For the military, the institutional debacle that resulted from failed economic policies, a disastrous war against the United Kingdom in 1982, and international and domestic ridicule were also traumatic. For the country as a whole, the 1976–83 dictatorship was traumatizing in a way that promoted a search for a different way of doing politics. Political actors with radical agendas have almost completely disappeared. The radical right-wing temptation – the idea that Argentina could recover its golden era through right-wing radicalism – died. The defeat in the 1982 Falklands/ Malvinas war, the military regime's (1976–83) incompetent mishandling of economic policy, the international notoriety and condemnation that surrounded the state terror of the military regime, and the domestic repudiation of the human rights violations committed by the armed forces during the "dirty war" completely discredited the radical right.

The end of radicalism had profound consequences for democratic survival. In periods of economic downturn, some of which have been severe in the post-1983 period, most people, companies, and sectors have suffered losses, but democracy has given them an institutionalized, peaceful way of fighting for their policy preferences without resorting to coups or violence.

Between 2001 and 2002, popular mobilizations challenged the institutional structure and ultimately led to the downfall of the de la Rúa government in December 2001. When unemployment and poverty soared, the protestors (*piqueteros*) became an important actor. Although the *piqueteros* adopted a repertoire of contentious action, their policy demands seldom acquired radical overtones. The *piqueteros* employed confrontational tactics by blocking roads and highways, vandalizing toll booths, blocking the pay booths for subways, and encouraging people to ride the subways without paying (Cheresky 2008: 189). In 2004, some groups committed violent acts, including an attack on a police station (Botana 2006: 140). However, most factions were relatively moderate (Godio 2006: 307, 319).

International Factors. External influences have also supported democracy since 1983, reinforcing the positive trends established by changes in actors' normative preferences and the decline of policy radicalism. The demise of the revolutionary left in Brazil, Chile, and Uruguay and the quest to create a new democratic left in these countries and in much of Western Europe helped reorient Argentine intelligentsia. The rise of international human rights networks created new actors that worked on behalf of democracy and human rights (Keck and Sikkink 1998; Sikkink 2011). For the Reagan administration, the Malvinas/ Falklands war in 1982 was a turning point in reorienting attitudes about authoritarian regimes in Latin America. Rather than viewing right-wing authoritarian regimes as friendly dictators, the administration realized that these dictators were not always reliable. From 1982 on, Washington favored democracy in Argentina, and it signaled disapproval when military officers threatened coups in 1987 and 1989. By 1985, regime change had taken place in neighboring Bolivia (1982), Brazil (1985), and Uruguay (1985). The remaining dictatorships in South America (Chile and Paraguay) were becoming isolated.

The subsequent downfall of long-time dictators Alfredo Stroessner in Paraguay (1989) and Augusto Pinochet in Chile (1990) helped consolidate the democracy-friendly environment in South America. The fall of the Berlin Wall in 1989 and the disintegration of the Soviet Union reinforced the turn away from radical authoritarian leftist ideals. With the growing involvement of the OAS after 1991 and of Mercosur from 1996 on, the regional political environment became more protective of competitive regimes. As a result, external incentives for preserving democracy reinforced domestic democratic actors. During this period, U.S. policy continued to be favorable to democracy. We discuss these international factors in more depth in Chapters 7 and 8.

Table 5.3 summarizes the conditions for Argentine democracy since 1983 according to the three variables of our theory. By the early 1990s, thanks in good measure to a greater commitment to democracy on the part of key actors, the decline of authoritarian forces, the demise of radical politics, and changing international political and ideological currents, the fear of a successful coup had receded greatly. The changed international political environment was less crucial for Argentina than it was for El Salvador (Chapter 6), Guatemala, and Nicaragua in explaining the transition to a stable competitive regime, but it reinforced the positive effects resulting from more actors committed to democracy and the extinction of radicalism.

Table 5.4 aggregates the historical information about specific actors presented in earlier sections into an overall assessment of the situation during each administration. The table reports the average scores for normative regime preferences (−1 indicates support for dictatorship and 1 indicates support for democracy) and radicalism (0 reflects moderation and 1 radical policy preferences) for political actors during each administration. It also reports whether the international environment was generally favorable to democracy, based on the previous discussion. Table 5.4 also summarizes the behavior of the dependent variable (breakdown or stability of the competitive regime) during each administration.

ALTERNATIVE EXPLANATIONS

This section explores the usefulness of some alternative theories of democratization for understanding the Argentine experience.[18] Even if our theory appears to account for Argentina's transformation, without examining alternatives, a rival explanation might be better. Moreover and related, we have not yet considered whether some more distant causal explanations reasonably account for Argentina's transformation. We show that alternative explanations based on modernization theory (the level of development), the size and power of the working class (class theories), the level of inequality, and economic performance cannot reasonably explain this change. These findings for Argentina are consistent with the more general quantitative results in Chapter 4.

We follow an unstructured version of Mill's indirect method of difference, looking for explanatory conditions that covaried with the dependent variable over time, and discarding alternative explanations when they behaved inconsistently with the observed regime outcomes (Mill 1859: 551–53; Skocpol and Somers

---

[18] We do not discuss O'Donnell's (1973) famous theory about modernization and bureaucratic authoritarianism. See D. Collier (1979) for a detailed analysis.

TABLE 5.3. *Historical Conditions for Argentine Competitive Regimes, 1983–2010*

Administration	Normative regime preferences	Radicalism	International context
R. Alfonsín, 1983–89	Alfonsín and UCR: 1; Partido Justicialista: 1; Organized labor: 0.5; Military: 0	Military: 0.5 All others: 0	Favorable: wave of democratization; U.S. support for democracy since 1985.
C. Menem, 1989–99	Menem and PJ: 1; UCR: 1; Organized labor: 1; FREPASO: 1; Military: 0.5	Menem: 0.5 All others: 0	Favorable: Third wave of democratization. End of the Cold War.
F. de la Rúa, 1999–2001	de la Rúa (UCR): 1; FREPASO: 1; Partido Justicialista: 1; Social movements: 1	Social movements: 0.5 All others: 0	Favorable: Democratic stability in Latin America.
E. Duhalde, 2002–03	Duhalde and PJ: 1; UCR: 1; Social movements: 1	All actors: 0	Favorable: Adoption of OAS Democratic Charter in 2001. Unfavorable: U.S. focus on counterterrorism; Chávez in Venezuela.
N. Kirchner, 2003–07	Kirchner and FPV/PJ: 1; Social movements: 1; UCR: 1; ARI: 1	All actors: 0	Favorable regional environment, but emergence of radical leaders in Venezuela and Nicaragua.
C. Fernández de Kirchner, 2007–11[a]	Fernández and FPV: 1; UCR: 1; Rural sectors: 1	All actors: 0	Favorable regional environment, but consolidation of radical leaders in Venezuela and Ecuador, coup in Honduras (2009).

Note: Values show each actor's score for Normative regime preferences (1 is pro-democracy, –1 is pro-dictatorship) and Radicalism (0 is moderate, 1 is radical) for each administration.

[a] Information through 2010. Trends in radicalism and support for democracy changed after 2010.

TABLE 5.4. *Aggregate Conditions for Argentine Competitive Regimes, 1916–2010*

Administration	Period	Breakdown	Normative preferences	Radicalism	Favorable International Context
H. Yrigoyen	1916–22	No	0.50	0.17	Yes
M. T. de Alvear	1922–28	No	0.08	0.33	No
H. Yrigoyen II	1928–30	Yes	−0.17	0.50	No
J. D. Perón	1946–55	Yes	−0.30	0.50	No
A. Frondizi	1958–62	Yes	0.00	0.58	Yes
A. Illia	1963–66	Yes	−0.08	0.58	No
H. Cámpora; J.D. Perón; I. Perón	1973–76	Yes	−0.19	0.69	No
R. Alfonsín	1983–89	No	0.63	0.13	Yes
C. Menem	1989–99	No	0.90	0.10	Yes
F. de la Rúa	1999–2001	No	1.00	0.13	Yes
E. Duhalde	2002–03	No	1.00	0.00	Yes
N. Kirchner	2003–07	No	1.00	0.00	Yes
C. Fernández de Kirchner[a]	2007–11	No	1.00	0.00	Yes

Key:
Breakdown: The competitive regime broke down during this administration.
Normative preferences: Score for the average actor during the period (−1 indicates support for dictatorship, 1 indicates support for democracy).
Radicalism: Score for average actor during the period (1 indicates radical policy preferences).
Favorable context: Positive conditions for democracy in the international context outnumbered the unfavorable conditions.
[a] During the second Fernández de Kirchner administration, there was some deterioration in normative preferences for democracy and an increase in radicalism. The table reflects our codings through 2010.
Source: Based on Tables 5.1, 5.2, and 5.3. See the project's Web site for the aggregation of actor-level data into regime-level data for each administration.

1980). We also employ selected cross-national comparisons in order to calibrate our assessment of domestic conditions in Argentina in given historical contexts.

Modernization. A modernization explanation can explain the survival of democracy after 1983, but it cannot explain why democracy has fared better since 1983 than it did between 1973 and 1976, and it offers at best a weak explanation for why democracy has fared better since 1983 than in the breakdowns of 1930, 1951 (or 1955 for those who dispute our coding of the late Perón years as competitive authoritarian), 1962, and 1966. As the earlier discussion made clear, Argentina's vulnerability to breakdowns until 1976 did not stem from factors associated with a low level of development. When the first breakdown took place in 1930, Argentina was an upper-middle-income country by standards of the day. In fact, the country is unique in the world for its breakdowns of competitive regimes at high levels of development (Przeworski et al. 2000).

During much of the twentieth century, Argentina enjoyed the highest level of development in Latin America. In 1928, when Yrigoyen assumed the presidency for the second time, Argentina's per capita GDP was $4,497 (in constant 2000 U.S. dollars), 21 percent higher than the second-highest in Latin America at that time (Uruguay, $3,711 per capita), and more than double the per capita GDP of each of the other eighteen Latin American countries. According to Maddison's (1989: 19) estimates, in 1929, just before the country's first democratic breakdown, Argentina had a higher per capita GDP ($2,036 in international dollars in 1980 prices) than Finland ($1,667) and only slightly lower than Norway ($2,184) and Sweden ($2,242). Norway has enjoyed continuous democracy since 1898 and Sweden since 1912. Norway's per capita GDP ($1,218 in 1900) when it became democratic was well below Argentina's in 1929, and Sweden's when it became democratic ($1,792 in 1913) was well below Argentina's at the time of all five breakdowns (Maddison 1989: 19).

In 1960, Argentina's per capita GDP in 2000 constant U.S. dollars was $5,237. Only twenty-two countries among those for which the World Development Indicators provides an estimate for 1960 had a higher per capita GDP than Argentina. Twenty-one of the twenty-two have had competitive regimes continuously since at least 1958; Venezuela is the sole exception. Based on the level of development, Argentina's breakdowns are an anomaly.

Although Argentina's level of development has long been favorable to democracy, the per capita GDP in 1983 ($6,721) was slightly lower than it was at the beginning of the previous democratic regime in 1973 ($6,953). Per capita GDP was only 38 percent higher in 1983 than in 1958 ($4,856) and 36 percent higher than in 1963 ($4,943), when the previous two semi-democratic experiences began. Given that Argentina as early as the 1920s had a level of development favorable to democracy, the post-1983 democratic stabilization does not seem to be a product of a higher level of development during the current democratic experience compared to the previous ones.

Class theories of democratization based on the power of the working class do not explain Argentina's vulnerability to breakdown before 1983. By the time of Perón's ascent to power between 1943 and 1946, Argentina had a large and mobilized working class. It had the largest blue-collar labor force in Latin America from the 1940s until at least 1970.[19] Around 1946, Argentina's blue-collar labor force was almost exactly the same relative size as that of France, Finland, and Italy.[20] Rapid unionization occurred after Perón became secretary

---

[19] The exact indicator is the share of the economically active population engaged in manufacturing, mining, construction, and transportation. Source: International Labour Organization, *ILO Yearbooks 1955, 1960, 1965, 1970, 1975, 1980.*

[20] In Argentina, 28% of the economically active population (EAP) was engaged in manufacturing, mining, construction, and transportation in 1947. Similar figures for the most proximate years are

of labor in 1943 and provided incentives for workers to organize. By 1954, union density (the number of union members divided by the economically active population) was at 42.5 percent (Marshall 2006: Tables 1 and 2). From 1955 to 1976, Argentina had Latin America's most combative and powerful labor movement. If a powerful labor movement were an unqualified asset for democracy, Argentina should have been a stable democracy from at least the 1940s on.

A powerful union movement was an asset in overthrowing dictatorships, but because of its unconditional support for Perón and its indifference to democracy, it was a democratic liability under the competitive regimes of 1958–62 and 1963–66, both of which it helped destabilize (Levitsky and Mainwaring 2006). It was also a liability to democracy during both Perón periods. Between 1946 and 1955, organized labor unconditionally supported Perón notwithstanding the regime's descent into authoritarianism. Between 1973 and 1976, the labor movement consistently prioritized policy results over democracy.

The organized working class is smaller and less powerful now than it was during Argentina's competitive regimes of 1946–50, 1958–62, 1963–66, and 1973–76. The share of the economically active population engaged in manufacturing, mining, transportation, and construction declined from 28 percent in 1970 to 22 percent by 2005.[21] Union density declined steeply, from 42.5 percent in 1954 to 24.4 percent for the 1990–95 period.[22] Therefore, Argentina's post-1983 democratic stabilization cannot plausibly be a result of a larger or more powerful working class.

Inequality and Democracy. Theories of democratization based on income inequalities also fail to explain Argentina's transformation from repeated breakdowns to stable democracy after 1983. They claim that more equal income distributions are favorable to democracy.[23] They mispredict Argentina's democratic transformation and (as the limited evidence showed in Chapter 4 suggests) the democratic transformation in Latin America as a whole. Argentina's income distribution was relatively equal between 1960 (and almost certainly well before then) and 1976. Along with Costa Rica and Uruguay, Argentina was historically one of the three Latin American countries that in most of the twentieth century did not have highly skewed income distributions. During the 1960s and 1970s – the first decades for which hard data are available – Argentina's Gini coefficient for income distribution was almost always below .40 and was as low as .33 (1972), one of the lowest figures ever recorded in Latin America. In our dataset for the quantitative analysis in Chapter 4, 13 of the 19 lowest scores for income

29% for France in 1946, 29% for Finland in 1950, and 28% for Italy in 1951. Source: *ILO Yearbook 1955*.
[21] Sources: For 1970, *ILO Yearbook, 1975*. For 2005, International Labour Organization, LABORSTA Labour Statistics Database, online.
[22] Sources: For 1954, Doyon (1988, table 5). For 1990–95, Oficina Internacional del Trabajo, *Panorama Laboral 2002: América Latina y el Caribe* (Lima).
[23] This is Boix's (2003) claim. Acemoglu and Robinson (2006) posit that very even and very uneven income distributions are inimical to democracy.

inequality for the twenty Latin American countries, out of a total of 665 data points (country-years), were for Argentina before the 1976 coup.

Income inequalities became much worse in Argentina in the decades after the 1976 coup. From 1976 to 2003, Argentina experienced the greatest increase in inequality of any country in Latin America. The Gini index increased from .35 in 1973 (the inaugural year of the last competitive regime before the current one) to .53 in 2003. Few countries in the world outside the former communist countries experienced such a staggering increase in inequality in this time. In terms of inequalities, Argentina had relatively favorable conditions for democracy from at least the second half of the 1940s through the late 1970s (Waisman 1987: 71–75), and much less favorable conditions during the post-1983 period.

Economic Performance. Hypotheses based on economic performance also cannot explain Argentina's democratic transformation. Faltering economic performance contributed somewhat to the breakdowns of 1962 and 1966, and clearly contributed to the breakdowns of 1930 and 1976.[24] But in none of these cases was economic performance the primary reason for the breakdown. In 1929, Argentina's per capita GDP was flat, and the following year it fell 5 percent as the Great Depression set in. The depression flamed the passions of actors that were already opposed to Yrigoyen and indifferent to democracy. However, economic growth had been robust in the decades prior to the 1930 breakdown. For this reason, it is implausible that in and of itself, the Great Depression had a decisive impact on the political regime by 1930. If a regime is legitimate, actors do not lead or support coups because of a short-term economic downturn caused by international factors. The depression had a destabilizing effect because most actors were already indifferent or hostile to democracy.

Economic performance under Perón was poor from 1949 on, including five consecutive years of decline in per capita GDP (1949–53). Poor economic performance solidified some opposition against Perón, and it probably tilted some previously neutral actors into the pro-coup camp. But economic decline took place when competitive politics had already been compromised. The reason why this regime is coded as authoritarian from 1951 on is that the government engaged in gross violations of political and civil rights and of the principles of free and fair elections. These violations were well under way before the recession of 1949–53, and they were probably not affected by the recession. In fact, the recession pushed Perón into recurrent efforts to be more conciliatory toward business.

The breakdown of 1962 did not stem primarily from poor economic performance. From 1958 to 1962, per capita GDP growth was sluggish but not terrible by Argentine standards of the last eighty years (0.0 percent, 1.0 percent, 6.6 percent, 3.7 percent, and 2.4 percent). Inflation was very high (124 percent) in 1959, but a stabilization plan brought it down to 12 percent in 1960 and 13

---

[24] Given the lack of data on wages for earlier periods, we use per capita growth and inflation as our indicators of economic performance.

percent in 1961. Several powerful actors conspired against the regime from the outset, before the economic results were known.

The breakdown of 1966 occurred despite relatively good economic performance by Argentine standards of the post-1930 era. Per capita GDP growth rates under Illia declined steeply (7 percent) in 1963, but Illia took office late in the year (October 12), so this recession could not be attributed to his administration. A brisk recovery took place in 1964–65, with growth rates of 8 and 9 percent, respectively. The growth performance between 1964 and 1965 was the best two-year record in the twentieth century until 1991–92. Another recession began in 1966, and the coup took place in June 1966 (Monza 1966). The recession probably solidified some defections to the coup coalition and away from the democratic coalition (Rouquié 1982b: 254–55), but several powerful actors had been highly disposed to sabotage the regime since 1963.

The competitive regime of 1973–76 mishandled economic policy, with negative political consequences. Per capita GDP fell 2 percent in 1975 and 4 percent in 1976. Inflation surged to 183 percent in 1975 and 444 percent in 1976. Poor economic performance added to the sense that democracy could not resolve pressing issues and facilitated the coup, but this explanation is thoroughly overshadowed in Argentine historiography by the intense radicalization on the left and the right of the political spectrum. Moreover, political radicalization contributed to bad economic performance by undermining economic agents' confidence in the stability of the rules of the game.

If faltering economic performance provides partial explanations for some of the coups between 1930 and 1976, this variable utterly fails to predict democratic survival from 1983 to 2002. Argentina has experienced periodic profound economic crises since the transition and has had an anemic average rate of economic growth since 1983. The early years of the democratic regime were particularly bad. A brutal recession occurred in 1985, followed by another between 1988 and 1990. Per capita GDP was 17 percent lower in 1990 than it had been in 1983. Another recession followed in 1995, and then a prolonged and deep recession began in 1999, with four consecutive years of downturn. The country experienced chronically high inflation from 1983 until 1992, with only one year (1986) of consumer price increases below triple digits, and barely at that (90 percent). Inflation peaked at 3,080 percent in 1989 and 2,314 percent in 1990, with devastating social consequences.

Per capita GDP plunged from $8,211 in 1998 to $6,425 in 2002 after four consecutive years of decline.[25] The incidence of poverty doubled from 1999 (23.7 percent) to 2002 (45.4 percent) and almost tripled from 1994 (16.1 percent) to 2002 (ECLAC 2005: 317). A country that for generations had had a large middle class and moderate income inequalities suddenly experienced a dramatic surge of poverty, and inequalities intensified.

---

[25] In 2000 U.S. dollars (World Bank Development Indicators, online).

In December 2001 the economy collapsed, again with devastating social consequences. By then the de la Rúa administration had no institutional support and was deeply discredited and isolated. A series of riots broke out, and on December 20, 2001, de la Rúa resigned in the face of multitudinous social protest. He was replaced by four short-lived interim presidents between December 21, 2001 and January 2, 2002. Finally, Eduardo Duhalde (January 2, 2002 to May 5, 2003) of the PJ was appointed by Congress to complete de la Rúa's term. Despite the deep crisis, de la Rúa was replaced following the rules stipulated by the constitution – a clear indication that Argentina's post-1983 regime stood on much firmer ground than its predecessors.

The economic crisis deepened, and poverty and social exclusion reached unprecedented levels. Yet the regime itself was not challenged, as all major parties were committed to democracy. The popular mobilizations of December 2001 never turned into anti-system actors. These mobilizations condemned the political parties and the political class as a whole, but they did not ally themselves with antidemocratic leaders or parties. "The streets issued a veto, but they did not seek to appropriate a decision-making power that would replace the legal institutions" (Cheresky 2008: 135, 136; also Novaro and Palermo 2004: 12–13). Surprisingly, the main actors remained moderate. At a different historical moment, some of the social movements that mobilized against the de la Rúa government in 2001 might have turned into radical anti-system actors. Notwithstanding the profundity of the crisis, the military refused to patrol the streets (a role that was forbidden by law) and remained on the sidelines, not tempted to assert its voice and coercive power into the dynamics of regime politics (Diamint 2006: 163; Levitsky and Murillo 2005: 40).

From 1983 to 2002, Argentine society had many economic losers and few winners. Actors did not support the regime because it generated good results for them. Organized labor supported the regime despite a 35 percent drop in average real wages and a 73 percent decline in real urban minimum wages from 1984 to 1992 (ECLAC 1992: 44, 45), a sharp increase in urban unemployment from 5.9 percent in 1987 to 18.6 percent in 1995 and 19.7 percent in 2002 (ECLAC 1995: 50; ECLAC 2009: 237), hyperinflation between 1989 and 1990, and the stunning increase in the poverty rate. For most Argentine workers, the period from 1983 to 2002 was terrible. The PJ and UCR supported the democratic regime in the face of far worse economic results than had triggered their defection to coup coalitions in earlier episodes. Business, which had frequently conspired against competitive regimes until 1976 (C. Acuña 1995), supported democracy after 1983 even during terrible times such as the 2000–02 period, when the stock market plunged by 65 percent (ECLAC 2006: table A-20). In 2001, 200 of the country's 500 largest companies reported losing money (compared to an average of 95 in 1993, 1994, and 2004, which were years of economic growth) (INDEC 2009), yet big business did not turn against the regime.

Moreover, during the Alfonsín administration, sectors of the armed forces were disposed to overthrow the government. Thus, neither simple instrumental logic (the regime generated good policy results for actors) nor more sophisticated instrumental logic (an actor would defect to the coup coalition if policy results were bad *and* if there was a plausible coup coalition) can explain actors' adherence to democracy after 1983.

Mass Values. Argentina's mass political culture could help explain the breakdown of multiple competitive regimes between 1930 and 1976. At the mass level, Argentina's political culture from 1946 through 1976 was unfavorable to democracy (O'Donnell 1973: 148–54). Argentina shifted from a mass political culture that was generally indifferent and sometimes hostile to democracy between 1930 and 1976 to one that has embraced it since 1983. Many leading Argentine scholars have underscored this transformation (Botana 1995: 18; Cheresky 1999: 15–18; Cheresky 2008: 249; Fontana 1987: 417–18; Godio 2006: 29; Novaro and Palermo 2004: 18–19; Peruzzotti 2005: 229–41; Portantiero 1987b: 164).

The lack of systematic survey data makes it virtually impossible to disentangle mass and elite preferences before the 1980s. Yet if we assume that mass values are relatively stable, the short-term fluctuations in political regimes during the first two historical periods are difficult to explain. It is not clear that Argentine *mass* culture was less supportive of democracy in 1930, when democracy broke down, than in 1916, when the first democratic period was inaugurated. And it is not clear that Argentines were less supportive of democracy in 1966, when President Illia was ousted, than seven years later, when President Cámpora was inaugurated. Even if mass preferences create a social environment that facilitates certain outcomes, other explanations must be considered in order to explain the timing and the sequence of particular episodes of regime change.

In any case, Argentina's authoritarian political culture from the 1930s through 1976 did not stem from long-standing cultural legacies of the country's Catholic or Iberian heritage. Democratization in Argentina got off to an early and in many respects promising start. If the country's Catholic or Iberian legacy were the primary obstacle to democratization, it would be impossible to explain this promising start or democratic survival since 1983. An authoritarian political culture was the product of Argentina's regime history more than the cause of it (Potter 1981).

A COMPARATIVE ANALYSIS OF COMPETITIVE ADMINISTRATIONS, 1916–2010

In this section, we undertake a comparative qualitative analysis (QCA) of the thirteen democratic and semi-democratic administrations in Argentina between 1916 and 2010 to complement the within-case process tracing of previous sections. This analysis has two advantages: it allows us to assess the interaction of our main independent variables and to reflect systematically on counterfactuals, that is, historical conjunctures that could have taken place but did not occur in Argentine history. This configurational analysis complements other modes of causal inference in within-case studies.

The qualitative comparative analysis loses the nuance provided by process-tracing in the previous sections, but it is helpful in laying bare the logic of an explanatory argument and in ensuring its consistency (Ragin 1987, 2000, 2008; Rihoux and Ragin 2009). It also allows us to assess the specific role of each variable in the causal process and to compare the explanatory power of different causal paths. In conjunction with the within-case qualitative analysis presented above, this approach helps address some common problems of inference in small-N comparison.[26]

Table 5.5 presents a causal typology defined by eight possible configurations resulting from the interaction of our three explanatory factors (George and Bennett 2004). For simplicity, we classified the thirteen administrations depicted in Table 5.4 according to three criteria: (1) whether a majority of political actors during the period had a normative preference for democracy; (2) whether a majority of political actors embraced radical policy preferences; and (3) whether international conditions were generally favorable to democratization. The interaction of the three dichotomous conditions generates the eight causal types identified in the table. All administrations fit one of the historical configurations, and they are classified according to their regime outcomes (breakdown or survival).

The first three columns of the table identify the causal types. The Argentine experience provides historical examples of five of the eight possible configurations, but three types (nos. 2, 7, and 8) are "remainders" or counterfactual situations with no historical examples in Argentina (Ragin and Sonnett 2005). The following three columns list the cases and the regime outcomes falling under each configuration. The term "survival" in the table refers to the competitive regime, not the president. President de la Rúa, for instance, resigned before the end of his term, but democracy did not collapse.

The last column of Table 5.5 reports the proportion of administrations that were overthrown under each configuration – that is, the consistency score for a hypothesis of sufficiency linking each casual type with democratic breakdown (Ragin 2006). Breakdowns cluster under types nos. 1, 3, and 4, while episodes of

---

[26] Lieberson (1991) claimed that small-N comparison usually relies on three unrealistic assumptions: that there is a single (rather than a multivariate) explanation, that there are no interactions among the causes, and that the causal mechanism is deterministic rather than probabilistic. Our analysis in this section relaxes all three assumptions while recognizing the limitations of QCA pointed out by Seawright (2005). Moreover, Lieberson's criticism underestimates the insight provided by process-tracing in within-country studies. See Appendix 5.1 for technical information about the QCA procedure.

TABLE 5.5 Historical Configurations Leading to Breakdowns: Argentina, 1916–2010

#	Commitment to Democracy	Prevailing Radicalism	Favorable International Context	Regime Breakdowns	Regime Survivals	N	Consistency (breakdown)
1	No	No	No	Yrigoyen II Perón		2	1.0
2	No	No	Yes			0	n.a.
3	No	Yes	No	Illia Cámpora-Perón-Perón		2	1.0
4	No	Yes	Yes	Frondizi		1	1.0
5	Yes	No	No	Alvear		1	0.0
6	Yes	No	Yes		Yrigoyen I Alfonsín Menem de la Rúa Duhalde Kirchner Fernández de Kirchner	7	0.0
7	Yes	Yes	No			0	n.a.
8	Yes	Yes	Yes			0	n.a.

Key:
Normative commitment to democracy: Most actors had a normative preference for democracy (i.e., score for normative preferences in Table 5.4 is greater than zero).
Prevailing radicalism: Most actors expressed radical policy preferences (score for radicalism in Table 5.4 is greater than 0.5).
Favorable context: Positive conditions for democracy in the international context outnumbered the unfavorable conditions.
Source: Tables 5.1 to 5.4. We relied on fs/QCA and Tosmana for the identification of essential prime implicants.

survival cluster under types nos. 5 and 6. This comparative analysis suggests some conclusions.[27]

Two historical configurations consistently led to the breakdown of competitive politics in Argentina: the lack of normative commitment to democracy combined with radicalism, *or* the lack of normative commitment to democracy combined with an adverse international context. The absence of a normative preference for democracy among a majority of political actors thus emerges as a common denominator for all instances of breakdown. Combined with radicalism, weak preferences for democracy undermined the regime even under relatively favorable international conditions, as in the case of Frondizi. In an adverse international context, weak normative commitments were enough to undermine the regime even when most actors were not radical, as during the second Yrigoyen administration.[28]

By contrast, the combination of a normative preference for democracy and moderate policy preferences among a majority of political actors consistently allowed the survival of democracy in Argentina. This conjuncture of domestic conditions preserved the competitive regime even in a deteriorating international context, as during the Alvear (1922–28) administration.[29] The probability that these casual patterns are the product of historical chance is very low ($p < .05$). Appendix 5.1 presents technical details about the QCA procedure and about our use of the binomial test to assess the likelihood of these results.

Taken together, these findings reinforce the quantitative results presented in Chapter 4 and the disciplined qualitative narratives presented earlier in this chapter. The combination of a normative commitment to democracy and the absence of radical policy preferences among the main actors seems to immunize competitive regimes against their enemies. Indeed, the Argentine case provides

---

[27] For clarity of presentation, we have omitted all technical notations from the text of the chapter. See Appendix 5.1 for additional information.

[28] We cannot assert, however, that the lack of normative preferences for democracy alone is enough to destabilize competitive regimes unless we admit a counterfactual claim: that breakdown would have taken place in the absence of normative commitments even if actors were not radical and if the international context was favorable. We do not have any empirical instances of this type (#2) in Table 5.5, but this is a "hard" counterfactual because it contradicts previous evidence (presented in Chapter 4) about the casual effects of international conditions (Ragin and Sonnett 2005).

[29] Moreover, if we entertain the possibility – consistent with the available evidence – that a lack of normative commitment to democracy was necessary for democracy to break down, it follows that the presence of such commitment (alone) would be enough to prevent a breakdown. However, this assertion also demands the acceptance of two counterfactuals (represented by types nos. 7 and 8). Although not completely implausible, counterfactual #7 is harder to accept because it implies that democracy would have survived if actors were committed to democracy, even under adverse external conditions and if players were radical. The absence of historical configurations with strong preferences for democracy *and* high radicalism underscores the empirical connection between radicalism and normative preferences documented in Chapter 3.

evidence that a breakdown will be unlikely if most actors value democratic politics intrinsically.

CONCLUSIONS: ON DEMOCRATIC SURVIVAL
IN THE THIRD WAVE

The Argentine experience illustrates some of the factors that explain the capacity of competitive regimes to survive even in the face of poor economic performance, hyperinflation, rapid increases in inequality, and the downfall of many presidents. By implication, this analysis helps account for the absence of a counterwave in Latin America after 1978. An in-depth analysis of actors as summarized by our disciplined narratives and the qualitative comparative analysis indicates that the combination of actors' normative commitment to democracy, low radicalism, and a favorable international context created an environment that has enabled democracy to survive in the face of many profound challenges since 1983. The evolution of these factors helps explain the historical trajectory of Argentine politics.

Most actors' indifference to democracy from the 1920s until 1976 consistently put competitive regimes at peril. Extreme radicalism from 1973 to 1976 helped doom the short-lived democratic experiment of the 1970s. In all five breakdowns, most major actors were indifferent or hostile to democracy. Radical actors were relevant for the demise of democracy in all cases. An unfriendly regional environment contributed to the breakdowns of 1930, 1951, 1966, and 1976.

After 1983, most actors became committed to democracy, and radicalism diminished among powerful actors in Argentine politics. The international political environment became friendlier to democracy. Although this factor was less important in explaining regime change in Argentina than in many Latin American countries, the disappearance of negative international influences had a salutary effect for democratic survival. The results of the qualitative analysis therefore reinforce the quantitative findings of Chapter 4.

The evidence in this chapter provides some hints about the more distant causes of radicalization and low commitment to democracy. In Argentina, the peak of radicalization (1969–78) coincided with an era of moderately low income inequality, and low support for democratic norms coexisted with high modernization and a strong middle class (O'Donnell 1973). Radicalism and a weak normative preference for democracy emerged from a combination of external influences and domestic historical legacies. Among external influences, Spanish and Italian authoritarianism in the 1920s, the Cuban Revolution in the 1960s and 1970s, U.S. willingness to support authoritarian regimes during most of the period from 1948 to 1977 and support of national security policies in the 1960s and 1970s, and the rethinking of leftist politics that took place in the southern cone and Western Europe in the 1970s and 1980s reoriented some

Argentine actors. Argentine political actors also responded to the apparent lack of democratic commitment and the intransigence of their adversaries with an escalation of antidemocratic practices and a radicalization of their own policy positions.

The distribution of historical cases in Table 5.5 underscores some possible empirical connections among the three explanatory factors that find strong empirical support in an in-depth analysis of actors. As we pointed out in Chapter 2, for individual actors, it is difficult to embrace radical policy preferences and normative support for democracy simultaneously. To the extent that support for democracy or radicalism are limited, those preferences may coexist, but at the extremes they are very hard to reconcile for any actor. Moreover, at the collective level, there are tensions between radicalism and a normative preference for democracy, even though different actors could presumably embrace each principle. Table 5.5 offers no historical instances of widespread radicalization at the aggregate level combined with extensive commitment to democracy, suggesting that in equilibrium such a configuration is hard to preserve.

In many democracies, some actors with strong normative commitments to democracy (and typically moderate policy preferences) coexist with others who have radical policy preferences (and usually weak commitments to democracy). But if radical policy preferences become prevalent, actors committed to democracy lose their centrality in the political process. Most actors, anticipating that radical players will seek to impose their goals on society, prepare for a different political game. The progressive displacement of moderate actors is illustrated by the Argentine case from 1930 to 1976. The radical policy preferences of some powerful actors in the competitive regimes from 1946 through 1966 escalated into intense radicalization by 1973–76. Moderate actors such as the UCR (1973–76) were drowned out in the cacophony of political violence.

This example suggests that waves of democratization may stabilize when most actors in a region develop strong democratic norms and moderate policy preferences, but they may recede if key actors in key countries renege from democratic commitments in order to gain short-term political advantages or if they embrace radical positions. In this context, successful antidemocratic examples may disseminate across the region, creating a reverse wave. This conclusion helps explain the sustainability of the third wave in Latin America in contrast to what has occurred in the former Soviet countries. It also brings to the fore the role of international mechanisms in disseminating democratic values and policy models, linking domestic conditions across different national units. We turn to this issue in Chapter 7 after the case study of El Salvador.

6

From Persistent Authoritarianism to a Durable Democracy: El Salvador

In this chapter, we analyze the dramatic and surprising shift from persistent and often brutal authoritarianism to stable democracy in El Salvador. We focus on three questions. First, what explains the persistence of authoritarianism for such an extended time into the twentieth century? With the exception of a few months in 1931, El Salvador had uninterrupted authoritarian rule until 1984. Second, what explains why a transition to a competitive regime occurred despite this profoundly authoritarian past? Third, albeit much more briefly, why has a democratic regime survived notwithstanding performance deficiencies?

Authoritarian rule was chronic because of a consistent severe imbalance between a powerful and fairly stable authoritarian coalition and an extremely weak democratizing coalition. Notwithstanding occasional rifts between big business and some factions of the military, these two actors formed a stable authoritarian coalition that lasted until it was rendered asunder by the civil war in the 1980s. Official governing parties were a third important partner in the authoritarian coalition. In contrast, democratizing coalitions were chronically extremely weak until the emergence of the Christian Democratic Party (PDC) in the 1960s.

A transition to democracy occurred between 1984 and 1994 because of deep and rapid changes in the balance between the authoritarian and democratic coalitions. Powerful actors that had supported extremist agendas and had normative preferences for dictatorship in the 1980s underwent extraordinary transformations. Over the course of a long sanguinary civil war (1980–92), three key actors defected from the conservative authoritarian coalition: ARENA (*Alianza Republicana Nacionalista* or Nationalist Republican Alliance), which was created in 1981 as an extreme-right party with a normative preference for dictatorship; big business; and the military. The latter two had been the key pillars of the authoritarian regimes that ruled from 1931 to 1979. The FMLN (Farabundo Martí Front for National Liberation, *Frente Farabundo Martí para la Liberación Nacional*), which was created in 1980 as a revolutionary leftist guerrilla organization, defected from the revolutionary left authoritarian coalition. The extraordinary polarization of the 1970s and 1980s receded.

These defections occurred in part because of the brutal civil war. The cost in lives, injuries, privations, human and physical capital, destroyed crops, and infrastructure was huge. By late 1989, the war appeared to be at an interminable stalemate. The extraordinary cost of the status quo, coupled with the fact that neither side seemed capable of militarily defeating the other, led the more moderate factions of the guerrillas, ARENA, and big business to defect from the authoritarian left and authoritarian right coalitions. When the two sides showed signs of being willing to negotiate and de-radicalize, fears about possible policy losses under democracy decreased for ARENA and big business, and the possibility of meaningful policy gains under democracy appeared for the FMLN. In addition, some sectors of the FMLN and ARENA changed their normative preferences about the political regime in the late 1980s and 1990s and embraced democracy as an intrinsically desirable regime.

Consistent with our emphasis on the importance of international influences in understanding regime dynamics, the United States played a major role in fostering some of these transformations, even if not always fully by design. Because of its geopolitical interests, and because of domestic political conflicts related to U.S. policy toward Central America, the United States made elections a highly important political currency in El Salvador in the 1980s. In turn, the need to win votes in this new political context transformed the Salvadoran right.

Democracy has survived despite major shortcomings because the major actors have a normative preference for democracy and are much more moderate than they were in the 1970s and 1980s. The combination of well-entrenched political parties (including a strong leftist party) and decent government performance (except for public security) has made radical populism a remote possibility. In addition, the regional political environment for democracy remains largely positive.

Because of the persistent pattern of authoritarianism and the limited number of transitions, in this chapter we modify our analytical strategy in the interest of saving space. Rather than comparing specific administrations as units of analysis as we did in Chapter 5, we engage in a paired comparison (Tarrow 2010) of longer-term historical periods for 1900–1983 and for 1984–2010. Our discussion identifies the most powerful actors and their transformation over time, their normative regime preferences and policy positions, and the main international forces that influenced them.

COUNTRY CASE SELECTION: WHY EL SALVADOR?

The eight countries that had deep authoritarian pasts before the third wave of democratization are listed in Table 6.1. For our qualitative case study, we wanted one with a competitive political regime today that has survived for an

TABLE 6.1. *Level of Development and History of Competitive Regime, Eight Latin American Countries*

	Years of competitive regimes, 1900–77	Number of breakdowns of competitive regimes, 1900–77	Per capita GDP (2009)	Poverty rate circa 2008 (%)	Year of inauguration of current competitive regime	Number of breakdowns of competitive regimes since 1978
Mexico	1	1	6,099	34.8	1988	0
Dominican Republic	4	1	3.697	41.1	1978	0
El Salvador	0	0	2.597	47.9	1984	0
Guatemala	14	2	1,867	54.8	1986	0
Paraguay	0	0	1,433	48.2	1989	0
Bolivia	8	1	1,192	54.0	1982	0
Nicaragua	7	1	877	61.9	1984	0
Haiti	0	0	390	ND	2006	2

Sources: For columns 1, 2, 5, and 6 on political regimes, the Appendix to Chapter 1. Per capita GDP is in 2000 constant US dollars. Source: World Bank (2007).
Poverty rate: ECLAC, *Social Panorama of Latin America and the Caribbean 2010* (table A-4, pp. 224–25).

extended time in the post-1977 period. This is by far the more common pattern in the contemporary era. This criterion eliminated Haiti.

Countries in which a competitive regime emerged and has been stable despite many formidable obstacles pose a more interesting intellectual puzzle than countries with socioeconomic conditions favorable to democracy. What accounts for regime transition and survival despite these obstacles? In this sense, Bolivia, El Salvador, Guatemala, Nicaragua, and Paraguay are better country cases than Mexico, which has a significantly higher standard of living, less poverty, a more solid state, and stronger institutions. Given the regional political environment in Latin America, Mexico's level of development, its relatively solid state, and the long-term prevalence of political moderation from 1940 on, it is not surprising that Mexico eventually (in 1988) moved to a competitive political regime and later (2000) to democracy. The Dominican Republic is an intermediate case, with a higher level of development and less poverty than all but Mexico of the eight countries in Table 6.1. The intellectually more interesting question is why the six poorer countries with histories of brutal authoritarianism experienced the end of dictatorships and the emergence of what became stable competitive regimes.

Table 6.1 provides some comparisons along these dimensions of the eight countries that transitioned from a strongly authoritarian past to enduring competitive political regimes in the third wave. The boldface cells highlight country conditions that do not meet our preferred criterion for case selection.

Bolivia, El Salvador, Guatemala, Nicaragua, and Paraguay are therefore the intellectually most interesting and suitable for our case selection. Finally, because political dynamics have historically been different in Central America and the Caribbean compared to South America, and because the other qualitative chapter focused on Argentina, we preferred a country in Central America or the Caribbean. International influences have had a distinctive flavor in Central America and the Caribbean given the United States' history of intervention in this subregion. U.S. influence weighed heavily in the transitions to competitive regimes in the three Central American countries, and much less so in Bolivia and Paraguay. Moreover, the three Central American countries exercised a strong common influence as civil wars ravaged all three at the same time. Choosing one of the Central American countries enabled us to include a case of pronounced international influence. Within these parameters, the specific country case in Central America does not matter much on theoretical grounds.

THE PERSISTENCE OF AUTHORITARIANISM, 1900–84

Along with Haiti and Paraguay, El Salvador is one of only three Latin American countries that in our classification never had a competitive political regime until the third wave of democratization.[1] During the lengthy period from 1900 to 1984, Salvadoran politics underwent many changes, but the pro-authoritarian coalition consistently and readily defeated every democratizing impulse. Many *governments* were unstable, but coalitions to support authoritarian *regimes* always prevailed. Different actors that supported dictatorship competed for power, but they consistently coalesced in opposition to democratization.

The authoritarian right ruled El Salvador until 1927 without any challenge from a pro-democratizing coalition, although the country was rife with coups and governmental instability as competing *caudillos* battled for power from independence in 1841 until 1885. During some periods, including 1932 and 1977–84, El Salvador had particularly brutal authoritarian regimes.

The authoritarian coalition consistently included most of big business and most of the military, the country's two most powerful actors from 1931 to 1984, as well as the official governing parties. From 1927 to 1984, the year of a transition to a semi-democratic regime, big business included coffee growers and exporters, other export agriculture (such as cotton), big industry, and big banking and financial firms.[2] Until the 1980s, big business consistently

---

[1] For a few months in 1931, from the inauguration of President Arturo Araujo in March to his imposition of martial law in July, the regime was semi-democratic. Because we did not code regimes that did not survive a single end of the year (December 31), our coding in Table 3.1 does not register this short-lived experiment.

[2] We usually treat big business in El Salvador as one actor because some important formal organizations represented big business as a whole, and these organizations converged politically far more than they diverged. They included the *Asociación Salvadoreña de Café* (ASCAFE), created in 1929 to represent coffee growers; the *Asociación Salvadoreña de Beneficiadores y Exportadores de Café*

supported authoritarian rule and elite privilege (Johnson 1993). The same big firms and wealthy families often engaged in business activities across multiple sectors, thus reducing the likelihood of political conflict based on divergent economic interests (Guidos Béjar 1988: 195–96; Wood 2000a: 39).

By the 1960s and 1970s, El Salvador was a more modern, urban, and industrial country than it had been in earlier decades. Popular class organizations were more widespread (Almeida 2008; Brockett 2005), and the first organized democratic mass party, the PDC, was created in 1960. Nevertheless, authoritarian actors and coalitions continued to prevail. The military, big business, and the official party were the core of the authoritarian coalition.

From 1961 until 1979, a regular succession of military dictators ruled the country, albeit with growing challenges from actors that preferred democracy or revolutionary socialism. In 1960, inspired by the reformist spirit of the immediate aftermath of the Cuban revolution and by the innovations taking place within the Catholic Church, reform-minded democrats created the Christian Democratic Party (PDC) (Webre 1979; Williams and Seri 2003; Zamora 1998: 137–79). Until the 1990s, the PDC was by far the most important actor in Salvadoran politics with a normative preference for democracy. It spearheaded the prodemocratic coalition that challenged the old order in the 1960s and 1970s. It represented a new and important democratizing force, but electoral fraud and repression thwarted its rise.

The hope of establishing a democratic path toward social reform was dashed in 1972, when PDC leader José Napoleón Duarte headed a coalition (UNO) as the leading opposition candidate for president. Duarte won the popular balloting only to lose the fraudulent official vote count. In the context of leftist and rightist radicalization that enveloped most of Latin America in the 1960s and the 1970s, the electoral fraud in 1972 had significant long-term consequences. The democratic electoral route to political and social change became discredited. Repeated electoral fraud in 1972, 1974, 1976, and 1977 demonstrated to opposition actors that peaceful democratic change was not possible.[3] The visible closing of this possibility at a time of regional leftist veneration of revolutionary socialism – more than widespread poverty or social inequality – spurred the escalation of the revolutionary insurgency (Brockett 2005; C. McClintock 1998; Zamora 2003). Social inequality and widespread poverty had existed since the country's independence, so they do not explain the outbreak of insurgency in the 1970s.

Some opposition leaders gave up on the electoral route and joined leftist organizations and peasant or labor groups. The oligarchy and death squads

(Salvadoran Association of Coffee Processors and Exporters, ABECAFE), founded in 1961; the *Asociación Nacional de Industria* (ASI), created in 1963; ANEP (*Asociación Nacional de la Empresa Privada*), created in 1966, which became the most important business organization until the 1980s; the *Cámara de Comercio e Industria*; and the *Frente de Agricultores de la Región Oriente* (Farmers' Front of the Eastern Region), created to combat the 1976 agrarian reform and defend landowners' interests.

[3] On the radicalizing effects of electoral fraud on the opposition in El Salvador, see the reflections of the secretary general of the Salvadoran Communist Party from 1973 to 1994, Schafik Handal, in Harnecker 1988: 21–27, and of other FMLN leaders interviewed in Harnecker 1993: 187–90.

undermined the Molina government's (1972–77) proposed agrarian reform and fueled further skepticism about reformist, democratic paths. The elimination of the democratic path encouraged the formation of revolutionary groups. In turn, the surge in the guerrilla's capacity unleashed a wave of repression with few precedents in twentieth-century Latin America.

President Carlos Humberto Romero (1977–79) represented the hard-line, radical, and repressive faction of the military, and his government had a further polarizing effect. The guerrilla movement expanded its efforts. Popular mobilization under the aegis of revolutionary Marxist and leftist Catholic leaders burgeoned. In response, the right organized new death squads and became more radicalized. In this context of profound polarization and growing resort to violence as the primary currency of political power, the space for reformist democratic options vanished (Stanley 1996: 107–32).

Consistent with our argument about the importance of international influences, the Sandinista overthrow of the Somoza dynasty in July 1979 in Nicaragua catalyzed revolutionary and counterrevolutionary mobilizations in El Salvador (Almeida 2008: 168; Brockett 2005: 18, 93; Dunkerley 1982: 119–31; Harnecker 1993: 203–06). Revolutionary struggles gained new fervor as the left became convinced that it could follow the Sandinistas and overthrow the regime. Popular groups mobilized against the regime. Counterrevolutionary measures intensified in response to the gathering revolutionary tide; the Sandinista victory inspired deep fear in conservative sectors of Salvadoran society.

On October 15, 1979, a coup ousted Romero. The military initially installed a junta that included prominent reformist democratic civilian politicians, military leaders who also favored social reform, and conservative officers whose primary concern was putting down the insurrection. Violence quickly spiraled out of control as the hard-right National Guard, military, and death squads sought to thwart the rise of the revolutionary left and to undermine the agrarian reform announced by the junta. By early 1980, the country descended into civil war.

The civil war raged until 1992, costing an estimated 75,000 Salvadorans their lives. The vast majority of deaths were at the hands of the military, the National Guard, the police, and extra-official death squads. Even though the civil war exacted a horrific toll into the early 1990s, in 1984 a transition to a semi-democratic regime began.

EXPLAINING PERSISTENT AUTHORITARIANISM

Authoritarianism consistently prevailed until 1984 because the resources of the authoritarian coalition overwhelmed those of every democratizing coalition. The most powerful actors during the long period from 1931 to 1984 consistently included the military, the official governing parties, big business, and presidents. Notwithstanding occasional rifts between the military and big business, they generally had an amicable alliance, and both supported authoritarian rule. These actors had very powerful resources. Big landowners had wealth and land, controlled jobs and the local labor force, and for the most part co-opted and controlled the local police and judiciary. The military had the arms and sufficient internal cohesion to guarantee order. The ruling parties provided clientelistic benefits that won some popular support and quiescence. All of the presidents except Pío Romero (1927–31), Arturo Araujo (1931), and Andrés Ignacio Menéndez (1934–35 and May 9–October 20, 1944) supported an authoritarian project.

From December 1931 to October 1979, the military with the support of an official party ruled El Salvador in an occasionally uneasy coalition with big business (Stanley 1996). The military defended the economic elite from the threat of major social and economic upheaval, and the economic elite allowed the military to rule and sometimes plunder the country. Some military leaders had reformist impulses, but the hard-line military and the economic elite always vetoed major economic and social reform and political democratization. Shared fear of social reform and democracy, along with policy outcomes that reasonably satisfied big business, the military, and the governing parties, cemented this coalition.

Because the authoritarian regimes suppressed the formation of actors that could present a challenge, pro-democratizing coalitions were chronically weak. Structural factors such as a fairly low level of development, a limited manufacturing base, and a small urban working class also impeded the formation of powerful opposition actors. With the partial exceptions of Presidents Pío Romero during part of his term, Araujo during the first months of his very short presidency, and Menéndez, no major actor supported a democratizing project until the creation of the PDC in 1960. Because the democratizing coalitions were so weak, Romero and Araujo quickly retreated from their reformist initiatives. Araujo and Menéndez were quickly toppled in 1931 and 1944, respectively, as a result of opposition to their reformist impulses. The huge imbalance between a relatively stable and powerful authoritarian coalition and a very weak democratizing coalition explains the persistence of authoritarianism and the consistent and rapid crushing of democratizing impulses.

Four actors occasionally opposed military authoritarianism from 1931 to 1979, but they never formed a solid democratizing coalition. First, reformist military factions favored economic and social reform, but they consistently either lost to the hard-liners or won for very brief interregnums (1944, 1960–61, 1979–80) before giving way again to the hard-liners. Even the reformists typically favored authoritarian rule; they combined social reform with political authoritarianism.

Second, the PDC fought for liberal democracy. From the time of its creation in 1960 until the late 1980s, it was the only consistent pro-democracy actor. Electoral fraud and coercion kept it from displacing the authoritarian coalition.

Third, in the late 1960s, a range of vibrant popular organizations (peasant groups and urban labor unions) emerged (Almeida 2008; Brockett 2005). Initially, these organizations worked for peaceful social reform. With the electoral fraud of 1972 and the closing of space for a democratic reformist option, many leaders of these organizations became more radical.

Finally, in 1931–32 and from 1972 to 1992, some radical left authoritarian actors challenged the extant order. In 1931–32, this coalition was easily and rapidly crushed, but its existence fueled a violent counterresponse and changed Salvadoran politics for decades. In the 1980s, the revolutionary left put forward a powerful challenge to the status quo. As occurred in 1931–32, the radical-left challenge generated fear in both the military and the big business, leading to intensified state repression to preserve the authoritarian coalition in power. This time, consistent with our empirical finding in Chapter 4, the radical left ultimately helped spawn democracy – but only after it renounced its radical left views. Although the coalition that opposed specific military rulers was often strong, the pro-democracy coalition never was until the 1990s.

In sum, even though *governments* were often unstable, a stable and powerful coalition of actors consistently favored authoritarian regimes. This coalition was vastly more powerful than its democratic challengers, and the result was persistent authoritarianism.

Modernization and Structural Explanations of Persistent Authoritarianism

Many works have argued that economic backwardness and poverty are unfavorable to democracy and foster authoritarianism. This approach could potentially explain persistent authoritarianism in El Salvador because it was a poor country. A second common structural explanation of persistent authoritarianism in El Salvador is coffee-based agriculture. Both accounts offer important insights but overstate the direct effects of social structures on regime outcomes.

Modernization, Poverty, and Persistent Authoritarianism

The eight Latin American countries with persistent histories of authoritarianism from 1900 to 1977 (see Table 6.1) were not uniformly those that faced the most daunting structural obstacles to democratization throughout the course of the twentieth century, even though they faced greater structural obstacles than Argentina, Chile, and Uruguay. Table 6.2 shows how seven of these countries compare with twelve other Latin American countries in per capita GDP in 1950, 1960, 1970, and 1978, the beginning of the third wave of democratization. The seven countries with histories of persistent authoritarianism are in bold. The nineteen countries are ordered from highest to lowest per capita GDP in 1950.

On average, the seven countries with persistent authoritarianism until 1978 were considerably poorer than the other twelve countries in the region. However, Mexico (especially) and El Salvador were exceptions to this rule. In all four years, Mexico had the region's fourth-highest per capita GDP. El Salvador was tenth in 1950, tied for ninth in 1960, tenth in 1970, and ninth in 1978. Two of the three countries (along with Uruguay) with the strongest democratic heritages until 1978 – Chile and Costa Rica – did not have exceptionally high per capita incomes by regional standards. Moreover, El Salvador had a consistently higher per capita

TABLE 6.2 *Per Capita GDP, Nineteen Latin American Countries, 1950–78 (constant 2000 U.S. dollars)*

	1950	1960	1970	1978
Argentina	4,613	5,237	6,606	6,768
Venezuela	4,438	5,425	6,279	6,447
Uruguay	4,224	4,340	4,496	5,260
Cuba	2,046	2,052	1,775	2,533
Mexico	2,029	2,554	3,576	4,489
Chile	1,569	1,842	2,202	2,188
Costa Rica	1,528	1,798	2,369	3,181
Panama	1,443	1,713	2,740	3,151
Peru	1,332	1,647	2,074	2,179
El Salvador	1,312	1,448	1,859	2,286
Brazil	1,077	1,448	1,991	3,184
Colombia	1,030	1,188	1,489	1,927
Bolivia	1,001	896	928	1,135
Guatemala	906	963	1,257	1,627
Dominican Republic	843	901	1,151	1,650
Nicaragua	786	914	1,301	1,371
Ecuador	759	820	928	1,315
Honduras	731	750	889	1,126
Paraguay	667	662	776	1,165

Source: World Bank, World Development Indicators (2007) for 1960–78. Figures for 1950 are based on *Penn World Table Version 6.2*. All figures are in constant 2000 U.S. dollars.

GDP than Colombia, which in 1958 inaugurated a competitive regime that has survived until today. Thus, economic backwardness and poverty do not suffice to explain El Salvador's persistent authoritarianism, although they generated structural conditions supportive of it. Countries with roughly the same level of development had far more experience with democracy.

Likewise, although the social science and historical literature correctly underscores El Salvador's high level of inequality, and although high inequality favors authoritarianism, El Salvador's level of inequality was not an *insurmountable* obstacle to democratization. According to the World Bank's data, El Salvador usually had a lower Gini coefficient of income inequality than Brazil, Chile, Colombia, and Panama, countries that had considerable experience with democracy before 1978. Inequalities and poverty favored authoritarianism in El Salvador, but they do not fully explain it.

Coffee and Authoritarian Politics

Some works on El Salvador have explained chronic authoritarianism on the basis of the country's coffee economy and a highly inegalitarian landowning structure dominated by large coffee estates. Paige (1997) primarily emphasizes labor-repressive agriculture and the dominance of coffee elite to explain long-term authoritarian persistence. Although at times he emphasizes the impact of actors' ideas on political outcomes, he often embraces strong structural claims. Many other accounts of chronic authoritarianism in El Salvador likewise emphasize coffee production or the political control of a small group of coffee-producing families (e.g., Cáceres Prendes 1988; North 1985). Some versions claim that fourteen or some other small number of coffee-based families dominated politics until the 1980s.

El Salvador's economic structure favored authoritarian rule, but reliance on coffee exports and/or coffee production is not a sufficient explanation of chronic authoritarianism. Figures 6.1 and 6.2 situate El Salvador relative to other Latin American countries in terms of coffee exports as a percentage of total exports and coffee production per capita, respectively. On both measures, El Salvador ranks toward the top of Latin American countries, consistent with a hypothesis that coffee production goes a long way toward explaining persistent authoritarianism. However, Colombia usually surpassed El Salvador on reliance on coffee to obtain export revenue, and Costa Rica consistently surpassed El Salvador in coffee production per capita. Colombia and Costa Rica were among the Latin American countries with most extensive experience of competitive regimes before the third wave (see also Lehoucq 2012: 28). Brazil and Guatemala also score high on both measures. Brazil had an extended competitive regime (1946–64), and Guatemala had brief competitive regimes in 1926–31 and 1945–54 before the third wave.

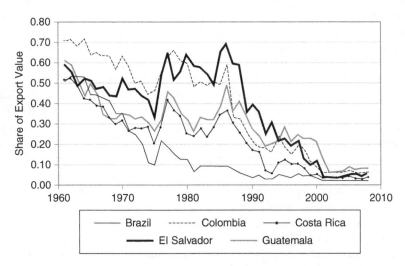

FIGURE 6.1. Share of Coffee Exports over Total Exports, Five Latin American Countries
Source: UN Food and Agriculture Organization, FAOSTAT (http://faostat.fao.org/). Data reflects the value of green coffee exports over total exports.

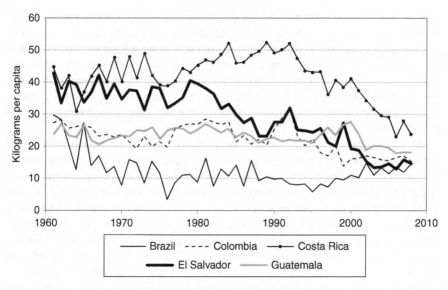

FIGURE 6.2. Coffee Production per Capita, Five Latin American Countries
Source: UN Food and Agriculture Organization, FAOSTAT (http://faostat.fao.org/).
Data reflects kilograms of green coffee per inhabitant.

Some of the literature claims or implies that a highly inegalitarian landholding structure was a key (or the key) ingredient in chronic authoritarianism in El Salvador. Comparative data on landholding do not unequivocally support this claim. Deininger and Squire (1998) built a dataset with 261 observations from 103 countries of estimates of the Gini index of inequality of landownership. It includes thirteen Latin American countries for around 1961. At that time, three Latin American countries (Uruguay, .778; Venezuela, .779, and Costa Rica, .784) had slightly more inegalitarian land distribution than El Salvador (.775). Despite highly inegalitarian landholding structures, Uruguay and Costa Rica were among the countries with the strongest democratic heritages in Latin America. Nine Latin American countries (Argentina, Brazil, Colombia, the Dominican Republic, Panama, Mexico, Nicaragua, Peru, and Paraguay) had lower Gini indices of inequality in landholding than El Salvador, but none of them were bulwarks of democracy at the time. The mean Gini index for the five authoritarian regimes (.74) was barely indistinguishable from the mean for the five democracies (.75) or the three semi-democracies (.71). High inequality in landownership favored an authoritarian regime, but it is hardly a sufficient explanation for it.

Deininger and Squire (1998) also estimated the Gini index of landholding inequality for thirteen Latin American countries in the 1970s. El Salvador had the sixth-lowest Gini index (.808) among these thirteen. One of the countries that had a competitive political regime throughout the 1970s, Colombia, had a slightly lower Gini index (.800), while the two countries that had democracies throughout the decade, Venezuela (.813) and Costa Rica (.818) had slightly more inegalitarian land distribution. Again, landholding patterns do not offer anywhere close to a full explanation of persistent authoritarianism in El Salvador.

Our approach differs from structural accounts of persistent authoritarianism in how we conceptualize the actors, in our understanding of what motivates the actors (exclusively instrumental economic interests or a broader array of issues and concerns), and in the critical role of external actors and influences. First, we have a somewhat different understanding of who the key actors are. Structural accounts see social classes as the key actors. Class organizations were important actors in El Salvador, but we also emphasize the importance of the military and parties as autonomous actors and note occasional but important conflicts between the military and the oligarchy.[4] Structural accounts of authoritarianism downplay the importance of the military as an autonomous actor and minimize conflicts between the military and the oligarchy. From 1931 until 1992, the military was a powerful actor that did not respond mechanically to the interests of the coffee elite (Almeida 2008: 60). Conflicts occurred between the landed elite and military presidents who attempted to implement reforms that the oligarchy opposed in 1944, 1960–61, and 1976–77. Most of the landed elite attempted to undermine agrarian reform and favored a more draconian approach to the war against the FLMN in the 1980s. These conflicts demonstrated that the military was not consistently an agent of the dominant classes. Reformist military presidents and the reformist military leaders of the 1979–80 junta faced some-times savage opposition from most large landowners (Almeida 2008: 115–16). Moreover, from the late 1940s until roughly the 1980s, economic policy was more statist, more pro-urban, and more pro-industrial than large landowners preferred (Guidos Béjar 1988; Johnson 1993: 92–158). In the 1980s, under pressure from the United States, most of the military leadership grudgingly accepted agrarian reform while most landowners did their best to thwart it. Although the military was usually aligned with the bottom-line interests of the Salvadoran oligarchy, it was a powerful independent actor. This means grappling with its ideas, reasons for acting as it did, and worldview (Stepan 1971).

Some parties and presidents were also important political actors – more so than structural accounts acknowledge. The PDC was an important actor from the 1960s until its demise in the 1990s. ARENA, the conservative party that was born under the aegis of the extremist Roberto D'Aubuisson in 1981, almost immediately became an important actor and remains one. Since 1989, ARENA has been a more important political actor than the coffee oligarchy, and it is not a mere instrument of the landed elite or of big business. Parties and the military develop preferences, identities, and interests reasonably independently of structural conditions.

Second, our theory claims that structural factors have important but less direct and more mediated consequences on regime outcomes. It places actors' radicalism and normative regime preferences at the core of the analysis of the

---

[4] Ching (1997), Lauria-Santiago (1999), and Stanley (1996) converge with our analysis.

long-term persistence of authoritarian rule for the period from 1931 to 1984. Right-wing truculence fueled leftist radicalism, and conversely, leftist and peasant radicalism in the 1932 peasant uprising had profound and enduring effects on the Salvadoran right. As Wood (2000a: 32) notes, "Elite 'memories' of the uprising combined the elite's two worst nightmares, a communist insurrection and an Indian rebellion. ... Because the uprising had followed a brief period of political reform, any reformist initiatives were considered communist. ... These attitudes endured for many decades." (See also Anderson 1971: 158; Stanley 1996: 57; Almeida 2008: 51–53, 210.)

Structural arguments understate the degree to which *political* factors fostered persistent authoritarianism in El Salvador (Lehoucq 2012: 45–48). The combination of right-wing radicalism that generated a sense that democracy and peaceful reform were impossible, left-wing radicalism that fueled the fears of the right, and a paucity of actors with a normative preference for democracy consistently blocked the possibility of democratization and even timid reform.

Although most of the oligarchy supported authoritarian rule as a way of protecting its economic interests, interpretations that see economic elites as *intrinsically* wedded to authoritarian regimes are wrong for the Salvadoran case and more generally. In El Salvador, some families of the traditional oligarchy – those that played a leading role in the PDC – were leaders of the failed democratization efforts of the 1960s, 1970s, and early 1980s.[5] Moreover, in other contexts such as Chile, landowners and conservatives supported democratization (Valenzuela 1985). The idea that landowners consistently supported authoritarianism while workers and peasants consistently worked for it, as some class theories of democratization suggest, is historically inaccurate. We say more about this in Chapter 9.

Although Paige (1997) is an exception, most predominantly structural theories understate the impact of actors' ideas (including their policy radicalism/moderation and their normative preferences) on regime outcomes. In El Salvador, the ideals of revolutionary socialism inspired the left in the 1970s and 1980s, and the fear of revolution obsessed the right for decades. The national security doctrine penetrated and deeply affected the Salvadoran military in the 1960s, 1970s, and 1980s (M. McClintock 1985). Without taking these ideas seriously, we cannot understand what political goals actors had or why they pursued them the way they did.

Third, most structural accounts underplay the importance of international actors and influences, which in the Salvadoran case were highly consequential. Any effort to understand Salvadoran political regimes from the 1940s to the 1990s must consider the powerful effects of U.S. policy in the context of the Cold War. In the Salvadoran military as in most Latin American armed forces, the U.S. military helped disseminate a national security doctrine and helped with counterinsurgency training in the 1960s (see Chapter 7). U.S. support for the

---

[5] The reformist president, Arturo Araujo (1931), was a wealthy landowner.

Salvadoran military and pressure to clean up the human rights abuses had a huge impact in the 1980s.

Structural accounts usually do not emphasize the powerful demonstration effects of the Cuban and Nicaraguan revolutions on actors in El Salvador. In El Salvador as in most of Latin America, the Cuban revolution sparked a new wave of leftist radicalism that in turn reinforced right-wing truculence (Almeida 2008: 61, 87–88, 168; Brockett 2005: 74, 84).[6] In the direct aftermath of the Cuban revolution, some groups of the Salvadoran Communist Party undertook guerrilla struggle from 1961 to 1963, when they were easily defeated. In the 1970s and 1980s, the Cuban model inspired countless Salvadorans to work for revolution. As we have already noted, the Sandinista takeover of power on July 19, 1979 had an almost immediate catalyzing effect in El Salvador; the October 15, 1979 coup that overthrew President Romero came less than three months later. An actor-based approach that takes actors' goals and international influences seriously can better account for the trajectory of the left than structural approaches to political regimes.

THE TRANSITION TO SEMI-DEMOCRACY, 1984–92

If we refine our broad distinction between authoritarian and democratic coalitions, in the early 1980s, the regime battle in El Salvador included four blocs of actors. The powerful radical-right authoritarian coalition included most of the armed forces, the death squads, ARENA, and some big-business interests. A bloc of soft-line authoritarians included minority factions of the military and politically more moderate business interests. The PDC was the main actor in the democratic coalition. Until 1989, the democratic coalition sometimes appeared to be crushed between the authoritarian left and the authoritarian right blocs. Finally, the revolutionary guerrilla left constituted the core of the authoritarian left bloc. Some popular organizations and movements were also part of this coalition. This configuration of forces seemed entirely unfavorable for a democratic outcome; the right-wing authoritarian coalition was much more powerful than the democratic coalition.

The transition to semi-democracy began in 1984, when El Salvador had its first non-fraudulent competitive presidential election since 1931. José Napoleón Duarte of the centrist PDC won. We code Duarte's inauguration on June 1, 1984 as marking the transition to a semi-democratic regime for four reasons (following our four criteria of democracy). First, even though the 1984 election was marred by ongoing violence and the de facto proscription of the left, it was fiercely competitive. In the first round, Duarte won 43.4 percent and his main rival, Roberto D'Aubuisson of ARENA, garnered 29.8 percent. Duarte won the tightly contested runoff with 53.6 percent of the vote. Massive repression and

---

[6] For personal reflections of FMLN leaders on the influence of the Cuban revolution on their decision to take up armed struggle, see the interviews in Harnecker 1993: 23–29.

intimidation from the right did not prevent a PDC triumph. The vote count was generally accurate, although the playing field was not. Second, a majority of Salvadoran citizens were enfranchised and were able to vote, although citizens in many war-torn areas could not. Third, notwithstanding ongoing deep violations of civil and political rights, the PDC government of 1984–89 made efforts to protect these basic rights. In 1984, the level of political violence dropped from the horrific levels of 1980–82 (Wood 2003: 8–9). Finally, the government was able to pursue most policies without being fully subjected to military or death squad vetoes, although the armed forces and death squads continued to exercise profound influence in important policy areas.

We register 1984 as the first year of a semi-democratic regime because we consistently use fairly lenient criteria for coding a regime as semi-democratic. Until the signing of the peace accords in 1992 and the subsequent elections in 1994, the regime was very far from being a democracy. Our regime coding of El Salvador from 1984 to 1991 shows partial violations of all four dimensions of democracy. In April 1990, the government and the FMLN agreed to end the armed conflict, and in January 1992 they signed the peace accords. The agreement guaranteed that the FMLN could reconstitute itself as a political party and compete in elections.

We record 1994 as the first year of a democratic (as opposed to semi-democratic) regime. This was the first election in which a leftist party could compete under reasonably free and fair conditions,[7] and its electoral participation marks a critical difference in our regime coding. In addition, the end of the civil war led to an improvement in individual political and civil rights such as freedom of speech, freedom of assembly, freedom of the press, and so on. The changes brought about by the peace accords were absolutely fundamental for El Salvador's democratic process.

EXPLAINING THE TRANSITION TO A COMPETITIVE REGIME

The transition to a competitive regime was caused by a gradual strengthening of the democratic coalition and a gradual weakening of the authoritarian coalition over the course of the 1980s. By 1994, the democratic coalition was much stronger and the authoritarian coalition was weaker than it had been a decade earlier. The constellation of actors into these different coalitions had changed dramatically relative to the early 1980s. The hard-line right-wing authoritarian bloc was much weaker. The death squads, which had been a major part of this bloc in the early 1980s, largely disbanded. Most of the military had shifted to soft-line authoritarians or had ceased staking a clear position in the regime coalitions. The coffee elite was weakened by the civil war and the agrarian reform. Because the war had proven so costly, most business groups were

---

[7] In 1989, a center-left party, Democratic Convergence, competed, but violence against the left was still widespread.

anxious to end it, so they defected from the hard-line authoritarian coalition. ARENA's electoral success convinced many actors that had formed part of the authoritarian coalition that they could further their interests more effectively through democratic politics than through war. The FMLN shifted from the radical-left authoritarian coalition toward democratic politics (Almeida 2008: 188–90, 213). The democratic coalition expanded greatly, even though the primary actor that had been part of it in the early 1980s, the PDC, suffered pummeling electoral losses. In short, in little more than a decade, the relative power of the authoritarian and democratic coalitions had changed dramatically. How did this happen?

In light of how tentative, fragile, and still partial the transition to semi-democracy was in 1984, our question is not limited to what paved the way to holding competitive presidential elections that year. Rather, it extends to what explains how this war-ravaged country moved to successful peace accords in 1992 and to a fuller democracy that incorporated the former guerrillas in an electoral process in 1994.

As we noted in Chapters 2 and 5, regime change may occur because (1) new actors emerge and join the opposing coalition; (2) the relative distribution of political resources changes in favor of the opposition; or (3) enough political actors switch sides and tip the balance of forces against the current regime. One important new actor emerged around 1983: a more moderate business sector often linked to FUSADES (*Fundación Salvadoreña para el Desarrollo Económico y Social*). Created in 1983, FUSADES was a market-oriented think tank that played a pivotal role in the emergence of a more moderate, more democratic business sector, and in ARENA's transformation (Johnson 1993). In the late 1980s, this new business sector, which was closely linked to ARENA, provided crucial support for competitive politics and for peace negotiations.

Changes in the distribution of resources and actors that abandoned the authoritarian coalition were very important for explaining the transition in El Salvador. The United States significantly altered the distribution of political resources among domestic actors. In addition, key domestic actors, namely the Salvadoran military, the FMLN, ARENA, and big business, switched coalitions. These key actors made decisions and underwent transformations that led to dramatic change in balance between the authoritarian and democratic coalitions, which in turn led to the transition to a competitive political regime.

The U.S. Role

Throughout much of the twentieth century, the United States significantly influenced many political regimes in Central America and the Caribbean and, to a lesser degree, some South American countries. From 1979 until 1992, El Salvador was a textbook illustration of this point. The United States got much more involved in El Salvador's politics in the aftermath of the October 15, 1979 coup. In January 1981, when he assumed office, President Reagan made El Salvador one of the focal points of U.S. policy.

Until George H. W. Bush became president in January 1989, U.S. policy toward El Salvador was racked by many internal tensions. Although the U.S. role was complex and can be criticized for being excessively tolerant toward El Salvador's extremist right especially from 1981 to 1983, overall it buttressed the democratic coalition by strengthening its actors, giving them resources, and using a combination of resources and cudgels to nudge other actors to abandon the authoritarian coalition. U.S. military aid had an ambiguous impact. On the one hand, it helped avoid an FMLN victory, and for this reason blocked the emergence of a leftist authoritarian regime. On the other hand, it also empowered the military, which in the 1980s was an authoritarian actor. But it leveraged military aid by conditioning it on holding competitive elections and on an improved human rights record. It is unlikely that absent U.S. involvement, El Salvador would have had a semi-democracy by 1984 or a democracy by 1994 (Stanley 1996: 253–54). For those complex reasons, the United States became a hugely important actor in El Salvador's transition. In a variety of ways, it changed domestic actors' resources and incentives.

First, the United States pressured the Salvadoran government to hold competitive elections beginning in 1982. In turn, competitive elections radically altered the incentives for, and the behavior of, domestic Salvadoran actors. In July 1981, under trenchant international and domestic criticism for its policies toward El Salvador, the Reagan administration called for "prompt, free and open elections" (quoted in Karl 1986: 16; see also Arnson 1982: 85; LeoGrande 1998: 158, 219, 249; Stanley 1996: 231). Because of U.S. pressures and resources, the electoral path rather than military power became the primary way to winning executive power. Without U.S. pressure to hold free and fair elections, the Salvadoran right would almost certainly have preferred to wage war unconstrained by civilian power and by the need to seek votes. The need to win votes was a powerful incentive in Roberto D'Aubuisson's decision to create a party in October 1981, a mere three months after the U.S. call for elections, and in ARENA's transformation from an organization led by an extremist committed to annihilating the left into a political party respected by international public opinion.

Second, the United States pushed El Salvador's government to undertake an ambitious agrarian reform that expropriated the country's large (more than 1,250 acres) farms (Arnson 1982: 50, 99; Bonner 1984: 187–97; Browning 1983; Deere 1982; LeoGrande 1998: 166–70; M. McClintock 1985: 266–71). The agrarian reform and the war weakened the traditional oligarchy. A weaker traditional oligarchy helped pave the way to a transition into a competitive political regime (Johnson 1993; Wood 2000a).

Third, although the United States tolerated El Salvador's terrible human rights record, it nevertheless pushed the government and the military to improve the human rights situation (Arnson 1993: 73–74, 140, 150–51, 230–31, 256–57,

263–64; Bonner 1984: 44–46, 76, 182, 216–17, 359, 365–66; Bosch 1999: 69–72; Brockett 2005: 239–40; LeoGrande 1998: 160–66, 226–32; M. McClintock 1985: 275–85; C. McClintock 1998: 221–31; Sikkink 2004: 170–73; Williams and Walter 1997: 115). The Salvadoran military desperately needed U.S. military aid and support, and by decision of the U.S. Congress, this military aid was conditional on El Salvador's human rights record. Even though El Salvador continued to be plagued by horrendous human rights abuses throughout the 1980s, U.S. pressure tilted the balance within the Salvadoran armed forces toward those who wanted to limit killing and were later willing to negotiate peace. Even in the face of U.S. pressure and conditional aid, parts of the Salvadoran right favored a bloodbath (Stanley 1996: 247–49).

Fourth, massive U.S. military aid was probably decisive in enabling the Salvadoran military to avoid a defeat at the hands of the FMLN (Arnson 1993: 51, 64–65, 163; Bonner 1984: 87, 138, 165, 168–71, 180, 208–09, 213, 222–28, 270–84; LeoGrande 1998: 91–96; 157; 257–75; C. McClintock 1998: 9, 201, 221–23; M. McClintock 1985: 286–350; Williams and Walter 1997: 141–43). U.S. military aid to El Salvador increased from $40,000 in 1979 to $196.5 million in 1984 (Karl 1986: 20). If the FMLN had won the war, it probably would have implemented a left wing dictatorship. In this respect, U.S. military support decisively influenced the outcome.

Fifth, U.S. resources and support generally legitimated moderate and non-extremist conservative Salvadoran actors at the relative expense of extremist actors, even though the United States sometimes tolerated the extremists. In 1982, U.S. heavy pressure led the constitutional congress to elect the center-right leader Alvaro Magaña rather than extremist Roberto D'Aubuisson as provisional president (Arnson 1993: 95–98; Karl 1986: 19; LeoGrande 1998: 160–61; Stanley 1996: 232). In the 1984 presidential election, the United States clearly favored PDC candidate José Napoleón Duarte (Arnson 1993: 152–58; Stanley 1996: 233). In the first half of the 1980s, the United States bolstered the PDC and worked against D'Aubuisson. High-level U.S. officials, including Vice-President George Bush during a visit to El Salvador in December 1983 and U.S. Ambassador Thomas Pickering, criticized death squads and called for an end to the most atrocious human rights violations. Although U.S. pressure was far from successful at ending human rights atrocities in the 1980s, it strengthened the hand within the military of factions that kept the death squads at arm's lengths. U.S. support for non-extremist actors helped pave the way for the move toward semi-democracy, peace, and later democracy. U.S. resources also helped *create* new actors: the United States helped fund FUSADES.

By conditioning military support on El Salvador's human rights record, U.S. suasion helped transform two critical actors in El Salvador: the military and ARENA. After 1980, the United States more often than not strengthened the hand of groups within the Salvadoran military that were willing to curb human rights abuses and mass killings (Arnson 1982: 51; LeoGrande 1998: 235; Williams and Walter 1997: 134). The Salvadoran military was sufficiently worried about losing the war that U.S. pressure tilted the balance toward the factions that were willing to largely follow the U.S. line. Absent U.S. pressures, the hard-liners who wanted the bloodshed to continue would most likely have prevailed, as they did in 1979–81 before the U.S. involvement escalated. U.S. repudiation of the extreme right wing also helped tip the scales toward moderation in ARENA – for example, by blocking D'Aubuisson's path to serving as president.

Domestic Actors

Although the United States had a powerful influence on the Salvadoran transition, actors within the country made the decisions and underwent the transformations that led to the transition and to peace. In a short time in the late 1980s and the early 1990s, powerful actors defected from the competing authoritarian coalitions. ARENA and the FMLN tentatively decided to bet on democracy during this time. Both shifted from a normative preference for dictatorship in 1980s to a (not fully consistent) normative preference for democracy by the end of the 1990s, and both changed from being very radical actors to greater moderation. The military and big business left the authoritarian coalition and took a wait-and-see approach.

As we noted in Chapters 2 and 5, actors can shift regime coalitions either because of changes in their perceptions about the likely policy benefits of regime change or because of changes in their normative preferences. Both factors explain why powerful actors defected from the competing authoritarian coalitions in El Salvador. First, the civil war made the incumbent regime very costly, especially when it became clear to all sides in late 1989 that the protracted military stalemate could continue for a long time.[8] During the 1980s, real wages plummeted (by as much as 84 percent for seasonal coffee workers; Wood 2000a: 62). Investment as a share of GDP dropped from 19.1 percent in the 1970s to 12.9 percent in the 1980s (Wood 2000a: 59). The death toll was huge for a country with El Salvador's population. A few business sectors flourished, but losers outnumbered winners.

U.S. influence and resources made it seem likely that the policy payoffs of a negotiated settlement and a new competitive regime would outweigh those of the incumbent regime. Also, when ARENA and the FMLN showed willingness to moderate, it created the possibility that a settlement could be non-disastrous for all major players.

In addition, in the late 1980s and early 1990s, several powerful actors changed their normative view about what constitutes a desirable political regime. Throughout most of the 1980s, the FMLN embraced revolutionary socialism, but at the end of the decade, two of the five organizations that had formed the FMLN expressed a normative preference for democracy. Under President Cristiani's

---

[8] On the impact of the stalemate on the FMLN's top leadership, see the interviews in Harnecker 1993: 299–302.

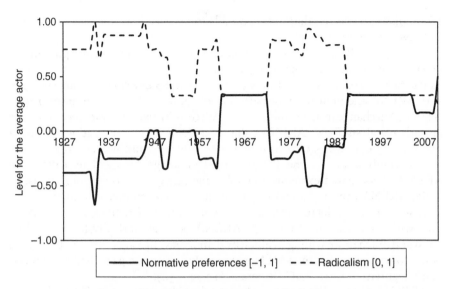

FIGURE 6.3. Evolution of Normative Preferences and Radicalism, 1927–2010
Source: Database on political actors (see Chapter 3).

leadership, ARENA began to articulate a normative preference for democracy as well. Big business and the military gave up on the normative ideal of right-wing dictatorship even if they did not become convinced democrats.

Appendix 6.1 shows the changing set of actors and their preferences from 1979 until 2010. Figure 6.3 indicates the mean scores for actors' normative preferences and policy radicalism from 1927 to 2010. It registers the steep drop in radicalism in the late 1980s, the fading of one radical actor (death squads) with a normative preference for dictatorships after 1990, and the gradual development of some normative preferences for democracy in the late 1980s and 1990s.

ARENA. Founded in September 1981 by Roberto D'Aubuisson, ARENA became one of the most successful conservative parties in the democratic history of Latin America. It was initially an extreme right-wing party with a nationalistic and viscerally anticommunist ideology (L. A. González 2003a: 1177–83) and implacable opposition to the PDC. In a context in which the United States was insisting on elections, however, ARENA quickly focused on winning popular support and building a party organization. Only six months after its creation, it achieved notable success in its first electoral foray, winning nineteen of sixty seats in the 1982 contest for a constitutional congress. In 1984, D'Aubuisson came close to defeating Duarte for the presidency, capturing 46.4 percent of the second-round vote despite U.S. funding and other support for Duarte.

ARENA's early electoral success galvanized the private sector and considerable public support and made it clear that the electoral path might protect its supporters' policy interests. Equally important, early electoral success reinforced incentives for party building and focusing on expanding its voter base. By 1985,

D'Aubuisson perceived that to fare even better in elections, the party needed to shift away from the far right.

After 1985, ARENA became less zealous in its anticommunism and promoted a neoliberal economic message (Artiga González 2001; Johnson 1993: 221–27; Koivumaeki 2010; Zamora 1998: 55–57). FUSADES developed strong synergies with ARENA and influenced the party's ideological development (Johnson 1993). A leadership change from D'Aubuisson to Alfredo Cristiani in September 1985 was an early manifestation of ARENA's shift away from extremist positions (Colburn 2009: 144; Johnson 1993; Koivumaeki 2010; Williams and Walter 1997: 140).

The combination of the PDC's tarnished image by the late 1980s and ARENA's modulated extremism enabled the party to reap electoral gains. In 1988, ARENA captured a majority in the national assembly, with thirty-one of sixty seats. In 1989, its presidential candidate, Alfredo Cristiani, won in a landslide with 58.3 percent of the vote. ARENA became markedly less radical by 1989 and much more willing to abide by democracy. In 1989, President Cristiani began to negotiate with the FMLN; in the early 1980s, the party had proclaimed that "negotiation is treason" (Ribera Sala 1996: 54).

ARENA's electoral success transformed the Salvadoran right. When the right realized that it could win by ballots, it no longer needed to win by bullets. As a result of ARENA's electoral success, the military's inability to defeat the FMLN, and international pressures against human rights abuses, part of the far right became less radical and migrated away from the authoritarian coalition. It became willing to play by democratic rules of the game (Johnson 1993; Ribera Sala 1996; Stanley 1996: 232–42; Wood 2000a).

As we noted in Chapter 2, actors may change their regime coalition either because of their instrumental policy preferences or because of changes in their normative preferences. Wood (2000a: 54–67; 2000b) convincingly argues that instrumental policy preferences help explain ARENA's transformation from a bedrock of the authoritarian coalition into part of the democratic coalition by 1989–94. The cost of the civil war, the prospect that ARENA would win elections and hence control the policy agenda, and the FMLN's moderation after 1989 made democracy more appealing and the status quo unacceptable. The FMLN's growing willingness to renounce war softened positions in ARENA. If the FMLN was willing to put down its arms, ARENA had less to lose by negotiating. Negotiation no longer meant the possibility of radical policy losses. The prolonged military stalemate convinced President Cristiani that it was time to give peace and democracy a chance. The war had a high economic cost for ARENA's support base and for the country.

ARENA also changed its normative preferences. It changed from an extremist party with a normative preference for dictatorship (1981–84), to a party willing to play by democratic rules of the game (1984–89), to one with a solid but not fully consistent normative preference for democracy (1989–present) (L. A. González 2003a; Guido Béjar 1996; Johnson 1993; Ribera Sala 1996; Wood 2000a, 2000b; Zamora 1998, 2003). Wood (2000a: 245) wrote that "by the late 1980s, elite ideology accepted a limited procedural notion of democracy and a negotiated resolution to the civil war."[9]

In Chapters 2 and 5, we argued that actors sometimes change their normative preferences because of (1) traumatic events that led to reassessments; (2) routine processes of organizational change usually involving a change in leadership; (3) a gradual process of learning attributable to unexpectedly positive or negative experiences; and (4) international influences. All four processes were central to ARENA's normative reorientation. First, the civil war and the military stalemate created an opening for new normative perspectives about democracy. Second, the emergence of Cristiani and a more moderate leadership was an essential component in ARENA's transformation. The new leadership moved ARENA away from its extremist positions of 1982–84 and from a normative preference for a right-wing nationalistic dictatorship toward the center-right, with less intransigence, and eventually toward a normative preference for democracy. Third, from 1989 on, ARENA and other actors on the Salvadoran right saw that democracy would not produce catastrophic losses. Even if initially this logic was outcome-oriented (i.e., referring to policy preferences), it generated a previously unimaginable belief in the intrinsic value of democracy. And finally, U.S. pro-democracy pressures and messages influenced ARENA and other actors on the Salvadoran right regarding the intrinsic value of democracy.

ARENA again won the presidency in 1994, 1999, and 2004, giving it a run of twenty consecutive years to govern El Salvador (1989–2009). It won a plurality of seats in the unicameral national legislature in 1991 (thirty-nine of eighty-four seats), 1994 (the same result as in 1991), 1997 (twenty-eight seats), and 2006 (thirty-four seats), and it came a close second in 2000, 2003, and 2009.

Big Business

Big business underwent a transformation parallel to ARENA's. Big business had long supported authoritarian rule. Wealthy landowners financed death squads in the 1970s and 1980s. When the civil war broke out, some sectors of big business normatively supported right-wing authoritarianism, and the rest supported the conservative authoritarian coalition for instrumental reasons, namely to protect policy interests.

In the 1980s, agrarian reform and the civil war weakened the traditional oligarchy (Wood 2000a). The war prompted many large landowners to flee the country out of fear for their lives, while new business sectors such as the financial sector expanded. The dominant faction of the economic elite shifted from being hard-core proponents of extremely repressive authoritarianism to grudgingly accepting and eventually embracing democratic politics (Wood 2000a). Paige

---

[9] Ribera Sala (1996: 54) wrote that "ARENA's profound transformation is undeniable." Williams and Walter (1997: 140) stated that Cristiani and the moderate faction "voiced support for a negotiated settlement and limited democracy." According to Colburn (2009: 144), "Cristiani steered it (ARENA) firmly in the direction of democracy."

(1997: 217–18) wrote that "[e]vents of the last decade have moved the agro-industrial faction away from its agrarian allies and toward a kind of liberal democracy that is 'representative, but restricted and controlled.[10]'"

In the initial phases of big business's move away from steadfast support for authoritarian rule, instrumental policy calculations were decisive. The economic costs of the war were staggering for many elite families. By the end of the 1980s, they were ready to try something different. The FMLN's November 1989 offensive frightened the Salvadoran elite and convinced important factions thereof that militarily defeating the guerrillas would be more difficult, time consuming, and costly than hitherto imagined (Wood 2000a: 54–67).

ARENA's success at the polls persuaded the economic elite that they could defend their interests better through a political party than by trying to annihilate the left and center-left (Stanley 1996). Competitive elections created opportunities for the political ascension of more moderate business leaders. These leaders prioritized economic growth and reorienting El Salvador's economy in a market-oriented direction more than militarily annihilating the communist threat (Johnson 1993). By the time of the Cristiani administration, the business groups that had viewed right-wing dictatorship as intrinsically desirable for El Salvador were eclipsed.

The Military

The military underwent a more limited but nevertheless important transformation in the 1980s and 1990s. It entered the 1980s a deeply divided institution, with a minority reformist sector that headed the October 1979 coup; a dominant faction that, although it was conservative and authoritarian, partly acquiesced to U.S. demands for agrarian reform and competitive elections; and a far-right nationalistic faction that worked to undermine the Christian Democrats, wanted to wage war without constraints, engaged in death squad activity, and publicly scorned the United States. The extremists believed that they were uniquely prepared to govern El Salvador, that civilians could not govern effectively, and that democracy was intrinsically an inferior political regime given the country's situation.[11]

By September 1980, the conservative mainstream and the extreme-right factions defeated the reformists who had helped spearhead the October 1979 coup, pushing them out of power and into irrelevance (Bosch 1999: 41–57; Williams and Walter 1997: 106–11). In 1981 and 1982, the extreme-right faction had great power within the Salvadoran armed forces, fueling the high death toll and massive

---

[10] Johnson (1993: xiv, 140) showed that, "Whereas at the beginning of the 1980s, the business elite opposed democracy, by the end of the decade, they fully supported it. ... The new generation of leaders now in control of El Salvador's business associations has acquired an institutional stake in maintaining democratic practices." Córdova Macías (1996: 7) noted that big business had accepted "a democratic political framework."

[11] "The office corps continued to regard the armed forces as the only national institution able to defend the state and to guarantee public order" (Williams and Walter 1997: 122). The military believed that "civilian politicians put personal and partisan interests before the national interest" (Williams and Walter 1997: 123–24).

human rights violations. Over the course of the 1980s, however, the less extremist factions prevailed. In late 1983 and early 1984, several officers notorious for associations with death squads were relieved of their duties (Williams and Walter 1997: 133–34). The death toll dropped sharply. In April 1983, General Eugenio Vides Casanova replaced General José Guillermo García as minister of defense. Vides Casanova shifted away from the scorched-earth policy of 1980–82.

The military remained a powerful part of the conservative authoritarian coalition through the 1980s, but from 1989 onward the balance of power shifted away from it. The faith that big business and the armed forces had in Cristiani bolstered the president's power vis-à-vis the military. The military gradually lost credibility because of its inability to win the war. Demoralized by the long war, the military itself lost its faith that conservative authoritarianism would yield better policy outcomes than Cristiani's more moderate and democratic alternative. Finally, the transition from President Reagan (1981–89) to Bush (1989–93) meant less support from Washington for continuing the war, giving the less extremist faction of the military an advantage (Brockett 2005: 243–44). We code the military as no longer having a normative preference for right-wing authoritarianism from 1989 on. It gradually accepted civilian rule and no longer advocated that conservative authoritarianism was an intrinsically desirable political regime.

Subsequent changes in the armed forces occurred when peace negotiations were well under way and after the government and FMLN reached an agreement (Córdova Macías 1999; Williams and Walter 1997: 151–83). As part of the peace agreements, the military was reduced in size. The National Guard, Treasury Police, National Police, and National Intelligence Serve were dissolved because of their involvement in human rights abuses. Seventy-six officers were forced to resign because of human rights crimes (Córdova Macías 1999: 4–14). The removal of some officers who committed egregious human rights violations and the dismantling of some of the most authoritarian units of the armed forces helped foster the change from an institution with a normative preference for dictatorship (1979–89) to one that accepted democratic politics (Stanley 1996: 249–53; Williams and Walter 1997: 151–56).

The FMLN
Originally created in 1980 as a federation of five revolutionary socialist guerrilla organizations, since 1994 the FMLN has become one of the most electorally successful leftist parties in the history of Latin America. In its days as a revolutionary guerrilla organization, the FMLN defined itself as a Marxist-Leninist organization:

At the beginning of the 1980s, all of the groups within the FMLN agreed on the struggle for socialism; accepted armed struggle as a way to achieve revolution; shared Marxism as a theoretical and conceptual framework; rejected social democracy, reformism, and an electoral path as unviable; and believed that under capitalism, it was impossible to achieve democracy, social justice, and progress on behalf of the popular sectors. (Guido Béjar 1996: 64)

By 1988, two of the five organizations that had formed the FMLN in 1980, the *Ejército Revolucionario del Pueblo* (Revolutionary Army of the People, ERP), and the *Resistencia Nacional* (National Resistance, RN), began a rapid and profound ideological and political transformation (Guido Béjar 1996: 58–61). That year, the FMLN proposed new peace negotiations and expressed willingness to compete in elections as the route to power (Gaspar Tapia 1989: 110). In early 1989, ERP leader Joaquín Villalobos (1989b) published a document calling for a democratic revolution and peace negotiations.[12] The document renounced revolutionary socialism and single-party dictatorships and called for respecting freedom of the press, religion, and elections.

The FMLN's 1990 "Manifesto to the Nation" embraced representative democracy and turned away from the anti-imperialist, anti-oligarchy discourse that it had espoused in the 1980s (Ribera Sala 1996: 52). The FMLN ceased to exist qua revolutionary force after signing the peace accords in 1992. In September 1992, it registered as a legal party and implicitly decided to abide by democratic rules of the game.

After signing the peace accords, the FMLN ratified its ideological transformation (Allison and Martín Álvarez 2012; L. A. González 2003a: 1194–1201; Ribera Sala 1996: 45–54; Zamora 1998: 226–32; 2003: 64–75). By the time the party first wrote its postwar statutes in 1995, it had ceased defining itself as a Marxist-Leninist organization, had rejected violence as a means of effecting political change, and had ceased using traditional Marxist concepts such as class struggle. Instead, it embraced democracy and professed allegiance to the Universal Declaration of Human Rights. Whereas in the 1980s the FMLN saw itself as a vanguard party fighting on behalf of the working class, its Declaration of Principles proclaimed that it was a "democratic, pluralistic party for El Salvador. The FMLN ... functions as a democratic party, with a broad, popular base, participatory, and based on a pluralistic ideology" (quoted in Zamora 1998: 229). It rejected the traditional Marxist emphasis on the state and instead called for valuing civil society (Zamora 1998: 230). As Zamora (2003: 64–75) notes, the FMLN's ideology become social democratic or social Christian. These transformations were deeply conflictual, leading to schisms in 1994 and later (Allison and Martín Álvarez 2012: 98–103; Guido Béjar 1996: 64–78).

Notwithstanding the strong ongoing influence of orthodox Marxism, the FMLN embraced a new normative vision of a desirable political regime. Change in the party's discourse was not merely instrumental, designed to achieve some other policy goals. The party shifted decisively away from the earlier veneration of revolutionary socialism. It is implausible that Joaquín Villalobos's strong arguments on behalf of democracy, which were echoed in highly publicized party documents a few years later, were merely instrumental. The fact that the FMLN

---

[12] *Foreign Affairs* published part of Villalobos's paper (1989a). In 1992, Villalobos published a book with the revealing title, *Una revolución en la izquierda para una revolución democrática* (A Revolution on the Left for a Democratic Revolution) (Villalobos 1992).

adhered to the normative principles laid out by Villalobos and others despite many disappointing policy outcomes after 1989 suggests a genuine commitment to democracy among powerful sectors within the party. After 1992, the FMLN consistently accepted outcomes that were generated through the processes of representative democracy even when they did not like those outcomes. From 1994 on, most of the party embraced a democratic discourse, abided by democratic procedures, and rejected the use of violence. Still, because of the ambivalence of the traditional Marxist factions toward representative democracy (Allison and Martín Álvarez 2012; L. A. González 2003a: 1194–1201; Zamora 2003), we do not code the FMLN as having a normative preference for democracy until the 1999–2004 period – and even then, we regard its preference as not entirely consistent (the same way we coded ARENA).[13]

The FMLN first participated in the 1994 national elections and did fairly well in light of the massive repression it had faced until 1991 and the great challenges in transforming itself from a guerrilla organization into a political party. It won 22 percent of the vote for the national assembly and eclipsed the PDC as the country's second-largest party. For president, the FMLN formed a coalition whose candidate, Rubén Zamora, was the runner-up with 25 percent of the vote. In 1997, it came within 27,000 votes and two chamber seats of becoming the largest party in the national assembly. From then on, ARENA and the FMLN competed as near equals in legislative elections. In 2009, the FMLN candidate for president, Mauricio Funes, won with 51.3 percent of the vote. He took office on June 1, 2009. Throughout the 1980s, it would have been impossible to imagine that the FMLN would become a highly electorally successful political party.

The FMLN's decision to renounce revolutionary socialism and support democracy reflected both a changing normative conception about the political regime and a changing instrumental perception of how best to achieve its policy interests. International influences and the trauma of the civil war help explain the transformation in the FMLN's normative preferences. The end of the Cold War lowered enthusiasm about "real socialism." For the FMLN, the fall of the Berlin Wall in 1989 and the imminent collapse of Soviet Union changed world politics. Some of the FMLN leadership had close linkages to the Soviet Union, and this close relationship magnified the impact of these changes. The failures of the Sandinista regime in neighboring Nicaragua also fostered a change in the FMLN's normative preferences. The Sandinistas' struggles made clear that revolutionary regimes in small countries that faced the implacable opposition of the United States had a difficult path. Finally, the diffusion of a pro-democracy ideology among the Latin American and European left influenced some FMLN leaders.

---

[13] A more traditional Marxist sector of the FMLN won internal control of the party when Schafik Hándal was the presidential candidate in 2004. Given some ambiguity in the party's discourse around that time (L. A. González 2003b), we coded the FMLN as not having a normative preference regarding the political regime for the 2004–09 period.

Instrumental policy considerations about what was possible to achieve also influenced the FMLN's decision to abandon the revolutionary struggle and support the peace accords. The Sandinistas' defeat in the 1990 Nicaraguan elections changed the geopolitical landscape in Central America. The FMLN's most important ally in the western hemisphere was no longer in power and could no longer supply munitions. However, the Sandinistas' defeat occurred after the normative reorientation within two of the five organizations that constituted the FMLN had already begun, so instrumental logic based on the Sandinistas' defeat does not explain the genesis of change within the party.

The transformation of the Salvadoran right made it easier for the left to change as well. Just as the right's intransigent authoritarianism in the 1970s helped fuel a radicalization of many individuals who became revolutionary leftists, so the moderation of the right after 1989 encouraged a moderation of the left. Democracy promised the possibility of achieving policy gains through elections.

War weariness was also a factor in the FMLN's transformation (Harnecker 1993). The FMLN's recognition that a military victory was impossible coincided with profound internal ideological and political change (Guido Béjar 1996: 60). Finally, electoral success generated a self-reinforcing dynamic from 1994 on.

The PDC

The PDC, which was the country's most important pro-democracy actor from 1960 until 1989, was crushed in the shift toward democracy. In the hyperpolarized politics and war of the 1980s, the PDC got overwhelmed. The death squads, the economic elite, and the Salvadoran military deliberately undermined PDC programs. FMLN economic sabotage took a toll. The PDC got pummeled as the economy suffered and the war dragged on. It took an ARENA president, Alfredo Cristiani, to convince the Salvadoran right to try peace. The leaders of the right, some of whom saw the PDC as communist stooges, did not trust the PDC to conduct peace negotiations. Caught in this cross fire, the PDC presided over economic destruction and warfare, and its electoral support withered. The PDC could not find a voice in this process, and by 1999, when its candidate won only 5.6 percent of the presidential vote, it had ceased to be a major actor (Ribera Sala 1996: 33–39; Williams and Seri 2003; Zamora 1998: 137–79).

ALTERNATIVE EXPLANATIONS OF THE TRANSITION

Wood's book (2000a) is the iconic work on El Salvador's transition to democratic politics. Her explanation focuses on two variables. First, sustained and powerful popular insurgency ultimately led the Salvadoran elite to prefer compromise and democracy to continued war. Second, the war structurally transformed elite interests, weakening the coffee oligarchy that had been the linchpin of authoritarian rule.

These two processes were an important part of the causal chain, but we complement them with more attention to political factors. To explain the end of the war and the right's willingness to compromise, we pay more attention to the U.S. role in pushing the right toward the negotiating table and accepting compromise. Absent U.S. pressures and influences, the war would have gone in a different direction, with even greater power exercised by the far right, which wanted to intensify the war effort.

Structural transformations in the countryside had a facilitative role rather than as central a role as Wood ascribes to it. The structural transformations altered the odds of a transition by weakening the coffee oligarchy, which had historically buttressed the authoritarian coalition. However, the transformations in landholding patterns do not account for change in the political positions of the large landowners who remained in El Salvador or those who left the country and later returned.[14] They do not fully explain the profound changes in several actors' political positions and preferences and their decision to join the authoritarian or democratic coalition. Moreover, the structural transformations were themselves the product of political decisions of actors. For example, the United States prodded the Salvadoran government into the far-reaching agrarian reform of the early 1980s (Deere 1982).

Democracy was in part forged from below, as Wood's title correctly claims, but change from above (in ARENA), from within the FMLN (toward greater willingness to negotiate), and influences from a powerful outside actor (the United States) and key external events (the collapse of the Soviet Union and the defeat of the Sandinistas) were also important in El Salvador's transition. Although Wood's narrative mentions these facts, her theoretical argument focuses on "forging democracy from below" and underplays the role of external actors and influences. Even before the FMLN's 1989 "final offensive," ARENA had changed profoundly since its creation in 1981. Its electoral success encouraged other actors on the Salvadoran right (especially business interests and the military) to move away from extremist positions.

An approach that looks at actors, their transformations, the resulting changes in the democratic and authoritarian coalitions, and international influences must complement Wood's structural focus. Specific actors made the choices that led to a semi-democratic regime in 1984 and to a democracy ten years later. Their choices were influenced but not fully determined by the structural changes in the Salvadoran economy.

Modernization theory is not very helpful for explaining El Salvador's transition from authoritarianism to democracy. Modernization theory might correctly predict that as a relatively poor country, El Salvador would have had authoritarian regimes for much of the twentieth century. But El Salvador was wealthier than several Latin American countries that had extensive experience with

---

[14] Paige (1997: 215–18) documents these changes in the dominant political positions of the coffee elite.

competitive political regimes before the third wave. Modernization theory would predict that El Salvador's probability of experiencing a transition to democracy and building stable democracy would increase as the country modernized. At first blush, the evidence matches this prediction. El Salvador at the end of the twentieth century, when it was a democracy, was wealthier than in the first half of the century, when it had one dictatorship after another. We agree that El Salvador's economic backwardness in the first half of the twentieth century was an obstacle to democracy and that modernization over the long haul enhanced the odds of democratization.

But modernization theory does not explain when the transition to a competitive regime occurred or why it did. Substantial economic growth from 1945 to 1979 did not lead to democracy. Per capita GDP (in 2000 constant dollars) increased from $1,103 in 1945 to $2,152 in 1979, an increase of 95 percent. In the 1980s, when a competitive regime finally emerged, and in the 1990s, when it took firmer footing, it did so in the midst of economic decline. The country's per capita GDP plummeted from $2,152 in 1979 to $1,523 in 1984, when Duarte took office. Wood (2000a) convincingly argued that one aspect of economic decline – the erosion of traditional coffee growers – contributed to democratization.

Moreover, by implicitly positing a close relationship between the level of development and the distribution of regime preferences and relative power among domestic actors, modernization theory fails to explain how actors were constructed and reconstructed and how and why their regime preferences changed. It does not capture the profound role the United States played during the Salvadoran transition, the importance of international influences such as the Sandinista revolution and the end of the Cold War on the Salvadoran political process, or the interactions among actors that ultimately led to the 1992 peace accords. In sum, although modernization theory can help explain the long-term persistence of authoritarianism until 1984, it does not adequately account for when and why El Salvador became semi-democratic in 1984 and democratic a decade later.

THE AFTERMATH OF THE TRANSITION

A history of uncheckered and sometimes brutal authoritarianism and a horrific civil war (1980–91) augured very poorly for democracy. Yet the record since 1992 reveals some striking achievements in democratization (Wood 2005). The right quickly built El Salvador's most successful political party and captured four consecutive presidential elections from 1989 to 2004. The former revolutionaries gave up arms and also built a successful political party. The FMLN has governed the country since 2009 when Mauricio Funes captured the presidency with 51.3 percent of the vote in the first round.

Since 1994, democracy in El Salvador has deepened. Elections became freer and fairer as the left was able to fully participate. The left, which was the object of wide-scale massacres in 1932 and the 1980s, has become fully incorporated into the political system. The competition between the FMLN and ARENA ensures that, in contrast to what occurs in some Latin American countries, citizens can choose among competing parties with very different programmatic profiles.

Politically motivated human rights abuses have waned even though common crime has ravaged the country. Amnesty International, Freedom House, and the U.S. State Department, among others, have reported dramatic improvements in the human rights situation in El Salvador (excepting the treatment of common criminals). After ruling the country for nearly half a century (1931–79) and then acting as an independent agent that often undermined government policy during the first decade of the civil war (1980–89), the military underwent a major revamping with the peace accords of 1992. Over time, it gradually accepted civilian control. The level of democracy in El Salvador is considerably higher than it is in the other two Central American countries with histories of persistent authoritarianism: Guatemala and Nicaragua. For a country with El Salvador's past and a brutal civil war in the 1980s, these achievements are noteworthy.

Alongside these achievements, democracy in El Salvador has had serious shortcomings.[15] Democratic governments have not promoted much economic growth, income distribution, or social improvements. The Gini index of income inequality budged little between 1995 and 2004, improving ever so slightly from .507 to .493 (ECLAC 2009: 252). According to data of the Economic Commission for Latin America and the Caribbean (2009: 244), the poverty rate dropped from 54.2 percent of the population in 1995 to 47.5 percent in 2004 – a slow improvement. El Salvador remains much poorer than the more affluent countries of Latin America. Its per capita GDP ($2,597) in 2009 in 2000 constant dollars was less than half that of Argentina ($9,880), Chile ($6,083), Mexico ($6,099), Panama (5,738), Uruguay ($8,942) and Venezuela ($5,638) (World Bank 2007).

Crime soared in the 1990s and remains a huge problem. El Salvador has one of the highest homicide rates in the world, with a recorded 61.3 homicides per 100,000 population in 2005, the highest in Latin America and more than ten times the rate in Uruguay (PAHO 2007). For the citizens of El Salvador, these serious shortcomings limit life opportunities in deep ways.

THE STABILIZATION OF DEMOCRACY AFTER 1994

The third question of this chapter, which we answer much more briefly than the first two, is how democracy has survived in this relatively poor country with profound social deficits, anemic economic growth, awful crime rates, and stark

---

[15] See Cañas and Dada (1999); Wood (2005); Zamora (2001: 67–84) for balanced assessments of achievements and shortcomings under democracy.

inequalities. Our answer points to the transformation in actors' normative preferences, their policy moderation, and international influences and context.

The Salvadoran story until the end of the 1980s primarily involves instrumental actors seeking to advance their policy interests, but democracy would not have stabilized if extremist actors with normative preferences for right-wing or revolutionary dictatorships[16] had remained powerful or without a profound transformation in the FMLN and ARENA. Over time, the FMLN and ARENA developed reasonably solid if not fully consistent normative preferences for democracy. Business interests saw that they could achieve some important policy goals under democracy (and conversely, the extreme conflict of the 1980s had terrible economic consequences for many businesses). They did not develop a normative preference for democracy, but they accepted it. Whereas historically some powerful actors had a normative preference for a left- or right-wing dictatorship, today none do. These changes in actors' normative preferences have been crucial for democratic stabilization. No disloyal oppositions have emerged despite meager economic and social results. The extreme polarization and radicalization that prevailed in the 1970s and 1980s has receded. In this context, a regime breakdown is farfetched.

Why did actors' normative preferences change? To repeat, changes in normative preferences can stem from (1) traumatic experiences, (2) routine processes of organizational change including new leadership, (3) positive or negative learning experiences under the existing regime, and the (4) international diffusion of normative principles about political regimes. In El Salvador, the trauma of the civil war by itself did not immediately provoke change in actors' normative preferences, but eventually it did reshape how the FMLN and ARENA perceived a desirable political regime.

Routine processes of organizational change were important for ARENA and the military. The displacement of Roberto D'Aubuisson as ARENA leader in 1985 ushered in the possibility of significant change in the party's normative preferences (the second explanation). Part of the extremist right abandoned ARENA in the 1990s, reinforcing the party's shift away from its earlier positions. The removal of some officers implicated in human rights abuses helped shift the armed forces away from a normative preference for military authoritarianism. President Mauricio Funes, who took office in 2009, represented the most pro-democracy faction of the FMLN, so leadership displacement also affected the FMLN's reorientation.

Over time, all of the main actors in El Salvador came to believe that they could achieve some policy goals under competitive politics. The contrast between acceptable, if far from laudable, policy results for most actors under democracy (our third explanation presented earlier), and the destruction during the 1980s (our first explanation) reinforced change in normative preferences and policy moderation. Finally, on the left, as we discussed earlier, international influences

---

[16] In Linz's (1978a, 1978b) terms, these are disloyal oppositions.

were important in the FMLN's changing views of a desirable political regime (our fourth explanation).

In a context in which the main actors have a normative preference for democracy, none has a normative preference for dictatorship, and radicalization has receded considerably from the extreme levels of the 1970s and 1980s, democracy has not been challenged. The stunning transformation of ARENA and the FMLN from radical, authoritarian actors into parties with a normative preference for democracy has been key. The fear of the past led these two parties away from policy radicalism.

A relatively favorable regional context for democracy has bolstered the situation of democratic actors and has prevented the formation of antidemocratic ones. The emergence of an authoritarian populist left (led by Hugo Chávez until his death in 2013) has made the regional environment for democracy less favorable than it was in the 1990s, but the FMLN has steadfastly rejected the authoritarian populist path. For these reasons, the significant deficits in democratic governance have not prevented or overshadowed the country's remarkable transformation from a past of persistent and often brutal authoritarianism to a stable democracy.

CONCLUSION

In this chapter, we addressed the reverse question from the core question in Chapter 5: What explains why a country with a chronic and often brutal history of authoritarianism unexpectedly and against many odds became and remained a democracy?

Our explanation of chronic authoritarianism in El Salvador focused on the construction of a powerful and stable authoritarian coalition of the military, big business, and official parties from 1931 until 1979. By using repression, patronage, and fraud, this coalition easily staved off all democratic challenges. El Salvador's relatively low level of development, moderately high inequalities, and class structure worked against the establishment of a competitive regime, but they did not fully determine this outcome. Rather, the political forging of a durable authoritarian coalition of powerful business interests, the military, and governing parties, coupled with the weakness of democratizing coalitions, were decisive. Occasional outbursts of leftist radicalism, especially in 1932, helped cement this durable authoritarian bloc. The absence of actors with a normative preference for democracy until the emergence of the PDC in 1960 precluded the formation of strong democratizing coalitions.

Political processes are more important than structural changes in understanding the emergence of a competitive regime (in 1984) and democracy (in 1994) in El Salvador. The United States was a key actor in sparking political change. Partly in response to U.S. pressures and incentives, major political actors in El Salvador underwent dramatic transformations. Over the course of a decade, the extremist parts of the conservative authoritarian bloc became much weaker. In part in response to external events, the FMLN renounced revolutionary authoritarian politics. The democratic coalition became much stronger in the 1990s.

The historical narrative in this chapter revolved primarily around the formation of regime coalitions. This analysis of specific processes leading to regime change allows us to conclude this chapter by returning to the hypotheses introduced in Chapter 2.

Our first hypothesis was that the presence of radical actors increases the risk of breakdown of a competitive regime while policy moderation facilitates its survival. Except for the short period from 1984 to 1989, the Salvadoran case supports this hypothesis. The country's first competitive regime broke down quickly in 1931, and radicalization was a major contributing factor. De-radicalization occurred steadily after 1989, and it was a hugely important factor in making democracy sustainable after 1989. After 1989, the radical actors, especially ARENA and the FMLN, were themselves keenly aware that the viability of a competitive regime depended centrally on their willingness to de-radicalize.

The Salvadoran experience also illustrates an extension to our first hypothesis already documented by the quantitative analysis in Chapter 4: a radical opposition to an authoritarian regime may facilitate a transition to competitive politics by destabilizing the incumbent authoritarian government (Wood 2000a). The establishment of a competitive regime may not be the first choice for radical insurgents, but military stalemate sometimes leads to competitive politics as a compromise for both camps (Rustow 1970).

Profound de-radicalization was a necessary condition for the peace terms in 1992. The FMLN agreed to lay down its arms only under the condition that a more democratic regime be established, with political rights and civil liberties for all Salvadorans and with significant changes in the armed forces and the justice system, among many other concessions. ARENA and the military agreed to the peace only under the condition that the FMLN relinquish its arms. Thus, consistent with H1, significant de-radicalization was a necessary condition to move beyond a minimalist semi-democracy and to stabilize democracy.

Our second hypothesis was that a normative preference for authoritarianism (or the weakness of actors with a normative preference for democracy) helps stabilize an authoritarian regime and reduces the likelihood of a transition to a competitive regime. The Salvadoran case is inconsistent with H2 if we use 1984 as the year of a transition. Many actors had a moderate normative preference for dictatorship, and only the PDC and the leadership of the Catholic Church had a normative preference for democracy. A transition occurred nevertheless, but it was an extremely fragile and partial transition. However, the Salvadoran case strongly supports H2 if we consider the years between 1984 and 1994 as an extended transition period and if with think about the solidity of the transition. A transition to a minimalist semi-democracy in 1984 was possible, but it would not have occurred absent U.S. pressures. If we focus on a less fragile and more complete transition, achieved by 1994, the Salvadoran case strongly supports H2.

The Salvadoran case also strongly supports the third hypothesis, that normative preferences for democracy among powerful actors reduce the likelihood of competitive regime breakdowns. Democracy has been stable despite mediocre policy results. The transition in ARENA and the FMLN from normative preferences for authoritarianism to normative commitments to democracy has enabled the regime to endure.

Finally, the Salvadoran case overwhelmingly supports our two hypotheses about the role of international factors. Notwithstanding the complexities and contradictions of U.S. policy toward El Salvador in the 1980s, it is very unlikely that El Salvador would have transitioned to a semi-democracy by 1984 or a peace agreement in 1992 absent U.S. pressures and support for an electoral solution. Moreover, every time in the 1980s that the right-wing authoritarian factions of ARENA and the military threatened to derail competitive politics, the United States intervened to keep things on track. Consistent with H4 and H5, U.S. involvement was decisive in facilitating the transition and preserving a competitive regime.

In many ways, the Salvadoran case is a stark contrast to the Argentine case discussed in Chapter 5. Whereas El Salvador had a stable authoritarian coalition with no serious democratic challenge until 1984 except for the PDC-led coalition in the 1972 election, Argentina had a rapid succession of unstable regimes from 1930 until 1983, with five breakdowns and five transitions to competitive regimes. The change in regime dynamics in El Salvador was heavily influenced by the United States, which was much less influential in Argentina. The shift to stable competitive politics in Argentina was caused foremost by a change in critical actors' normative preferences that antedated the transition to democracy in 1983. In contrast, the initial shift to competitive politics in El Salvador occurred because of U.S. pressures. Further advances toward democracy resulted when ARENA, big business, and the FMLN concluded that the policy cost of the existing regime was prohibitively high and perceived an opportunity to build a competitive regime that would advance some of their core policy interests. Changes in actors' normative preferences were important in stabilizing democracy and in bringing about peace, but not in establishing a semi-democratic regime in 1984.

The two cases also share important similarities. In both countries, democracy has been stable despite some deeply adverse circumstances. In both cases, traumas from the past – the civil war in El Salvador and the brutal dictatorship of 1976–83 in Argentina – helped induce change in actors' normative preferences. In both countries, it is impossible to understand democratic stabilization in the third wave without emphasizing actors' relatively new normative preferences for democracy.

7

International Actors, International Influences, and Regime Outcomes

The quantitative analysis in Chapter 4 showed that a favorable regional political environment helped account for both the increased transition rate and the sharp drop in the breakdown rate after 1977. And in Chapter 6 we argued that international actors and influences decisively affected the outbreak of civil war, the transition to a competitive regime, the peace accords of 1992, and the establishment of a democracy in 1994 in El Salvador.

Consistent with our evidence in Chapters 4 and 6, a growing body of literature has recognized the importance of international effects on political regimes (Beissinger 2007; Brinks and Coppedge 2006; Brown 2000; Bunce and Wolchick 2011; Farer 1996; Gleditsch 2002; Gleditsch and Ward 2006; Huntington 1991: 72–106; Levitsky and Way 2010; Lowenthal 1991; O'Laughlin et al. 1998; Pevehouse 2002a, 2002b, 2005; Pridham 1991, 1997; Starr 1991; Stepan 1986; Weyland 2010; Whitehead 1986b, 1991, 1996). The importance of international effects on political regimes has become a consistent finding in quantitative analyses of regime survival and fall and of the level of democracy. As we noted in Chapter 1, the importance of international effects on political regimes suggests a need to rethink conventional comparative politics approaches to the survival and fall of political regimes, which focused exclusively on domestic factors. When they study political regimes, social scientists cannot ignore transnational actors and influences or the interaction between domestic actors and transnational actors and influences.

But what is the role of international influences in creating waves of democratization and authoritarianism? What are the mechanisms through which transnational actors and influences work? And which actors are responsible for these transnational effects? These are the questions we address in this chapter. The literature on international influences on political regimes has not resolved these issues. Quantitative work has shown a causal impact of the regional or neighborhood political environment on the level of democracy, transitions, and breakdowns, but it has done little to explain its aggregate consequences or the causal mechanisms behind this statistical effect (cf. Yee 1996).

This chapter fleshes out the role of international influences and actors in regime outcomes that was described more briefly in Chapters 1 and 2. We have three primary goals. First, we show that international factors exercise a dynamic effect that is critical to explaining regional waves of democratization. By dynamic effect we mean that the regime in a given country at a point in time not only (on average) influences other countries in the region at the time, but also reinforces the prospects for democracy (dictatorship) in the same country in the future, as the regional neighbors return the influence back through international mechanisms. Thus, transnational forces not only disseminate models of regime change across countries; they also help reinforce those models over time. Regional influences produce important feedback effects that the literature until now has generally ignored. We simulate regional dynamic effects based on the statistical results of Chapter 4 and show that they emulate the evolution of the third wave in Latin America with considerable accuracy.

Second, we discuss six mechanisms by which international forces influence domestic regime outcomes. We explicitly link these six mechanisms to the theory outlined in Chapter 2. Previous authors have discussed causal mechanisms to explain international influences in regime outcomes, but very few have linked international influences to a theory about the domestic political game in an explicit manner.

We then discuss the transnational dissemination of normative regime preferences and radicalism (our first mechanism) in greater detail. We focus on this causal mechanism because of the importance of normative preferences and policy moderation/radicalism in our theory and in the history of Latin American political regimes. We illustrate this point with three historical examples: the dissemination of conservative anticommunism in the 1960s and 1970s, of revolutionary radicalism in the 1960s through the 1980s, and of the norms of liberal democracy and human rights from the late 1970s to the 1990s.

Our third objective is to analyze four international actors that have had region-wide reach and influence on regime outcomes in Latin America: the U.S. government, the Organization of American States (OAS), the Catholic Church, and the international human rights movement. The conclusion to the chapter emphasizes that although international influences provide a powerful explanation for democratization, they have important limitations.

THE THIRD WAVE OF DEMOCRATIZATION: DYNAMIC INTERNATIONAL EFFECTS

The statistical results presented in Chapter 4 showed that international factors play a major role in the process of regime change at the domestic level. International influences also play an intuitive role in creating regional waves of democratization. It is very unlikely that multiple episodes of regime change of similar characteristics will take place in neighboring countries within a short time period unless they are connected in some way. Domestic explanatory factors would have to behave similarly in all countries at the same time for this convergence to occur simply by chance. This is highly implausible in Latin America, where domestic conditions vary considerably within the region.

In this section we analyze the specific role of regional influences in the creation of the third wave of democratization. Several simulations reconstruct how the empirical findings in Chapter 4 explain the evolution of region-wide levels of democratization in Latin America between 1978 and 2010.

At the end of Chapter 4, we reached three conclusions related to this problem. First, the average rate of transitions from authoritarianism into democracy (.042) or semi-democracy (.064), and the average risk of breakdown for democracies (.002) or semi-democracies (.030) predicted by our statistical models (Models 4.2.5 and 4.4.5), were very close to the actual rates for the 1978–2005 period (see Table 4.7). Second, if we know the average probability of transitions and breakdowns for countries of a region in a given year, we can anticipate the proportion of competitive regimes that the region will sustain over the long run (i.e., the equilibrium level for the "crest" of the wave), provided that those probabilities remain steady (see Equation 4.3 and Appendix 4.1). Third, based on this information, we showed that the equilibrium for the proportion of competitive regimes in Latin America expected on the basis of our statistical models was 96 percent – roughly consistent with the aggregate level of democratization in Latin America since 1995 (92 percent of regimes were competitive on average).

While the discussion in Chapter 4 focused on the contrast between the 1945–77 and 1978–2005 periods, here we focus on the impact of regional influences in the post-1977 period. Following the terminology introduced in Chapter 3, the analysis in Chapter 4 showed that our models can explain the *magnitude* of the third wave in Latin America (i.e., the level of democracy achieved by the region in the long run), but it did not show to what extent our models can account for the wave's *duration* (i.e., the time required to achieve that level in the absence of a counterwave).

Regional influences played an essential role in setting the pace and the duration of the latest wave of democratization. We prove this point by simulating the wave-like behavior of levels of democracy in Latin America in the years between 1978 and 2010, using the empirical estimates from Chapter 4 as the main input for the simulations. This exercise also shows that the impact of international forces is always constrained by domestic conditions.

Figure 7.1 compares the results of two simulations against the actual proportion of competitive regimes observed in Latin America between 1978 and 2010. The first simulation, derived from the equilibrium analysis in Chapter 4, treats regional effects as static, while the second simulation adds a dynamic component to the analysis.

The first simulation, summarized by Figure 7.1.1, applies the average probability of transitions and breakdowns predicted by our statistical models (4.2.5

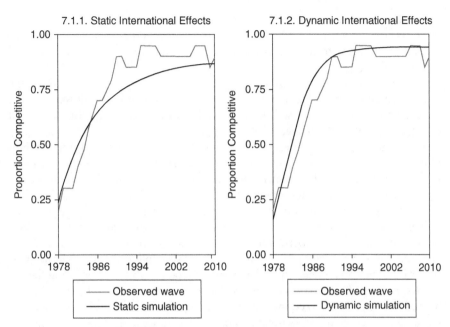

FIGURE 7.1. Simulated Proportion of Competitive Regimes in Latin America, 1978–2010
Note: Figure 7.1.1 applies the average probability of transitions and breakdowns predicted by our statistical models to the observed proportion of democratic, semi-democratic, and authoritarian regimes observed in 1977. The expected proportion of regimes in each category was updated iteratively through 2010, using the same transition and breakdown rates for all years. In Figure 7.1.2, we created a sample representing the 20 Latin American countries. The simulation used the coefficients of our statistical models to predict the expected probability of transitions and breakdowns for each country in 1978. Based on this information, the simulation estimated the probability that each country would be democratic, semi-democratic, or authoritarian by the end of the year. This information was used to create an expected value for the *Region* variable in 1979. The process was repeated iteratively through 2010.

and 4.4.5) for the 1978–2005 period to the proportion of democratic, semi-democratic, and authoritarian regimes observed in 1977. This calculation gave the proportion of regimes in each category expected for 1978. We then took those predicted values and calculated the proportion of regimes expected for 1979, assuming that the transition and breakdown rates were constant for the whole period. Following this iterative procedure, we estimated the proportion of competitive regimes through 2010, using the formula:

$$D_t + S_t = D_{t-1} + S_{t-1} \\ + (.042 + .064)(1 - D_{t-1} - S_{t-1}) - (.002\, D_{t-1} + .030\, S_{t-1}),$$

$$(7.1)$$

where D_t is the proportion of democracies and S_t is the proportion of semi-democracies in year t. This formula is equivalent to Equation 4.1, but it substitutes the generic transition and breakdown rates for the average predicted values in Table 4.7.[1]

The sequence of estimates for the proportion of competitive regimes produces the upward curve shown in Figure 7.1.1. Because transition and breakdown rates are assumed to be constant, based on the equilibrium Equation 4.3, this curve will converge asymptotically to a value of 0.96 over the long run. This trend mimics quite well the patterns in Latin America between 1978 and 2010. However, the duration of the simulated wave is too long compared to the actual wave of democratization. By 1995, 95 percent of the countries in Latin America had established a competitive regime, while the simulation anticipates just 80 percent. And because the curve decelerates after that year, it takes a very long time to converge on the target level.

This inconsistency between the observed series and the underpredicted values of the simulation underscores the dynamic effect of international factors. The literature has not theorized such dynamic effects systematically, but their foundation is intuitive. An increase in the level of democracy in the neighborhood (i.e., in our *Region* variable) expands the probability of transitions and reduces the risk of breakdowns in any given country. In turn, changes in those rates for any country will alter the expected proportion of competitive regimes in the region for the next year. This sequence determines a dynamic effect. Changes in aggregate regional conditions at time t affect domestic conditions at time $t + 1$, and domestic conditions at $t + 1$ in turn affect aggregate regional conditions at $t + 2$. Thus, the regional variable helps us understand not only the dissemination of regime change across space, but also the replication of regime change over time.

Simulation 7.1.1 does not capture such dynamics because regional effects are treated statically. The *Region* variable was included in the statistical models to estimate predicted probabilities of transitions and breakdowns for countries in our sample in Chapter 4, but we employed the average value of those probabilities for the third-wave era (1978–2005) as a constant rate for all years in the simulation. For this reason, the first simulation reflects the effects of regional influences imperfectly.

To reconstruct the dynamic effects of regional influences during the third wave, we followed a more complex approach. For the second simulation, we created a synthetic sample of twenty cases representing the Latin American countries. Each case had constant values for the independent variables in our statistical models (4.2.5 and 4.4.5), fixing them at the national mean for the 1978–2005 period.[2] The values were fixed so that changes in the proportion of

---

[1] The numbers in Figure 7.1 represent the rates of transition from authoritarianism to democracy (.042) or semi-democracy (.064) and the average risk of breakdown from democracies (.002) and semi-democracies (.030) predicted by Models 4.2.5 and 4.4.5.

[2] As exceptions, to simplify the simulation, we set the age of all regimes at 1 year in 1978 and treated all competitive regimes as two-party systems with a score in the presidential powers index of 16 (the average for the region in this period).

democracies over time could be attributed to international influences alone and not to variance in domestic predictors. The *Region* variable was initially set at the actual levels observed for each country in 1978. The simulation relied on those values and on the coefficients obtained from our statistical models – taken as fixed parameters – to predict the probability of transitions and breakdowns for every country in the first year (1978). Based on this information, it estimated the probability that each country would be democratic, semi-democratic, or authoritarian by the end of the year. This information about the distribution of political regimes by the end of 1978 was then employed to create an expected value for the *Region* variable in the following year. Using the updated scores for the *Region* variable, the constant values for the other predictors, and the fixed coefficients from the statistical models, the simulation recalculated the expected probabilities of transition and breakdown for each country in 1979. This process was repeated iteratively through 2010.[3]

The results of this exercise, summarized in Figure 7.1.2, indicate that the dynamic effects of democratic diffusion help explain the duration of regime waves. The predicted share of competitive regimes in Figure 7.1.2 is closer to the observed values and is more consistent with the pace of the historical transformation in Latin America. The dynamic simulation predicts that competitive regimes should represent 94 percent of the region in the nineteenth year of the wave – that is, in 1996 (in fact, the observed proportion by 1996 was 95 percent) – whereas the static simulation would take about a century and a half to reach an equivalent level.

In spite of these powerful results, it would be a mistake to conclude that because diffusion effects operate across borders iteratively, a small positive change in the regional context will inevitably trigger a region-wide wave of democratization. Because the probability of transitions and the risk of breakdowns are also driven by domestic conditions, international influences can be offset by national factors.

To illustrate this point, we reran the dynamic simulation, altering the initial values of normative regime preferences and radicalism. The results of this exercise are shown in Figure 7.2. In the original simulation (Figure 7.1.2), each country had a constant value representing the average scores for normative regime preferences as well as government and opposition radicalism between 1978 and 2005 (the same was true for other independent variables). In the revised simulations, we assigned hypothetical values for these variables in order to create different regional scenarios. Figure 7.2.1 presents the results of a favorable counterfactual in which all countries had positive values for normative preferences (0.5) and no radicalism. In this case the values of the sequence overpredict the levels of democracy actually achieved by Latin America, and indicate that the region should have been completely populated by competitive regimes by 1990. Figure 7.2.2, by contrast, presents the results of an adverse

---

[3] We do not offer a formal representation of the sequence to simplify the presentation here, but the computer code for the simulation is available on the Web site for this book: http://kellogg.nd.edu/democracies-materials.shtml

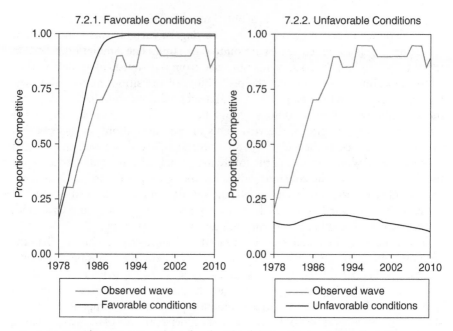

FIGURE 7.2. Alternative Scenarios for the Third Wave (Dynamic Simulation)
Note: All 20 countries are assigned the same values for normative regime preferences and radicalism. Favorable conditions include limited support for democracy (0.5) and no government or opposition radicalism (0). Unfavorable conditions include limited support for dictatorship (–0.5) as well as government and opposition radicalism (0.5).

counterfactual in which all countries had preferences for dictatorship (–0.5) and somewhat radical policy preferences (0.5). In this case, hostile domestic conditions would have offset the effects of democratic diffusion, and the third wave of democratization would have never taken off.[4]

SIX MECHANISMS OF TRANSNATIONAL INFLUENCE ON REGIME OUTCOMES

This analytical reconstruction of regional waves shows that transnational forces have powerful and complex effects on the dynamics of democratization. Political scientists traditionally thought of the actors in regime games as domestic actors. However, international actors regularly affect domestic actors' attitudes about democracy and dictatorship, their policy preferences, the resources of the

[4] This exercise can also help explain reversals. If we allow the initial conditions in Figure 7.1.2 to operate for a decade, and then introduce the conditions for the unfavorable scenario in Figure 7.2.2, the proportion of competitive regimes expands to 86% by 1988 and a counterwave drives the share of democracies and semi-democracies to 31% by 2010.

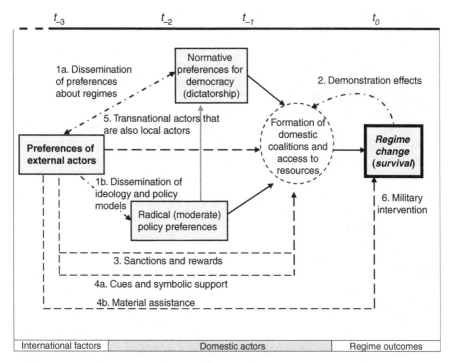

FIGURE 7.3. Mechanisms Linking International Factors and Regime Change
Key: 1. Short dashes indicate indirect (bidirectional) influences. 2. Long dashes reflect direct influences.

competing regime coalitions, and actors' perception of the probability of different regime outcomes.

The fundamental theoretical question is how the preferences of *external* actors (i.e., players located outside of the national territory) can affect the probability of regime change (or survival) at the *domestic* level. In this section, we argue that there are six mechanisms by which this happens. The first mechanism is indirect and reciprocal – it refers to the iterative process replicated in the dynamic simulations of the previous section. The other five mechanisms involve the direct intervention of powerful international actors in the domestic arena. Figure 7.3 expands on Figure 2.2, the graph that summarized our argument in Chapter 2, in order to represent these six mechanisms.

First, international actors can influence domestic actors through the transnational diffusion of normative preferences about democracy and dictatorship, and the dissemination of policy preferences involving moderation or radicalization. This diffusion of preferences can lead some domestic actors to change their choice of a regime coalition. Dissemination of value preferences about the regime and policy preferences is (as reflected in Figure 7.3) a two-way process:

domestic actors both receive influences from the outside and also influence actors in other countries.

Belief systems including normative regime preferences are profoundly international. Domestic political actors do not operate in a vacuum, sealed in by national borders. They act in a world of permeable borders and freely flowing information. Books and journals, television and radio, electronic communication, international conferences; international actors such as the Catholic Church and the Christian Democratic and Socialist Internationals; and international travel and exchanges of ideas and communication by scholars, politicians, policy makers, and activists disseminate worldviews (Htun 2003; Keck and Sikkink 1998; Markoff 1996; Pedrosa 2012; Walker 1990). Cross-country dissemination of information and norms has become more intense since the 1990s with the advent of a powerful internationalized media (e.g., CNN) and the Internet.

A second way in which external factors can influence regime change is through demonstration effects. In this mode of external influence, domestic actors in one country are inspired by highly visible political events or processes in another country, and they mobilize to achieve regime change or to preserve the status quo. This concept differs from the transnational diffusion of norms and beliefs (the first mechanism) because demonstration effects precipitate changes in actors' calculations about what the likelihood of different outcomes, not about their fundamental preferences. For example, many individuals who participated in demonstrations against communist rule in Eastern Europe between 1989 and 1991 already opposed the incumbent regimes. Mass demonstrations in other Soviet bloc countries did not fundamentally change their assessment of the undesirability of communist rule, but they did change their assessment of the possibility of demonstrating without ending up in prison and of effecting change through such opposition. Demonstration effects contributed significantly to opposition uprisings that overthrew communist rule in parts of the Soviet bloc in 1989 and the early 1990s (Brown 2000; Huntington 1991: 100–06; Kuran 1991; Lohmann 1994), to revolutions against incumbent regimes in the post-Soviet region in the 2000s (Beissinger 2007; Bunce and Wolchik 2011), and to uprisings against entrenched authoritarian regimes in Egypt, Libya, and Syria in 2011–12. The Nicaraguan revolution in July 1979 inspired the left in El Salvador to believe that revolution was possible and inspired the right to intensify its repression almost immediately. Whereas the diffusion of preferences works through identifiable *actors*, this is not generally true of demonstration effects. Instead, they work through identifiable *events*.

The other four mechanisms involve external actors with sway in the international arena purposefully attempting to influence domestic regimes. In most cases these actions facilitate (or restrain) the operation of local coalitions that already have their own regime preferences. For this reason, some of these mechanisms depicted in Figure 7.3 act through domestic coalitions on the final regime outcome.

A third causal mechanism involves the imposition of sanctions and the provision of rewards to sway domestic actors to join (or refrain from joining) a domestic regime coalition. Confronted with the possibility of sanctions or positive rewards, domestic actors may adjust their calculation of the policy benefits expected from certain regimes, and therefore withdraw (or increase) their support for a given regime coalition (see path 3 in Figure 7.3).

Economic assistance and benefits (such as free trade agreements, open borders, etc.) offered by external actors can help stabilize political regimes or promote regime change. The European Union offered economic subsidies to new members provided that they remain democratic, thus making it more attractive to domestic actors to support the democratic coalition. This economic assistance nurtured democracy in southern Europe in the 1970s and 1980s (Whitehead 1991). The promise of economic benefits through membership in the EU served as an inducement to central and eastern European governments to become or remain democratic in the 1990s during the process of accession.

Sanctions and other measures against regimes, including trade embargos and the removal or denial of benefits such as economic assistance, also affect the policy benefits of domestic actors under competitive regimes or dictatorship. These sanctions can be enshrined in international law, as has occurred with the development since 1991 of Inter-American international legal mechanisms for the defense of democracy (e.g., Resolution 1080) (Lutz and Sikkink 2001). They can weaken governments, strengthen the opposition, and discourage certain actors from joining particular regime coalitions. For example, in 1993, Guatemalan President Jorge Serrano attempted to pull off a palace coup by eliminating the congress and exercising greater control over the judiciary. The United States, the United Nations, and the OAS made it clear that Guatemala would pay an economic price if Serrano succeeded. The economic sanctions imposed by external actors would have adversely affected the domestic economy, and accordingly some business interests that might otherwise have supported Serrano's coup refrained from doing so.

Fourth, external actors may support members of a particular regime coalition or undermine their relative position by offering resources to their adversaries. This set of mechanisms is closely related to the previous one, but it is analytically distinct. The goal in this case is not to reward or punish domestic players in order to induce them to join a regime coalition, but rather to empower (or weaken) domestic players who are already part of existing blocs. Rewards and sanctions affect the probability that particular actors will join regime coalitions by increasing or reducing the policy costs and payoffs associated with democracy or dictatorship. Direct assistance, by contrast, empowers actors that already share the regime or policy preferences of the external donors.

U.S. aid to El Salvador in the 1980s both swayed some actors to shift coalitions (the third mechanism) and empowered other actors whom the United States wanted to support (the fourth). The United States gave the Salvadoran military massive resources in the 1980s, helping it prevent a military defeat at the hands of the revolutionary left coalition. The Salvadoran military had previously been part of the authoritarian right coalition; U.S. assistance empowered it (the fourth mechanism). But by conditioning aid on an improved human rights record in the Salvadoran military, the United States also supported change within the Salvadoran military, toward forces that did not favor a scorched-earth policy. U.S. policy nudged the dominant position in the Salvadoran military from an extremist actor in the authoritarian right-wing coalition during the early 1980s to being willing (albeit begrudgingly) to refrain from actively supporting authoritarian rule and to accepting peace negotiations and democratic politics (the third mechanism). In the 1980s, the United States also provided funding for the Christian Democratic Party in an effort to strengthen the fledgling democratic coalition (the fourth mechanism).

Support for domestic players may be symbolic or material. International actors often offer information cues that tell domestic actors what their (the international actors') preferences are. The most important actor by far in the western hemisphere in this respect is the United States. When the United States lets it be known that it will support or accept a coup, this fact emboldens the authoritarian coalition. When the United States provides unflinching support for democracy, it encourages domestic democrats to work to preserve democracy or to protect it.[5]

External actors may also provide material support for certain regime coalitions. For instance, between 1990 and 2005, the U.S. Agency for International Development invested more than \$1.7 billion to support democracy programs in twenty-two Latin American and Caribbean countries (Azpuru et al. 2008: 155). Finkel et al. (2007) show that these programs generally enhance the level of democracy by small but statistically significant amounts.[6] By strengthening democracy, these programs can reduce the likelihood of regime breakdowns.

Conversely, an infamous example of covert action against a competitive regime was the CIA's support for overthrowing Chilean President Salvador Allende between 1970 and 1973. When Allende won a plurality of the vote in 1970, U.S. officials tried to persuade (including through bribes) members of the Chilean congress to vote for the runner-up in the presidential election, Arturo Alessandri. (Under the 1925 constitution, if no candidate won a majority in the popular vote, the congress chose the president from among the two candidates

---

[5] In some historical contexts, U.S. support for domestic actors has backfired. For example, the activist position of U.S. Ambassador Spruille Braden in favor of liberal democracy undermined the power of Fulgencio Batista and facilitated the coming to power of the *Auténtico* Party in Cuba in 1944. But when Braden attempted to replicate the move at his new post in Argentina a year later, his intervention in favor of the Democratic Union strengthened Juan Perón's nationalistic appeal among voters (Ameringer 1996, 2000; Bosoer 2011; Guadagni 2007).

[6] Democracy assistance may have unintended consequences when external donors support a local opposition that itself lacks clear democratic credentials. For instance, the National Endowment for Democracy (NED) funded some groups in Venezuela that eventually backed the failed military coup in 2002, leaving the NED in an embarrassing position. It also tends to have weaker effects when democracy programs are part of a broader package of foreign assistance deployed for national security or geostrategic reasons (e.g., U.S. democracy assistance in Egypt).

with the most popular votes.) When this tactic failed and the congress elected Allende, the CIA tried to persuade the military to launch a coup to block him from taking office (Schoultz 1981: 173–77, 243–47; U.S. Senate 1975; A. Valenzuela 1978: 48–49). The CIA funded parts of the Chilean opposition, including the truckers' union, which went on strike and paralyzed the country in October 1972. U.S. action to destabilize Allende's government strongly supported the formation of an adversarial bloc. U.S. action created new resources for the emerging authoritarian coalition, deprived the governing coalition of resources, and, by fueling the economic crisis, lowered the policy benefits (and increased the policy costs) of democracy for domestic actors.

The fifth mechanism depicted in Figure 7.3 represents the role of transnational actors that are simultaneously domestic actors. The Catholic Church is the most important example. It is a worldwide organization with its head in the Vatican, a regional Latin American organization (through CELAM, the Latin American Bishops' Conference), and a domestic actor. As a domestic actor, the Catholic Church has often formed part of regime coalitions. It affected regime outcomes directly by mobilizing Catholic organizations and the faithful in support of particular regime outcomes. In contrast, purely external actors (such as the United States or the OAS) exercise an influence on regime outcomes primarily by swaying or empowering domestic actors – except in the case of a military invasion.

Finally, external actors can affect regime outcomes directly through military intervention (or withdrawal). Overt military intervention of the United States in the Caribbean was common between 1898 and 1933, but it became less frequent afterward. In post-1945 Latin America, only four regime outcomes were determined by U.S. military interventions: arguably Guatemala in 1954, the Dominican Republic in 1965, Panama in 1989, and Haiti in 1994. U.S.-funded mercenaries overthrew the semi-democratic regime led by Guatemalan President Jacobo Arbenz (1951–54) and installed a dictatorship that lasted until 1986 (with many different presidents). The U.S. invasion of the Dominican Republic blocked the possible return of democratically elected Juan Bosch, who had been overthrown in a coup in 1963. In April 1965, military leaders supportive of Bosch rebelled, hoping to restore him to the presidency. U.S. President Lyndon Johnson (1963–69) sent in troops, who helped defeat Bosch loyalists. The U.S. invasion sustained an authoritarian regime that lasted until 1978 (when, paradoxically, the United States helped end the dictatorship by insisting on clean elections). The invasion of Panama led to a democracy that has lasted since the 1990s. The invasion of Haiti in 1994 restored President Jean Bertrand Aristide to power, but in this case the competitive regime eroded in the next few years. Although the number of regime outcomes determined by military invasion in the post-1945 period is only four, because three of these interventions had long-lasting impacts, their total effect is more than marginal.

By contrast to the cases of Panama, Haiti, and the Dominican Republic, the invasion of Guatemala in 1954 illustrates the grey zone between direct military intervention and foreign assistance to domestic coalitions. In Central America and the Caribbean, military invasions sometimes were conducted (and more often attempted) by exiles organized with foreign assistance. Such plans were not always backed by the U.S. government. For instance, in the late 1940s, the competitive regimes in the Caribbean (mainly Cuba and Guatemala, and for some time Venezuela and Costa Rica) supported several plans to overthrow Rafael Trujillo in the Dominican Republic and Anastasio Somoza in Nicaragua (Ameringer 1996). In such cases, foreign governments operated at the boundary between direct military intervention (e.g., Ramón Grau's administration recruited Cuban volunteers to join the Dominican exiles against Trujillo) and material assistance (providing safe haven, equipment, training, and funding for the exiles).

These six causal mechanisms often function together and are mutually reinforcing. For example, the cross-national diffusion of normative preferences about political regimes can lead countries to reject past forms of external military intervention and to new formal norms to protect competitive regimes. In this respect, new value preferences and external resources and sanctions can work in conjunction with changes in patterns of external military interventions.

TRANSNATIONAL DISSEMINATION OF REGIME PREFERENCES AND RADICALISM

The transnational dissemination of beliefs affects whether (and how much) domestic actors develop preferences for democracy or dictatorship, as well as preferences for moderate or radical policies. We devote this section to the transnational dissemination of beliefs because it is crucial to our theory, and because it has been an important part of international influences on political regimes in Latin America.

The cross-national dissemination of actors' preferences is usually decentralized, and it usually results from the reciprocal influence exercised recursively, albeit often inadvertently, by domestic actors in different countries and by actors (such as the U.S. military) that influence domestic actors in multiple Latin American countries. Shared regime and policy preferences are common across borders among generations of activists and political leaders inspired by a shared political spirit in a certain historical context.

We discuss three examples of international diffusion of regime and policy preferences in Latin America. The first illustrates the reciprocal cross-national influence of domestic actors in a context shaped by exogenous shocks. From the outset of the Cold War until roughly 1982, conservative anticommunism held that national security interests were often not compatible with support for democracy in Latin America. The diffusion of conservative anticommunism led actors to devalue democracy and often to embrace radical (conservative) policy preferences. Second, from 1959 until its demise in the 1970s in some countries, and later in others, the revolutionary left in Latin America believed that revolution was possible and desirable and that liberal democracy was a sham. The diffusion of revolutionary left ideas led some actors on the left to devalue democracy and to embrace radical leftist policy preferences. Third, from the mid-1970s on, more voices in the United States and Latin America believed that democracy and human rights are intrinsic values that must be respected and advanced. In the late 1970s, these groups created an international human rights network. By the early 1990s, the pro-democracy beliefs led to new legal norms to protect democracy. The dissemination of the ideals of democracy and human rights encouraged actors in Latin America to develop a normative preference for democracy and to become more moderate on the policy spectrum.

Our argument is not about general cultural dispositions or disembodied beliefs, but rather about how preferences embraced by specific actors disseminate across borders. In the following examples, we attend to four tasks that are central to understand this theoretical problem. First, we identify the transnational actors that helped disseminate attitudes toward democracy and dictatorship across country borders. The process of diffusion of ideas usually requires carriers of those ideas. Second, we indicate the channels through which these international actors influenced the attitudes toward democracy and dictatorship of actors in Latin America. Third, we indicate new practices, norms, and formal organizations that resulted from actors' changing beliefs about democracy, human rights, and dictatorship. Finally, we discuss how these attitudes toward dictatorship, democracy, and radicalization affected political regimes in the region.

Of course, the international diffusion of normative preferences and policy preferences takes place in country contexts that are very different, and hence diffusion does not have the same impact everywhere. Actors within their countries interact in strategic ways to advance their goals even as normative preferences and policy preferences diffuse across borders.

The Transnational Diffusion of Conservative Anticommunism

The case of conservative anticommunism is an example of how exogenous factors can accelerate the dissemination of certain beliefs among domestic players within a region. It also illustrates how peer-to-peer dissemination is fostered by powerful actors.

From the late 1940s until the end of the Cold War, but with greatest intensity from 1954 until around 1977 and between 1981 and 1985, most of the U.S. political elite, military, and media embraced and "exported" the idea that communism represented a realistic and grave threat in the western hemisphere. This idea was appropriated in Latin America by elites who were fearful of leftist and reformist political mobilization, by traditional Catholics who feared revolutionary governments' actions against the Church, by an emerging middle class that increasingly embraced U.S. consumption patterns and feared radical redistributive efforts, and by "modern" military officers who saw themselves as the guarantors of national security and integrity. Although these Latin American groups pursued different goals, held different worldviews, and had unequal leverage in different countries, they converged on the idea that communism was a great evil and the main enemy facing western civilization. The diffusion of anticommunism led many actors in Latin America to reject a normative preference for democracy. Conservative anticommunists prioritized "national security" above and beyond democracy and feared that left-of-center democratic governments could pave the way to communism. Conservative anticommunism was also linked to somewhat radical or radical policy positions.

The question of how to contain Soviet influence in Latin America challenged U.S. policy makers soon after the end of World War II. Cold War liberals – to use Schwartzberg's (2003) term – believed that reformist democracies in Latin America were the best antidote for communism. They argued that the United States should support democracy in Latin America and shy away from backing repressive governments (Schwartzberg 2003: 45–90). President Kennedy embraced this philosophy, especially in his first two years in office (1961–62), and created the Alliance for Progress. In contrast, Cold War conservatives doubted that democracy could work in most of Latin America and argued that fighting communism should be a higher priority than promoting democracy. They believed that the United States should support friendly Latin American governments regardless of regime type. Most of the U.S. military adhered to and exported this latter version of anticommunism. So did most of the foreign policy establishment during the presidencies of Eisenhower (except for 1959–60), Johnson (1963–69), Nixon (1969–74), and Ford (1974–77), and during Reagan's first term (1981–85).

The Cold War conservatives saw left-of-center democratic governments in Latin America as vulnerable to communist influence, and ultimately as potentially opening the doors for communism. Accordingly, they perceived most left-of-center democratic governments as threats. The dissemination of this belief had damaging consequences for democracy in Latin America. One paradigmatic example was the semi-democratic Guatemalan government of Jacobo Arbenz (1951–54), who was elected in reasonably free and fair elections in November 1950. Motivated by exaggerated fears of communist influence in Arbenz's administration, the United States helped topple his government. A military invasion of expatriates organized and funded by the CIA terminated the Guatemalan democratic experiment after nine years in 1954, with tragic consequences.

When the revolutionary nature of the Cuban regime started to become clear in the early 1960s, U.S. officials and many Latin American elites adopted the view that international communism was a grave threat to the region (Child 1980: 143ff; T. Wright 1991: 61–72). Because of Castro's success in seizing power, the fear that communists could take over had some empirical justification. Cuba's eagerness to support revolutionary struggles elsewhere in Latin America and

Africa, and the perilous situation created by the Cuban missile crisis in 1962, reinforced concern among U.S. policy makers and their conservative (as well as many moderate) allies in Latin America. Their fears were compounded by guerrilla struggles in most countries in the region in the 1960s and the 1970s.

After the Cuban revolution, Cold War conservatives and liberals converged in developing a new conception of threats in the western hemisphere. The U.S. military created new programs and organizations to intensify its contact with Latin American armed forces (Child 1980). U.S. officers helped train Latin American militaries in counterinsurgent tactics and in institutional development (Schoultz 1981: 219–21, 227–47). The U.S. military became the main vehicle for disseminating the new, more vigorous anticommunism to Latin American armed forces.

U.S. military officers helped structure the curriculum and training for Latin American officers in some countries. For example, a U.S. mission advised the Brazilian military when it created the Escola Superior de Guerra (ESG, Superior War College) in 1948–49 (Stepan 1971: 175), and it advised the fledgling ESG from 1948 to 1960. Brazilian officers who trained at the ESG played a prominent role in rethinking the role of the Brazilian military in a way that legitimized long-term military rule. ESG graduates were among the coup leaders in 1964 and among the highest leaders of the military governments from 1964 to 1985 (Stepan 1971).

The United States expanded its resident military missions in Latin America in the 1960s. The U.S. military also hosted training programs for Latin American military officers. According to T. Wright (1991: 68–69),

Latin American officers received regular and counterinsurgency training (from the US military) in the Panama Canal Zone and at over 100 service schools in the United States. ... Over 20,000 Latin American officers underwent training in Panama alone during the 1960s. ... The Inter-American Defense College, founded in 1962 at Fort McNair in Washington, D.C., offered annual ten-month courses on social, economic, and political problems of the Americas as well as military matters for 40 to 60 officers of colonel rank or above. (See also Barber and Ronning 1966: 141–78.)

Beginning in the early 1960s, the heads of the Latin American armies, navies, and air forces met annually or biannually with their U.S. counterparts (Child 1980: 160–162). Moreover, Latin American militaries had high-level contacts with each other. These contacts provided opportunities for the dissemination of beliefs about counterinsurgency, communism, and military roles. Conservative anticommunism helped spawn the national security doctrines that justified torture and authoritarian rule in Latin America. The national security mentality was an important factor in the emergence of bureaucratic-authoritarianism (O'Donnell 1973), The region-wide dissemination of anticommunist ideologies during the Cold War reinforced the willingness of domestic actors to support military rule.

Although it is tempting to conclude that dissemination occurred in a top-down fashion, with the United States exercising hegemonic influence over Latin American elites, this conclusion is too simplistic. Conservative actors in Latin America exercised considerable agency whenever they embraced an anticommunist discourse. Latin American militaries and governments did not uncritically adopt all of the doctrines and policy initiatives the United States proposed. The Mexican government, for example, resisted an expansion of U.S. military influence and ideas even though at times it repressed the leftist opposition harshly. The Peruvian army embraced the role expansion promoted by the U.S. military, but it followed a leftist variant under the military government of Juan Velasco Alvarado (1968–75). The Mexican and Peruvian examples illustrate a critical point about the diffusion of beliefs: even if one core actor (in this case the U.S. military) is primarily responsible for disseminating these beliefs, similarly situated actors (i.e., the armed forces) in different countries do not respond to these ideas in exactly the same way. Because normative and policy preferences are the glue that holds domestic and international coalitions together, political actors often embrace or reject ideas strategically according to their needs. Nevertheless, the U.S. military exercised considerable influence over most Latin American militaries in the aftermath of the Cuban revolution, with a tendency toward promoting role expansion of the Latin American armed forces, a greater concern with counterinsurgency, greater propensity to develop a normative preference for military dictatorship (seen by some military leaders as the best kind of regime because of its efficiency, rationality, and capacity to thwart the left), and more radical policy positions.

It would also be a mistake to assume that the diffusion of conservative anticommunism occurred only through social networks of military officers. Power (2002) documented the presence of well-organized and interrelated conservative women's movements in Latin America in the 1960s and the 1970s. "The US Government and conservative forces in Latin America learned from each others' experiences in mobilizing women against progressive or leftist movements and applied these lessons to their own situations" (Power 2002: 85). Operation "Pedro Pan" in Cuba (1960–62) encouraged families to send their children to the United States in order to save them from communism; about 14,000 children were airlifted during this period. Shortly after, Brazilian women began to organize against President João Goulart; their activism escalated between 1962 and 1964. A massive "March of the Family with God for Liberty," attended by hundreds of thousands of demonstrators, set the tone for the Brazilian military coup in 1964 (Dulles 1970: 274–78). In Chile the Christian Democratic Party and the National Party built women's networks, and the United States and the Catholic Church encouraged the mobilization of female voters against Salvador Allende in the elections of 1964 and 1970. The Brazilian experience served as one of the sources of inspiration for Chilean women in their mobilization against the Allende administration between December 1971 and September 1973 (Baldez 2002; Power 2002).

The Transnational Diffusion of Revolutionary Leftist Radicalism

The Cuban revolution had important demonstration effects and diffusion effects (the first two mechanisms in Figure 7.3). It demonstrated the feasibility of socialist revolution in the western hemisphere and inspired many people to work for revolution in their own countries (a demonstration effect). In addition, revolutionary leftist ideals hostile to liberal democracy disseminated across borders with impacts on actors in many countries (a dissemination of policy and normative preferences).

The revolutionary leftist ideal is old in Latin America, but it had limited influence until Fidel Castro came to power in Cuba in 1959. Before the Cuban revolution, most Communist parties in Latin America accepted the idea that in the short term, conditions for a revolutionary uprising were unfavorable. These parties embraced Marxism and advocated revolution in the long term, but they rejected as misguided and ill-advised revolutionary uprising in the short term.[7] Communists embraced the "popular front" strategy in Chile between 1937 and 1946, allied with Fulgencio Batista in Cuba between 1938 and 1944, and sided with Isaías Medina Angarita in Venezuela between 1943 and 1945.

With the advent of the Cuban revolution, the Marxist left grew in influence, and much of it became radicalized (Wright 1991). After Cuba, part of the Latin American left embraced the belief that conditions in Latin America would allow for a revolutionary takeover of power in the short term.[8] It espoused a normative preference for a socialist dictatorship along with more radical policy preferences. Revolution in short order was seen as feasible and desirable, regardless of structural conditions. In his 1961 book, *On Guerrilla Warfare*, Che Guevara popularized the idea that small guerrilla groups could ignite the revolution. French intellectual Régis Debray's (1967) book, *Revolution within the Revolution: Armed Struggle and Political Struggle in Latin America*, struck a similar theme. Both books generalized from a highly questionable interpretation of the Cuban experience, idealized revolutionary socialism, and made it seem within reach in the short run.

Whereas earlier generations of Latin American Marxists had accepted the view that structural conditions were unfavorable for revolution, Guevara and Debray argued that these conditions were not an insuperable obstacle. These

---

[7] Communist Party support for the 1932 uprising in El Salvador was an exception.

[8] In an interview, Schafik Hándal, the long-time (1973–94) secretary general of the Salvadoran Communist Party (PCS) and later (2004) presidential candidate of the FMLN, strongly underscored the impact of the Cuban revolution in pushing the PCS to adopt armed struggle. "The Cuban revolution influenced us profoundly. Because of its influence and based on the objective conditions in the country, the Party decided to prepare for armed struggle" (Harnecker 1988: 9). Likewise, Mario Firmenich, leader of the Argentine Montoneros, referred to the impact of the Cuban, Algerian, and Vietnamese revolutions in an interview in 2002 to explain why the Montoneros took up arms. Interview with Felipe Pigna, online at http://www.elhistoriador.com. ar/entrevistas/f/firmenich.php

ideas, disseminated by countless writers, artists, university teachers, and social leaders at the time, inspired voluntaristic conceptions of the revolutionary struggle. Between 1960 and 1990, tens of thousands of mostly young people embraced this conception and joined revolutionary movements (Moyano 1995: 109–10).

For example, in Chile, in the second half of the 1960s, the Socialist party espoused Leninism (1966) and moved far to the left (Roberts 1998). In 1967, the party congress issued a declaration that "revolutionary violence is inevitable and legitimate" (Walker 1990: 146). Young leftists rejected working within the confines of "bourgeois democracy" and split off to form radical left parties (MIR, *Movimiento de Izquierda Revolucionaria*, and MAPU). In Uruguay, radical leftists formed a new organization, the Tupamaros, in 1963. By the end of the 1960s, they were kidnapping enough people to purchase sophisticated weaponry and to alarm the Uruguayan establishment.

As discussed in Chapter 5, in Argentina the two radical left guerrilla groups that became powerful actors in the 1970s, the Montoneros and the ERP (*Ejército Revolucionario del Pueblo*), were created in 1969. In contrast to most of the revolutionary left, the Montoneros had Peronist rather than Marxist origins, but they embraced revolutionary Marxism after their fusion with the Argentine Revolutionary Armed Forces (FAR) in 1973 (Gillespie 1982). From 1969, when guerrilla activity began in earnest, until 1976, the revolutionary left had a major impact in Argentine politics. Moyano (1995: 52) located press accounts of 4,402 guerrilla attacks from 1969 until 1979, when the revolutionary left was annihilated.

In Brazil, the Communist Party splintered in 1962. The more moderate faction (the Brazilian Communist Party, PCB) adhered to the Soviet line, whereas the more radical organization (the Communist Party of Brazil, PC do B) favored Maoism (Vinhas 1982). At the time of the schism, the PC do B charged the "right wing revisionist majority" of the PCB's Executive Committee with betraying the communist cause (Vinhas 1982: 187). After the military coup of 1964, the left underwent further radicalization. In the late 1960s, some far-left groups in Brazil split from the Communist parties and took up armed struggle. In Brazil, revolutionary Marxism did not cause a regime change, but it prompted the military dictatorship to dig in further and to intensify the repression in the late 1960s and early 1970s.

These are but four examples of a broader phenomenon. Throughout most of the region, a revolutionary left emerged in the 1960s. The revolutionary guerrilla model spread because of transnational demonstration and diffusion effects. The success of the Cuban revolutionaries in winning state power and in creating a new regime and society was idealized by the left throughout Latin America. The activation of similar movements in multiple locations created a sense of transnational solidarity and of shared historical mission.

Several mechanisms helped disseminate the revolutionary leftist ideal throughout the region. First, many leaders of the revolutionary left went to

Cuba or the Soviet Union for training. There they interacted with radical left leaders from other Latin American countries. Second, parts of the revolutionary left received instructions from and interacted with Soviet and Cuban leaders. Third, the revolutionary left from multiple Latin American countries interacted in various forums and traveled to different countries. Che Guevara was the iconic example. An Argentine by birth, he fought with Fidel in Cuba, engaged in battle in Congo, and ultimately died in a guerrilla struggle in Bolivia. Fourth, leftist intellectuals published books that disseminated ideas across country borders. These books did not all advocate socialist revolution, but they drew tens of thousands of university students into a leftist worldview, especially in sociology, anthropology, philosophy, and history. In those years, the distance from a leftist worldview to sympathizing with the revolutionary left was often not great.

The penetration of revolutionary leftist ideals was greater in some countries than others, and it had very different consequences in different countries depending on domestic political conditions. But the Cuban revolution profoundly affected leftist politics throughout almost all of Latin America. In much of the region, the rise of a revolutionary left had dramatic consequences for political regimes. The radicalization of the left triggered strategic reactions from other actors in the political spectrum, consistent with our finding in Chapter 4 that radicalization erodes normative commitments to democracy and makes competitive regimes more likely to break down.

As we discussed in Chapter 5, in Argentina, the revolutionary left helped defeat the military governments of 1966–73 and bring about a restoration of democracy in 1973 (Gillespie 1982; Moyano 1995; O'Donnell 1982; Viola 1982). But its embrace of violence (Leis 2012; Ollier 1998) also fostered the strengthening of a reactionary and militarized right during the second Peronist period (1973–76). Had the revolutionary left been a weak actor, the 1976 military coup might not have taken place.[9]

In Chile and Uruguay, too, the growing strength and the radicalization of the left in the late 1960s and early 1970s created right-wing counterresponses, leading to democratic breakdowns in 1973. Leftist radicalization was critical in the breakdowns of long-lasting democratic regimes in both countries in 1973 (Scully 1992: 136–70; A. Valenzuela 1978; Walker 1990: 146–71 on Chile). The radical left closed off opportunities to resolve conflict within the space of democracy. It pushed the Allende government to the left. The right and by 1972 much of the center was deeply worried about the intentions and actions of the Allende government. The revolutionary left considerably intensified the right's and center's fears.

The left was never a serious contender for power in most countries, but it was seen as a threat by privileged elites, conservative Catholics, large parts of the

---

[9] This counterfactual regresses into a previous one: had the revolutionary left been a weak actor, Perón's return to Argentina in 1972 and the subsequent transition might not have taken place either.

middle class, the militaries, and the United States. In most Latin American countries, the right was authoritarian even before the youthful revolutionaries burst on the scene, but the far left spurred the right toward more truculent positions. In the 1960s and 1970s, conservative actors feared, not without foundation, that revolutionary change would lead to their destruction. They reacted intransigently, supporting authoritarian governments. In turn, as we saw in Chapter 6 on El Salvador, right-wing authoritarianism led leftist forces to conclude that effecting political change through democratic channels was impossible.

The Transnational Diffusion of a Norm of Democracy and Human Rights

A third example of dissemination was the greater value attached to the ideals of democracy and human rights in Latin America. This ideational transformation began in the late 1970s, especially on the left of the political spectrum. The broad dissemination of prodemocratic attitudes and norms raised the costs of coups and increased many actors' tolerance of competitive regimes despite poor economic and social performance in most of Latin America. The cross-national dissemination of prodemocratic beliefs and norms also inspired activists to fight for democracy where it did not exist (Keck and Sikkink 1998; Sikkink 2004).

Normative attitudes about democracy changed significantly in many countries in a relatively short time. This rapid change is consistent with the model of diffusion presented in Figure 7.1.2, and it is inconsistent with older approaches that emphasized Latin America's long-established Catholic Iberian tradition, which was seen as inherently antidemocratic (e.g., Wiarda 2001), or that focus on entrenched mass values (e.g., Inglehart 1990, 1997). The former approach is too static and too homogeneous for the region as a whole, and it ignores important transformations within the Catholic Church (Levine 1992; Mainwaring 1986). If the Iberian tradition were intrinsically inimical to democracy, it would be hard to explain the demise of authoritarianism in the late 1970s and the 1980s, as well as the persistence of competitive regimes in the following decades.

The greatest change in attitudes toward democracy in Latin America came on the left. As explained in the previous section, the traditional revolutionary left was authoritarian in its practices as well as in its regime preferences (Gillespie 1982; Ollier 2009; Roberts 1998; Walker 1990). By the mid-1980s, however, most of the revolutionary left in Brazil and in the southern cone had reassessed and rejected its earlier political convictions and practices (Castañeda 1993; Ollier 2009). Intellectuals and political leaders increasingly embraced democratic regime preferences and more moderate policy preferences. This process of ideational transformation occurred later in Peru, El Salvador (Chapter 6), Guatemala, and Nicaragua.

Intellectuals have historically had more political influence in Latin America than in the United States, and this remains the case to this day (Rama 1996). In the 1960s and 1970s, most politically influential Latin American intellectuals were on the left, hostile to capitalism and ambivalent (or worse) about liberal democracy. Dependency theory was in its heyday. Most intellectuals considered radical social change a more urgent priority than liberal democracy. Many doubted that "bourgeois" democracy was possible under conditions of dependent development.

In the third wave, by contrast, progressive intellectuals became more convinced of the importance of democracy. Leftist groups in one country witnessed the futility of trying to win power through revolutionary means in neighboring countries. Intellectuals met at international conferences and exchanged ideas. Parties that were members of the Socialist International observed parallel transformations in Western Europe and Latin America (Pedrosa 2012; Walker 1990). These changes occurred as part of an international trend; intellectuals in Europe, too, increasingly questioned the authoritarian left, renounced radical Marxism, and embraced liberal democracy.

In 1980, two leading intellectuals formerly in the Brazilian Communist Party published books that defended the normative value of liberal democracy. Carlos Nelson Coutinho's 1980 book, *A Democracia Como Valor Universal* (Democracy as a Universal Value) called for a positive reappraisal of democracy's intrinsic value. Leandro Konder's *A Democracia e os Comunistas no Brasil* (Democracy and Communists in Brazil) argued that Brazilian communists should fight for democracy. In a book published the following year, Bolivar Lamounier (1981) argued that Brazilian intellectuals had underappreciated the importance of formal liberal democratic institutions. Lamounier was a social democrat who was clearly identified with the opposition to military rule. In 1984, Francisco Weffort's book *Por que Democracia?* (Why Democracy?) captured the spirit of the reappraisal of democracy. He argued that democracy is an intrinsic value (pp. 51–62), and that it would enable progressive social-change. At the time, Weffort was the secretary general of the Workers' Party (PT).

Change on the left was not limited to intellectuals; it extended to electorally significant parties. Committed to Leninist ideals and rhetorically favorable to a revolutionary uprising in the 1960s and 1970s, the Chilean Socialist Party became a stalwart of liberal democracy in the 1980s (Walker 1990). In 1972, the Central Committee of the Socialist Party criticized Salvador Allende's government for respecting "bourgeois mechanisms that are precisely what impede us from accomplishing the changes that we need" and called for a dictatorship of the proletariat (Walker 1990: 159). By 1982, a mere decade later, the wing of the party that had most vigorously denounced bourgeois institutions explicitly rejected "real" socialism, affirming that it had failed to "create mechanisms of democratic governance capable of resolving the conflicts that emerge in a modern society" (Walker 1990: 188; see also Roberts 1998). Before the 1973 breakdown, the Frente Amplio in Uruguay was dominated by a revolutionary left that disdained liberal democracy. By the early 1990s, most party leaders fully accepted democracy. Their exercise of power after 2005 confirmed this profound transformation.

Following the argument in Chapters 2, 5, and 6 about changes in actors' preferences, both domestic and international factors contributed to this widespread ideational transformation on the left. First, traumatic experiences (including the repression under military dictatorship and exile) encouraged leftist actors to reassess their views simultaneously in multiple countries. The tragic fate of the left under the dictatorships in Argentina (1976–83), Bolivia (1971–78), Brazil (1964–85), Chile (1973–90), Paraguay (1954–89), and Uruguay (1973–85) meant the physical disappearance of important radical leaders. It eventually inspired a revaluing of democracy and of human rights throughout multiple countries of Latin America (Roberts 1998). Defeat and destruction inspired reassessment of goals and methods, as the left came to realize that its actions had failed to produce positive political change and had come at great personal cost (Ollier 2009).

International political and intellectual networks facilitated the exchange of new ideas among those actors, and transnational institutions (such as human rights organizations, the Catholic Church, and the Socialist International) allowed for the expansion and consolidation of those new ideas (Pedrosa 2012).The experience of exile also fostered cross-national critical reflections. Activists and intellectuals who went into exile in the Soviet bloc countries often were disillusioned with what they experienced. Those who went into exile in Western European countries with social democratic orientations enjoyed freedom, high living standards, and robust debates about social democracy. This positive experience helped stimulate a reappraisal of the value of democracy.

The fall of the Berlin Wall in 1989 and the collapse of the Soviet Union in 1991 affected the left in Latin America. Real socialism no longer appeared as a desirable model. The moral bankruptcy of the Soviet Union, Cuba's economic crisis in the 1990s, China's turn to the markets and repudiation of the Cultural Revolution of 1966–76, and the Tiananmen Square massacre in 1989 deprived most of the left of a communist model to emulate. The transformation of the left in Latin America was not a simple effect of the end of the Cold War, however. In most of South America, Costa Rica, and Mexico, this transformation substantially antedated the end of the Cold War, so it would be wrong to attribute this transformation to those later events. But these global changes antedated the transformation on the left in El Salvador, Guatemala, Nicaragua, and Peru, where they had a greater impact.

The Sandinistas' electoral defeat in Nicaragua's presidential election in 1990 triggered a reevaluation of the revolutionary ideal in Nicaragua itself, El Salvador, and Guatemala. The withering of the Sandinista regime and its defeat at the polls accelerated a process of critical reflection among Central American revolutionaries. The crushing defeat of *Sendero Luminoso* in Peru in the early

1990s and the decision of the revolutionary left to give up arms in El Salvador (1992) and Guatemala (1996) moved the tide further away from revolution. By the mid-1990s, the revolutionary fervor was even weaker than it had been a decade before, and the civil wars in Central America came to a gradual halt. Most FMLN survivors in El Salvador joined the democratic process with the signing of the peace accords in 1992. The M–19 in Colombia, one of the country's biggest guerrilla groups, became integrated into electoral politics after 1991, even though Colombia remained an outlier in the 1990s, with a sizable revolutionary guerrilla left.

As they reflected on those experiences, scholars and political leaders on the left exchanged ideas through conferences and books. First in Europe in the late 1960s, then in Latin America in the 1970s, a new "left" emerged – not an authoritarian radical left, but a prodemocratic left involved in social movements committed to human rights, environmental issues, and women's issues (Viola and Mainwaring 1984). The cross-national scholarly exchange of ideas was especially important for the Latin American countries with stronger, more internationalized scholarly communities. At the same time, transnational actors such as the human rights movement and the Catholic Church (discussed in greater detail later in the chapter) helped consolidate a new worldview.

Since the election of Hugo Chávez in 1998, a new left that is more critical of representative democracy has emerged. Other leading political figures of this new left include Evo Morales, president of Bolivia since 2006; Rafael Correa, president of Ecuador since 2007; and Daniel Ortega of Nicaragua, president since 2007 (and previously from 1979 to 1990).[10] We discuss this new left in Chapter 8.

So far, the discussion has focused on changing attitudes on the left. Change in the right's normative attitude about democracy and dictatorship was equally important. Historically, the right was the greatest obstacle to democracy in most Latin American countries. In much of the region, traditional elites maintained virtually unfettered power until some time (varying greatly by country) in the twentieth century (Hagopian 1996a, 1996b; Paige 1997; Wood 2000a). They refused to accept democracy when doing so could threaten their core policy preferences. As the revolutionary left became more significant in the aftermath of the Cuban revolution, the right became more disposed to undermine democracy (where it existed) to protect its interests and less willing to contemplate democracy where it did not. Conservative political elites frequently conspired against democracy in Brazil between 1946 and 1964 (Benevides 1981) and in Argentina between 1930 and 1976 (Gibson 1996).

As the specter of communism faded, much of the right became willing to abide by democratic rules of the game, and the rest became less eager to support coups. The left's transformation in a more democratic direction fostered a similar

---

[10] This radical left is another example of the diffusion of similar ideas about democracy and similar policy preferences. It is no accident that these leaders emerged in such close historical proximity.

trajectory on the right. As we discussed in Chapter 6, one of the most dramatic transformations occurred with ARENA, the right-wing party in El Salvador. Likewise, the Argentine right, which supported coups in 1930, 1966, 1962, 1966, and 1976, has played by democratic rules of the game even when faced with disastrous policy results in 1989–90 and 2001–02. Business groups have not been at the forefront of democratization, but they have lived peacefully with it in most countries (C. Acuña 1995; Cardoso 1986; L. Payne 1994). The right does not universally subscribe to democracy (L. Payne 2000), but the mere fact that most of it accepts democracy marks a historic change.

Changing attitudes toward democracy in Latin America thus further disseminated *within countries* as actors adjusted their behavior strategically. Changing attitudes in one actor fostered change in others. The conversion of leftist groups to democratic politics, for example, reduced the fears of rightist actors that democracy could lead to their destruction. Similarly, the growing willingness of rightist groups and governments to abide by electoral politics signaled to the left that some positive change could occur through democracy. Where this process of mutual reassurance was disrupted (as with the case of the Patriotic Union in Colombia between 1985 and 1992), the ideational transformations faltered.[11]

Changes in actors' normative beliefs about democracy and dictatorship led to the creation of new formal institutions and norms. For example, the growing commitment to democratic values led to the creation of new actors (e.g., a human rights network) and to new formal norms that empowered the OAS to become a prodemocratic actor after 1990. The establishment of new formal organizations and norms gave an organizational and legal embodiment to changes in actors' beliefs.

INTERNATIONAL ACTORS AND REGIME OUTCOMES

Whereas the previous two sections focused on mechanisms that underpin international influences in regime outcomes, in this section we discuss four transnational actors that help account for these influences: the U.S. government, the OAS, the Catholic Church, and the international human rights movement. The four actors changed in ways that favored democracy in Latin America in the third wave.

Changes in these actors were mutually reinforcing. Change in U.S. foreign policy, for instance, helped drive the OAS's decision to protect democracy more assertively. Thinking about mutually reinforcing effects among international actors – rather than thinking of them as discrete actors operating independently – helps explain why they create "waves." Feedback among international actors

---

[11] The Patriotic Union was a leftist party formed by the Colombian Communist Party and the Colombian Revolutionary Armed Forces (FARC) after the government signed a ceasefire in 1984. Its members were assassinated in droves.

creates the wave-like effects. If this argument about mutually reinforcing effects among international factors is correct, it would be difficult and even misleading to try to isolate the impact of individual international actors or to attribute all of the change in the international environment to any one of them.

U.S. Government's Impact on Political Regimes in Latin America

Our discussion of conservative anticommunism highlighted the role the U.S. government played in its dissemination. Given the hegemonic position acquired by the United States in the Western hemisphere after 1898, some analysts have explained regional regime trends in the twentieth century as the product of changing U.S. priorities and policies toward Latin America (Robinson 1996). However, the statistical results presented in Chapter 4 indicated that the orientation of U.S. policies toward democracy in Latin America was not sufficient to determine regime outcomes in Latin American countries. In models analyzing both transitions and breakdowns during the postwar era (1945–2005), the effects of the U.S. policy indicator were often statistically insignificant. Our findings indicated that on average, Latin American regimes have been more responsive to the regional political environment than to the dictates of Washington.

However, there are two reasons to not discard U.S. influence altogether. First, the variable for U.S. policy toward democracy in Latin America is based on general tendencies, not on policies toward specific countries. Although U.S. policies may not have discernible effects on the probability of transition or breakdown for the *average* country in the region, targeted U.S. policies (interventions, diplomatic support) toward specific countries clearly contributed to specific regime outcomes at given historical moments.[12] A statistical model that measures U.S. policy toward the region would not pick up such effects. If we had been able to measure U.S. policy toward each country in every year, our indicator would have been more valid, and its explanatory power would probably be greater. And because outcomes in those countries helped define the overall regional trend at a given point in time, U.S. bilateral policy might have influenced regional conditions indirectly. Second, as stated earlier, U.S. policies may reinforce or retard the impact of regional trends (for instance, by backing or resisting certain initiatives in the OAS). Therefore, U.S. policies had important indirect effects on regime outcomes in Latin America in addition to the direct ones. The U.S. government has influenced actors in Latin America through

---

[12] From 1945 until 2005, there were thirty-seven transitions from authoritarian to competitive regimes in Latin America (see Chapter 4, Table 4.1). The United States (sometimes in conjunction with the OAS) arguably played a decisive role in eleven of them: Ecuador in 1947–48, the Dominican Republic in 1961–63 and in 1978, Nicaragua in 1984, El Salvador in 1984–94, Guatemala in 1986–96, Chile in 1988–90, Panama in 1990, Peru in 1992–95, and Haiti in 1995. By "decisive" we mean that the regime transition would probably not have occurred when it did without U.S. (and in some cases OAS) involvement.

offering sanctions and rewards (the third mechanism discussed earlier) and by empowering actors in Latin America that share common interests (the fourth mechanism), as well as by invading countries to effect or prevent regime change (the sixth mechanism).

Historically, the United States often supported Latin American dictators who were friendly to U.S. interests. Secretary of State Elihu Root stated in 1907 that Mexican dictator Porfirio Díaz was "one of the great men to be held up for the hero worship of mankind" (quoted in Schoultz 1998: 237). The United States intervened militarily dozens of times in Central America and the Caribbean during the first three decades of the twentieth century (Munro 1964; Schoultz 1998: 176–289; Smith 2000: 50–62),[13] often to prop up or install dictators. President Franklin Delano Roosevelt (1933–45) purportedly said of Nicaraguan dictator Anastasio Somoza (1937–56), "He's a son of a bitch, but he's our son of a bitch."[14] From the early twentieth century until the late years of World War II (1944–45), this cozying up to friendly dictators was commonplace. Until that time, the only notable effort at promoting democracy in Latin America occurred during the first six years (1913–18) of Woodrow Wilson's administration (see Figure 3.7 in Chapter 3). Wilson's efforts, however, were inconsistent, and they were undercut by frequent U.S. military occupations and persistent paternalism (Munro 1964; Tulchin 1971). During his final two years as president, Wilson retreated from the policy of democracy promotion.

U.S. policy was more favorable to democracy for short periods from 1944 to 1948 (Schwartzberg 2003) and from 1959 to 1963, but otherwise U.S. policy makers did not make democracy in Latin America a high priority until 1977. Except from 1959 until 1963, between 1948 until 1977, the U.S. usually subordinated support of democracy to national security concerns (Packenham 1973; Schoultz 1998; P. Smith 2000). As noted in previous sections, the United States supported several coups against reformist and leftist governments, including those in Guatemala in 1954, Brazil in 1964, and Chile and Uruguay in 1973. A U.S. military intervention prevented the return of elected President Juan Bosch to power in the Dominican Republic in 1965. The United States helped create an ideological environment in which conservative actors in Latin America believed that the United States would not object if they fostered coups (Robinson 1996; Sanchez 2003). Presidents Lyndon Johnson (1963–69), Richard Nixon (1969–74), and Gerald Ford (1974–77) strongly prioritized anticommunism over democracy, as did Presidents Eisenhower (1953–61) and Reagan (1981–89) during considerable parts of their terms (1953–58 and 1981–85, respectively).

The U.S. Congress began to adopt a pro–human rights agenda in 1973 (Sikkink 2004: 48–73). Beginning with the presidency of Jimmy Carter

---

[13] P. Smith (2000: 51) lists thirty U.S. military interventions in the Caribbean basin from 1898 to 1934.

[14] *The Washington Post*, April 30, 1952, p. B15.

(1977–81), with the exception of President Ronald Reagan during his first term (1981–85), U.S. policy makers have been relatively consistent in supporting democracy since 1977. President Carter changed the policy of supporting friendly dictatorships. He publicly criticized human rights violations committed by authoritarian governments until then friendly to the United States (Argentina, Brazil, Chile, Nicaragua, and Uruguay, among others). Carter's commitment to human rights was a cornerstone of his foreign policy (Schoultz 1981: 257–66), especially until the troika of foreign policy challenges that confronted him in 1979: the Nicaraguan revolution, the Iranian hostage crisis, and the Soviet invasion of Afghanistan.

Carter supported democratic transitions in the Dominican Republic (1978), Ecuador (1979), and Peru (1978–80). In the Dominican Republic in 1978, U.S. efforts blocked electoral fraud that would have enabled incumbent President Joaquín Balaguer to extend his period of authoritarian rule (1966–78) (Hartlyn 1991). By promoting an honest vote count, Carter helped pave the road for the first democratic transition of Latin America's third wave. Most importantly, Carter legitimized a new norm that human rights should be a part of U.S. foreign policy. The change that began under Carter was rooted in changing normative conceptions about how the United States should operate in world politics and in a different conception of how best to advance U.S. interests in the world (Sikkink 2004).

The first Reagan administration coddled the southern cone dictators until Argentina invaded the Falkland Islands in 1982, and it propped up sagging repressive regimes in El Salvador (Chapter 6) and Guatemala (LeoGrande 1998: 52–146; Sikkink 2004: 158–74). But surprisingly, and notwithstanding its visceral opposition to leftist governments, the Reagan administration's foreign policy efforts began to emphasize democracy during the president's second term (Carothers 1991a, 1991b; Sikkink 2004: 148–80). The 1982 war in the South Atlantic between Britain and Argentina contributed to the administration's reorientation by unveiling the potential bellicosity and erratic behavior of authoritarian regimes. Human rights and democracy remained on Congress's foreign policy agenda, and this fact pushed the Reagan administration to pay more attention to these issues. To bolster the credibility of its much-criticized military offensive against the Sandinistas, the administration used pro-democracy rhetoric and ultimately criticized authoritarianism of the right (Arnson 1993; Carothers 1991a, 1991b; LeoGrande 1998).

The Reagan administration declared its opposition to military uprisings in Argentina in 1987 and 1988, and it pressured for democratic change in Chile from 1985 on, as well as in Paraguay, Panama, and Haiti. Even in Central America, where anticommunism dominated the administration's agenda, it took some steps to further the cause of democracy. As we noted in Chapter 6, as the United States pumped hundreds of millions of dollars into arming the Salvadoran military, it also applied pressure to hold elections, attempted to prop up the centrist Christian Democrats over the right wing, and favored less extremist elements in the military and ARENA. Similar U.S. pressures pushed the Guatemalan military to hold elections in 1985, leading to the inauguration of civilian president Vinicio Cerezo in 1986.

The Reagan administration took some initiatives that helped institutionalize a pro-democracy policy. For the first time, the United States Agency for International Development (USAID) provided ample technical assistance for the 1982 election in El Salvador. USAID's Latin American and Caribbean Bureau began a Democracy Program for Latin America in 1984, funding a variety of initiatives intended to facilitate democratization (those activities later evolved into worldwide democracy and governance programs). Although USAID had worked in Latin America since the 1960s, programs explicitly designed to facilitate elections, promote the rule of law (human rights and judicial reform), strengthen civil society, and support governance (legislatures, local governments, and institutional reforms) consolidated only in the 1990s. These efforts have enjoyed mixed success, but they signal the U.S. commitment to foster democracy.

The George H. W. Bush (1989–93) and Clinton (1993–2001) administrations promoted democratization in Haiti, criticized authoritarian involutions in Peru (1992) and Guatemala (1993), and applied pressure against coup mongers in Peru (1989 and 1992), Venezuela (1992), and Paraguay (1996). The 1989 invasion of Panama ousted dictator Manuel Noriega and led to the installation of a government that had been denied office through electoral fraud. The United States has used diplomatic pressure, public pronouncements, and economic sanctions to bolster democracy and hinder authoritarian regimes (Pastor 1989; Sikkink 2004: 181–220). The George H. W. Bush administration also expanded democracy assistance programs, which henceforth became an important part of U.S. foreign policy (Carothers 1999; Finkel et al. 2007).

During the George W. Bush administration (2001–09), the United States retreated slightly from the support for democracy that characterized his predecessors between 1985 and 2000. In April 2002, a military coup temporarily deposed Venezuelan President Hugo Chávez. Because the U.S. administration had some antipathy toward Chávez, it did not rush to condemn the coup. When the OAS did so, however, the Bush administration went along (Sikkink 2004: 209–10). The U.S. government supported the removal from power of Haitian President Jean Aristide in February 2004, notwithstanding the fact that he came to power in free and fair elections.

Nevertheless, the contrast to the frequent pre-1977 pattern of supporting coups and propping up dictators is significant. To the extent that U.S. policy reinforced regional trends, the historical transformation of U.S. policy making after 1977 helps account for greater democratic survivability in the third wave.

The Organization of American States

Created in 1948, the OAS represents the views of the member states, each having one vote in the General Assembly (established in 1970). A limited number of democracies in the region – combined with limited commitment on the part of the United States, its most influential member – made the OAS an ineffective force for democracy until 1990. The OAS put the principle of sovereignty above democracy promotion. In these earlier decades, the OAS issued some declarations espousing democracy, but they had no teeth. Moreover, the organization exercised little autonomy with respect to the United States in promoting democracy.

With a few exceptions such as its support for the 1954 coup against the semi-democratic regime of Guatemala, pressures against the Trujillo dictatorship in the Dominican Republic in 1961, and pressures against the Cuban communist regime after the revolution, the OAS's role in democracy intervention began in 1990 with the monitoring of the Nicaraguan elections. OAS involvement in Nicaragua helped ensure free and fair elections that produced an alternation in power – the first time that the OAS had monitored the election of a member nation. This precedent established an important new international norm. After that experience, which successfully ensured a fair vote count, the organization monitored elections and promoted peace talks in El Salvador, Guatemala, and Haiti (McCoy, Garber, and Pastor 1991).

In the 1990s, the OAS was a meaningful actor for protecting existing democracies in Latin America. In 1991, the OAS approved Resolution 1080 (also known as the Declaration of Santiago), an important new measure for the multilateral defense of democracy. It called for an automatic meeting of the organization's Permanent Council within the first few days of a democratic breakdown and legitimated OAS intervention in such cases. Resolution 1080 prompted OAS interventions in Haiti (1991), Peru (1992), Guatemala (1993), and Paraguay (1996). Through Resolution 1080, the OAS influenced several political regime outcomes in Latin America by thwarting coup attempts.

Never before in the Americas had there existed anything like the legal norms to support democracy that have been present since the approval of Resolution 1080. Even in this context, democratic breakdowns can occur, as happened in Peru in 1992 and Honduras in 2009. But they have been vastly less common. At almost any other time in the history of Latin America before 1978, coups such as those in Venezuela (2002), Guatemala (1993), Paraguay (1996, 2000), and Ecuador (2000) probably would have succeeded. The OAS and the United States lowered the benefit of regime change to potential coup supporters, increased the cost of a failed coup, and lowered the likelihood of a successful coup.

In December 1992, the OAS approved the Protocol of Washington, which established that by a two-thirds majority, the General Assembly could suspend a member state whose democratically elected government had been overthrown by force (Burrell and Shifter 2000; Perina 2000). Resolution 1080 and the Washington Protocol significantly raised the costs of a coup (the third causal mechanism of the six discussed previously) and in several crisis moments altered the calculations and behavior of domestic political actors. OAS action can also trigger sanctions by the United States or by subregional groups such as Mercosur, whose sanctions have real bite. On September 11, 2001, coincidentally the day of Al Qaeda's attacks on New York and Washington, the OAS unanimously adopted the Inter-American Democratic Charter, reinforcing the commitment to democracy.

The possibility of sanctions changed the game of regime politics in the international arena. Verbal criticisms of international actors against dictators in earlier eras usually had little impact except in the unusual cases when they were accompanied by tough economic sanctions (e.g., the Dominican Republic, 1959–61). The threat of economic sanctions in the contemporary period puts more bite into the efforts to promote or sustain democracy.[15]

Although the OAS was an important pro-democracy actor in the 1990s, its limitations became apparent in the 2000s. It has meager financial resources, so, to exercise leverage on political regimes, it must build internal consensus among member nations. Consensus is likely only under situations of clear attacks on democracy, with a coup serving as the clarion example. The OAS has been more vocal in addressing egregious violations of democratic principles than in responding to quotidian abuses of power or less flagrant electoral infractions. It can build consensus in cases of outright coups or threats of coups, but it has not been effective when presidents gradually curb political and civil rights or undermine formal democratic institutions without frontally attacking them.

The OAS has not invoked Resolution 1080 since 1996 notwithstanding several crises when it could have done so: the deposal of Ecuador's President Jamil Mahuad in 2000; the Venezuelan coup of April 2002 (the OAS did invoke the Democratic Charter on this occasion); more controversially, the deposal of Bolivian President Gonzalo Sánchez de Lozada in October 2003; and the deposal of Haitian President Jean Aristide in February 2004. If the 1990s underscored the OAS's capacity to intervene on behalf of democracy in Latin America, in the 2000s, its ability to do so has receded (Boniface 2007; Disi Pavlic 2011). The OAS is more able to intervene effectively in attempted coups, as occurred in the four cases in the 1990s when it invoked Resolution 1080, than in cases of the erosion of democracy (Venezuela in the 2000s) or of popular mobilization leading to presidential resignations (Bolivia 2003).

In addition, the OAS is more able to intervene on behalf of democracy when there is a high degree of consensus among member nations. With the rise of presidents Hugo Chávez (1999–2013) in Venezuela, Evo Morales (2006–present) in Bolivia, Rafael Correa (2007–present) in Ecuador, Daniel Ortega (2007–present) in Nicaragua, and George W. Bush (2001–09) in the United States, there was less consensus in the 2000s than in the 1990s. The OAS has some influence on regime outcomes primarily because of its ability to impose costs on nondemocratic regimes (the third of our six mechanisms). But its

---

[15] As U.S. sanctions against Cuba illustrate, sanctions are not always effective in inducing regime change, but they do reinforce verbal criticisms.

sanctioning capacity depends on the support of the member nations. The limits of the OAS in the more polarized 2000s became clear when the organization was rebuffed and failed in its efforts to reverse the Honduran coup in 2009.

There is an asymmetry in the effects of the OAS and other international actors such as Mercosur. The OAS and Mercosur have considerably increased the price of overtly authoritarian regimes except for Cuba (which already paid the price of an international boycott), but they are powerless to prod semi-democratic regimes into further democratization. Even in the face of openly authoritarian regimes, the OAS faces a delicate balance: At what point is it going too far in intervening in the internal affairs of another country? When a regime sponsors reasonably free and fair elections but falls short of other criteria of democracy, this dilemma has been insurmountable for the OAS. The OAS has also been powerless against erosions of democratic regimes. In a similar vein, the OAS and other multilateral actors have had almost no capacity to nudge semi-democracies into becoming more democratic. As we show in the next chapter, these actors are often key to encouraging transitions from authoritarianism to competitive politics and in discouraging democratic breakdowns, but developing a more robust democracy hinges overwhelmingly on domestic politics.

The Catholic Church

Some international actors function simultaneously as domestic actors in many or all countries in the same region. Their change in orientation over time can affect political regimes in multiple countries, either by direct involvement in the regime game (i.e., by joining one of the competing regime coalitions) or by changing individuals' value beliefs about democracy and dictatorship or their policy preferences. In this way, they influence regime outcomes in multiple countries. The Catholic Church is the prime example. It is a worldwide organization that experiences common trends in theology, has highly centralized (through the Vatican) appointments of bishops, and some shared understanding of mission even though it has a different orientation in different countries. It is organized and acts both within countries and globally. No quantitative indicator allowed us to measure the effects of changes in the Catholic Church in Chapter 4. However, there are good reasons to believe that these changes have contributed to democratization in Latin America.

The Catholic Church traditionally was an actor of political import in many Latin American countries. Until the 1960s, whenever there was a possibility or a reality of a secularizing, left-leaning democratic government, the Church more frequently sided with authoritarians than with democrats (Gill 1998: 25–36). In the twentieth century, the Church was a protagonist in several coups against democratic or semi-democratic governments. The revolutions in France, Mexico, and Cuba were trenchantly anticlerical, and in response the Church consistently opposed leftist movements and governments. The Franco regime in

Spain also provided the Latin American right with a model that linked Catholic ideals with authoritarian conservatism.

The conservative sectors of the Church formed part of the successful pro-coup coalitions against competitive regimes in Venezuela in 1948 (Levine 1973: 62–93), Colombia in 1948 (Hartlyn 1988: 46; Wilde 1978: 49–50), Guatemala in 1954 (Berryman 1984: 167–69; Handy 1984: 132–33), Brazil in 1964 (Bruneau 1974: 119–21), and Argentina in 1976 (Gill 1998: 149–71; Mignone 1986). In all of these cases, the conservative sectors of the Church had the dominant position at the time of the coups. In these intense conflicts, the Church's moral standing and organizational capacity enabled it to mobilize other actors against the competitive regime. Conservative sectors of the Church also formed part of the pro-dictatorship coalitions in many authoritarian regimes, including some of the most notorious dictatorships in the history of Latin America. For example, until the late 1950s, the Catholic Church fulsomely supported Rafael Trujillo, the tyrant who ruled the Dominican Republic from 1930 to 1961 (Hartlyn 1998: 32–33, 50).

Since the 1970s, the Catholic Church has usually supported democratization (Huntington 1991: 74–85). Under the sway of the Second Vatican Council (1962–65), the Church came to accept and promote democracy in most of the region, with isolated ignominious exceptions.[16] Progressive Catholic bishops' and clergy's commitments to human rights and social justice led them to denounce military rule in several countries.

The Catholic Church is a very pluralistic political actor; every diocese has its own specificities, and every bishop has great latitude about how to lead the Church in his diocese. Nevertheless, it is at the same time a very hierarchical organization (Poggi 1967; Vaillancourt 1980). The Church leadership has powerful means of promoting diffusion of its theology, policy preferences, and pastoral practices, and hence, in our terminology, also in its normative preferences for dictatorship or democracy and its policy moderation or radicalism. Chief among them is the Vatican's control over episcopal nominations, which determine the leadership of the Church. Religious congregations (such as the Jesuits) and the Latin American Bishops' Conference (CELAM) also generate important cross-national influences in how the Church acts in different countries and dioceses.

Change in the Catholic Church affected democracy in three ways. First, the Church became an important member of the democratizing coalitions in countries such as Brazil from the 1970s until 1985 (Mainwaring 1986), Chile after 1973 (Gill 1998: 121–48; Smith 1982: 283–355), El Salvador during the 1970s and early 1980s (Cáceres Prendes 1989), Nicaragua in the late 1970s (Berryman

---

[16] On balance, the Church in Argentina (Mignone 1986) and Guatemala (Berryman 1984: 169–200) supported repressive authoritarian regimes in the 1970s and early 1980s. The Church leadership in Bolivia and Uruguay was largely acquiescent under the military dictatorships of the 1970s and 1980s.

1984: 65–89; Crahan 1989: 42–44; Williams 1989: 64–67), and Peru from 1975 until 1980 (C. Romero 1989). In these countries, the Church was a new prodemocratic actor. It strengthened the coalition of forces that worked for a transition to democracy.

Second, further changes in the Catholic Church during the 1980s and the 1990s reinforced the transformation of the left discussed in previous sections. During the 1960s and 1970s, in many countries of the region, the Catholic Church provided the ferment that led many young people to embrace the political left (Beozzo 1984; Berryman 1984; de Kadt 1970; Gómez de Souza 1984; Pásara 1989; Souza Lima 1980). Change in the Church during the long papacy of John Paul II (1978–2005) made the religious route to becoming a revolutionary leftist far less likely. By the end of his papacy, John Paul II had appointed a majority of the world's Catholic bishops, in most cases relatively conservative individuals. In addition, John Paul II's Vatican criticized some aspects of liberation theology, which had provided the theological underpinning for the involvement of committed young Catholics to leftist political causes. The radical left impulses in the Catholic Church in Latin America were much weaker by 2005 than they had been in the 1970s. Instead, the Church largely positioned itself in favor of representative democracy (Hagopian 2009).

Third, even where the Church did not embrace an activist pro-democracy stance, it no longer was a member of the coalitions that conspired against competitive regimes. Almost uniformly, the Church broke the pattern of alliances with right-wing dictators and reached a peaceful modus vivendi with democratic regimes once they were established (Levine 1981). The Argentine and Guatemalan Churches, which bolstered authoritarian rule in the 1970s and early 1980s, have supported the competitive regimes that were inaugurated in 1983 and 1986, respectively. Nowhere in Latin America has the Church been a pro-authoritarian actor since the transitions to competitive regimes occurred in the 1970s and 1980s. The issue today is how the Church inserts itself into democratic politics (Hagopian 2009), not whether it will be part of the authoritarian coalition. The fact that the Church no longer supports coups or dictatorships removes one player from potential authoritarian coalitions.

The International Human Rights Network

The international human rights network became important in recent decades in Latin America. It first emerged to protest widespread human rights violations committed by the military dictatorships of Brazil and the southern cone in the 1970s. Dictatorships in Latin America had committed human rights violations for generations, but the creation of an international human rights network was a new phenomenon notwithstanding the prior existence of some earlier human rights organizations such as Amnesty International, which was created in 1961. As Keck and Sikkink (1998: 89) explain, "Although some organizations are much older, in the 1970s and 1980s human rights NGOs proliferated and diversified. .... Human rights organizations also formed coalitions and communications networks. .... As these actors consciously developed linkages with each other, the human rights advocacy network emerged."

This network shined a bright light internationally on the dark sides of dictatorships. It strengthened the efforts of domestic foes of dictatorship. Acting in isolation, domestic human rights activists would have had little impact, and they would have faced even greater personal risks in confronting dictatorships. A network provided a means of disseminating information and mobilizing opinion in the advanced industrial democracies and elsewhere in Latin America against the barbaric acts committed by dictatorships.

It is not clear whether there have been any cases in Latin America in which the human rights network was a powerful actor in causing the demise of an authoritarian regime. However, human rights activists have collected and disseminated systematic and reliable information on human rights practices. By doing so, they facilitated the regional dissemination of democracy in three ways: by increasing the visibility of human rights violations (i.e., through "shaming"), by lobbying other domestic and international actors to condemn such violations, and by redefining the normative framework within which other actors (including the United States and the traditional left) assess the normative desirability of democracy and dictatorship.

By publicizing human rights abuses that previously received far less international attention, the human rights network has made dictatorship normatively less appealing to conservative domestic actors than it used to be. Thanks in part to the dogged efforts of human rights networks and to the changes in international law that the network helped stimulate, regimes that engage in gross violations of human rights face greater international opprobrium and sanctions today than ever before. The human rights movement helped change the Western world's normative and cognitive frameworks in the late twentieth century, with implications for domestic political coalitions (Forsythe 1989; Keck and Sikkink 1998; Schoultz 1981; Sikkink 2011).

In this respect, human rights groups have been critical in safeguarding competitive regimes and in supporting the transformations of U.S. foreign policy and the OAS. They contributed to the efforts to establish an international legal framework for the protection of democracy and helped change U.S. policy toward Latin America in a way more favorable to competitive regimes and less favorable to dictatorships (Schoultz 1981). By making violations a highly visible issue, human rights organizations helped pave the way for the OAS to get involved in democracy protection. They helped generate new formal legal norms that safeguard competitive regimes.

The human rights movement also facilitated the transformation of the Latin American left discussed in previous sections. Many leaders and activists in these networks originally came from the left. The growth of these networks created an alternative worldview opposed to that of the traditional revolutionary left, which had little or no regard for human rights and liberal democracy. These networks disseminated new norms regarding the value of human rights and democracy and created a new space for progressive actors that opposed right-wing dictatorships but did not share the regime and policy preferences of the radical left (Keck and Sikkink 1998; Risse, Ropp, and Sikkink 1999).

CONCLUSION

Since Whitehead's (1986b) seminal contribution, many social scientists have emphasized international actors and influences in studies of democratization. But the mechanisms of influence have not been thoroughly studied. Much remains unanswered about why there are regional effects. The most obvious answer for the western hemisphere is U.S. policy –but this answer is inadequate for reasons sketched out earlier in the chapter.

Pevehouse (2002a, 2002b, 2005) is among the few authors who provided a detailed discussion of mechanisms in connection to empirical results. He argued that the OAS and similar regional organizations in other parts of the world are the key external actors and that they account for the regional influences. To explain the high survival rate of competitive regimes since 1990, we give the OAS less credit than Pevehouse. Although the OAS contributed to the very high survival rate of competitive regimes in the 1990s, the third wave of democratization was well under way before it made major contributions to supporting democracy. The most rapid period of democratization had already taken place. Moreover, in the 2000s and 2010s, in the face of growing hemispheric divergence in normative preferences about political regimes and of the new kinds of threats to democracy that we discuss in more length in Chapter 8 – incremental paths toward competitive authoritarianism – the OAS became a less important player.

We proposed six mechanisms by which international actors affect domestic regime outcomes: (1) the transnational diffusion of beliefs alters the normative preferences or policy moderation of domestic actors; (2) highly visible events in one country inspire actors to mobilize, usually against the incumbent regime, in another; (3) external resources and sanctions induce some actors to change their regime coalition; (4) external actors provide resources that empower domestic actors of one of the regime coalitions; (5) a transnational actor that is simultaneously a domestic actor forms part of regime coalitions; and (6) an external military intervention directly produces regime change (or prevents it).

If these six mechanisms are variables that change over time, five of them changed in a favorable direction for stabilizing competitive regimes in Latin America after 1977. First, the diffusion of a normative valuing of democracy and of an abandonment of radical policy preferences in the 1980s and the 1990s facilitated the emergence and sustainability of competitive regimes. Changing cross-national beliefs about the desirability of democracy after 1977 promoted a safer environment for competitive politics and a less friendly environment for dictators. The transformation of regime and policy preferences increased the stability of competitive regimes where they existed and increased the likelihood of transitions where authoritarian regimes existed. And once ignited, the success of democratic transitions reinforced the belief among domestic actors in neighboring countries that authoritarianism could be toppled.

It is less clear whether the net effect of demonstration effects changed in a direction favorable to the stabilization of democracy after 1977. In the earlier era, the Cuban and Nicaraguan revolution demonstrated to both the left and the right that revolution was possible, and it catalyzed polarization and action on both sides. It is more difficult to pinpoint powerful demonstration effects during the third wave, with the exception that the rise to power of Hugo Chávez bolstered the perception that it was possible to challenge market-oriented economic policies and to find incremental paths to consolidate plebiscitarian competitive authoritarian regimes. Demonstration effects did not have the dramatic impact in Latin America that they did in Western Europe in 1848, in the Soviet region in 1989–91, or during the Arab Spring of 2011–12 (Weyland forthcoming).

Third, after 1990, the United States, the OAS, and intra-regional international organizations such as Mercosur persuaded some actors to join the pro-democracy coalition and convinced others to refrain from joining a coup coalition. These international actors devised more powerful means to reward competitive regimes and punish overtly authoritarian regimes. As a result, domestic actors in Latin America that might otherwise have been open to dictatorship believed that their policy preferences would more likely be realized under a competitive regime than under a dictatorship. These international incentives to support democracy and reduce the likelihood of authoritarian regressions increased some domestic actors' policy benefits under competitive regimes. They thereby reinforced the stability of competitive regimes.

Fourth, for most of a generation, from 1953 until 1977, the United States never opposed a coup against a democratic leftist government and often actively supported them. This behavior emboldened potential dictators and empowered dictators already in power. In contrast, after 1977, except for Ronald Reagan's first term (1981–85), the United States has often empowered pro-democracy actors and has rarely encouraged coup mongers.[17] This position was matched by increasing international cooperation with democratic actors: the United States Agency for International Development expanded democracy assistance for Latin America and the Caribbean from $93 million in 1990 (the first year for which there is systematic data) to $157 million in 2005 (in constant 2000 dollars; Azpuru et al. 2008, 156).

Fifth, some international actors that are simultaneously domestic actors became pro-democracy players. The Catholic Church and international human rights networks evolved in ways far more favorable to democracy.

---

[17] The most prominent exception was Venezuela in 2002. The United States initially supported the coup that sought to remove Hugo Chávez from power.

With important cross-national differences, the Catholic Church became more favorable to democracy in the 1970s and 1980s than it had been before. Although some human rights groups existed before the 1970s, a human rights network came into being in the mid- to late 1970s.

Finally, U.S. military interventions have declined in frequency and have shifted from almost always being detrimental to democracy before 1977 to being more positive for democracy in the third wave. Before 1978, several U.S. military interventions undermined competitive regimes or prevented them from coming into power; few had democratizing intentions or effects. Since 1978, the only two U.S. military interventions in Latin America – the invasions of Panama in 1989 and Haiti in 1994 – resulted in the overthrow of dictators and the installation of competitive regimes.

These favorable changes in the regional environment accelerated the rapid transformation of Latin America after 1977, documented in Figure 7.1. Yet they were not a sufficient cause for this transformation. International diffusion influences the normative regime preferences and policy orientations of domestic actors, but it cannot substitute for them. As we showed in Figures 7.2.1 and 7.2.2 simulations, the effects of international forces can be thwarted or compounded depending on domestic actors. The blunt instruments deployed by international actors often prevent the most egregious breakdowns of competitive regimes, but they are unable to prevent subtler forms of democratic erosion. We turn to this problem in the next chapter.

8

Political Regimes after the Third Wave

Our primary empirical purpose in this book is to document and explain the long-term transformation of political regimes in Latin America. For this reason, Chapters 4 through 7 focused on explaining two opposite processes: transitions from authoritarianism and the breakdown of competitive regimes. Changes in the likelihood of these processes, acting together, account for the wave of democratization experienced by Latin America after 1977.

This emphasis on basic regime types prevented us from analyzing subtler transformations within the set of competitive regimes. Figure 4.1 in Chapter 4 identified two important changes within the family of competitive regimes: the *deepening* of semi-democratic systems into full democracy and the *erosion* of democracies into semi-democratic politics. Although less dramatic, these transformations suggest that democratization is a latent, continuous process and that levels of democracy may vary considerably even within the set of competitive regimes.

An analysis of the different levels of democracy achieved by competitive regimes is crucial to understand the evolution of Latin America in the aftermath of the third wave. This analysis is our purpose in this chapter.[1] In the first section we show that, although all countries in Latin America except for Cuba have experimented with competitive regimes in recent decades, the level of democracy varies considerably among them. Chile, Costa Rica, and Uruguay have established what are fairly widely regarded as high-quality democracies, whereas many other countries including Bolivia, Colombia, Ecuador, Guatemala, Haiti, Honduras, Nicaragua, Paraguay, and Venezuela today have significant infringements of at least one of the four defining features of democracy. Post-transition countries have followed different democratic trajectories, making contemporary Latin America a politically diverse region.

In the second section we explore whether, and to what extent, the theory introduced in Chapter 2 helps explain the different trajectories observed among

---

[1] See also Pérez-Liñán and Mainwaring (2013).

post-transition countries. Our analysis focuses on two questions. Why did some countries begin their period of competitive politics in the third wave at higher levels of democracy than others? And why have countries experienced different trends over time since the establishment of a competitive regime? Strictly speaking, both of these questions fall outside the purview of our theory, which focuses on regime survival and fall rather than on levels of democracy once a competitive regime is established. However, the variables introduced in Chapter 2 might be relevant for understanding the quality of democracy in the contemporary period.

By higher-level or higher-quality democracy we mean a regime that comes close to realizing the four dimensions of democracy described in Chapter 3. In a high-quality democracy, elections are free and fair, and the playing field is even. Almost all adult citizens are able to vote, and the regime should make it easy for them to vote. Protection of civil liberties and political rights must be robust, and the state and civil society organizations intended to promote accountability and defend rights should function in an untrammeled manner. Finally, the military should be firmly under civilian control. These are all procedural issues, but they demand an exacting standard in order to qualify as a high-quality democracy. In lower-quality competitive regimes, the gap between at least one of these four democratic ideals and actual practice is greater.

The third section of the chapter presents an empirical analysis of contemporary levels of democracy. We employ latent growth-curve models to analyze the democratic trajectories of nineteen countries between the time of the transition and 2010. The results suggest that normative regime preferences have exercised a long-term historical influence over the third wave. Countries in which political actors were historically committed to democracy entered the third wave at higher levels of democracy than other countries, once they established a competitive regime. Radical policy preferences have exercised an immediate negative influence on competitive politics. The presence of radical governments or oppositions has eroded the levels of democracy achieved during the current era.

We explore the consequences of radical policy preferences more extensively in the fourth section, linking government radicalism with the emergence of political projects that pursue presidential hegemony and with the erosion of democratic politics. The case of Venezuela illustrates how this process of gradual erosion may ultimately compromise the competitive nature of the regime.

In the penultimate section, we discuss recent region-wide trends in the three independent variables at the core of our theory and assess the consequences of those trends for the future of democracy. We argue that an increase in radicalization and a mild dip in normative preferences for democracy create new perils for democracy in a few countries, but that there is little prospect of a wholesale reverse wave of authoritarianism. The variety of radicalism in the early twenty-first century is milder than the one from 1959 until roughly 1989. At the same time, in some countries, signs of weak commitment to democracy among some powerful actors became more acute in the 2000s. We also argue that international actors face serious constraints in preventing the erosion of democracy.

Although international actors and influences have helped greatly reduce the incidence of overt democratic breakdowns, they have important limitations in preventing subtler forms of democratic erosion.

COUNTRY TRENDS IN DEMOCRATIZATION

The period since 1990 has been by far the most democratic in the history of Latin America. Notwithstanding a common impression that Latin America is a region of political instability, at the level of basic regime types as conceptualized in this book – democracy, semi-democracy, and authoritarianism – the region has enjoyed considerable stability since the third-wave transitions. Only in Bolivia (1980),[2] Peru (1992), Haiti (1991 and 1999), and Honduras (2009) did competitive regimes break down, and all five breakdowns lasted for short periods. Venezuela is a more ambiguous case because it reflects a pattern of progressive erosion that is hard to date with precision. We have coded this case as non-democratic since 2009 when the government redid a constitutional referendum to reverse a prior popular decision preventing the indefinite reelection of the president. At that point, the cumulative evidence suggested that the regime had become "competitive authoritarianism" (Corrales and Penfold 2011; Human Rights Watch 2012; Levitsky and Way 2010).

The main challenge confronting competitive regimes in most countries is not sheer survival, but rather a panoply of problems such as poor economic and social performance from the 1980s until 2002, weak states, weak protection of the rights of poor citizens, high crime rates, and citizen disgruntlement. Remarkably, competitively elected regimes have survived in the face of all this, although several countries in the region have experienced near-breakdowns, including Ecuador in 2000, Guatemala in 1993, Paraguay in 1996 and 2000, and Venezuela in 1992 and 2002.

Figure 3.2 in Chapter 3, which provides a highly aggregated picture of trends in democracy, showed that the proportion of competitive regimes remained relatively stable between 1992 and 2010, while the proportion of full democracies suffered a minor decline after 2000. This highly aggregated picture reflects a few cases of democratic deepening, a few of erosion, some stable democracies, some persistent semi-democracies, and one case (Cuba) of persistent authoritarianism.

Figure 8.1 summarizes our regime classification for the Latin American countries, starting with the first year in which they experienced competitive politics after 1977. Post-third-wave cases fall into four categories: (1) countries that by our trichotomous classification have generally had reasonably "full"

---

[2] The Bolivian case could alternatively be counted as two breakdowns, one occurring on November 1, 1979 and the other on July 18, 1980, but the leader of the coup that took power on November 1, 1979 remained in power only sixteen days. The first democratic attempt in 1979 broke down after less than three months (August 8 to November 1). Because we coded regimes at the end of a year, this breakdown does not appear in Table 3.1.

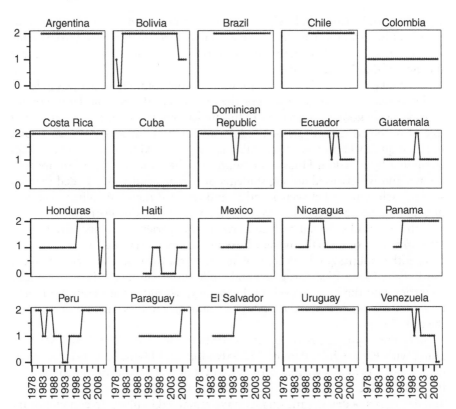

FIGURE 8.1. Regime Classification for Twenty Countries after the Third Wave
Note: Vertical axis is the Mainwaring et al. (2001, 2007) classification of political regimes (0 is authoritarian, 1 is semi-democratic, and 2 is democratic). Countries that enter the sample in the first year experienced a competitive regime after 1977. Cuba is included in the picture for reference only.

democracies since the transitions (Argentina, Brazil, Chile, Costa Rica, the Dominican Republic, Panama, and Uruguay); (2) countries that have become fuller democracies after an extended time as semi-democracies in the 1980s and 1990s (Mexico, Peru, and El Salvador); (3) countries that have stagnated as semi-democracies or with persistent difficulty in creating a higher-quality democracy (Colombia, Guatemala, Haiti, and arguably Honduras, Nicaragua, and Paraguay[3]); and (4) countries that have experienced democratic erosions (Bolivia, Ecuador, and Venezuela).

Although our trichotomous classification is useful to pinpoint the occurrence of transitions and breakdowns (central to the analysis in Chapter 4), it does not

---

[3] Paraguay experienced some democratic deepening after 2008 when the Colorado Party transferred power peacefully to an elected competitor. However, the constitutionally dubious and rushed impeachment of President Lugo in 2012 casts new doubts on this trend.

capture subtler changes in levels of democracy among competitive regimes. Our classification assumes an underlying continuous variable that ranges from highly authoritarian to highly democratic, but it reflects regime change only as a step function of that latent variable.

We need a more sensitive indicator to assess the continuous changes in levels of democracy in recent decades. For the recent period, Freedom House scores provide a very good measurement of this underlying variable. The series are not free of problems (Mainwaring, Brinks, and Pérez-Liñán 2001; Munck 2009), but their quality improved considerably in the 1990s. Moreover, the two indices computed by Freedom House (for political rights and civil liberties) are well known and widely used among students of regime change. We added the two scores, each ranging between 1 and 7, and rescaled the total value to create a measure ranging between 0 (authoritarian) and 12 (fully democratic).[4]

Table 8.1 ranks the nineteen countries that experienced competitive politics after 1977 according to the average Freedom House scores since the transition to competitive politics (or 1978 for Colombia, Costa Rica, and Venezuela). In the third wave, Costa Rica, Uruguay, and Chile stand out as the Latin American countries with the highest levels of democracy. We agree with Freedom House that there is a gap between the quality of democracy in these three countries and the rest of the region.

Since the 1990s, the two largest countries in the region, Brazil and Mexico, along with Peru, Chile, Panama, El Salvador, and Haiti, have become more democratic. As of this writing in early 2013, Latin America continued to enjoy its most democratic period ever. Nevertheless, in most countries, persistent and deep gaps in democratic quality have remained in place. In contemporary Latin America, the dimension of democracy that is most fragile and problematic is the protection of civil liberties and citizen rights, including opposition rights. Most semi-democratic regimes since 1978 have involved a partial violation of the protection of civil liberties. From 1978 through 2010, there were 182 semi-democratic regime-years in Latin America. In 85 percent of those cases ($n = 154$), there were partial violations of civil liberties. Some problems on this dimension of democracy stem from weak states; others, from deliberate efforts of radical presidents to curb opposition activities. Partial violations of the other three dimensions of democracy were considerably less common.

Table 8.1 also reports information about the level of stability in Freedom House scores (i.e., the standard deviation) in the post-third-wave era. Although the level of democracy in principle can be quite fluid and historically has been so for many Latin American countries, the region has experienced remarkable stability in the level of democracy in recent years. For the twenty countries, the

---

[4] For more information, see http://www.freedomhouse.org/report-types/freedom-world

TABLE 8.1. *Freedom House Scores in the Third Wave, Latin America*

Country	First year of competitive regime	Average FH score, 1978[a]–2010	Standard deviation	Average change, 1978–2010
Costa Rica	(1949)	11.7	0.48	0.00
Uruguay	1985	11.2	0.83	0.08
Chile	1990	10.8	1.04	0.10
Panama	1990	9.9	1.37	0.15
Argentina	1983	9.6	0.95	0.07
Dominican Republic	1978	9.4	0.97	0.00
Ecuador	1979	8.9	0.83	−0.06
Brazil	1985	8.9	1.08	0.04
Venezuela	(1959)	8.5	2.24	−0.22
Bolivia	1979	8.4	1.81	0.00
El Salvador	1984	8.3	0.90	0.12
Honduras	1982	8.2	0.79	−0.07
Mexico	1988	7.9	1.49	0.05
Peru	1980	7.7	1.93	0.00
Colombia	(1958)	7.6	1.23	−0.06
Paraguay	1989	7.5	0.51	0.05
Nicaragua	1984	6.6	1.76	0.08
Guatemala	1986	6.6	0.96	−0.08
Haiti[b]	1991	3.1	1.92	0.26

[a] Original Freedom House scores are rescaled using the formula: 14 − (Civil liberties + Political rights) to create a 0–12 scale. Average scores were computed since the transition from authoritarianism, or since 1978 in the cases of Colombia, Costa Rica, and Venezuela. Cuba is excluded from the analysis.
[b] President Aristide took office in February of 1991, so we code that year as the beginning of competitive politics. He was ousted in September of that year, so in Table 3.1, Haiti is coded as authoritarian for 1991.

bivariate correlation in Freedom House scores was .93 from 2007 to 2012 and .86 from 2002 to 2012, reflecting very high aggregate stability even over a decade.[5]

This stability in the regime type (democratic, semi-democratic, and authoritarian) and in the underlying continuous level of democracy coexists with considerable government instability in some countries, as reflected in the large number of presidents who have failed to finish their terms in recent years (Pérez-Liñán 2007). It also coexists with important political, economic, and social changes: the reemergence of the left as a powerful electoral contender in many countries (Levitsky and Roberts 2011; Weyland et al. 2010), a period of sustained economic growth and low inflation for the region (2003–08), and notable decreases in poverty in Chile, Brazil, Mexico, Argentina, and

[5] By contrast, the correlation from 1975 to 1980 was only .54, and the correlation from 1972 to 1982 was only .32.

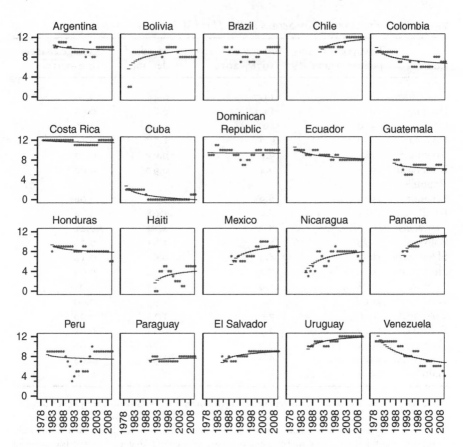

FIGURE 8.2. Freedom House Scores for Twenty Latin American Countries
Note: Vertical axis is Freedom House scores, rescaled between 0 and 12. Curves reflect the latent trend for each country. Cuba is included in the picture for reference only.

Venezuela since 2003. Unfortunately, in many countries the stability in Freedom House scores reflects stagnation in the process of democratization.

The last column of Table 8.1 summarizes the average change in Freedom House scores since the inauguration of a competitive regime. Positive values reflect a democratic trend while negative values reflect erosion toward authoritarianism. Several countries (Venezuela, Guatemala, Honduras, Colombia, and Ecuador) present negative values, indicating that their level of democracy in 2010 was lower than the initial level of democracy at the time they entered the sample of third-wave countries. This pattern suggests that both the initial post-transition level of democracy achieved by Latin American countries and their trajectories over time deserve analysis.

In order to reconstruct those trajectories, Figure 8.2 plots yearly levels of democracy by country, using Freedom House scores. The graphics also show the trend followed by each country after the transition.[6] Overall, Figure 8.2 confirms the patterns identified in Figure 8.1, but the Freedom House scores present a more nuanced picture of democracy in the region.

In recent years, Venezuela and Haiti have anchored the low end of the spectrum on democracy scores (we exclude Cuba from the discussion because it never experienced a competitive regime after 1977). The competitive regimes with low levels of democracy have features of what Diamond (1999, 2002) and Zakaria (1997) called illiberal democracies and Karl (1995) called hybrid regimes. In extreme cases, they have turned into what Brooker (2009: chapter 8) labeled semi-dictatorship and Levitsky and Way (2010) called competitive authoritarianism. Although the latter category differs from our regime classification, it reflects the fact that some nondemocratic regimes are located at the boundary between semi-democratic and authoritarian politics. We occasionally employ the label "competitive authoritarianism" in this chapter to highlight this ambiguity. Venezuela is an example of this phenomenon, with other countries such as Nicaragua and Ecuador (and to a lesser degree Bolivia) acquiring some of its features.

REGIME CHANGE, STAGNATION, AND EROSION

Can the theory presented in Chapter 2 help explain the trajectories observed in Figure 8.2? Our theoretical framework is intended to account for major episodes of regime change (transitions and breakdowns) rather than subtler variations within regime types. However, if regime coalitions sometimes strengthen or undermine competitive regimes gradually, producing incremental shifts in levels of democracy, some insights of Chapter 2 may be relevant for the post-1977 era. Two problems that coexist alongside important democratic advances in some countries deserve attention from the perspective of our theory: democratic stagnation and democratic erosion.

By stagnation we refer to a situation in which countries are trapped in persistent semi-democratic politics. Guatemala, Honduras, and Paraguay exemplify this pattern. Democratic stagnation results from two combined conditions: a limited level of democracy achieved in the aftermath of the transition, and the inability of political actors to deepen the process of democratization in the ensuing period. A stable country trajectory, in this case, reflects the maintenance of a mediocre competitive regime.

Cases of erosion represent a very different pattern. Countries may have entered the third wave of democratization at high levels of democracy, but gradual changes progressively undermined the competitive nature of the regime. Venezuela is the most visible example in Figure 8.2, although other countries have shown indications of erosion in recent years as well. The case of Venezuela reminds us that a sustained negative trend may ultimately induce a shift in the

---

[6] The growth curve was estimated using Equation 8.1, presented later in this chapter.

nature of the political regime, as continuous downward movement along the continuous variable will eventually lead into the terrain of nondemocratic politics.

A clear understanding of stagnation and erosion therefore demands answers to two different empirical questions. Why did some countries enter the third wave at higher levels of democracy than others? And why is it that some countries suffered changes (positive or negative, large or small) in levels of democracy over time? Our theory may shed some light on both issues.

Initial Levels of Democracy

The first question refers to cross-national variance in the initial levels of democracy achieved by countries in the aftermath of the transition.[7] An answer to this question must invoke some initial condition (or set of conditions) that made transitions to semi-democracy likely in some countries and transitions to full democracy more likely in others. To address this issue, an important observation is in order. Figure 8.2 suggests that transitions into semi-democracy were more likely in countries – such as Haiti, Nicaragua, Guatemala, and Paraguay – that had long histories of authoritarianism before the third wave. By contrast, countries with a long history of competitive politics, such as Chile and Uruguay, entered the third wave at higher levels of democracy and enhanced those levels in subsequent decades.

This observation is consistent with our argument about organizational legacies presented in Chapter 2. When political actors in previous historical periods established transparent electoral procedures, strong political parties, independent courts, and civic-minded security forces, they created an institutional infrastructure necessary to sustain the four principles of democracy over the long run. These organizations survived their founders and evolved over time, socializing new members, and creating an institutional memory of the democratic process available to new political actors after 1977. Even where those organizations were undermined by periods of authoritarianism or transformed by traumatic learning experiences, their principles, practices, and sometimes their old leaders reemerged after the transition, providing a solid foundation for the *re-democratization* of societies with prior democratic experience (Pérez-Liñán and Mainwaring 2013; J. S. Valenzuela 2011).

More importantly, such institutions were built by past political actors with normative preferences for democracy. Thus, political actors operating in the distant past created a stock of democratic institutions that benefitted some countries during the third wave of democratization (Gerring et al. 2005).

---

[7] In the unusual cases of Colombia, Costa Rica, and Venezuela, the initial level of democracy refers to the 1978 level (i.e., the beginning of the third wave). Although the discussion focuses on post-transition cases for clarity in the exposition, the argument presented in this chapter applies to these cases as well.

Conversely, countries in which no actors cared about the intrinsic value of democracy before 1978 were more likely to become low-quality competitive regimes in the third wave. Political actors failed to invest in the development of democratic institutions during the twentieth century, and the absence of a preexisting democratic infrastructure ultimately made civil liberties and accountability more difficult to achieve. As a result, those countries entered the third wave of democratization at a disadvantage compared to countries with longer democratic trajectories, such as Chile or Uruguay.

We do not assume that organizations and political leaders did not suffer transformations over time. In Chapters 5 to 7, we showed that regime and policy preferences may evolve, sometimes rapidly, as a result of dissemination, traumatic events, and learning. Our point is simply that past actors with strong preferences for democracy helped build solid institutions that undergird democracy, such as parties and courts.[8] For this reason, we hypothesize that a prior (1945–77) history of normative preferences for democracy promoted higher-quality democracy in the aftermath of the transitions and that, by contrast, the lack of sustained efforts to build democratic institutions in the past made it more difficult to establish full democracies in the third wave.

Post-Transition Trajectories

The second question refers to changes in levels of democracy once the competitive regime had been established. What explains fluctuations in levels of democracy after the transition? An answer to this question may adopt two alternative forms. The first possibility is that changes in levels of democracy are driven by transformations in causal conditions operating over the short run. If this is the case, the trajectories depicted in Figure 8.2 may be the cumulative result of a sequence of yearly changes in explanatory variables.

In Chapters 1 and 2 we theorized that radicalism increases the risk of breakdowns, and that normative preferences for democracy decrease such risk. If regime coalitions can alter levels of democracy in an incremental way, it follows that democratic erosions should be more likely with higher radicalism and that democratic deepening should be more likely with stronger normative preferences for democracy. For instance, a common source of democratic erosion in the third wave has been presidents who deliberately undercut mechanisms of accountability. These presidents often have radical policy agendas and do not value democracy on intrinsic grounds, inducing a deterioration of civil liberties and political rights.

The second possibility, less likely but not completely implausible, is that initial conditions at the time of the transition set countries in particular

---

[8] Elsewhere (Pérez-Liñán and Mainwaring 2013) we have shown that a history of party and Supreme Court institutionalization under democracy enhances the level of democracy in post-1977 Latin America.

trajectories – increasing, declining, or stagnant democratization paths – such as the ones depicted by the latent trends in Figure 8.2. The literature on "modes of transition" (e.g., Karl 1990; Fishman 2011) claimed that the historical circumstances surrounding transitions into competitive politics later constrain the trajectory of new democracies. If this is true, initial conditions may set competitive regimes on a given path, irrespective of other factors affecting levels of democracy over the short run. This argument is less attuned to the hypotheses presented in Chapter 2, but we will explore this possibility as part of our empirical analysis in the next section.

AN ANALYSIS OF LEVELS OF DEMOCRACY AFTER 1977

The previous discussion indicates that our theory can inspire some tentative hypotheses about stagnation and erosion in the post-transition era. These hypotheses potentially address three separate issues: (1) the initial level of democracy, (2) changes in levels of democracy in the short run, and (3) sustained long-term trends, provided that discernible trends exist after we account for short-term changes in levels of democracy. Although the three issues aggregate into a single observed outcome – the quality of the competitive regime in the post-transition period – this distinction is useful to disentangle different causal mechanisms.

In order to clarify this analytical distinction, we represent the level of democracy for each country i at time t using the following equation:

$$y_{it} = b_{oi} + b_{li} \, ln \, (T_{it}) + \varepsilon_{it} \qquad (8.1)$$

where y_{it} is the country's Freedom House score in a given year, b_{oi} is the initial level of democracy in country i in the year of its transition to a competitive regime ($t = 0$), and b_{li} is the change in the level of democracy expected to occur every year after the transition (i.e., the slope of the latent trend). T_{it} represents the total number of years elapsed since the transition in a given country by year t. Because Figure 8.2 suggests that democratization often does not follow a straight path, we employ a logarithmic transformation of T to allow for nonlinear trajectories. Finally, ε_{it} represents the residual variance in levels of democracy that remains unexplained after accounting for the initial level of democracy and the latent trend. This is the distance between the latent curve and the value for any specific point observed in Figure 8.2.

The parameters for the intercept (b_{oi}) and the latent growth curve (b_{1i}) in Equation 8.1 are subscripted by country (i), indicating that their size may vary cross-nationally. Some countries entered the sample at higher levels of democratization than others and thus have a higher intercept, whereas others followed a positive democratic trajectory and thus present a higher coefficient for the time trend. If we assume that those parameters follow a normal distribution, we can estimate Equation 8.1 using a latent growth-curve model, in which the two parameters are treated as random coefficients (Bollen and Curran 2006; Hox 2010; Preacher 2008).

To model the impact of contemporaneous, time-varying predictors on yearly changes in the level of democracy, we expand Equation 8.1, estimating levels of democracy as a function of the time elapsed since the transition, plus the contemporaneous values for our indicator of radicalism, our measure of normative regime preferences, and a battery of controls. The estimating equation thus becomes:

$$y_{it} = b_{oi} + b_{li} \, ln(T_{it}) + b_2 \, Radicalism_{it} + b_3 \, Normative_{it}$$

$$+ \, b_4 Region + \sum b_k X_{it} + \varepsilon_{it} \tag{8.2}$$

where y_{it} is the Freedom House score, *Radicalism* is our measure of radical policy preferences for each country-year (i.e., the proportion of radical actors in the country; see Chapter 3), *Normative* is our measure of normative regime preferences (ranging from –1, or full support for dictatorship, to 1, or full support for democracy), and X represents the set of control variables.

The dependent variable in this analysis (level of democracy) is different from the dependent variable in Chapters 4 through 6 (changes in regime type). For the sake of consistency, we use largely the same control variables here as we did in Chapter 4, understanding that we may get different results for some of them. The control variables are the natural logarithm of per capita GDP measured in 2000 dollars, the average rate of economic growth over the past ten years (or since the transition), a dichotomous variable for resource dependence (coded as 1 when oil and mineral exports surpass 10 percent of gross national income), and the proportion of the labor force in the industrial sector. We also include the Gini index of income inequality in a separate model because of problems of missing data.

Following Abente Brun (2007) and Ottaway (2003), we anticipate that wealthier countries will be more likely to develop high-quality democracy. Also, countries with better governance records, as measured here by per capita GDP growth, may sustain higher levels of democracy. Bad governance in the context of widespread poverty and high inequalities could generate dissatisfaction with the regime among citizens and political actors, making it easier for populists who are not committed to competitive politics to come to power. Finally, we suspect that higher income inequalities could make it more difficult to build high-quality democracy. Controlling for these possible effects, we hypothesize, as noted earlier, that contemporaneous preferences about the political regime and radicalism will affect changes in the level of democracy over the short run.

Given the high stability of Freedom House scores between one year and the next, documented in Table 8.1, we employ a first-order autoregressive specification, such that $\varepsilon_{it} = \rho \, \varepsilon_{it-1} + v_{it}$. The model represented by Equation 8.2 therefore estimates the short-term effects of radicalism, normative regime preferences, regional conditions, and other explanatory factors, while allowing for the possibility that countries also follow a long-term trajectory, captured by the time trend.

This strategy allows us to model the initial post-transition level of democracy as a function of past historical conditions. If countries with a prior history (1945–77) of normative preference for democracy established higher levels of democracy after 1977, specific country intercepts (b_{oi}) would be shaped by inherited country characteristics. These historical legacies are "fixed" attributes by the time our cases enter the third wave of democratization; they vary across countries but not over time in the post-1977 period. Thus, we model the constant for each country as a function of the prior history of normative regime preferences and prior levels of radicalism:

$$b_{oi} = b_{oo} + b_{o1} \, Normative \, (1945-77)_i + b_{o2} \, Radicalism(1945-77)_i + u_o.$$
$$(8.3)$$

Equation 8.3 is a cross-sectional model in which the intercept for Equation 8.2 (b_{oi}) is estimated as a function of the average value for our measure of normative preferences during the 1945–77 period, the average level of radicalism in the country during the same period, and a country-specific residual that follows a normal distribution (u_o).

Table 8.2 presents the results of the analysis, using Freedom House scores for nineteen Latin American countries after 1978. Our unit of analysis is country-years ($N = 503$). Countries enter our sample after the transition (dated in Table 8.1) or in 1978 in the cases of Colombia, Costa Rica, and Venezuela. (Cuba is excluded from the analysis because of the lack of a regime change during the third wave). The top panel reports the coefficients for the time-varying covariates introduced in Equation 8.2. The second panel reports the information for the random intercept. Following the convention for hierarchical models, we report the value for the baseline intercept (b_{oo}), followed by the coefficients for the country-level predictors identified in Equation 8.3. The third panel has the coefficient for the variable measuring the number of years elapsed since the transition (i.e., the latent trend), and the bottom of the table reports the variance of random coefficients and autocorrelation parameter ρ.

The evidence in Table 8.2 suggests that radicalism has an immediate (negative) effect on contemporary levels of democracy, while normative regime preferences operate cumulatively over the long run. In the top panel, the coefficient for normative preferences is insignificant, indicating no discernible effect of regime preferences on the level of democracy in the short run (i.e., in the same year). By contrast, models 8.2.1 and 8.2.2 show that radical policy preferences have had an instantaneous influence on third-wave levels of democracy. The shift from a system populated by moderate actors to one dominated by radical actors involves an average loss of one point in the Freedom House scale in the immediate future.

TABLE 8.2. *Latent Growth Models for Levels of Democracy, 1978–2010*

	8.2.1	8.2.2	8.2.3	8.2.4
Normative preferences (all)	−0.236	−0.278	−0.299	0.354
	(0.292)	(0.291)	(0.295)	(0.394)
Radicalism (all)	−1.112***	−1.050***		
	(0.393)	(0.391)		
Radicalism (ruler and allies)			−0.491**	−0.483*
			(0.226)	(0.275)
Radicalism (opposition)			−0.584*	−0.460
			(0.312)	(0.370)
Region, $t-1$	−1.506*	−1.255	−1.200	−1.543*
	(0.812)	(0.820)	(0.820)	(0.927)
Per capita GDP, ln $t-1$	0.757**	0.872**	0.894**	0.565
	(0.372)	(0.370)	(0.374)	(0.368)
Growth, 10 years	5.715	3.380	3.254	6.396
	(4.199)	(4.240)	(4.249)	(5.502)
Oil and minerals (> 10% GNI)	0.274	0.302	0.321	0.301
	(0.566)	(0.568)	(0.578)	(0.499)
Industrial labor, $t-1$	0.059**	0.053**	0.054**	0.035
	(0.024)	(0.024)	(0.024)	(0.027)
Gini index				0.014
				(0.022)
Intercept	2.002	1.627	1.456	3.476
	(3.015)	(3.062)	(3.092)	(3.345)
Normative preferences, 1945–77	2.316***	3.436***	3.415***	2.705**
	(0.850)	(1.169)	(1.182)	(1.170)
Radicalism, 1945–77	−0.066	−1.118	−1.244	−0.846
	(1.216)	(1.730)	(1.749)	(1.737)
Years from the transition (ln)	0.255	−0.093	−0.115	−0.076
	(0.166)	(0.364)	(0.366)	(0.394)
Normative preferences, 1945–77		−0.704	−0.699	−0.455
		(0.462)	(0.464)	(0.493)
Radicalism, 1945–77		0.715	0.770	0.745
		(0.713)	(0.717)	(0.772)
Variance components				
Standard deviation of the intercept	0.161	0.395	0.412	0.000
	(1.256)	(0.539)	(0.523)	(0.000)
Standard deviation of the trend	0.333**	0.241*	0.241*	0.171
	(0.117)	(0.126)	(0.126)	(0.153)
Rho (ρ)	0.835***	0.841***	0.844***	0.826***
	(0.040)	(0.039)	(0.039)	(.038)
Number of observations	503	503	503	366
(Countries)	(19)	(19)	(19)	(18)

Note: Dependent variable is Freedom House scores (rescaled in the 0–12 range). Residual structure assumes autoregressive (ar1) process.
* $p < 0.1$, ** $p < 0.05$, *** $p < 0.01$

Because radicalism is the main political predictor for short-term influences on the level of democracy, in models 8.2.3 and 8.2.4 we distinguish the radicalization of government forces from the radicalization of opposition actors to verify whether it makes a difference which actors are radical. By contrast to the distinctive effects identified in Chapter 4 for transitions from authoritarianism, the results in Table 8.2 indicate that the radicalization of *all* actors is harmful to the level of democracy once a competitive regime is in place. This is consistent with the view that radical governments undermine democracy by pursuing hegemony, while radical opposition parties and social movements undermine democracy by promoting instability. In model 8.2.4 (with a smaller sample) the coefficient for opposition radicalism is insignificant but retains the negative sign.

The second block of coefficients shows the impact of historical preferences for democracy and radicalism from 1945 to 1977 on the initial level of democracy established after 1977. Countries in which past political actors held normative preferences for democracy established higher-quality competitive regimes during the third wave. The difference between an ideal-typical country in which all actors from the 1945–77 period upheld authoritarian preferences (−1) and another hypothetical country in which all actors preferred democracy (1) is between five (in model 8.2.1) and seven points (in model 8.2.2) – a very large difference on the thirteen-point Freedom House scale. A past history of radicalism, on the other hand, does not adversely affect the average levels of democracy after 1977.

The presence of historical continuities connecting the normative principles of past leaders and the achievements of contemporary democracies does not prove that some countries are predetermined to be more democratic than others. Rather, it shows that early investments made by political elites in the construction of a democratic infrastructure pay off in the long run (Pérez-Liñán and Mainwaring 2013). Cumulative investments in the creation of institutions such as competitive parties and independent courts allowed for considerably higher levels of democracy after 1977. By contrast, some of the greatest shortcomings in competitive regimes are in countries – such as Guatemala, Paraguay, Nicaragua, and Haiti – that had a limited (or no) history of democratization prior to the third wave. Democratic stagnation at the present is partly explained by legacies of political regimes in the past.

The table also reports information for several control variables, with some surprising results that run contrary to our initial expectations. In models 8.2.1 to 8.2.3, per capita GDP has a positive impact on the level of democracy, at the .05 level of significance. A higher per capita GDP might favor a higher level of democracy.[9] The coefficients for economic growth are insignificant; they do not support our expectation that higher growth would be favorable to a higher level of democracy. Model 8.2.4 includes the Gini index of income inequality.

[9] A higher per capita GDP also indirectly affects the level of democracy by boosting normative preferences for democracy. See Table 3.3 and the discussion related to it.

Because Gini data are not available for all observations (for instance, Haiti completely drops from the sample when we consider this variable) the results across models 8.2.3 and 8.2.4 are not fully comparable. Against our expectations, in model 8.2.4, income inequality has no impact on levels of democracy for the Latin American cases. With the possible exception of the level of development and the size of the industrial labor force, these potentially important structural and performance variables do not explain differences in the level of democracy in contemporary Latin America when we include the variables for normative preferences and radicalism.

Although the regional political environment powerfully affects the probability of transitions and breakdowns (see Chapters 4 and 7), it does not influence the level of democracy once a competitive regime has been installed. The coefficients are negative but generally insignificant.[10] The fact that the *Region* variable has a large effect on transitions and breakdowns – documented in Chapter 4 – but does not influence the level of democracy suggests that the power of regional institutions and the United States to prevent breakdowns is greater than their ability to contain the erosions taking place within competitive regimes and to support democratic deepening. It is much easier for the OAS, Mercosur, and the United States to act in the face of flagrantly authoritarian regimes and of clear-cut breakdowns than in cases of more subtle and gradual erosions to competitive authoritarianism.

The variance of the random coefficient for the time trend (reported in the bottom panel) is significant, indicating that individual countries have followed different democratic trajectories. To account for this variance, in models 8.2.2 through 8.2.4 we allowed this random coefficient to vary in response to historical levels of normative support for democracy and radicalism, adding a cross-sectional equation:

$$b_{1i} = b_{10} + b_{11} \ Normative \ (1945-77)_i + b_{12} \ Radicalism \ (1945-77)_i + u_1.$$
$$(8.4)$$

The lack of statistically significant estimates for coefficient b_{11} in all models indicates that, by contrast to the initial level of democracy established in the aftermath of the transition, country trajectories were not determined by prior national histories of normative support for democracy. This contrast in the

---

[10] The negative coefficients in part reflect the nature of the independent variable. Because the *Region* variable measures the average level of democracy in the neighborhood excluding the country in question, the regional average for highly democratic countries is influenced by cases at the bottom of the Freedom House scale, and the average for weakly democratic countries is influenced by cases at the top of the distribution. This creates a weak negative correlation between levels of democracy in each country and the mean for the rest of the region. This effect is magnified in our sample by the fact that two groups of countries in the region have followed opposite trajectories. Whereas high-quality regimes such as Chile and Uruguay have sustained a moderate upward trend, others such as Venezuela have sustained a downward trajectory, making the contrast between these polar cases and their neighbors starker over time.

results is not surprising, and in part may be driven by a mechanical effect. Because levels of democracy have a ceiling (e.g., the Freedom House measure is capped at the maximum value of 12), if a past history of democracy facilitates a high initial level of democracy, it may not also facilitate a rising trend. A steeper *upward* trend would require a *lower* point of departure, thus imposing a trade-off between the coefficients for Equations 8.3 and 8.4.

RADICALISM, PRESIDENTIAL HEGEMONY, AND DEMOCRATIC EROSION

While persistent deficiencies in the competitive regime have prevented democratic *deepening* in many countries, a few countries have experienced a process of democratic *erosion*. The data analysis in the previous section indicates that political radicalism is a key factor behind democratic erosions. This is consistent with what we see in the country cases. According to Freedom House's scoring, Venezuela and Nicaragua stand out as the prime examples. Venezuela slipped seven points from its highest score of 11 (1976–88) to 4 in 2011, reflecting Hugo Chávez's increasingly authoritarian turn. Nicaragua fell from a Freedom House score of 9 in 1998 to 5 in 2011. Our trichotomous classification registers these two cases as eroding from reasonably full democracies (Venezuela, 1959–98; Nicaragua, 1990–96) to semi-democracies and, in the former case, competitive authoritarianism by 2009. By our classification, Ecuador declined from a (borderline) democracy to semi-democracy in 2004, and Bolivia declined in 2007. All four countries have experienced somewhat radical governments headed by presidents with hegemonic aspirations.

By contrast to the enduring violations of civil liberties observed in cases such as Colombia, the source of recent democratic erosions is not the unwillingness or the inability of elected officers to rein in the abuses of security forces and to guarantee citizen access to justice. Rather, presidents have acted purposively to neutralize or to capture the institutions of democracy. These presidents have weakened or entirely displaced the previous democratic coalitions and built new plebiscitarian coalitions. Rather than brutally suppressing democratic actors as most military dictatorships did, contemporary rulers have used less coercion and more institutional manipulation to displace the old coalitions. They have also deployed state resources and political power to help create new actors that are part of their coalition. And unlike most governments that undermined democracy in previous generations, they have relied on significant popular support, as manifested in many elections.

In the current historical context, the costs of overtly authoritarian rule have been prohibitively high. But some presidents have concentrated power by undermining the role of institutional veto players: legislatures, supreme courts, constitutional tribunals, and other institutions designed to hold the executive branch accountable. In Venezuela, Bolivia, and Ecuador, presidents have radically displaced the parties that formed the backbone of the competitive regimes from 1959 to 1999, 1982 to 2006, and 1979 to 2007, respectively. The major parties in these countries – AD and COPEI in Venezuela; the MNR, MIR, and ADN in Bolivia; and the DP, ID, and PSC in Ecuador – have largely disappeared (Mayorga forthcoming; Morgan 2011; Pachano 2011; Seawright 2012). These parties were undermined not only by their own governing failures, but also by aggressive presidential strategies, as popular presidents dismantled the coalition that underpinned the previous competitive regime to build their own.

In addition to undermining opposition parties, these presidents helped create new political actors favorable to their radical policy agendas. For example, the Venezuelan state created or nurtured a large number of popular organizations that were highly committed to Chávez (Hawkins 2010; Smilde and Hellinger 2011). It also transformed the armed forces, which were under civilian control (and hence not a major actor) from the early 1960s until 1990s, into a powerful political actor committed to the regime.

These presidents have also concentrated power by securing control of the judiciary. Attempts to manipulate the judiciary are not uncommon in Latin America, but systematic takeovers have profound implications for competitive regimes. If the government packs the Supreme Court or the Constitutional Tribunal with minions, attacks the legitimacy of those bodies (as opposed to merely voicing disagreement over specific decisions or rulings), or cuts their budgets in order to avoid adversarial decisions, political actors and ordinary citizens are increasingly deprived of their capacity to challenge the government in court in order to protect their rights. This outcome undercuts the normal operation of checks and balances and usually empowers the party controlling the executive branch vis-à-vis the opposition. This argument also applies to other institutions of intrastate accountability designed to protect the law, such as comptrollers, prosecutors, and electoral councils. Our discussion focuses on the takeover of the Supreme Court because it is the most prominent body designed to protect the rule of law, but other institutions of intrastate accountability have confronted similar challenges.

The Venezuelan case again provides a distinctive example of this process. After winning the 1998 presidential election, Hugo Chávez called an election for a Constituent Assembly in order to replace the 1961 Constitution. Although the president's allies held a minority of seats in Congress, they won 94 percent of the seats in the Constituent Assembly. The Assembly deprived Congress of most legislative powers and temporarily replaced it with a standing legislative committee, which remained in place until the election for a new, unicameral assembly took place in 2000 (Ellner 2001). The formation of the Constituent Assembly and the decision to largely strip Congress of its powers dramatically weakened the old pro-democracy coalition.

The Venezuelan Constitutional Assembly declared that the judiciary was in a state of emergency and suspended the tenure of judges. In October 1999, it announced the dismissal of more than 100 judges who faced legal charges. Approved in 1999, the new constitution also disbanded the Supreme Court and replaced it with a new, twenty-member body (the *Tribunal Supremo de Justicia*, TSJ). The new National Assembly, in which the ruling party obtained 56 percent of the seats in 2000, confirmed these new justices appointed by the constituent body.

Within two years, the new Supreme Court was profoundly divided between a pro- and an anti-government faction, and observers reported "an even, ten-ten split, with each camp controlling some of the Court's six chambers" (Human Rights Watch 2004, section 4). The increasing politicization of legal decisions was reflected in a highly controversial ruling that absolved military officers who participated in the failed coup against President Chávez in 2002.

In May 2004, the largely pro-Chávez National Assembly passed a new law expanding the Court from twenty to thirty-two members, thereby giving the government an opportunity to gain control of it. It also established that any nominee who failed to receive two-thirds of the legislative votes in three successive rounds could be designated by a simple majority of the Assembly's members.[11] This clause allowed the government coalition in Congress to unilaterally determine the new composition of the Court. The law also empowered the National Assembly to suspend justices through an impeachment process and to nullify an appointment to the Court by a simple majority of votes if it determined that a justice had undermined the workings of the judiciary. This clause effectively reduced the threshold to remove justices because an impeachment required two-thirds of the legislative votes. The very approval of the law induced some justices to leave office, creating some additional vacancies. In December 2004, the Assembly appointed seventeen new justices (and thirty-two alternates) to secure the government's control of the Tribunal.[12]

The erosion of intrastate accountability, which was already weak by 1998, has had important consequences for competitive politics in Venezuela. The playing field became skewed enough that we coded a partial violation of the principle of free and fair elections after 2003. Although the vote count is not fraudulent, the Chávez administration undermined the ability of the National Electoral Council (*Consejo Nacional Electoral*, CNE) to operate as an impartial arbiter of the electoral process (Álvarez 2009; Kornblith 2005). It also used public resources to reinforce incumbency advantage during electoral campaigns (Ojo Electoral 2008, 2009; Freedom House 2007) and adopted electoral rules to overrepresent the plurality (or majority) in each district. The government has increasingly discriminated against the opposition.[13]

---

[11] http://www.tsj.gov.ve/legislacion/nuevaleytsj.htm

[12] As a result of scattered episodes of violence and government pressures against the opposition, we coded Venezuela as a case of partial violation of civil liberties in 2002–03. The complete takeover of the Court in 2004 and subsequent pressure on opposition media outlets led us to code Venezuela as a partial violation also after 2004.

[13] For instance, the government discriminated against individuals who signed lists in support of the 2004 recall election against President Chávez. It fired public-sector employees who signed the list, discriminated against government contractors who did so, and audited taxes of individuals who supported the recall (Hsieh et al. 2007).

Venezuelan officials have increasingly interpreted the law to secure incumbency advantage in the electoral process. Rulings of the Supreme Court and the National Electoral Council have generally upheld these interpretations of the law. Between 1998 and 2009, elections in Venezuela remained competitive, but the fairness of the electoral *process* declined over time. None of these problems by itself necessarily constitutes a partial violation of democracy in our coding scheme, but their cumulative effect clearly does.

Similar takeovers of the judiciary have taken place in Bolivia, Ecuador, and Nicaragua, although the undermining of political rights has not been equally extreme in those cases – at least so far. What makes the cases of Venezuela, Nicaragua, Ecuador, and Bolivia distinctive are the timing of the events and the boldness with which elected presidents undermined the independence of high courts and other institutions of accountability. Those events took place in the early twenty-first century at the crest of the third wave of democratization, when concerns about democratic survival had been superseded in most countries by new debates about economic growth and equity, institutional development, accountability, and the protection of citizen rights. Yet presidents and legislators in those countries sought to dismantle or control high courts and other independent institutions overtly, without hiding their intentions. They wanted to undermine opposition actors in order to pursue the government's policies without meaningful constraints. In order to achieve that goal, these presidents subjected the courts to recurrent attacks until they secured submissive bodies. An erosion of the competitive regime followed as a result.

OUR THREE INDEPENDENT VARIABLES AND THE FUTURE OF DEMOCRACY

As we have noted, the period since about 1990 has been one of remarkable stability in Latin American political regimes. In contrast to earlier waves of democratization, there have been few breakdowns. Now that almost the entire region has competitive regimes, there are few remaining authoritarian cases that can transition to democracy. Stability in Freedom House scores is very high. A cluster of countries has achieved a fairly high level of democracy; many others have stagnated, with pronounced deficiencies in the quality of democracy. Such stability in regime types and the level of democracy over an extended period of time suggests a probability of continuity into the short- to medium-term future.

Nevertheless, this temporary equilibrium could be upset. In light of our theory, regime outcomes in Latin America are likely to be heavily influenced by trends in radicalism, attitudes toward democracy and dictatorship, and the hemispheric political environment. If our theory is valid, the idea that history has a democratic teleology (Fukuyama 1992) or that Latin America could not experience a new counterwave is not accurate. If the three core variables of our theory change in a significantly negative direction, some reversion to authoritarianism could occur.

The Limits of De-Radicalization

Among post-transition countries, levels of radicalism declined steeply between the early 1980s and the late 1990s. Using our measure of radical policy preferences described in Chapter 3, about 39 percent of national political actors were radical in the average competitive regime in 1984, but only 16 percent of them were radical by 1998 ("somewhat" radical actors are counted as 0.5). After that year, however, the proportion of radical actors showed a moderate recovery, reaching 22 percent by 2010. Since the late 1990s, several countries have shown growing radicalism and a reduced commitment to democracy, raising the specter of additional erosions of democracy in countries with weak states and poor records of democratic governance. A massive counterwave is unlikely, however, because the recent negative trends are very modest and because the international environment is still generally supportive of democracy.

The 1990s were characterized by uncommon moderation and by an unusual and ephemeral narrowing of policy debates. Not surprisingly, when market-oriented policies generated disappointing results in most Latin American countries in the 1990s and early 2000s (Williamson 2003), some actors turned to more radical alternatives and rejected the market-oriented path, which had seemingly failed. Radicalism has risen in recent years in some Latin American countries, especially those with disappointing governance records. In Venezuela, Ecuador, Bolivia, Nicaragua, and Argentina increasingly after 2011, presidents embraced a somewhat radical leftist discourse. Radical actors on the right and left have been powerful players in Colombia since the late 1980s.

Democratic erosion – most dramatically expressed in episodes of presidential instability and in trends toward presidential hegemony – is the likely result of a (limited) revival of radical policy preferences, possibly followed by a limited erosion of normative preferences for democracy. The radicalization of presidents and their allies has played an important role, as radical governments sought to dismantle the judiciary and other institutions of accountability. But the radicalization of opposition forces may have had a negative impact on democracy as well, as radical oppositions sought to unseat elected presidents – often invoking some constitutional procedure.

With his confrontational style and left-leaning positions, President Hugo Chávez became emblematic of the new, somewhat radical left. With Chávez's rise to power, Venezuelan politics became dramatically polarized between pro- and anti-Chávez forces (López Maya 2005: chapter 11). In Bolivia, the outbreak of violent social mobilization in 2000, the nearly successful presidential candidacy of Evo Morales in 2002, and renewed anti-system mobilization in 2003 that led to the forced resignations of Presidents Sánchez de Lozada (2002–03) and Carlos Mesa (2003–05) indicated rising radicalism (Mayorga 2005). During Evo Morales's presidency (2006–present), polarization has increased considerably.

We describe the policy preferences of most of these actors as *somewhat* radical to mark the contrast with the past. Although radical leftist actors were more powerful at the end of the first decade of the twenty-first century than they were in the 1990s, these actors were markedly less radical than the guerrillas who took power in Cuba in 1959 and those that attempted to win power throughout much of Latin America in the 1960s, 1970s, and 1980s. Similarly, even in the late 1980s, a retrograde right was still committed to intransigently preserving traditional privileges and political power in many countries. The radical right is much weaker today than it once was, with very little prospect of a full-scale resurgence. Much of the radical right survived under the aegis of openly authoritarian regimes.

Still, the resurgence of a somewhat radical discourse combined with the dismantling of institutional veto players has triggered radicalized responses from parts of the opposition. Some members of the opposition embraced insurrectional strategies when they felt that government policies were particularly threatening to their interests and found that no institutional venues were effective to challenge such policies. The course of action adopted by the Venezuelan opposition in 2002–03 (a failed military coup, violent riots, and a strike that paralyzed the oil industry and therefore much of the economy) illustrates this risk (López Maya 2005: chapter 11). The insurrection of some regional elites in Bolivia after 2005 and the strong elite support for the military ousting of President Zelaya in Honduras in 2009 also reflect this peril.

This revival of radicalism is analytically separate from the expansion of the left in the 2000s. Although the wave of electoral victories by leftist presidential candidates has attracted much attention, right- or left-wing policies by themselves do not indicate radical policy preferences. Radicalism involves intransigence in the agenda-setting process, impatience in the relation with veto players, and willingness to impose high costs on other sectors of society. The left-leaning presidents with strong ties to established parties – Lula da Silva (2003–11) and Dilma Rousseff (2011–present) in Brazil, Ricardo Lagos (2000–06) and Michelle Bachelet in Chile (2006–10), or Tabaré Vázquez (2005–10) and José Mujica (2010–present) in Uruguay – were moderate and deeply committed to democracy (Levitsky and Roberts 2011; Weyland, Madrid, and Hunter 2010).

Normative Preferences

Consistent with our claims in previous chapters, a slight decline in normative preferences for democracy has accompanied the modest increase in radical policy preferences. As is the case of radicalism, the degree of commitment to democracy is still very favorable to competitive politics compared to the 1960s or in the 1970s. Ambiguous or instrumental attitudes toward democracy are not widespread, and explicit authoritarian projects are currently rare. Over the long run, our measure of normative preferences (ranging between –1 and 1) increased steeply among competitive regimes in the region, expanding from an average of 0.37 in 1984 to 0.66 in 2006. This indicator experienced a slight decline afterward, but the average score still was 0.60 in 2010.

Several facts suggest a decline in the dominance of actors committed to democracy in some countries. First, although military coups have failed in most cases, coup leaders sometimes gained popularity and electoral support as a result of those actions. In 1998, Hugo Chávez, who led a coup attempt in 1992, was elected president of Venezuela. In 2002, Lucio Gutiérrez, the leader of the military coup that deposed President Mahuad two years earlier, won the presidency in Ecuador. Not surprisingly, an erosion of democratic practice occurred during their administrations. President Fujimori won presidential reelections in 1995 (and, although accusations of fraud made the situation confusing, again in 2000) despite leading a coup against Congress in 1992. Powerful actors and significant segments of public opinion accepted the military ousting of presidents in Ecuador in 2000, Venezuela in 2002, and Honduras in 2009.

Second, several presidents have attacked and undermined opposition parties as legitimate mechanisms of representation (Mayorga 2006; Tanaka 2006). Antiparty politics has been present since the early days of the third wave of democratization – as illustrated by Presidents Alberto Fujimori in Peru and, to a lesser extent, Fernando Collor in Brazil (Kenney 1998). However, several leaders in the early twenty-first century dismantled the existing party system (e.g., Hugo Chávez in Venezuela, Rafael Correa in Ecuador, Evo Morales in Bolivia, and Alvaro Uribe in Colombia). The rise of antiparty politicians – especially in the case of former coup leaders – often spells troubles for democracy. Whatever the flaws of a particular party and the shortcomings of a particular party system, parties remain an indispensable mechanism of representation in democratic politics.

Third, some presidents have also displayed an instrumental attitude toward competitive elections and independent institutions such as the legislature and the courts, respecting them when they served their goals but undermining them when they constrained their objectives. In the 1980s and the 1990s, most presidents with a limited normative commitment to democracy were on the right of the political spectrum (e.g., Joaquín Balaguer in the Dominican Republic, León Febres Cordero in Ecuador, and Alberto Fujimori in Peru). By contrast, in the 2000s, several leftist candidates with ambivalent attitudes toward democracy made successful runs at the presidency. Some of these leaders disdained representative democracy and espoused participatory democracy. The presumed trade-off between representation and participation sometimes operated as a justification to dismantle institutional veto players, centralize decision making in the executive branch, and legitimize semi-democratic rule through popular mobilization (Coppedge 2005; Kornblith 2005).

Given the results of the analysis in Table 8.2, weak normative commitments to democracy at the present may not have an immediate impact on the regime, but will have long-term consequences for the quality of democracy in Latin America. Because committed actors make considerable efforts at building strong institutions, their normative preferences have enduring effects for the operation of competitive regimes. The main risk created by eroding normative preferences among some Latin American leaders may not be an immediate breakdown of competitive regimes, but a persistent trap of low-quality institutions.

The Limit of International Support for Democracy

International actors and transnational dissemination have reinforced de-radicalization and more favorable attitudes toward democracy since 1978. However, the contribution of international factors to the wave of democratization also showed important limits in the 2000s. These limits emerged from the combination of three factors: a decline in commitment to democracy among some influential actors in the region; the constraints of international organizations, which are able to condemn episodes of democratic breakdown but find it difficult to confront subtler forms of democratic erosion; and the dissemination of domestic practices and exemplars that eroded competitive regimes rather than strengthening them.

During the 2000s, hemispheric support for democracy waned slightly. In the aftermath of the terrorist attacks in the United States in 2001, the George W. Bush administration focused more on terrorism and less on democracy building in Latin America than any other U.S. administration since President Reagan's first term (1981–85) (see Figure 3.7 in Chapter 3). The U.S. government had an equivocal attitude toward the April 2002 coup against Venezuelan President Hugo Chávez, initially tacitly condoning the coup. The United States also supported the ouster of Haitian President Jean Bertrand Aristide in 2004, but the implications of this episode for democracy are harder to assess because the ousted administration already showed authoritarian tendencies after Aristide took office in 2001.

International forces, crucial to explain the emergence and consolidation of the third wave of democratization, have limited influence to prevent democratic erosion in the absence of a full-blown military coup. Regional responses to the ousting of Paraguayan President Fernando Lugo in 2012 clearly illustrate this point. Several South American leaders attempted to "stretch" the concept of a coup to cover the impeachment of President Lugo under this rubric, and the members of Mercosur suspended Paraguay. Yet the OAS and the United States declined to act. Not surprisingly in the absence of a broader coalition of international actors determined to thwart Lugo's removal, Mercosur's action did little to undermine the Liberal administration that replaced Lugo in office.

Most Latin American countries sustained a common front in order to condemn the open breakdown of competitive regimes. Activist networks, often supported by governments, helped change the region-wide discourse and norms regarding human rights. A full reversal of these propitious developments is highly unlikely in the foreseeable future. The formal norms that the OAS instituted between 1991 (Resolution 1080) and 2001 (the Democratic Charter) remain fully in place. In 2009, for the first time since the adoption of the Democratic Charter, the OAS suspended a member country in response to the coup that ousted President Manuel Zelaya of Honduras. The international community coherently backed this response. The United States suspended military aid to Honduras, the World Bank and the Inter-American Development Bank suspended new credit lines, and several Latin American countries and the European Union withdrew their ambassadors to the country.

The Honduran coup illustrates the deeper challenge confronted by international actors at the end of the third wave of democratization. In spite of the united international front and the consistent response, the OAS could not overcome the Honduran leaders' resistance to allow President Zelaya to return to office. The opposition adamantly claimed that President Zelaya had violated the constitution by trying to overturn a constitutional ban on presidential reelection. Zelaya had repeatedly defied the Supreme Electoral Tribunal, Congress, and the Supreme Court, which had declared his proposal for a referendum to call for a constitutional assembly to be illegal. Honduran elites resented that international actors had remained silent as the president moved forward with his plan against the will of all other institutions.

The OAS's capacity to deal with presidents who win relatively free and fair elections but subsequently undermine democracy is very limited, especially if those leaders command substantial support domestically and regionally. The OAS can act decisively when unambiguous events such as a military coup or overt electoral fraud take place – and even then only to the extent that member countries widely support such action. It is unable, however, to muster the high degree of consensus needed to challenge presidents who enjoy domestic popularity and the support of a substantial number of presidents in the region, even if those presidents flagrantly undermine or bypass important democratic institutions (Legler, Lean, and Boniface 2007; McCoy 2006; Policzer 2003).

Regional dissemination has acted not only to motivate transitions and to dissuade breakdowns (as documented in Chapter 4) during the 1980s and the 1990s, but also to spread new patterns of democratic erosion in more recent years. Ambitious incumbents have learned that loyal constitutional assemblies provide a veneer of democratic legitimacy to the dissolution of an adversarial Congress, that supreme courts can be dominated by expanding the number of justices, that antiparty politics can be a popular strategy to neutralize the opposition, and that referendums may help overturn term limits. Unfortunately, their opponents have also learned that insurrectional strategies intended to create presidential instability sometimes work as a blunt instrument against presidential hegemony.

CONCLUSION

After the great transformation of the 1978–95 period, Latin America continued evolving in a slightly more democratic direction. The period since the mid-1990s has been characterized by stable competitive regimes and by stable underlying levels of democracy despite poor governing performance from the 1980s until 2002 in most countries, significant instability in the presidency, and occasional attempts to establish presidential domination. From a long-term perspective, the biggest surprise in Latin America is not that democracy has had serious shortcomings, but that it has survived. To a degree that is without any historical precedent until 1990, Latin America today is a region of competitive regimes.

In the 2000s, change in the independent variables at the core of our theory has been slightly negative, with adverse effects on regime outcomes in only a few countries so far. It would be premature – indeed, a downright folly – to proclaim the definitive triumph of democracy in Latin America, but dictatorship is much less pervasive than ever before. Full-fledged dictatorship has virtually disappeared for the time being, with little prospect that it will return in the foreseeable future.

The main weaknesses of competitive regimes in the post-1977 era have involved the third dimension in our definition of democracy: respect for civil liberties and political rights. This shortcoming has kept many competitive regimes at relatively low *levels* of democracy (Figure 8.2). We have argued in this chapter that instances of democratic stagnation partly reflect the absence of a prior history of normative commitments to democracy. When political actors before 1978 embraced democratic ideals, they invested efforts in the development of democratic institutions such as political parties, independent courts, and professional security forces. Such institutions constituted the democratic infrastructure that allowed for a higher level of democracy after 1978.

In other countries, by contrast, an erosion of our third dimension of democracy has triggered a negative *trend* in democratization. Negative trends in democratization have been particularly acute in countries where presidents consistently attempted to concentrate power, undermining opposition parties and independent institutions with potential to hold them accountable. In Venezuela, Nicaragua, and – to a lesser degree – Bolivia and Ecuador, presidents with somewhat radical agendas have attempted to reshape regime coalitions by weakening parties from the earlier periods of democracy and using state resources to help create new actors. In this sense, they have followed an old script in Latin American politics by which presidents with radical agendas dramatically alter the balance of power in their own favor. In the contemporary cases, favorable international conditions have prevented full-fledged breakdowns but have been ineffective at preventing democratic erosions. In these cases, government radicalism and the creation of hegemonic coalitions have driven the erosion of democracy in the short run.

Previous chapters showed that conventional theories of regime change provide limited theoretical insights on the reasons leading to the wave of democratization that transformed Latin America since 1978. In the same vein, the analysis of radicalization, normative attitudes toward democracy, and the dissemination of preferences and values in the regional arena are essential to understanding the challenges that Latin American competitive regimes will confront in the future.

9

Rethinking Theories of Democratization in Latin America and Beyond

We began this book because we wanted to understand regime survival and fall in twentieth-century Latin America. As we studied these issues, we developed doubts about many theoretical approaches to understanding political regimes. It became essential to engage in a broader effort to theorize about the rise and fall of democracies and dictatorships.

Therefore, we developed a theory to explain the survival or fall of democracies and dictatorships. Starting from assumptions about how actors are constituted and what motivates them to join regime coalitions, we deductively derived five hypotheses about regime survival or fall. We particularly drew on three literatures: (1) transitions, breakdowns, and the survival of political regimes; (2) international factors in regime change and survival; and (3) the impact of ideas and beliefs on political outcomes. But we go beyond most of the existing work in these literatures by articulating an integrated theory and testing it in new ways. We believe that this theory is more realistic than competing theories; that there are benefits to systematizing it as a theory; and that it explains regime change and survival in twentieth-century Latin America better than alternative theoretical explanations.

This chapter undertakes three main tasks. First, we summarize our theoretical arguments and contributions. Our theory is based on more realistic microfoundations than most alternatives, and it has stronger empirical support. In addition, we devised an original research strategy to test hypotheses about actors across a much broader range of countries and time than previous actor-based theories. We also articulate our contributions to the literatures on actors' normative regime preferences, their policy radicalism or moderation, and international influences on regime outcomes.

Second, we briefly argue that the theory could fruitfully be extended beyond Latin America. As examples of this potential, we claim that prominent analyses of the breakdowns of democracy in Spain (1936) and Germany (1933) and of the transition to democracy in Spain (1977) are fully consistent with our approach.

We then use the Latin American experience and some broader evidence to reflect on the theoretical approaches commonly employed to understand the emergence and fall of democracies and dictatorships. We argue that the Latin American experience in the twentieth century is not consistent with modernization theory, class theories, works based on economic performance, mass political culture approaches, works based on formal institutions, and theories that strongly emphasize leadership and agency. We do not question all the results that have stemmed from these theoretical approaches, but the evidence in this book suggests modifications, boundaries, and nuances to these theories.

RETHINKING REGIME SURVIVAL AND CHANGE

We offer an alternative theoretical framework with more realistic microfoundations than existing theories. In agreement with Coppedge (2012) and Munck (2001), we believed that it could be fruitful to articulate a theory that makes explicit how we conceptualize the actors and what drives their behavior. Articulating how to conceptualize the actors, making explicit assumptions about what motivates them, and linking different levels of analysis (actors and coalitions at the country level, as well as international forces) integrates different elements in potentially useful ways. Hypotheses that could otherwise seem ad hoc instead are grounded in the theory.

Our theory integrates the analysis of actors' normative preferences about political regimes and policy moderation or radicalism in an explicitly articulated way rather than just presenting discrete hypotheses. Our primary contribution is not the discrete hypotheses, but rather the theory and the testing of it.

Likewise, we followed many works that established the empirical importance of international factors in regime change and survival, but with few exceptions, this work did not integrate the findings about international factors into a theory of regime change and survival. In order to advance understanding of how international forces and influences in democratization function, we concluded that it would be useful to connect domestic and international factors into a theory.

A second contribution of this book is our effort to test an actor-based theory of political regimes across a wide time period and over a sizable number of countries (twenty), using both quantitative and qualitative tests. Actors make history, although structures, cultures, and formal rules of the game condition those actors. Many authors have enriched the understanding of democratic transitions and breakdowns through case studies, usually using one or a small number of countries or through inductive generalizations such as those presented by Linz (1978b) and O'Donnell and Schmitter (1986). The work in this qualitative tradition has bumped up against some limits. How can we go beyond case studies and examine how far in time and space these insights travel? How can we aggregate and test the knowledge built through these case studies? How can we test hypotheses about actors across a broader range of cases?

To build on insights of previous studies and to test them, we integrated some hypotheses through a theory and then coded actors in the twenty Latin American countries for each presidential administration from 1944 to 2010. This endeavor required developing clear and explicit coding rules, ensuring consistency across different coders, and undertaking substantial historical research on political regimes and actors in the twenty Latin American countries. In order to test hypotheses about the impact of actors' preferences on regime outcomes, it was essential to actually look at actors' preferences rather than using inadequate aggregate proxies. The coding of actors enabled us to test hypotheses about radicalism and actors' normative preferences with greater validity, and much greater extension across time and space, than we otherwise would have been able to. This kind of historical qualitative coding grounded in explicitly articulated coding rules could be useful for other research projects.

International Actors and Regime Outcomes

Prior to 1986, theoretical works on regime change that emphasized the role of political factors focused largely, and usually exclusively, on domestic processes. Research beginning with Stepan (1986) and Whitehead (1986b) established that this traditional approach had neglected international influences. Over the last twenty-five years, a substantial body of literature has emphasized international influences in regime outcomes.

Our book adds to the literature that has shown that it is essential to examine regional political and ideological trends, the policy of hegemons, and the interconnection between domestic and transnational actors. Transnational trends and actors profoundly influence domestic regime outcomes. It is impossible to understand regime dynamics exclusively in terms of the cumulative effect of isolated political processes in individual countries. What happens in one country affects others. Moreover, developments among transnational and international actors affect political regimes in multiple countries.

We drew on many insights from this literature, but only a few works in this field are richly theoretical, and none integrated their emphasis on international factors into a theory of regime change and survival.[1] Our treatment of this issue added to the existing literature on international influences in democratization in four ways. First, we incorporated international influences into a theory of regime change that links domestic and international factors. Second, we quantitatively disentangled different international effects (U.S. policy toward authoritarian and democratic regimes in Latin America, the regional political environment, and the average world level of democracy) more than most previous work has.

---

[1] The excellent work of Levitsky and Way (2010) is a partial exception, but their dependent variable is different from ours. They analyzed whether competitive authoritarian regimes that existed in the early 1990s became democratic or remained authoritarian subsequently.

Third, our analysis in Chapters 4 and 7 documented the dynamic consequences of international influences. International effects not only operate across countries; they also sustain democratization trends over time. Regional influences affect domestic actors in individual countries, and those actors in turn refract those influences back into the regional arena. Waves of democratization as well as counterwaves of authoritarianism are hard to explain without understanding such dynamic effects.

Fourth, this literature has not adequately theorized the mechanisms by which international actors influence regime outcomes. International actors may influence some regime outcomes directly, but their effects are often mediated by other variables. In Figures 2.1 and 7.3, international actors influence domestic actors' attitudes toward democracy and dictatorship, their policy preferences, and their political resources. These variables in turn shape domestic actors' decisions about which regime coalition to join and how many resources those coalitions have.

International actors can influence regime outcomes by (1) generating policy preferences and attitudes about dictatorship and democracy that disseminate across country borders; (2) creating demonstration effects; (3) swaying domestic actors' decisions to join one of the competing regime coalitions; (4) providing resources to domestic actors and thereby influencing the power of the two competing regime coalitions; (5) joining one of the competing regime coalitions (e.g., the Catholic Church) and thereby swaying the regime outcome; and (6) undertaking a military invasion that topples or preserves the political regime.

We also emphasized that there are limits to the explanatory power of international variables. International actors usually exercise their influence indirectly, by affecting domestic actors' calculus of policy benefits under the competing regime coalitions and their normative preferences about the political regime. They explain change over time better than change across countries at a given point in time, and in Latin America they have infrequently been the main cause of a regime change. Moreover, international support does little to enhance the quality of democracy in contexts where it is low. The international community has devised mechanisms to deal with overt attempts to impose authoritarian rule, but it is ill equipped to deal with more subtle or gradual authoritarian regressions.

Normative Preferences for Democracy and Dictatorship

Our emphasis on the central role of actors' normative preference for democracy or dictatorship in explaining regime outcomes theoretically resonates with works by Berman (1998), Capoccia (2005); Dahl (1971: 124–88), Levine (1973), Lijphart (1977), Linz (1978a, 1978b), and O'Donnell (1986: 15–18).[2]

[2] Few of these scholars argued that attitudes toward democracy affect its odds of survival, but they made related points. For example, Dahl (1971: 124–88) argued that activists' beliefs influenced regime outcomes. His discussion of beliefs included the legitimacy of polyarchy (pp. 129–40), which coincides with our focus on normative commitment to democracy. Lipset (1959: 90) claimed

We added to this literature in four ways. First, we brought together two bodies of literature that have been largely divorced from one another: work that emphasizes the impact of actors' beliefs on different political outcomes and the scholarship on political regimes. Little of the expanding literature on actors' beliefs focuses on regime outcomes (Berman 1998 is an exception), and little of the work on political regimes emphasizes the importance of actors' beliefs (Dahl 1971: 124–88, Linz 1978b, and Stepan 1971 are exceptions).

Second, we tested arguments about the impact of actors' normative preferences on regime survival or fall in new ways. The coding of 1,460 actors across 290 presidential administrations in Latin America from 1944 to 2010 enabled us to undertake a more extensive test of the impact of actors' beliefs on regime outcomes than any previous work. The qualitative analysis in Chapters 5 and 6 enabled us to look at causal mechanisms intensively.

Third, we confronted in new ways some challenges that causal claims about normative preferences must address (see the discussion in Chapter 2). Other scholars have devised strategies for assessing the causal impact of beliefs in qualitative small-N studies. We add to this discussion by confronting these challenges for an intermediate number of countries over a long period of time. Our strategy includes devising careful coding rules to distinguish between sincere and strategically stated preferences and to ensure a clear separation between the independent and dependent variables; undertaking statistical tests for reverse causality; looking at reverse causality and examining causal mechanisms in the qualitative case studies; ensuring that normative preferences are not reducible to structural or broader cultural variables; and verifying in the qualitative case studies that actors' regime choices cannot be readily explained by their material gains.

Fourth, we added to the discussion of why actors' normative preferences sometimes change. Actors' preferences are not static (Bowles 1998), but social scientists have not often systematically addressed why they change.

We do not claim that democracy emerges or stabilizes because political actors have the "right values." Actors derive procedural utility from political regimes (Frey et al. 2004), and they measure the performance of incumbent regimes against their normative preferences. If actors are normatively committed to democracy, they are willing to tolerate disappointing policy outcomes that might tip uncommitted actors to join the authoritarian coalition. Actors that are committed to democracy are less likely to understand policy failures as a *regime* failure. Instead, they might accept policy failures as a consequence of negative legacies inherited from a previous regime, of negative trends in a country's terms of trade, of a poor leader who can be replaced through the democratic process, of a difficult time in the world economy, or of policies that are not tightly conditioned by the political regime and therefore might not change even if the regime

that citizen beliefs in democratic legitimacy help protect the regime from the destabilizing consequences of low effectiveness (i.e., poor performance).

changed. Given this reasoning, a change of regime would not necessarily produce better policy outcomes (Linz 1988; Remmer 1996). A normative preference to democracy extends actors' time horizons.

It is impossible to understand regime fall and survival in Latin America without examining changing normative views about democracy and dictatorship. For example, the Cuban revolution inspired a generation of revolutionary struggle in the region based on the belief that socialist revolution was desirable and possible, with negative consequences for democracy including a powerful counterreaction from conservative forces, leading to many military coups. Similarly, the embracing of liberal democracy as an ideal by actors across the political spectrum in the 1980s and the 1990s facilitated the establishment and survival of competitive regimes in bad economic times.

Radicalism and Moderation

Actors' radicalism or moderation is another important determinant of regime outcomes. Greater radicalism makes it more difficult to sustain a competitive regime. This argument builds on but refines the insights of Bermeo (1990, 1997, 2003), Figueiredo (1993), Przeworski (1991), Sani and Sartori (1983), Santos (1986), and Sartori (1976), among others. We modify this literature by how we conceptualize and define the continuum from moderation to radicalism. Whereas Sartori (1976) focused exclusively on ideological distance among actors, we define radicalism as policy positions toward the left/right pole in combination with urgency to achieve these positions in the short to medium term where these positions do not represent the status quo or with an intransigent defense of these positions where these positions represent the status quo. Although we build on Sartori's insights, his formulation overstates the destabilizing effects of polarization on competitive regimes when leftist or rightist actors perceive their projects as long term.

Sartori's formulation also misses the deleterious impact of actors that are not extreme in ideological terms, yet whose policy impatience coupled with policy preferences toward the left or right of center makes them threatening to other actors and contributes to regime breakdown. Chapter 5 discussed two somewhat radical actors par excellence: Juan Perón in the period from 1946 to 1970 and Argentina's labor unions from 1955 through 1976. Although most unions were not ideologically extremist, they combined policy preferences to the left of center (statist, nationalistic, pro-union, etc.) with considerable policy impatience, as manifested by factory takeovers, general strikes, and repeated willingness to support military coups to achieve policy gains. Similarly, although Perón rejected socialism, his confrontational discourse and behavior, his somewhat left-of-center policies, and his willingness to run roughshod over the opposition in order to achieve his policy goals made him a somewhat radical and deeply polarizing figure.

The analysis of radicalism poses questions for bargaining models of policy making and regime change. Conventional representations of impatience assume positive payoffs and thus identify a first-mover advantage: impatient actors are willing to accept a discounted offer today rather than wait until tomorrow (Rubinstein 1982; Sutton 1986). Our historical analysis of radical actors in Latin America identified a very different pattern of behavior that calls for a different formal setup (Primo 2002). If the incumbent regime promises to deliver the player's ideal policy in the future but demands some policy loss or patience today, a radical actor will endure large immediate loses and may prefer to gamble on an alternative regime. In this sense, radical players display a behavior inclined toward risk (Kahneman and Tversky 1979). This reverses the first-mover advantage, as governments need to offer additional benefits in the short run to appease radical players, who appear to be disloyal opponents exercising blackmail (Linz 1978b; Sartori 1976).

CAN THE THEORY TRAVEL BEYOND LATIN AMERICA?

For reasons outlined in Chapter 1, we focused on Latin America rather than a broader set of countries. This raises a question: Can the theory travel beyond Latin America? We cannot extend the theory empirically to other regions of the world here except by way of brief illustration, but two observations are in order.

First, our theory is compatible with several extant *theoretical* traditions in democratization studies. For example, it is compatible with Linz's (1978b) emphasis on orientations toward the democratic regime (loyal, semi-loyal, and disloyal oppositions); with O'Donnell and Schmitter's (1986) and Przeworski's (1991) delineation of actors into blocs depending on their orientation toward the political regime; and with Berman's (1998) argument that Social Democratic parties' programmatic beliefs strongly affected their behavior in interwar Sweden and Germany, which in turn affected the survival or breakdown of democracy in the 1930s. It is also compatible with the extensive literature that has documented international influences in regime outcomes. These compatibilities suggest that our theory can travel beyond Latin America.

In addition, analyses of many non–Latin American cases of breakdowns of competitive regimes, transitions from authoritarian rule to competitive regimes, stabilizations of authoritarian regimes, and democratic stabilizations are fully consistent with our theory. We illustrate this point by briefly indicating the strong compatibility of our theory with existing analyses of (1) the breakdown of democracy in Spain in 1936; (2) the breakdown of democracy in Germany in 1933; and (3) the stabilization of democracy in Spain after 1978.

Without using exactly the same concepts as we do, many scholars have argued that democracies broke down because actors had weak normative preferences for democracy or had normative preferences for dictatorship, or because radicalism made it impossible for some actors to be willing to abide by democracy. Most interpretations of the breakdown of democracy in Spain in the 1930s mesh with our theoretical approach. Casanova (2010) and Linz (1978a: 144, 151, 169) emphasized the negative impact of international influences, especially the rise of fascism in Germany and Italy, on Spanish democracy. No powerful actors had a steadfast normative preference for democracy (Casanova 2010: 95, 111, 116, 122; Linz 1978a: 149, 160–68, 180–81; S. Payne 2006: 41–45, 346–47, 350–54[3]). When this is the case, especially in a polarized high-stakes environment, actors easily turn against democracy. Powerful radical actors from the far left to the far right were willing to use violence to pursue political ends (Casanova 2010; Linz 1978a: 145, 153–54, 157–58, 187–94; Malefakis 1996: 644–46; S. Payne 2006; Preston 2006: 53–64). They were decisive in the spiral of violence, revenge, and hatred that led to the breakdown. Right-wing radicalism fueled left-wing radicalism, and vice versa. No actors were willing to make significant policy sacrifices in order to save democracy. By the time Franco launched his coup in July 1936, several powerful actors on the right had a normative preference for dictatorship (Casanova 2010: 124, 137).

Many scholars have also analyzed the German breakdown of democracy in 1933 along the lines that are fully consistent with our theory. Some extremely radical actors, no actors with solid normative preference for democracy, several (including the Nazis, the Communists, and some traditional right-wing parties) with a normative preference for dictatorship, and an inhospitable international political environment – all in the context of a severe economic crisis – led to the breakdown. The German Social Democrats (SPD), the largest party during much of the Weimar Republic, embraced some radical policy preferences including orthodox Marxism (Berman 1998: 77–95, 123–31, 180–98). They did not have a clear normative preference for democracy (Berman 1998: 85–88, 130–31, 180–81). Berman argues that if the SPD had been more flexible, less radical, and more oriented toward preserving democracy, it could have undercut the Nazis' appeal. Chancellor Heinrich Brüning (1930–32) and the Center Party were willing to sacrifice democracy in order to achieve other policy goals (Berman 1998: 187; Weitz 2007: 122–23). The Communists and the Nazis had very radical policy preferences and a normative preference for different kinds of totalitarian dictatorship. The rightist German People's Party (*Deutsche Volkspartei*) was somewhat hostile to democracy, and the German National People's Party (*Deutschnationale Volkspartei*) combined radical right-wing policy preferences with a normative preference for authoritarian and monarchical rule (Lepsius 1978: 37, 43, 45; Weitz 2007: 92–97). The *Landvolkbewegung* was a right-wing peasant movement with radical policy preferences and antidemocratic normative preferences (Lepsius 1978: 53–54). The army and the Protestant and Catholic churches were hostile to democracy (Weitz 2007: 115–21).

A third case that has often been analyzed in ways entirely consistent with our theory is the stabilization of democracy in Spain after 1978. Many conditions

---

[3] Echoing our terminology, S. Payne (2006: 354) wrote that "[m]ost major actors had limited or no commitment to democracy."

favored democratic consolidation in Spain, but this favorable outcome was by no means a foregone conclusion (Agüero 1995: 18–22; Linz and Stepan 1996: 87–115). Democratic consolidation was facilitated by strong support from the European Union (Linz and Stepan 1996: 113). De-radicalization of the Socialist Party (Tussell 2005: 285, 327), the Communist Party, the labor movement (Fishman 1990b), and the right (Share 1986) also facilitated democratic survival. By the time of the transition in 1978, actors with a normative preference for dictatorship were weak (G. Alexander 2002: 138–81). Finally, by 1978, most actors either already had a normative preference for democracy or quickly developed one. This includes the right (G. Alexander 2002: 138–81); Prime Minister Adolfo Súarez (1976–81) and his party, the Union of the Democratic Center (*Unión de Centro Democrático*, UCD) (Share 1986: 86–153); and labor (Fishman 1990b). The fact that most powerful actors have had an unambiguous normative preference for democracy and the highly supportive international political environment enabled the democratic coalition to thwart difficult challenges including the Basque terrorist organization ETA (*Euskadi Ta Askatasuna*, Basque Homeland and Freedom), a military that had strong *golpista* factions until 1981 (Agüero 1995), and a bruising depression in recent years.

ALTERNATIVE THEORIES OF DEMOCRATIZATION

Throughout this book, especially in Chapters 4 through 6, we have compared our theory with alternatives, but without an extended discussion of the implications of our results for these alternative theories. In this section, we examine the implications of our analysis and empirical results for modernization theory, class theories, work on the impact of economic performance on regime fall or survival, mass culture theory, work on the impact of formal institutions on regime fall or survival, and work that strongly emphasizes political agency and leadership.

Some of our observations in this section focus on inconsistencies between the evidence for Latin America and broader research findings. Other arguments hold beyond Latin America. For example, our criticisms of class and mass cultural theories of democratization, while initially inspired by the Latin American experience, go beyond it.

Modernization Theory

One of the most influential theoretical approaches to studying democracy is modernization theory, which was famously formulated by Lipset (1959, 1960: 27–63) and subsequently empirically supported by many other scholars.[4] Modernization theory claims that more economically developed countries are

---

[4] The second part of Lipset's classic (1959) article made a different claim about the effects of regime legitimacy and efficacy that anticipated some points in our book.

more likely to be democratic, and proposes causal mechanisms to explain this relationship.

Lipset argued that wealthier countries are more likely to be democratic for several reasons. Higher education, which is associated with greater wealth, promotes more tolerant worldviews. Greater wealth tends to reduce political extremism and to increase the size of the middle class, which he claimed tended to be more prodemocratic than the poor. In developed countries, the lower strata tended to have more reformist political perspectives (Lipset 1959: 83), and the upper strata tended to have more democratic values (Lipset 1959: 83–84).

Many subsequent authors have demonstrated that higher levels of development are strongly associated with a greater likelihood of democracy (Bollen 1980, 1983; Bollen and Jackman 1985a,1985b; Burkhart and Lewis-Beck 1994; Coppedge 1997; Dahl 1971: 62–80; Diamond 1992; Epstein et al. 2006; Huntington 1984, 1991: 59–72; Jackman 1973; Lipset et al. 1993; Londregan and Poole 1996; Przeworski et al. 2000).[5] Recent work has demonstrated that the likelihood of democratic breakdowns diminishes and the likelihood of democratic transitions increases at higher per capita income (Epstein et al. 2006).

However, the seemingly robust association between income and democracy does not hold for Latin America for the lengthy period from 1945 to 2005 (Landman 1999; Mainwaring and Pérez-Liñán 2003; O'Donnell 1973). During this period, competitive regimes were as vulnerable to breakdown at a higher level of development as at lower levels (Tables 4.4 and 4.5). The level of development likewise had no impact on the probability of a transition from authoritarianism to a competitive regime (Tables 4.2 and 4.3).[6] As we discussed in Chapters 5 and 6, modernization theory does not go very far toward explaining regime outcomes in Argentina and El Salvador.

Building democracy in poor countries *is* difficult, and yet as the experience of poor countries in Latin America shows, the obstacles are not insurmountable. We reject Lipset's (1960: 40) argument that a certain level of development is a requisite for democracy or that "a high level of education ... comes close to being a necessary" condition for democracy. Costa Rica was a relatively poor country with a relatively low level of education at the inauguration of its competitive regime in 1949, with a per capita GDP of $1,546 in 2000 constant dollars, below the mean value of $1,846 for our entire dataset. Yet this regime has now lasted for more than six decades, becoming the longest-lasting democracy *ever* outside countries that today are part of the advanced industrial democracies.

---

[5] Acemoglu et al. (2008) argue that using a proper model specification, the level of development does not affect regime outcomes across all countries for which data was available. They advocate fixed effects models.

[6] In model 4.3.3 with the Gini index of income inequality, a higher per capita GDP seemed, against conventional expectations, to lower the probability of a transition. However, because of the large number of gaps in the data on income inequality, the number of observations fell from 576 to 222. Given the consistency of the results across many model specifications with 576 observations, it seems very likely that the result in model 4.3.3 stems from the reduced number of observations.

A low per capita income did not preclude building what has become a high-quality democracy. Competitive regimes have also endured at fairly low levels of development in countries such as Ecuador since 1979 and Nicaragua and El Salvador since 1984, or (a non–Latin American example) India from 1947 until Indira Gandhi's declaration of a state of emergency from 1975 until 1977, and then again since 1977.

We do not claim that modernization theory is wrong, but the relationship between the level of development and democracy has been far from determinate in Latin America until a high level of development makes radicalization unlikely. At a high level of development, democracy has historically never broken down (Przeworski et al. 2000; Epstein et al. 2006). It therefore seems that a high level of development is a sufficient condition to ensure the survival of a competitive political regime. It is possible, as Przeworski (2006) suggests, that the reason is that at high levels of development, few actors are radical, and radical actors are isolated. If this argument is correct, then the core causal mechanism linking high income to democracy is de-radicalization. Below that high level of wealth, for Latin America, the relationship between the level of development and democracy has been overpowered by the political factors to which we call attention.

High levels of poverty and glaring inequalities provide grist for radicalism and dampen the likelihood of strong normative commitments to democracy. Yet as the examples of the southern cone suggest, this effect is far from linear. As Lipset (1959: 90–91) himself recognized, poverty and inequality do not directly produce radicalization and do not automatically suppress normative preferences for democracy (see also Dahl 1971: 81–104; Moore 1978; Portes 1971; Powers 2001; Weyland 2002).

Class, Inequality, and Democratization

The Latin American evidence and broader evidence are largely at odds with class theories of democratization. These theories see some social classes as being consistently prodemocratic when democracy is possible and others as consistently supporting authoritarian regimes when stable dictatorship is feasible. The most prominent class theories include Acemoglu and Robinson (2006), Boix (2003), Moore (1966),[7] and Rueschemeyer, Stephens, and Stephens (1992).

Rueschemeyer et al. (1992) argued that prospects for democracy rest on the balance of power among social classes. In their general theoretical statements, they claimed that the working class is the agent of democratization par excellence (p. 8). Therefore, a strong working class is favorable to democracy. Conversely,

---

[7] Moore (1966) argued that a historical coalition of a strong landed aristocracy, a relatively weak bourgeoisie, and a modernizing state produced fascism; the combination of a recalcitrant aristocracy and an absolutist state triggered socialist revolutions; and the hegemony of the bourgeoisie over the aristocracy, the agricultural labor force, and the state led to the establishment of liberal democracy. See J. S. Valenzuela (2001) for a compelling critique.

they saw the landed elite (pp. 60–61) and the bourgeoisie as usually favorable to the status quo before democracy and as resistant to democratization.

Acemoglu and Robinson (2006) and Boix (2003) assume that classes try to maximize income and choose a political regime accordingly. They posit that democracy will economically benefit the poor and redistribute away from the rich. They conclude that the poor favor democracy over any nonrevolutionary authoritarian regime, whereas the wealthy concede democracy only to avoid revolution. The wealthy have more to lose with democracy in more inegalitarian societies. According to Boix, the rich block the emergence of democracy in unequal societies unless the cost of repression is high, but they accept democracy if capital mobility prevents high taxation.

Although they differ in many ways,[8] these class theories share four assumptions: (1) classes are the most important political actors; (2) members of social classes value political regimes exclusively for economic reasons; (3) democracies redistribute income in favor of the poor; and (4) given this outcome, the working class and the poor are strong supporters of democratization while the bourgeoisie or the rich concede democracy only reluctantly.[9] In addition, Acemoglu and Robinson (2006) and Boix (2003) assume that (5) high inequality reinforces resistance among the rich, making the establishment and survival of democracy unlikely.

These assumptions are not consistently realistic, and shortcomings of class theories result. First, classes as Boix and Acemoglu and Robinson conceptualize them (i.e., the poor and the rich) do not form cohesive political actors. Members of the same class are divided by religious, national, ethnic, and other value questions. These divisions make it difficult to act cohesively, and rich and poor face daunting collective action problems (Olson 1965). Moreover, in the struggles for and against democracy in most countries, political parties, militaries, and other nonclass organizations are key actors. This is clear in our analysis of Argentina (Chapter 5) and El Salvador (Chapter 6). The history of both countries involved important class-related actors. But in both countries, political parties, militaries, churches at some periods, and guerrillas in others were powerful actors whose behavior was not reducible to class interests. Throughout the region, actors other than classes have been powerful.

Second, class theories assume that the only issue that drives political conflict in all countries is income distribution and resource allocation. Classes prefer

---

[8] Rueschemeyer and colleagues and Moore employ class categories, and they delve into the historical development of democracy in different parts of the world. Acemoglu and Robinson (2006) and Boix (2003) base their analysis on income categories (poor, middle sector, rich) rather than class understood structurally, and Boix's evidence is largely quantitative. For Boix, the relationship between inequality and democracy is linear: more inequality generates a lower probability of democracy. In contrast, Acemoglu and Robinson posit an inverted-U-shape relationship; democratization is very unlikely at high or low levels of inequality.

[9] Rueschemeyer and colleagues make these assumptions in their general theoretical propositions, but their analysis of Latin America clearly breaks from the first and fourth.

political regimes for purely instrumental material reasons – to advance their economic interests. However, an extensive literature has argued otherwise (Haggard and Kaufman 2012). Again, it is difficult to understand the history of political regimes in Argentina (especially) or El Salvador as a battle exclusively over material goods.

As we have argued throughout this book, value divides about democracy and authoritarianism are not reducible to economic issues, and they often strongly influence regime outcomes (Berman 1998; Dahl 1971: 124–89; Ollier 2009; Viola 1982). So do conflicts over religion (Casanova 2010; Huntington 1996; Levine 1973; Linz 1991; Pérez-Díaz 1993; Stepan 2001; J. S. Valenzuela 2001), urban/rural and regional cleavages, nationalism (Linz 1997; Linz and Stepan 1996: 24–33; Stepan 1994, 2001: 181–212; 323–28; Stepan et al. 2011), and ethnicity (Diamond 1988; Rabushka and Shepsle 1972; Snyder 2000). Empirical analyses of post-Soviet countries in the 1990s underscored that citizens value democracy independently of economic results (Hofferbert and Klingemann 1999; Rose and Mishler 1996). In addition, international ideational currents – the Zeitgeist of an epoch – affect the survival and fall of political regimes. For most countries, it is impossible to understand the survival or fall of political regimes by looking exclusively at class conflict related to income distribution. A range of policy issues, not just economic distribution, affects regime outcomes (Haggard and Kaufman 2012). By emphasizing that actors do not join or defect from regime coalitions based exclusively on the regime's material payoffs, we are better able to understand the survival of competitive regimes in the third wave despite dismal economic performance in the 1980s, 1990s, and early 2000s.

Third, these class approaches rest on the questionable assumption that democracy is consistently good for the working class's material interests and that noncommunist authoritarian regimes are detrimental to the income of the poor. The empirical evidence however, is mixed, as our book and other works show. Huber and Stephens (2012) made a compelling argument for why competitive regimes, by allowing left parties to organize and gain office, may promote redistribution over the long run. They also documented that in the short run these effects are subject to constraints imposed by international factors (Chapters 6–7), and that Latin America has also experienced an authoritarian path to redistribution illustrated by Argentina and Brazil in the twentieth century (Chapter 4; Segura-Ubiergo 2007: chapter 2).

Whether we look at changes in real wages or income distribution, it is far from evident that Latin American workers have fared better materially under competitive regimes than under authoritarianism. Real wages fell in most countries after the establishment of competitive regimes in the third wave of democratization, including quite dramatically in Argentina after re-democratization in 1983. In Peru, the real urban minimum wage declined an astonishing 84 percent between 1980 and 1992. Real urban minimum wages fell drastically after the transitions to democracy in five of the six countries for which ECLAC reported data in 1992.[10] Conversely, real wages increased under many authoritarian regimes between 1945 and 1980. In the 1970s, real income improved at least 30 percent in all deciles of the Brazilian population under the military dictatorship. Real mean income for the poorest decile increased 50 percent from 1970 to 1980 (Skidmore 1988: 287).

For Latin America, the average currently existing competitive regime has not promoted income distribution in favor of the poor. For the seventeen countries for which data are available (all but Cuba, Haiti, and Nicaragua[11]), mostly from the World Bank inequality dataset, from the year of a transition to a competitive regime until 2010,[12] income distribution improved on average by a trivial 1.2 points (from 52.0 to 50.8) on the 100-point Gini index (weighting every country equally). Conversely, some populist and nationalist left-of-center (but not revolutionary) authoritarian regimes have redistributed income to the poor – a possibility that these works often neglect.[13]

The evidence beyond this book about the impact of regime type on income distribution and social policy is mixed. Huber and Stephens's (2012) analysis of eighteen Latin American countries between 1970 and 2007 suggests that a longer history of democracy may lead to greater investments in social programs and to a reduction in income inequality over time (chapter 5). On the other hand, Mulligan et al. (2004) show that on average, democracies do not spend more than dictatorships on social programs, that they tax less than dictatorships, and that they promote less income redistribution than dictatorships (p. 60). Bollen and Jackman (1985b) also showed that democracies are not more redistributive than dictatorships. Nelson (2007) reports converging findings about the impact of democracy on health and education. Democracies do not have demonstrably better results than dictatorships do in these social domains. Burkhart (1997) shows that democracies improve income distribution only at a fairly low level of democracy.

The fourth shortcoming of these class theories is that the empirical evidence to substantiate their claims about the relationship between class position and support for democracy is thin. Boix and Acemoglu and Robinson present little evidence to support the claim that the poor actually prefer democracy and have fought for it on a consistent basis. Rueschemeyer et al. (1992: 8) note that the

---

[10] ECLAC 1992, tables 6 and 7, pp. 44–45. ECLAC also reported data for urban real minimum wages for Rio de Janeiro and São Paulo, but did not give an average figure for Brazil. ECLAC 1995: 131–34, and ECLAC 1994: 127–28, also report figures for urban minimum wages. In most third-wave democracies, urban minimum wages fell after the transitions to competitive regimes.

[11] For Nicaragua, there are no data points close to 1984, the year of the transition to semi-democracy. For Cuba and Haiti, there are none whatsoever.

[12] For Colombia, Costa Rica, and Venezuela, no data were available for the transition years (1958, 1949, and 1959, respectively). We used the earliest available data points: 1970, 1961, and 1962, respectively.

[13] Along similar lines, Albertus (2011) showed that in Latin America, authoritarian regimes have undertaken more agrarian reform than democracies have.

Latin American cases do not fully conform to their general theory. R. Collier (1999: 33–76) argues that their theory does not work for many Latin American and Western European cases because elites and middle sectors rather than the working class were primarily responsible for establishing democracy.

The relationship between class and support for democracy is more mediated and less linear than class theories suggest. The historical evidence about which classes were more likely than others to support democratization is more mixed than class theorists claim (R. Collier 1999; Levitsky and Mainwaring 2006; J. S. Valenzuela 2001). In many cases, some sectors of the elite were at the forefront of democratization even in the absence of a credible revolutionary threat, and in some cases, the poor actively preferred a nonrevolutionary authoritarian regime to democracy.

Until recent decades, organized labor in most Latin American countries did not consistently support democratic regimes. As an illustration, in Argentina (Chapter 5), organized labor supported Peronism from 1945 on, notwithstanding its frequently authoritarian character. In 1962 and 1966, labor supported military coups against competitively elected governments. In Latin America, populist leaders with radical policy preferences and authoritarian proclivities often captured organized labor's support because of their promises or delivery of benefits for workers and their symbolic appeals to the poor (Germani 1974: 169–92, Lipset 1960: 87–126; Ostiguy 2009).

Rather than understanding democratization in terms of consistent democratic or authoritarian proclivities of class actors (Rueschemeyer et al. 1992) or of consistent first choice preferences that shift only if the first choice regime is not feasible (Boix 2003), we see classes as being *conditional* authoritarians and conditional democrats (Bellin 2000). As the Argentine case discussed in Chapter 5 showed – and our coding of actors in other countries confirmed – under some circumstances, organized labor will support authoritarian leaders, movements, parties, and regimes even if democracy is feasible. Whether labor supports democracy depends on (1) its normative preferences regarding the political regime and (2) whether it believes authoritarian or democratic leaders and parties better serve labor's policy goals. The fact that the working class does not consistently support democracy helps explain why the size of the working class had no impact on reducing the probability of democratic breakdowns in our quantitative analysis in Chapter 4 (Tables 4.4 and Tables 4.5).[14]

Voting patterns and public opinion surveys also show a mixed relationship between class position and support for democracy. For example, in Mexico, during the democratization process from 1988 to 1997, the poor and least educated solidly supported the PRI (the ruling authoritarian party). The middle and upper classes and the most educated were more likely than the poor to support the largest democratic opposition party, the PAN (Domínguez and

---

[14] A large working class was favorable to democratic transitions in the regressions in Table 4.4 but at most weakly favorable to transitions in Table 4.3.

McCann 1996: 99–100, 203–04; Klesner 2004: 103–07, 112, 116; Magaloni 1999: 228–31; 2006: 122–50; Magaloni and Moreno 2003: 268–69).

An analysis that sees the poor as the bearers of democracy and the rich as its opponents must also confront the fact that in public opinion surveys, respondents with lower income usually evince less democratic attitudes than those with higher income. In eleven of the nineteen Latin American countries included in the 2008 AmericasBarometer,[15] wealthier respondents displayed stronger pro-democracy attitudes (at $p < .05$) than poor respondents in response to the statement "Democracy has problems, but it is better than any other form of government."[16] Interestingly, in light of the 2009 coup, Honduras was the only country in which higher-income respondents gave less democratic answers. In the remaining seven countries, income did not have a statistically significant effect on responses to this question. The 2010 AmericasBarometer surveys confirmed this finding. The correlation between household income and support for democracy was positive and significant ($p < .05$) in fifteen of the nineteen countries, positive but insignificant in two cases (Brazil and Nicaragua), and negative but insignificant in only two countries (Bolivia and Honduras). The results of the bivariate correlations do not prove that poor citizens are generally less supportive of democracy, but they call into question a fundamental assumption of class theories of democratization.[17]

Fifth, most of the empirical evidence does not support the core claim that inequalities have a powerful impact on regime survival and change. Teorell (2010: chapter 3) finds no impact of inequality on democracy. According to Muller (1988: 61), the level of inequality had no impact on the probability of a democratic transition, although high inequalities made democracies more vulnerable to breakdown (pp. 61–65). Burkhart (1997) found that high inequality lowered the level of democracy (a different dependent variable than we use in this book), but the effect was modest.

The evidence in this book is consistent with these broader findings. For Latin America, income inequality had no statistically significant impact on the survival or fall of democracies or dictatorships (see Tables 4.3 and 4.5). According to some class theories, the deterioration of the already skewed income distributions during the 1980s and 1990s should have made competitive regimes more vulnerable and wealthy elites more resistant to democratization. In fact, competitive regimes

[15] The AmericasBarometer is conducted by the Latin American Public Opinion Project (LAPOP) at Vanderbilt University. All countries in our sample, with the exception of Cuba, were covered by the 2008 and 2010 waves of the project.

[16] Responses to the statement are captured by a seven-point scale, ranging from "Disagrees a lot" to "Agrees a lot." We ran a bivariate OLS regression for each country using this item as the dependent variable. The income variable is calibrated for local currency and coded using an eleven-point scale in all countries.

[17] In a study of mass attitudes in eight Latin American countries, Booth and Seligson (2009) found that household wealth is uncorrelated with support for core principles of democracy or demands for democracy, in statistical models that also control for educational levels (tables 4.3 and 7.1).

became far less susceptible to breakdown during the third wave. Even in the absence of a revolutionary threat, wealthy elites were critical actors in supporting democratization in many countries, including Chile in the nineteenth and early twentieth centuries (J. S. Valenzuela 1985, 2001), Brazil in the 1970s and 1980s (Cardoso 1986; L. Payne 1994), El Salvador in the late 1980s and early 1990s (Johnson 1993; Wood 2000a, 2000b; Chapter 6 in this book), and Mexico in the 1980s and 1990s. Bad income distribution did not prevent a large number of transitions to competitive regimes from occurring, and the further exacerbation of glaring inequalities did not lead to the breakdowns of competitive regimes after 1978.

Boix's (2003) own results provide weak support for the idea that better income equality increases the likelihood of transitions to democracy and decreases the likelihood of democratic breakdowns. In only one of four models for all countries (Model 3A) in his book did income distribution affect the likelihood of transitions to democracy at $p < .10$ (Boix 2003: 79–81). Income inequality had a significant impact on democratic breakdowns in three of the four models for all countries, but in one of the three (Model 1A), contrary to the theory, inequality facilitates democratic survival. Additional interactions of income inequality with other variables in the model do not provide unequivocal support for Boix's theory.

Boix qualifies his argument by asserting that high capital mobility (or high asset specificity) makes it easier for the rich to invest outside their country, and hence lowers the probability of major redistributive efforts. He argues that in contexts of high capital mobility, governments are forced to keep taxes low; otherwise, capital flight will result (pp. 12, 19, 25, 39). Because taxes are low, elite resistance to democracy will diminish.

In Latin America, however, increasing capital mobility after 1985 coincided with notable *increases* in tax collection in most countries. According to ECLAC data, between 1990 (the earliest data point) and 2010, total central government tax revenue increased substantially (at least 5 percent of GDP) in nine Latin American countries (Nicaragua, +14 percent; Bolivia, Ecuador, and Argentina, +10 percent; Colombia, +7 percent; Brazil and the Dominican Republic, +6 percent; Paraguay and El Salvador, +5 percent) under competitive regimes. In most other countries, tax revenue increased somewhat. Only in Venezuela (–7 percent) did central government tax revenue decrease at least 5 percent of GDP during this period of increasing capital mobility.[18] Therefore, for Latin America greater capital mobility did not reduce the capacity of democratic governments to collect taxes. A cross-regional comparison between Western Europe and Latin America further underscores the problematic nature of this argument. Both capital mobility *and* tax collection are higher in Western Europe than Latin America. Circa 2003, the average total tax revenue for fifteen EU countries was 41 percent of GDP, while according to 2005 estimates, nine Latin American countries had central government tax revenue of less than 15 percent

---

[18] ECLAC's data on central government tax revenue are online at http://www.eclac.org/estadisticas/

of GDP (ECLAC 2008). No Latin American democracy approached the level of the average EU country.

The impact of inequalities on democratic regime stability depends on what is going on in different countries at different times (Frey et al. 2004: 389–90).[19] In the 1990s, in times of deep economic crisis, poor people accepted the exacerbation of inequalities in order to achieve macroeconomic stability (Powers 2001; Stokes 2001; Weyland 2002).

We believe that our theory better interprets the survival and fall of democracies and dictatorships in and beyond Latin America than class theories. The main differences are as follows: (1) we view organizations, not classes, as the most important actors – some but not all organizations primarily defend class interests; (2) we assume that actors are interested in a broader range of policy outcomes than just material and distributive issues; conflicts over religion, ethnicity, and nationality, among others, influence regime outcomes; (3) we believe that many actors have normative preferences about the political regime in addition to policy preferences; (4) we situate our theory in an international context more than most class theories; and (5) we see the relationship between class and regime preference as highly conditional.

Economic Performance

Some authors have shown that democratic and authoritarian regimes are more likely to survive if their economic performance is better. Most of this literature is empirical and does not invoke strong theoretical claims about the relationship between economic performance and regime stability. We do not dispute the empirical assertions made by these authors. Among well-known works that peg democratic stability to economic performance are Gasiorowski (1995), Haggard and Kaufman (1995) and Lipset (1960: 64–70).[20]

The general theoretical proposition that government performance affects regime stability in developing countries is sensible. Consistent with this literature, we expected the regime's economic performance to affect actors' adhesion to the incumbent regime – but we expected this impact to be modest, especially in competitive regimes.

By the logic of our theory, poor economic performance creates a threat to the survival of democracy only if (1) some actors conclude that authoritarianism offers net policy advantages to them – that is, they believe they would be better

---

[19] Moore (1978: 41) comments that in popular perception, "a high degree of inequality may not only be acceptable but even regarded as very desirable, as long as in the end it somehow contributes to the social good as perceived and defined in that society."

[20] Lipset argued that regimes needed a combination of good performance and legitimacy. A reservoir of legitimacy can enable a democracy to remain stable despite poor performance. Thus, his was not a simplistic performance-based argument. See also Linz (1978b: 16–23) on the relationship between legitimacy and performance.

off under an authoritarian regime; (2) this net policy advantage is not offset by a normative commitment to democracy; and (3) the authoritarian coalition is powerful enough to consider overthrowing a democratic regime. Actors' decisions about whether to work to overthrow a competitive regime hinge on all of their policy preferences and their normative preferences about the political regime, as well as a strategic calculation about the odds of successfully subverting the regime. Democratic regimes can win support on bases other than regime performance (Linz 1988; Remmer 1996). Citizens do not necessarily attribute performance failures to the regime; they normally blame particular administrations or parties in office.

Consistent with our expectation, the most democratic period in the history of Latin America (since the mid-1980s), and the period with by far the highest-ever rate of survival of competitive regimes (since 1978), coincided with a prolonged period of dismal economic and social performance in most countries (1982–2002). The logic of our theory correctly predicts that actors' normative preferences for democracy, low radicalism, and strong regional support for democracy could protect competitive regimes in times of bad performance. Bad performance had adverse effects on democracy, but it has rarely led to regime breakdown in the post-1977 period.[21] For a generation, regime survival has not depended on economic performance, suggesting that the impact of bad economic performance on political regimes is mediated by citizen expectations, which vary over time; by the way political leaders do or do not politicize bad economic performance; and by actors' normative commitment to democracy.

In Latin America, the rate of economic growth had little or no impact on the survival of competitive (Table 4.4) or authoritarian regimes (Table 4.2). Inflation also had no impact on regime change (Tables 4.3 and 4.5). Competitive regimes have been vastly less vulnerable to breakdown since 1978 compared to 1945–77, even though the median regime's economic performance fell from solid in the earlier period to poor. The average per capita GDP growth rate of competitive regimes was 1.9 percent for the 1945–77 period and a meager 1.1 percent for the 1978–2005 period, and the mean inflation rate jumped from 19 percent in the earlier period to 257 percent in the later years. Yet the breakdown rate of these regimes was more than ten times greater (9.3 percent in the earlier period versus 0.8 percent in the post-1977 period).

The Latin American experience since 1978 shows that the impact of economic performance on regime survival is mediated by actors' understanding of what is possible in a given moment (i.e., their view of constraints and opportunities) and can be overcome by their normative attitudes about political regimes. Democracy in Latin America would be in better shape in many countries if

---

[21] There have been only six breakdowns since 1978: Bolivia in 1980; Peru in 1992; Haiti in 1991 and 1999; and Honduras and Venezuela in 2009. Because the Haitian regime of 1991 lasted only a few months before giving way to a coup before the end of the year, our regime classification registers only the other five breakdowns.

economic performance had been better during the third wave. Nevertheless, competitive regimes survived despite economic and social disappointments, a deterioration of public security, and rampant corruption in many countries. Although poor economic performance has weakened many competitive regimes, it has doomed few. Poor governing performance has bred citizen disaffection and paved the way to populist politicians with dubious democratic credentials, but it has rarely caused regime breakdowns during the third wave.

At some historical junctures, because of ideological currents, some actors might conclude that an authoritarian regime is more likely to be efficient and therefore more effective at fostering growth. This was the case in Argentina in 1965–66 (Chapter 5), when many actors concluded that democracy was inefficient and suboptimal despite the Illia government's respectable record in economic growth. However, even if government performance is deficient, actors might doubt that an authoritarian regime would be better for them. In the aftermath of bad economic performance and the accumulation of huge foreign debts under authoritarian regimes in the 1970s and early 1980s, citizens in most Latin American countries gave competitive regimes great leeway in managing the economy until the late 1990s (Powers 2001; Stokes 2001; Weyland 2002).

In many countries, citizens and elites had little reason to believe that a new round of authoritarianism would ease their economic troubles. The new competitive regimes inherited challenging and in several cases ruinous economic legacies. The dismal economic performance of these antecedent authoritarian regimes helps explain the disappearance of actors that have a normative preference for dictatorship and the high tolerance for poor economic performance under competitive regimes in most of Latin America from 1982 to 2002 (Powers 2001; Remmer 1996; Weyland 2002).

Assuming that some actors anticipate a net policy advantage under some form of authoritarian rule, policy preferences may still be offset by a normative commitment to democracy (Frey et al. 2004). Even where past achievements have not built a cushion to buffer democracies from poor performance, good economic performance might not be necessary for regime stability at some historical moments. Actors' policy expectations and their normative preferences about the regime mediate the relationship between government performance and regime stability. Actors that are committed to democracy have a reservoir of goodwill toward competitive regimes; they do not readily jump ship to further their policy goals.

Finally, even if some actors anticipate net gains from authoritarianism and lack a strong normative preference for competitive politics, the authoritarian coalition must be powerful enough to overthrow a democratic regime. In contexts where international actors might impose sanctions against coup leaders, only actors unusually concerned with economic growth are likely to believe that the growth advantage they presume an authoritarian regime would offer is sufficient to offset the risk of supporting a coup.

We do not claim that Latin American democracies have been permanently inoculated against instability resulting from bad performance. Citizen tolerance for poor economic performance under competitive regimes appears to have dropped somewhat in many countries in the late 1990s. At that time, a new period of prolonged stagnation (1998–2002) in the region as a whole and of increased poverty in many countries fueled growing disgruntlement in Argentina, Bolivia, Ecuador, and Venezuela. The theoretical lesson is that citizen and elite sensitivity to poor economic performance varies widely across time and space (Kapstein and Converse 2008).

Mass Political Culture and Democratization

Political culture studies based on individual attitudes see democracy as emanating from democratic values among the citizenry; where citizens have democratic values, democracy flourishes (Almond and Verba 1963; Inglehart 1990; 1997: 160–215; Inglehart and Welzel 2005). We agree that mass support for democracy is a powerful resource for democratic actors. But our work diverges from political culture approaches based on mass surveys in several ways. First, we emphasize the role of leaders and organizations, not of ordinary citizens, in determining regime outcomes The beliefs of leaders and organizations usually have more weight than citizen views in determining regime outcomes (Berman 1998; Bermeo 2003; Dahl 1971: 124–88; Linz 1978b).

Second, whereas our theory calls for analyzing specific actors and coalitions that trigger regime change or stabilize the incumbent regime, mass political culture approaches usually do not establish convincing mechanisms by which mass attitudes determine regime outcomes. They usually lack a sense of agency – that is, of specific actors or mechanisms through which mass beliefs about politics affect regime change. Inglehart and Welzel (2005) discuss this issue in greater detail than most work on mass political culture. They argue that political regimes confront pressures for change when mass values are incongruent with the regime (pp. 158, 174, 186–91).The variable "demand for freedom" is at the core of their theory that mass values are the most important long-term determinant of democracy. However, based on how the variable is constructed, it is difficult to see why it represents citizen demands for democracy. It is based on a factor analysis that combines five items: postmaterialism, personal happiness, tolerance of homosexuality, willingness to sign a petition, and interpersonal trust. None of these five survey items constitutes a demand for democracy, and it is not clear how any of them facilitates a transition to democracy.[22]

---

[22] By contrast, Mattes and Bratton (2007) measured demand for democracy using a battery of indicators that capture whether respondents reject one-man rule, reject military rule, reject one-party rule, and prefer democracy above other forms of government. Booth and Seligson (2009) measured demand for democracy using a dichotomous indicator that captured if respondents preferred an elected leader to a strong but unelected leader (Chapter 7).

Booth and Seligson (2009: chapter 8) theorized a more specific causal mechanism that is consistent with our approach, arguing that elites with a low commitment to democracy find it easier to curtail civil liberties and political rights when large segments of the population simultaneously present low levels of support for democratic principles, national political institutions, and regime performance. However, their comparison of those "triply dissatisfied" citizens against satisfied citizens showed only modest differences in terms of support for confrontational politics, military coups, and unelected governments (Figure 8.3). The evidence supports their arguments but does not sustain more sweeping claims about the impact of mass political culture on political regimes.

In contrast to theories that claim that mass political culture determines regime outcomes through some difficult-to-specify mechanisms, we begin with concrete, identifiable historical actors. Citizen opinion affects these actors, but the relationship between citizen opinion and actors' behavior is very far from linear (Bermeo 2003).

Third, mass political culture approaches generally do not attempt to explain regime change, which is one of our primary concerns. They can attempt to explain regime stability on the basis of patterns of association between mass attitudes and regime type, for example, that authoritarian mass attitudes are conducive to authoritarian regimes. But because mass attitudes are putatively relatively stable over the medium term, they are less successful at explaining dramatic change.

Inglehart and Welzel (2005) assert that self-expression (which is exactly the same variable as "demand for freedom") values explain political regimes. However, their own data indicate that their cultural explanation of regimes based on self-expression values works only modestly for the 1995–2002 period and not well for the 1978–89 period. They report modest country-level correlations, ranging from about .32 to about .39, between self-expression values measured between 1990 and 1995 and levels of democracy (measured by Freedom House scores) from 1995 to 2002 (figure 8.3, p. 184). Even more problematic for their argument, the correlation between self-expression values (again measured between 1990 and 1995) and the level of democracy from 1978 to 1989 is consistently low, ranging from about .01 to about .16. Because they claim there is very high stability over time in self-expression values, the correlation between these values from 1978 to 1989 and democracy in those years must also be low. At best, their theory is valid to a very modest extent for the 1995–2002 period and generally not valid for a longer time period (1978–89).

Fourth, mass political culture approaches usually disregard the problem of reverse causality – that is, the possibility that a democratic political regime fosters a democratic political culture (Barry 1978: 47–74; Muller and Seligson 1994; Seligson 2002). For instance, Booth and Seligson (2009) showed that respondents in countries with a longer history of democracy tend to express stronger support for democratic principles (chapter 4). Inglehart and Welzel (2005: 176–209) explicitly addressed reverse causality, claiming that a democratic political culture causes democracy and not vice versa. They correctly noted that "[i]f self-expression values cause democracy, they must be in place before democracy" (Inglehart and Welzel 2005: 178). Their statistical work thus implicitly assumes that all democracies in their sample transitioned to democracy *after* their measurement of self-expression values (i.e., 1990 or 1995, depending on the country), but this is not the case. Twenty-three of the sixty-one countries in their sample were democracies for *generations* before their measurement of the independent variable.[23] Moreover, the history of democratization in these countries raises serious doubts about an argument that invokes self-expression values as the cause of democracy. Inglehart's (1990, 1997) own work indicates that self-expression values emerged in recent decades, which means that they cannot explain the emergence of democracy in many countries before then.

Many other countries in their sample (e.g., Argentina, Brazil, the Dominican Republic, Greece, Portugal, the Philippines, South Korea, Spain, Turkey, Uruguay) transitioned to democracy before their measurement of self-expression values. Most of the countries that underwent transitions to competitive regimes at the time that fits their argument (between 1989 and 1996 – see Inglehart and Welzel 2005: 176–80) were in the Soviet bloc. In this region, international influences, in particular Gorbachev's willingness to accept growing autonomy of countries dominated by the Soviet Union, followed by demonstration effects that spread across the region and later by the dissolution of the Soviet Union, were hugely important (Brown 2000; Kuran 1991; Lohmann 1994).

Finally, the empirical predictions of mass political culture approaches are not demonstrably fruitful for explaining regime patterns in Latin America. There is no convincing empirical basis for claiming that a change in mass attitudes was primarily responsible for transitions to competitive regimes after 1977 or for democratic stability in the third wave. In contemporary Latin America, mass attitudes are far from unequivocally supportive of democracy. In the 2011 Latinobarómetro, for eighteen Latin American countries (all but Haiti and Cuba), only 58 percent of respondents agreed that "Democracy is better than any other form of government." Seventeen percent agreed that "Under some circumstances, an authoritarian government can be preferable to a democracy," and 18 percent agreed that "For people like us, it does not matter whether the regime is democratic." Another 7 percent did not know or did not respond.[24] This distribution of responses does not support the hypothesis that democratic mass values explain stable democracy. Conversely, the available empirical evidence does not support the idea that mass attitudes caused earlier breakdowns (Bermeo 2003).

[23] Australia, Austria, Belgium, Canada, Colombia, Denmark, Finland, France, Great Britain, Iceland, India, Israel, Italy, Japan, Luxembourg, the Netherlands, New Zealand, Norway, Sweden, Switzerland, the United States, Venezuela, and West Germany.

[24] Corporación Latinobarómetro, *Informe 2011*, p. 40. Online at http://www.latinobarometro.org/latino/LATContenidos.jsp

In short, mass political culture (or public opinion) influences whether democracies and dictatorships survive or fall. But the empirical evidence does not support strong causal claims about the impact of public opinion on the survival and fall of political regimes (Bermeo 2003).

Mass political culture could determine regime types if elites were "sampled" from the larger population or if, in order to mobilize followers as a political resource, elites needed to embrace the policy and normative regime preferences of mass publics. These two statements are partially true, but elites do not faithfully reflect mass preferences, for two reasons. Given their location in the social structure, elites usually differ from the larger population in terms of preferences (Dalton 1985; Iversen 1994). Even when elites claim to represent mass publics, there are serious monitoring problems (Przeworski et al. 1999). Elites have significant autonomy and preferences of their own, and elections do not suffice to induce them to mirror mass preferences. Elites frame the menu of feasible policy and regime options for their followers, and in this way they also shape mass preferences (Chhibber and Torcal 1997; Przeworski and Sprague 1986; Sartori 1969; Torcal and Mainwaring 2003).

We expect a correlation between elite and mass attitudes at the national level, but this correlation might be modest, and the causal direction of the association is not obvious. Because elites play a critical role in all episodes of regime change while mass publics play an important role only in some episodes (mass actors are mostly absent from processes based on elite pacts or imposition), it is safer to assume that the main explanatory variable behind regime outcomes is the elites' normative and policy preferences rather than mass attitudes per se.

Agency and Democratization

Some social scientists have underscored the role of elite values and strategies in regime breakdowns and transitions, emphasizing the importance of leaders' decisions (Capoccia 2005; Di Palma 1990, Linz 1978b, O'Donnell and Schmitter 1986, Stepan 1978). Following these scholars, we acknowledge the importance of leaders' decisions, perhaps especially in moments of regime crisis. Whereas structural and cultural theories such as Inglehart's focus on causally more distant explanations, these works that focus on agency highlight more causally proximate explanations.

Our theory, which is situated in the causal chain between structural approaches and agency explanations, is compatible with an emphasis on leaders and agency. We almost always consider the president an actor, which is consistent with an emphasis on individual leadership. The core of our theory, however, emphasizes political factors that, although amenable to being influenced by agency, are not *primarily* a result of individual leaders' decisions. In the short term, the political variables that we highlight are key parts of the landscape that political leaders confront. In this respect, our theory is not primarily about agency or political leadership. Organizations and movements more than individual leaders are at the core of our theory and empirical analysis.

For example, after the United States began to emphasize democracy in its Latin American policy and after the OAS institutionalized a system of sanctions to support competitive regimes and reduce the incentives for coups in 1991, open coups in the western hemisphere have been a rare exception. Even relatively inept leaders of competitive regimes have rarely fallen to coups. The development of international mechanisms to sanction overt coups has had greater weight in determining broad regime outcomes than the quality of political leadership. This is a contrast to what occurred in the past, when presidents who exercised poor decisions could trigger a coup (Stepan 1978). In the current inter-American system, the effect of poor presidential leadership on regime survival is circumscribed by norms about the desirability of democracy and sanctions.

Formal Institutional Rules and Democratic Stability

Our theory also differs from those that focus on the impact of formal political institutions on regime continuity and change. Linz (1994) famously argued that presidential systems are more vulnerable to breakdown than parliamentary systems. However, other scholars have questioned this argument (Cheibub 2007; Shugart and Carey 1992). Presidentialism might help explain democratic breakdowns before the third wave, but during the third wave, the breakdown rate of competitive regimes has been very low with presidential systems still in place throughout Latin America. Presidentialism does not help explain variance across the twenty countries of Latin America or over time in the region because presidential systems have been a constant.

In another well-known argument based on formal institutional rules, Shugart and Carey (1992) theorized that systems with strong constitutional powers for the president might be more vulnerable to breakdown than those with more balance between the executive and legislature. In a converging argument, Fish (2006) argued that strong legislatures are good for democracy. Although these arguments about the impact of formal institutions are intuitively sensible, and although Fish's claim has solid empirical support for a broad sample of countries, this hypothesis does not hold up for Latin America. On this point, our skepticism is grounded in empirical observations rather than theoretical conviction. In Latin America, the constitutional powers of presidents actually expanded during the third wave of democratization (Negretto 2009). As a result, in the models presented in Chapter 4, greater presidential powers enhanced democratic survival.

Although formal rules shape actors' incentives and behavior, their impact on regime survival or fall is mediated by many other factors that seem to have more weight than the formal rules. The willingness of actors to accept policy losses does not depend directly on the formal rules of the game, and it has an important impact on the capacity of competitive regimes to survive. Intransigent actors stretch their legal prerogatives to the limit (and beyond it) in order to impose their preferred policies, and they seek to undermine the power of veto players by casting them as illegitimate institutions. By contrast, non-radical players accept the existing institutional design as exogenous and bargain to achieve their policy preferences within the constraints imposed by those rules. In its focus on actors, our theory is fully consistent with institutional approaches to regime change and survival. But we focus on organizational actors (parties, militaries, unions, etc.), not formal institutional rules.

LOOKING AHEAD

The inability of these alternative theoretical approaches to account for the historical transformation of political regimes in Latin America may portend well for the region. By 2010, at least ten of the twenty Latin American countries remained below the income level of Argentina in 1976, identified by Przeworski et al. (2000: 98) as the threshold above which "no democracy has ever been subverted."[25] If modernization were the main source of inoculation against coups, most Latin American competitive regimes would still be at risk.

Latin America also remains one of the most unequal regions in the world. Data compiled by the United Nations Development Program in its 2011 *Human Development Report* indicated that the richest 20 percent of the population in the typical Latin American country earns sixteen times more than the poorest 20 percent. As a comparative reference, the mean ratio between the richest and the poorest quintiles of the population is about nine times for countries at high levels of human development, eleven times for countries at medium levels of development, and ten times for countries at low levels of development. On average, Latin American countries lost nine positions in the international ranking of human development once income inequality was taken into account.[26] Even though a combination of social policy, leftist governments, and commodity booms led to an improvement of income distribution in the last decade covered by our study (Gasparini and Lustig 2011), prospects for democracy in Latin America would be bleak if inequality was an insurmountable threat to competitive politics.

Most of Latin America remained shielded from the recession that undercut the U.S. and EU economies in the years after 2008. Estimates by the Economic

[25] Nominal GDP has risen over time, but the comparison refers to income measured in constant (2005) purchasing power parity dollars (data from the Penn World Table 7.0 for 2009). Using the figures in our dataset (in constant dollars, but not PPPs), some eighteen countries still remain below the threshold.

[26] Adjustments for income inequality in the HDI world ranking ranged from a loss of twenty-four positions for Colombia to a moderate gain of three positions in the case of Nicaragua (http://hdr.undp.org/en/media/HDR_2011_EN_Table3.pdf).

Commission for Latin America and the Caribbean (ECLAC) indicate that the economy of the average Latin American country grew by one-third between 2004 and 2010, and by 8 percent even in the difficult global environment experienced between 2008 and 2010.[27] Yet at the turn of the decade, Latin American growth often remained volatile and dependent on primary export booms, inflation emerged as a pressing issue in several countries, and the typical unemployment rate fluctuated around 8 percent.

There is no clear evidence that Latin American leaders were savvier, more prudent, or more inclined to act as statesmen by 2010 than they were two decades earlier. The legacy of past leaders who navigated the stormy waters of democratic transitions, such as Raúl Alfonsín in Argentina or Patricio Aylwin in Chile, or those who tamed hyperinflation, such as Fernando Henrique Cardoso in Brazil, reminds us that Latin American leadership has always included a good measure of vision and talent, as well as – in more unfortunate instances – short-sightedness and negligence.

Presidential institutions will remain a feature of Latin American politics for years to come. Some constitutional rules that presumably compound the effects of presidentialism have even expanded over time. Repeated constitutional reforms have extended the legal prerogatives of Latin American presidents (Negretto 2013). Constitutional amendments (or acts of judicial review) have also relaxed restrictions on presidential reelection to accommodate the ambitions of popular incumbents in Argentina (1994), Bolivia (2008), Brazil (1997), Colombia (2005), Costa Rica (2003), the Dominican Republic (2002), Ecuador (2008), Nicaragua (2009), Peru (1993), and Venezuela (1999, 2009). If extraordinary leaders or particular institutions were necessary to sustain democracy, the future of competitive regimes in the region would be uncertain.

By contrast, normative regime preferences, policy orientations, and international forces changed over the long run in ways that made Latin American political actors more willing to accept democracy by 2010 than at any previous point. If the argument presented in this book is correct, this fundamental transformation involving organizational ideas and collective goals, transnational networks, and international organizations anticipates a more promising future for democrats in the region than most alternative theories would predict.

At the same time, there are reasons to temper this optimism with caution. Chapter 8 documented a slight increase in radical policy preferences and a modest decline in normative commitments to democracy since the late 1990s. It also showed that investments in the construction of democratic institutions (or the lack thereof) have lasting consequences for the quality of competitive regimes over the long run. In this context, democratic stagnation and erosion have been common phenomena. A surge in radicalism could have deleterious effects for the

---

[27] *Anuario Estadístico de América Latina y el Caribe* (2011), table 2.1.1.1 (http://www.eclac.cl/publicaciones/xml/7/45607/LCG2513b.pdf).

strength of twenty-first-century democratic coalitions in the countries plagued by weak states, bad governance, and social exclusion.

These findings open an exciting research agenda that we can only begin to sketch. Studies of democratization have usually relied on theories that invoke the power and motivations of specific *actors*, but they have tested their theories using aggregate cross-national data at the *country* level. This inconsistency between the level of analysis invoked by the microfoundations of the theory and the units of analysis employed for hypothesis testing is common in other subfields – including comparative studies of political economy, conflict, institutions, and policy making – and it poses three important challenges.

The first challenge that future studies of democratization (and other subfields) must confront is the generation of systematic indicators to portray political actors in multiple countries and different historical periods. We addressed such measurement issues in ways described in Chapter 3. Large collaborative efforts would be required to develop accurate measures for political actors – their preferences, goals, and resources – worldwide. Yet the payoff of such large-scale undertaking for the social sciences could be great.

Previous chapters have shown that normative orientations and policy preferences have powerful consequences for regime change and stability. But once those preferences are identified, several questions emerge. Where do these preferences originate? How do they change? Under what conditions certain preferences spread in society? The second challenge for comparative politics is to take those questions seriously. We explored the origin and changes of normative preferences in Chapters 2 through 6, partly to dispel concerns about endogeneity, but a full treatment of this issue transcends the scope of this book. This is an area in which interpretive and positivist approaches in political science will need to engage in a joint effort (Bowles 1998).

Third, we need to extend our models of how actors' preferences aggregate into collective outcomes. The theoretical literature has addressed this issue in many ways (for a classic example, see Schelling 1978), but *empirical* estimators to model such processes have lagged behind. Hierarchical models conventionally assume that variance in the outcome variable takes place at a lower level of aggregation than variance in explanatory factors (Raudenbush and Bryk 2002). Yet the combination of actors' preferences in social outcomes presents the opposite situation. We handled this issue by averaging actors' preferences at the country-year level in order to create summary measures. More powerful estimators of aggregate choices may become available in the future.

These analytical challenges comprise an agenda that transcends the study of regime change and has broader implications for the field of comparative politics. We started this book in search of an explanation for the emergence, survival, and fall of democracies and dictatorships in the past. We end this book by looking ahead – to the perils to be met by future democratic actors in Latin America, and to the questions to be met by future social scientists seeking to understand them.

APPENDIX 3.1

Coding Rules for Political Regimes

No violations	Partial violations	Major violations
Elections for the Legislature and the Executive		
The head of government and the legislature are chosen in free and fair elections.	a) There are systematic complaints of rigged elections and/or harassment of the opposition but there is still uncertainty about electoral outcomes. b) The military veto a few "unacceptable" but important presidential candidates; fraud affects but does not thoroughly skew electoral results; or the elections are conducted under substantially unequal playing rules.	a) The head of government or the legislature is not elected. b) The government uses its resources (patronage, repression, or a combination of both) to ensure electoral victory. There is certainty about the outcome of presidential elections. c) Through fraud, manipulation, or outright repression, the government makes it impossible for a wide gamut of parties to compete (or if they do compete, to take office).
Franchise		
The voter franchise is broad compared to other countries in the same historical period, and disenfranchised social categories (e.g., children) are not seen as politically excluded groups with distinctive electoral preferences.	Disenfranchisement of some social groups occurs in ways that are not likely to alter electoral outcomes.	A large part of the adult population is disenfranchised on ethnic, class, gender, or educational grounds in ways that: a) likely prevent very different electoral outcomes (or so is widely believed); b) are unusually exclusionary for that historical period; or c) trigger mass social protests.

No violations	Partial violations	Major violations
Civil Liberties		
Violations of human rights are uncommon, parties are free to organize, and the government respects constitutional guarantees.	a) Violations of human rights are not widespread but still affect the opposition's capacity to organize in some geographic areas or some social sectors. b) There is intermittent censorship of the media or regular prohibition of one major party or candidate. c) The government recurrently reshuffles or dismantles the courts and other institutions of accountability in order to prevent checks on its power, but these institutions still have some capacity to restrict the government.	a) Gross human rights violations or censorship against opposition media occur systematically. b) Political parties are not free to organize (i.e., most major parties are banned, just a single party is allowed to exist, or a few parties are tightly controlled by the government). c) The legal system is consistently biased against the opposition. Opponents regularly confront criminal charges.
Civilian Control		
Military leaders and the military as an institution have negligible or minor influence in policies other than military policy, and their preferences do not substantively affect the chances of presidential candidates. Foreign powers do not control the national territory.	a) Military leaders or the military as an institution are able to veto important policies in a few areas not related to the armed forces. b) Foreign countries exercise explicit veto power over some decisions of the elected officials.	a) Military leaders or the military as an institution openly dominate major policy areas not strictly related to the armed forces. b) The elected head of government is a puppet, such that the electoral process does not really determine who governs. c) The country is ruled by a foreign governor.

Source: Based on Mainwaring, Brinks, and Pérez-Liñán (2001, 2007).

APPENDIX 3.2

Coding U.S. Foreign Policy toward Democracy in Latin America

Using secondary sources, we coded each presidential term in the United States on eight questions, presented in Table A3.2. These questions focus specifically on U.S. government behavior regarding political regimes in Latin America. We did not code other aspects of U.S. government policy that might affect Latin America – for example, economic policy – or the role of U.S. companies, human rights organizations, or interest associations in the region. The index varies on a yearly basis, although U.S. administrations tend to have consistent scores over time. Policy shifts occurred for at least one of the eight questions during the presidencies of Woodrow Wilson, Franklin Roosevelt, Harry Truman, Dwight Eisenhower, John Kennedy, and Ronald Reagan.

Two individuals coded all administrations; no question presented problems of inter-coder reliability. Our aggregation rule was simple. We added each administration's score for the eight questions, producing a scale ranging from −4 to 4. We then rescaled the total score to range between 0 and 1, using the formula: *US Policy* = $(4 + \Sigma\, Q_k)/8$ where Q_k represents the score for the k-th question coded.

TABLE A3.2. *Coding Rules for U.S. Policy*

Highest score	Intermediate score (if any)	Lowest score

1. In public speeches and writings, did influential U.S. policy leaders express a preference for democracy in Latin America even when there were trade-offs with other important values such as stability, U.S. economic interests, and U.S. security interests? Or did policy makers express an opinion that meddling in other countries' political affairs was a bad idea, and hence that the United States should refrain from expressing a preference for democracy in Latin America? *(Public statements)*

+1: Yes, U.S. policy leaders usually expressed a preference for democracy even when there were trade-offs with other important values.	+0.5: U.S. policy leaders sometimes expressed a preference for democracy even when there were trade-offs with other important values, or they expressed a preference for democracy that was quite conditional.	0: No, U.S. policy leaders usually did not express a preference for democracy if they believed that there were important trade-offs with other values.

2. Did the United States support coups, armed rebellions, or U.S. military interventions against democratic and semi-democratic governments? To code this answer yes, the U.S. needed to support the coup ex ante or to have been sufficiently hostile to a government so that coup leaders could assume U.S. support. (Mere U.S. opposition to a government is not sufficient.) *(Diplomatic positions and covert operations)*

0: No	-1: Yes

3. Did U.S. military interventions limit sovereignty (and hence limit democracy) of democratic or semi-democratic governments? *(Military interventions)*

0: No	-1: Yes

4. Did the United States actively promote the democratization of authoritarian regimes and/or make efforts to bolster democracies when they were under threat? Did the United States encourage or pressure authoritarian regimes to move toward democracy? And did it actively support democratic regimes so as to minimize the likelihood of democratic breakdowns? *(Diplomatic positions and covert operations)*

+1: Yes, the United States actively promoted democratization of authoritarian regimes and/or made efforts to bolster democracies when they were under threat.	+0.5: On isolated occasions, and as an exception, the United States actively promoted democratization of authoritarian regimes and/or made efforts to bolster democracies when they were under threat.	0: No, the United States did not actively promote democratization of authoritarian regimes or make efforts to bolster democracies that were under threat.

5. Did the United States criticize authoritarian regimes that were not leftist? Did the United States criticize human rights abuses and infringements on civil and political rights by regimes that were not leftist? *(Diplomatic positions and public statements)*[a]

+1: Yes, the United States criticized authoritarian	+0.5: On isolated occasions, and as an exception, the	0: No, the United States did not criticize authoritarian

TABLE A3.2. (*cont.*)

Highest score	Intermediate score (if any)	Lowest score

regimes, human rights abuses, and infringements on civil and political rights.

United States criticized authoritarian regimes that were not leftist.

regimes, human rights abuses, and infringements on civil and political rights.

6. Did U.S. foreign policy leaders clearly support authoritarian regimes? By this we mean more than accepting the existence of an authoritarian regime. Did U.S. leaders praise those dictators and/or actively seek to help keep them in power? (*Diplomatic positions and public statements*)

0: No   -1: Yes

7. Did U.S. leaders express the view that Latin American countries could not be democracies because of cultural dispositions – that is, that Latin Americans by temperament or culture were indisposed to have democracies? (*Public statements or internal communications, personal writings*)

0: No   -1: Yes

8. Did the United States practice a policy of nonrecognition when a military coup or rebellion overthrew a competitive government or clearly and credibly articulate ex ante that it would impose a sanction in the event of a coup or rebellion? Or did the United States impose some other kind of sanction (e.g., economic) if a coup or rebellion against a democracy occurred? (*Diplomatic positions*)

+1: Yes, the United States imposed some kind of sanction when a military coup or a rebellion overthrew a competitive political regime, or it clearly and credibly articulated ex ante that it would impose a sanction in the event of a coup.

+0.5: In exceptional cases, the United States imposed some kind of sanction when a military coup or a rebellion overthrew a competitive political regime.

0: No, the United States did not impose a sanction when a military coup or a rebellion overthrew a competitive political regime.

---

a We exclude leftist authoritarian regimes (e.g., the Cuban regime after 1959, the Nicaraguan regime of 1979–90) because U.S. criticism of such regimes has been a historical constant. As such, U.S. criticisms could stem from the leftist nature of the regime or from the regime's authoritarian character.

APPENDIX 4.1

Long-Run Equilibrium for the Proportion
of Competitive Regimes

Equation 4.3 summarized the equilibrium conditions for the proportion of democracies $D^* = p^D_t b^S_t / (b^D_t b^S_t + p^D_t b^S_t + p^S_t b^D_t)$ and semi-democracies $S^* = p^S_t b^D_t / (b^D_t b^S_t + p^D_t b^S_t + p^S_t b^D_t)$. This appendix provides proof of those conditions.

1. Given the transition matrix presented in Figure 4.1, the proportion of democracies observed at time t can be defined as $D_t = D_{t-1} (1 - b^D_t - q^S_t) + S_{t-1} q^D_t + (1 - D_{t-1} - S_{t-1}) p^D_t$. Because we are only interested in changes from competitive politics to authoritarianism (and vice versa), and for the sake of consistency between the analytic solution and the empirical models, we shall assume no erosion or deepening, that is $q^S_t = 0$ and $q^D_t = 0$. The equation then reduces to $D_t = D_{t-1} (1 - b^D_t) + (1 - D_{t-1} - S_{t-1}) p^D_t$. Similarly, the proportion of semi-democracies reduces to $S_t = S_{t-1} (1 - b^S_t) + (1 - D_{t-1} - S_{t-1}) p^S_t$.

2. In equilibrium, the proportion of democracies and semi-democracies must remain steady such that, at the limit, $D_t = D_{t-1} = D^*$ and $S_t = S_{t-1} = S^*$. We can reexpress the proportion of democratic regimes in equilibrium as $D^* = D^*(1 - b^D_t) + (1 - D^* - S^*) p^D_t$, where for any relevant case in which $0 < D^* < 1$, $b^D_t > 0$ and $p^D_t > 0$. It follows that $D^* b^D_t = (1 - D^* - S^*) p^D_t$. For the same reason, $S^* b^S_t = (1 - D^* - S^*) p^S_t$.

3. As a result, in equilibrium, $p^D_t / b^D_t = D^* / (1 - D^* - S^*)$, and $p^S_t / b^S_t = S^* / (1 - D^* - S^*)$.

4. Solving the equation for democracies, $D^* = p^D_t (1 - S^*) / (p^D_t + b^D_t)$, and for semi-democracies we get $S^* = p^S_t (1 - D^*) / (p^S_t + b^S_t)$.

5. Substitute the equation for semi-democracies in step 4 into the equilibrium equation for democracies in step 3, such that $p^D_t / b^D_t = D^* / (1 - D^* - (p^S_t - p^S_t D^*) / (p^S_t + b^S_t))$.

6. Solving for D^*, we get $D^* = p^D_t b^S_t / (b^D_t b^S_t + p^D_t b^S_t + p^S_t b^D_t)$.

7. Repeating steps 5–6 for semi-democracies, we obtain $S^* = p^S_t b^D_t / (b^D_t b^S_t + p^D_t b^S_t + p^S_t b^D_t)$.

APPENDIX 5.1

Qualitative Comparative Analysis

This appendix presents technical information for the qualitative comparative analysis in Chapter 5. We relied on specialized software (fs/QCA 2.0 and Tosmana 1.3.2) to generate the results. Because QCA results for an outcome and for the absence of the outcome are not symmetric, we report information for democratic breakdowns (*break*) and for democratic survival (*~break*) separately.

Let *normative* reflect the presence of a majority of actors with a normative commitment to democracy, *radicalism* be the presence of a majority of radical actors, and *favorable* the presence of a favorable international environment. Following conventional notation, we employ the symbols ~ to indicate negation (*not*), * to indicate conjunction (*and*), and + to indicate inclusive disjunction (*or*).

Figure A5.1 offers a graphic representation of the property space presented in Table 5.5 (i.e., of the truth table). We follow the graphical rules introduced by Cronqvist (2003). The large rectangle represents the thirteen administrations under study. The right panel of the figure corresponds to cases of commitment to democracy (*normative*) and the left panel to cases without such commitment (*~normative*). Similarly, the top panel contains instances without dominant radical actors (*~radicalism*) and the bottom panel contains instances of dominant radicalism (*radicalism*). Finally, the rectangle at the center contains all administrations that operated under favorable international conditions. The plane is thus segmented into eight configurations. For example, the cell at the top left corner (denoted 000) corresponds to type #1 (*~normative***~radicalism***~favorable*) in Table 5.5, while the cell at the bottom right (labeled 110) corresponds to type #7 (*normative**radicalism**~favorable*).

Configurations leading to survival are shaded in dark grey and configurations leading to breakdown are shaded in light grey. Because remainders are colored in white, the figure allows for an immediate visualization of the counterfactual assumptions necessary to make any simplified claim. For example, to argue that

TABLE A5.1. *Prime Implicant Chart for Democratic Breakdowns*

Observed type:	#1	#3	#4
Prime implicants:	~normative*	~normative*	~normative*
	~radicalism*	radicalism*	radicalism*
	~favorable	~favorable	favorable
I. Complex solution			
~normative*~favorable	X	X	
~normative*radicalism		X	X
II. Parsimonious solution			
~normative	X	X	X
radicalism		X	X

Note: Essential prime implicants are in bold.

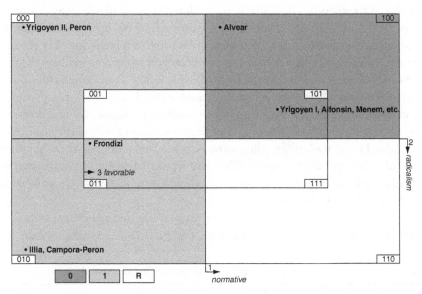

FIGURE A5.1. Representation of the Property Space in Table 5.5
Color coding: 0 refers to configurations leading to survival, 1 to configurations leading to breakdown, and R to remainders (that is, configurations with no empirical examples).

the lack of normative commitment to democracy was enough to undermine competitive regimes in Argentina, we would have to accept configuration 001 (*~normative*~radicalism*favorable*) as true.

Conditions for Competitive Regime Breakdowns. Table A5.1 presents the prime implicant chart for instances of breakdown (*break*). Prime implicants (listed in the rows) are corollaries resulting from minimizing the sufficient configurations originally identified in the truth table (listed in the columns). For example, if *~normative*radicalism*~favorable* (010) leads to breakdown and *~normative*radicalism*favorable* (011) leads to breakdown as well, it follows that the international context is not relevant once the first two conditions are present, and the explanation reduces to *~normative*radicalism*.

Entries in the table identify which empirical configuration is covered by each prime implicant. The first set of implicants refers to the "complex solution" that treats all remainders (counterfactuals, or white cells in Figure A5.1) as false; the second set corresponds to the "parsimonious solution" that treats remainders as true for the sole purpose of reduction (i.e., as *don't cares*). The inclusion of additional configurations (not listed in the columns of the prime implicant chart) allows for greater flexibility in the minimization process, and thus for more parsimonious outcomes in the bottom panel of the table. Essential prime implicants (those needed to cover all observed configurations) are noted in bold.

Table A5.2 reports additional information for each of the essential prime implicants. As in Table 5.5, consistency scores reflect the proportion of administrations falling under each configuration that suffered a breakdown. In the next column, coverage scores – a measure of explanatory power – indicate the proportion of all breakdowns covered by each explanation. For example, four out of five breakdowns (Yrigoyen, Perón, Illia, and Isabel Perón) took place when a majority of actors lacked a normative commitment to democracy and when the international environment was unfavorable, while three of the five (Frondizi, Illia, and Isabel Perón) took place when most actors lacked a normative commitment and had radical policy preferences. The third row in Table A5.2 indicates that the overall complex solution, ~normative*(~favorable + radicalism), covers all instances of breakdown in the sample.

In the last column of Table A5.2 we employ the binomial distribution to provide a test of statistical significance for each causal configuration. For

TABLE A5.2. *Report for Essential Prime Implicants (Breakdowns)*

Prime implicants	Consistency	Coverage	P-value
I. Complex solution			
~normative*~favorable	1.0	0.8	.02
~normative*radicalism	1.0	0.6	.06
~normative*	1.0	1.0	.01
(~favorable + radicalism)			
II. Parsimonious solution			
~normative	1.0	1.0	.01

Note: Intermediate solution in fsQCA is equivalent to complex solution. P-value corresponds to binomial test.

TABLE A5.3. *Prime Implicant Chart for Democratic Survival*

Observed type:	#5	#6
Prime implicants:	normative* ~radicalism* ~favorable	normative* ~radicalism* favorable
I. Complex solution **normative*~radicalism**	X	X
II. Parsimonious solution **normative**	X	X
~radicalism*favorable		X

Note: Essential prime implicants are in bold.

TABLE A5.4. *Report for Essential Prime Implicants (Survivals)*

Prime implicants	Consistency	Coverage	P-value
I. Complex solution normative*~radicalism	1.0	1.0	.02
II. Parsimonious solution normative	1.0	1.0	.02

Note: Intermediate solution in fsQCA is equivalent to complex solution. P-value corresponds to binomial test.

instance, what is the probability of observing four breakdowns out of four historical "trials" of the first configuration (~normative*~favorable) simply by chance, given that the unconditional probability of breakdown is 5/13? The resulting value ($.38^4$) yields $p < .05$. Even with a small sample of thirteen administrations, the p-values for the solutions generally achieve conventional levels of significance.

Conditions for Competitive Regime Survival. Table A5.3 presents the prime implicant chart for instances of regime survival (*~break*). As in the previous case, the complex solution treats all remainder configurations as false, and the parsimonious solution includes remainders for the purpose of Boolean minimization. Because the parsimonious solution involves the acceptance of some "hard" counterfactuals for both outcomes, our discussion in the text of the chapter generally focuses on the complex solutions for breakdowns as well as survivals.

Table A5.4 presents the empirical measures of consistency and coverage (Ragin 2006) for the complex and parsimonious solutions. All eight instances of democratic survival are covered by the resulting explanations. As additional support for the argument, the binomial test for eight successes in eight trials, given an unconditional probability of 8/13 results in $p < .05$.

Coding of Salvadoran Actors, 1979–2010

Administration	Years		Actor	Normative regime preference	Policy radicalism
First Junta	1979	1980	Reformist sectors of the military	0	0.5
			Hardline Military	−1	1
			Social Democrats/ MNR	0	0.5
			PDC	1	0
			Guerrilla Left	−1	1
			Death Squads	−1	1
			ANEP	0	1
			Catholic Church/ Romero	1	0
			Leftist Popular Organizations	−0.5	1
			FARO/extremist owners	−1	1
Second Junta	1980	1982	Duarte/PDC	1	0.5
			Military	−1	1
			CRM, leftist popular organizations	−0.5	1
			FMLN	−1	1
			ANEP/less extremist business	0	1
			Death Squads	−1	1
			FARO/extremist business	−1	1

Administration	Years	Actor	Normative regime preference	Policy radicalism
Magaña	1982 1984	Magaña/PCN/ARENA	-0.5	1
		Military	-1	1
		FMLN	-1	1
		PDC	1	0
		Death Squads	-1	1
		ANEP	0	1
		FARO/extremist big business	-1	1
Duarte	1984 1989	Duarte/PDC	1	0
		Military	-0.5	1
		FMLN	-0.5	1
		Death Squads	-1	1
		ARENA	0	1
		FUSADES/moderate business	0	0.5
		Coffee Elite/ANEP	0	1
Cristiani	1989 1994	Cristiani/ARENA	0.5	0.5
		FMLN	0	0.5
		Coffee Elite/ANEP	0	0.5
		FUSADES/moderate business	0.5	0
		Military	0	0.5
		PDC	1	0
Calderón Sol	1994 1999	Calderón Sol/ARENA	0.5	0.5
		FMLN	0	0.5
		Coffee Elite/ANEP	0	0.5
		FUSADES/moderate business	0.5	0
		Military	0	0.5
		PDC	1	0
Flores	1999 2004	Flores/ARENA	0.5	0.5
		FMLN	0.5	0.5
		Big business	0	0
Saca	2004 2009	Saca/ARENA	0.5	0.5
		FMLN	0	0.5
		Big business	0	0
Funes	2009 2010	Funes	1	0
		FMLN	0.5	0.5
		ARENA	0.5	0.5
		Big business	0	0

Bibliography

Abente Brun, Diego. 2007. "The Quality of Democracy in Small South American Countries: The Case of Paraguay," *Kellogg Institute Working Paper* #343 (November), available at: http://kellogg.nd.edu/publications/workingpapers/index. shtml.

Acemoglu, Daron, Simon Johnson, James A. Robinson, and Pierre Yared. 2008. "Income and Democracy." *American Economic Review* 98(3): 808–42.

Acemoglu, Daron, and James A. Robinson. 2006. *The Economic Origins of Dictatorship and Democracy*. Cambridge: Cambridge University Press.

Achen, Christopher, and Duncan Snidal. 1989. "Rational Deterrence Theory and Comparative Case Studies." *World Politics* 41(2): 143–69.

Acuña, Carlos. 1995. "Intereses empresarios, dictadura y democracia en la Argentina actual. (O sobre por qué la burguesía abandona estrategias autoritarias y opta por la estabilidad democrática)." In Carlos Acuña, ed., *La nueva matriz política argentina*, pp. 231–84. Buenos Aires: Nueva Visión.

Acuña, Marcelo Luis. 1984. *De Frondizi a Alfonsín: La tradición política del radicalismo*. Two volumes. Buenos Aires: Centro Editor de América Latina.

Agüero, Felipe. 1995. *Militares, civiles y democracia: La España postfranquista en perspectiva comparada*. Madrid: Alianza.

Albertus, Michael. 2011. "Political Regimes and Redistribution." PhD dissertation, Stanford University.

Alexander, Gerard. 2002. *The Sources of Democratic Consolidation*. Ithaca, NY: Cornell University Press.

Alexander, Robert J. 1951. *The Perón Era*. New York: Columbia University Press.

Allison, Michael E., and Alberto Martín Álvarez. 2012. "Unity and Disunity in the FMLN." *Latin American Politics and Society* 54 (4): 89–118.

Almeida, Paul. 2008. *Waves of Protest: Popular Struggle in El Salvador, 1925–2005*. Minneapolis: University of Minnesota Press.

Almond, Gabriel A., and Sydney Verba. 1963. *The Civic Culture: Political Attitudes and Democracy in Five Nations*. Princeton, NJ: Princeton University Press.

Álvarez, Ángel E. 2009. "El Consejo Nacional Electoral y los dilemas de la competencia electoral en Venezuela." *América Latina Hoy* 51: 61–76.

Amaral, Samuel. 2001. "De Perón a Perón (1955–1973)." In Víctor Tau Anzoátegui, ed., *Nueva historia de la Nación Argentina*, pp. 325–60. Buenos Aires: Planeta.

Ameringer, Charles D. 1996. *The Caribbean Legion: Patriots, Politicians, Soldiers of Fortune, 1946–1950*. University Park: Pennsylvania State University Press.

2000. *The Cuban Democratic Experience: The Auténtico Years, 1944–1952*. Gainesville: University Press of Florida.

Anderson, Thomas P. 1971. *Matanza: El Salvador's Communist Revolt of 1932*. Lincoln: University of Nebraska Press.

Arnson, Cynthia. 1982. *El Salvador: A Revolution Confronts the United States*. Washington, DC Amsterdam: Institute for Policy Studies.

1993. *Crossroads: Congress, the President, and Central America, 1976–1993*. University Park: Penn State University Press.

Artiga González, Álvaro. 2001. "El Salvador." In Manuel Alcántara Sáez and Flavia Freidenberg, eds., *Partidos políticos de América Latina: Centroamérica, México y República Dominicana*, pp. 135–78. Salamanca, Spain: Ediciones Universidad Salamanca.

Auyero, Javier. 2007. *Routine Politics and Violence in Argentina: The Gray Zone of State Power*. Cambridge: Cambridge University Press.

Azpuru, Dinorah, Steven E. Finkel, Aníbal Pérez-Liñán, and Mitchell A Seligson. 2008. "What Has the United States Been Doing?" *Journal of Democracy* 19(2): 150–59.

Baldez, Lisa. 2002. *Why Women Protest: Women's Movements in Chile*. Cambridge; New York: Cambridge University Press.

Ballester, Horacio. 1996. *Memorias de un coronel democrático: medio siglo de historia política argentina en la óptica de un militar*. Buenos Aires: Ediciones de la Flor.

Banks, Arthur. 2004. *Cross-National Time-Series Data Archive*. Available from http://www.databanksinternational.com/ (accessed August 2012).

Barber, William F., and W. Neale Ronning. 1966. *Internal Security and Military Power: Counterinsurgency and Civic Action in Latin America*. Columbus: Ohio State University Press.

Barros, Robert. 1986. "The Left and Democracy: Recent Debates in Latin America." *Telos* 68: 49–70.

Barry, Brian. 1978 (1970). *Sociologists, Economists, and Democracy*. Chicago: University of Chicago Press.

Beissinger, Mark R. 2007. "Structure and Example in Modular Political Phenomena: The Diffusion of Bulldozer/Rose/Orange/Tulip Revolutions." *Perspectives on Politics* 5(2): 259–76.

Bellin, Eva. 2000. "Contingent Democrats: Industrialists, Labor, and Democratization in Late Developing Countries." *World Politics* 52(2): 175–205.

Benevides, Maria Victória de Mesquita. 1981. *A UDN e o Udenismo: Ambigüidades do Liberalismo Brasileiro (1945–1965)*. Rio de Janeiro: Paz e Terra.

Benford, Robert D., and David A. Snow. 2000. "Framing Processes and Social Movements: An Overview and Assessment." *Annual Review of Sociology* 26: 611–39.

Benz, Matthias, and Alois Stutzer. 2003. "Do Workers Enjoy Procedural Utility?" *Applied Economics Quarterly* 49: 149–72.

Beozzo, José Oscar. 1984. *Cristãos na universidade e na política : História da JUC e da AP*. Petrópolis: Vozes.

Bergés Ame, Valpy FitzGerald, and Rosemary Thorp. 2007. *Oxford Latin American Economic History Database*. Latin American Centre, Oxford University. Available from http://oxlad.qeh.ox.ac.uk/.

Berman, Sheri. 1998. *The Social Democratic Movement: Ideas and Politics in the Making of Interwar Europe*. Cambridge, MA: Harvard University Press.

Bermeo, Nancy. 1990. "Rethinking Regime Change." *Comparative Politics* 23(3): 359–77.

——— 1997. "Myths of Moderation: Confrontation and Conflict during Democratic Transitions." *Comparative Politics* 29(3): 305–22.

——— 2003. *Ordinary People in Extraordinary Times*. Princeton, NJ: Princeton University Press.

Berryman, Phillip. 1984. *The Religious Roots of Rebellion: Christians in Central American Revolutions*. Maryknoll, NY: Orbis Books.

Bertoni, Lilia A. 1968. "Las transformaciones del partido y sus luchas políticas (1916–1930)." In Luis Alberto Romero et al., *El Radicalismo*, pp. 91–124. Buenos Aires: C. Pérez Editor.

Birdsall, Nancy. 1999. "Education: The People's Asset." Center on Social and Economic Dynamics, Working Paper No. 5 (September).

Blanksten, George. 1953. *Peron's Argentina*. Chicago: University of Chicago Press.

Blyth, Mark. 2002. *Great Transformations: Economic Ideas and Institutional Change in the Twentieth Century*. Cambridge: Cambridge University Press.

Boix, Carles. 2003. *Democracy and Redistribution*. Cambridge: Cambridge University Press.

Boix, Carles, and Susan C. Stokes. 2003. "Endogenous Democratization." *World Politics* 55(4): 517–49.

Bollen, Kenneth A. 1980. "Issues in the Comparative Measurement of Political Democracy." *American Sociological Review* 45(2): 370–90.

——— 1983. "World System Position, Dependency, and Democracy: The Cross-National Evidence." *American Sociological Review* 48(4): 468–79.

Bollen, Kenneth A., and Patrick J. Curran. 2006. *Latent Curve Models: A Structural Equation Perspective*. Hoboken, NJ: Wiley-Interscience.

Bollen, Kenneth A., and Robert W. Jackman. 1985a. "Economic and Noneconomic Determinants of Political Democracy in the 1960s." *Research in Political Sociology* 1: 27–48.

——— 1985b. "Political Democracy and the Size Distribution of Income." *American Sociological Review* 50(4): 438–57.

Boniface, Dexter S. 2007. "The OAS's Mixed Record." In Thomas Legler, Sharon F. Lean, and Dexter S. Boniface, eds., *Promoting Democracy in the Americas*, pp. 40–62. Baltimore: Johns Hopkins University Press.

Bonner, Raymond. 1984. *Weakness and Deceit: U.S. Policy and El Salvador*. New York: Times Books.

Bonvecchi, Alejandro. 2002. "El derrumbe político en el ocaso de la convertibilidad." In Marcos Novaro, ed., *El Derrumbe Político en el ocaso de la convertibilidad*, pp. 109–93. Buenos Aires: Grupo Editorial Norma.

Booth, John A., and Mitchell A. Seligson. 2009. *The Legitimacy Puzzle in Latin America: Political Support and Democracy in Eight Nations*. Cambridge: Cambridge University Press.

Bosch, Brian J. 1999. *The Salvadoran Officer Corp and the Final Offensive of 1981.* Jefferson, NC: McFarland and Co.

Bosoer, Fabián. 2006. "¿Crisis con salvataje? Una hipótesis sobre el componente parlamentario en el auto-rescate de las democracias sudamericanas: 1999–2004." In Giorgio Alberti, Elsa Llenderrozas, and Julio Pinto, eds., *Instituciones, democracia e integración regional en el Mercosur*, pp. 245–66. Buenos Aires: Bononiae Libris-Prometeo.

   2011. *Braden o Perón. La historia oculta.* Buenos Aires: El Ateneo.

Botana, Natalio. 1994. *El orden conservador: La política argentina entre 1880 y 1916.* Buenos Aires: Editorial Sudamericana.

   1995. "Las transformaciones institucionales en los años del menemismo." In Ricardo Sidicaro and Jorge Mayer, eds., *Política y sociedad en los años del menemismo*, pp. 11–18. Buenos Aires: Facultad de Ciencias Sociales, Universidad de Buenos Aires.

   2006. *Poder y hegemonía. El régimen político después de la crisis.* Buenos Aires: Emecé.

Bowles, Samuel. 1998. "Endogenous Preferences: The Cultural Consequences of Markets and Other Economic Institutions." *Journal of Economic Literature* 36(1): 75–111.

   2004. *Microeconomics: Behavior, Institutions, and Evolution.* Princeton, NJ: Russell Sage Foundation and Princeton University Press.

Bowman, Kirk, Fabrice Lehoucq, and James Mahoney. 2005. "Measuring Political Democracy: Case Expertise, Data Adequacy, and Central America." *Comparative Political Studies* 38(8): 939–70.

Bratton, Michael, and Nicolas van de Walle. 1997. *Democratic Experiments in Africa: Regime Transitions in Comparative Perspective.* Cambridge: Cambridge University Press.

Brinks, Daniel, and Michael Coppedge. 2006. "Diffusion Is No Illusion: Neighbor Emulation in the Third Wave of Democracy." *Comparative Political Studies* 39(4): 463–89.

Brockett, Charles D. 2005. *Political Movements and Violence in Central America.* New York: Cambridge University Press.

Brooker, Paul. 2009. *Non-Democratic Regimes.* 2nd ed. New York: Palgrave Macmillan.

Brooks, Clem, and Jeff Manza. 2007. *Why Welfare States Persist: The Importance of Public Opinion in Democracies.* Chicago: University of Chicago Press.

Brown, Archie. 2000. "Transnational Influences in the Transition from Communism." *Post-Soviet Affairs* 16(2): 177–200.

Browning, David. 1983. "Agrarian Reform in El Salvador." *Journal of Latin American Studies* 15: 399–426.

Bruneau, Thomas C. 1974. *The Political Transformation of the Brazilian Catholic Church.* Cambridge: Cambridge University Press.

Buchrucker, Cristián. 1987. *Nacionalismo y Peronismo: la Argentina en la crisis ideológica mundial, 1927–1955.* Buenos Aires: Editorial Sudamericana.

Bunce, Valerie. 1995. "Should Transitologists Be Grounded?" *Slavic Review* 54(1): 111–27.

   1998. "Regional Differences in Democratization: The East versus the West." *Post-Soviet Affairs* 14(3): 187–211.

   2000. "Comparative Democratization: Big and Bounded Generalizations." *Comparative Political Studies* 33(6/7): 703–34.

Bunce, Valerie, and Sharon Wolchik. 2011. *Defeating Authoritarian Leaders in Postcommunist Countries.* Cambridge and New York: Cambridge University Press.

Bunge, Mario. 1998 (1967). *Philosophy of Science, Vol. 1, From Problem to Theory.* New Brunswick, NJ: Transaction.

Burkhart, Ross E. 1997. "Comparative Democracy and Income Distribution: Shape and Direction of the Causal Arrow." *Journal of Politics* 59(1): 148–64.

Burkhart, Ross E., and Michael Lewis-Beck. 1994. "Comparative Democracy: The Economic Development Thesis." *American Political Science Review* 88: 903–10.

Burrell, Jennifer, and Michael Shifter. 2000. "Estados Unidos, la OEA y la promoción de la democracia en las Américas." In Arlene B. Tickner, ed., *Sistema interamericano y democracia: Antecedentes históricos y tendencias futuras*, pp. 27–50. Bogotá: Ediciones Uniandes.

Cáceres Prendes, Jorge. 1988. "La revolución Salvadoreña de 1948: Un estudio sobre transformismo." In Jorge Cáceres P., Rafael Guidos Béjar, and Rafael Menjívar Larín, *El Salvador: Una historia sin lecciones*, pp. 17–129. San José, Costa Rica: FLACSO.

    1989. "Political Radicalization and Popular Pastoral Practices in El Salvador, 1969–1985." In Scott Mainwaring and Alexander Wilde, eds., *The Progressive Church in Latin America*, pp. 103–48. Notre Dame, IN: University of Notre Dame Press.

Calello, Osvaldo and Daniel Percero. 1984. *De Vandor a Ubaldini 2.* Buenos Aires: Centro Editor de América Latina.

Calviño, Marta. 1968. "Las contradicciones del radicalismo durante la década infame." In Luis Alberto Romero et al., eds., *El Radicalismo*, pp. 175–208. Buenos Aires: C. Pérez Editor.

Camerer, Colin R., and Ernst Fehr. 2004. "Measuring Social Norms and Preferences Using Experimental Games: A Guide for Social Scientists." In Joseph Henrich et al., eds., *Foundations of Human Sociality: Economic Experiments and Ethnographic Evidence from Fifteen Small-Scale Societies*, pp. 55–95. New York and Oxford: Oxford University Press.

Cañas, Antonio, and Héctor Dada. 1999. "Political Transition and Institutionalization in El Salvador." In Cynthia J. Arnson, ed., *Comparative Peace Processes in El Salvador*, pp. 69–95. Washington, DC: Woodrow Wilson Center Press and Stanford University Press.

Capoccia, Giovanni. 2005. *Defending Democracy: Reactions to Extremism in Interwar Europe.* Baltimore: John Hopkins University Press.

Capoccia, Giovanni, and Daniel Ziblatt. 2010. "The Historical Turn in Democratization Studies: A New Research Agenda for Europe and Beyond." *Comparative Political Studies* 43(8–9): 931–68.

Cardoso, Fernando Henrique. 1986. "Entrepreneurs and the Transition Process: The Brazilian Case." In Guillermo O'Donnell, Philippe C. Schmitter, and Laurence Whitehead, eds., *Transitions from Authoritarian Rule: Comparative Perspectives*, pp. 137–53. Baltimore: Johns Hopkins University Press.

Carothers, Thomas. 1991a. "The Reagan Years: The 1980s." In Abraham F. Lowenthal, ed., *Exporting Democracy: The United States and Latin America, Themes and Issues*, pp. 90–122. Baltimore: Johns Hopkins University.

    1991b. *In the Name of Democracy: U.S. Policy toward Latin America in the Reagan Years.* Berkeley: University of California Press.

1999. *Aiding Democracy Abroad: The Learning Curve.* Washington, DC: The Carnegie Endowment for International Peace.

Carr, Edward H. 1961. *What Is History?* London: Penguin.

Carter, David B., and Curtis S. Signorino. 2010. "Back to the Future: Modeling Time Dependence in Binary Data." *Political Analysis* 18(3): 271–92.

Casanova, Julián. 2010. *The Spanish Republic and Civil War.* Cambridge: Cambridge University Press.

Casper, Gretchen, and Michelle M. Taylor. 1996. *Negotiating Democracy: Transitions from Authoritarian Rule.* Pittsburgh, PA: University of Pittsburgh Press.

Castañeda, Jorge G. 1993. *Utopia Unarmed: The Latin American Left After the Cold War.* New York: Alfred A. Knopf.

Cavarozzi, Marcelo. 1983. *Autoritarismo y democracia (1955–1983).* Buenos Aires: Centro Editor de América Latina.

Charosky, Hernán. 2002. "Honestos y audaces: Realizaciones y límites de la política anticorrupción." In Marcos Novaro, ed., *El derrumbe político en el ocaso de la convertibilidad*, pp. 195–252. Buenos Aires: Grupo Editorial Norma.

Chehabi, Houchang E., and Juan J. Linz, eds. 1998. *Sultanistic Regimes.* Baltimore: Johns Hopkins University Press.

Cheibub, José Antonio. 2002. "Minority Governments, Deadlock Situations, and the Survival of Presidential Democracies." *Comparative Political Studies* 35(3): 284–312.

2007. *Presidentialism, Parliamentarism, and Democracy.* Cambridge: Cambridge University Press.

Cheibub, José Antonio, and Jennifer Gandhi. 2004. "Classifying Political Regimes: A Six-Fold Measure of Democracies and Dictatorships." Presented at the Annual Meeting of the American Political Science Association, Chicago, September 2–5.

Cheresky, Isidoro. 1999. *La innovación política: Política y derechos en la Argentina contemporánea.* Buenos Aires: Eudeba.

2008. *Poder presidencial, opinión pública y exclusión social.* Buenos Aires: Ediciones Manantial.

Chhibber, Pradeep K. 1999. *Democracy without Associations: Transformation of the Party System and Social Cleavages in India.* Ann Arbor: University of Michigan Press.

Chhibber, Pradeep K., and Mariano Torcal. 1997. "Elite Strategy, Social Cleavages, and Party Systems in a New Democracy: Spain." *Comparative Political Studies* 30(1): 27–54.

Child, John. 1980. *Unequal Alliance: The InterAmerican Military System, 1938–1978.* Boulder, CO: Westview.

Ching, Erik Kristofer. 1997. *From Clientelism to Militarism: The State, Politics and Authoritarianism in El Salvador, 1840–1940.* PhD Dissertation, University of California, Santa Barbara.

Ciria, Alberto. 1968. *Partidos y poder en la Argentina moderna (1930–46)*, second edition. Buenos Aires: Editorial Jorge Alvarez.

1971. *Perón y el justicialismo.* Buenos Aires: Siglo XXI.

Cohen, Youssef. 1994. *Radicals, Reformers, and Reactionaries: The Prisoner's Dilemma and the Collapse of Democracy in Latin America.* Chicago: University of Chicago Press.

Colburn, Forrest D. 2009. "The Turnover in El Salvador." *Journal of Democracy* 20(3): 143–52.

Collier, David. 1979. "The Bureaucratic-Authoritarian Model: Synthesis and Priorities for Future Research." In David Collier, ed., *The New Authoritarianism in Latin America*, pp. 363–98. Princeton: Princeton University Press.

  1993. "The Comparative Method: Two Decades of Change." In Ada Finifter, ed., *Political Science: The State of the Discipline*, pp. 105–20. Washington, DC: American Political Science Association.

Collier, David, Henry E. Brady, and Jason Seawright. 2004. "Sources of Leverage in Causal Inference: Toward an Alternative View of Methodology." In Henry E. Brady and David Collier, eds., *Rethinking Social Inquiry: Diverse Tools, Shared Standards*, pp. 229–71. Lanham, MD: Rowman and Littlefield.

Collier, David, James Mahoney, and Jason Seawright. 2004. "Claiming Too Much: Warnings about Selection Bias." In Henry E. Brady and David Collier, eds., *Rethinking Social Inquiry: Diverse Tools, Shared Standards*, pp. 85–102. Lanham, MD: Rowman and Littlefield.

Collier, Ruth Berins. 1999. *Paths toward Democracy: The Working Class and Elites in Western Europe and South America*. Cambridge: Cambridge University Press.

Collier, Ruth Berins and David Collier. 1991. *Shaping the Political Arena: Critical Junctures, the Labor Movement, and Regime Dynamics in Latin America*. Princeton, NJ: Princeton University Press.

Colomer, Josep. 1991. "Transitions by Agreement: Modeling the Spanish Way." *American Political Science Review* 85(4): 1283–1302.

Comisión Nacional sobre la Desaparición de Personas (CONADEP). 1984. *Nunca más*. Buenos Aires: EUDEBA.

Coppedge, Michael. 1997. "Modernization and Thresholds of Democracy: Evidence for a Common Path and Process." In Manus I. Midlarsky, ed., *Inequality, Democracy, and Economic Development*, pp. 177–201. Cambridge: Cambridge University Press.

  2005. "Explaining Democratic Deterioration in Venezuela through Nested Inference." In Frances Hagopian and Scott Mainwaring, eds., *The Third Wave of Democratization in Latin America: Advances and Setbacks*, pp. 289–316. Cambridge: Cambridge University Press.

  2012. *Democratization and Research Methods (Strategies for Social Inquiry)*. Cambridge: Cambridge University Press.

Coppedge, Michael, and John Gerring, with others. 2011. "Conceptualizing and Measuring Democracy: A New Approach." *Perspectives on Politics* 9(2): 247–67.

Coppedge, Michael, Staffan Lindberg, and John Gerring. 2012. *Varieties of Democracy*. Available from https://v-dem.net/ (accesed November 2012).

Córdova Macías, Ricardo. 1996. "El Salvador. La nueva agenda de posguerra." *Nueva Sociedad* 145(September–October): 9–15.

  1999. *El Salvador: Reforma militar y relaciones cívico-militares*. San Salvador: FUNDAUNGO.

Corrales, Javier. 2011. "Why Polarize? Advantages and Disadvantages of a Rational-Choice Analysis of Government-Opposition Relations under Hugo Chávez." In Thomas Ponniah and Jonathan Eastwood, eds., *The Revolution in Venezuela: Social and Political Change under Chávez*, pp. 67–97. Cambridge, MA: David Rockefeller Center for Latin American Studies, Harvard.

Corrales, Javier, and Michael Penfold. 2011. *Dragon in the Tropics: Hugo Chávez and the Political Economy of Revolution in Venezuela.* Washington, DC: Brookings Institution Press.

Coutinho, Carlos Nelson. 1980. *A Democracia como Valor Universal.* São Paulo: Livraria Editora Ciências Humanas.

Crahan, Margaret E. 1989. "Religion and Politics in Revolutionary Nicaragua." In Scott Mainwaring and Alexander Wilde, eds., *The Progressive Church in Latin America*, pp. 41–63. Notre Dame, IN: University of Notre Dame Press.

Cronqvist, Lasse. 2003. "Presentation of TOSMANA: Adding Multi-Value Variables and Visual Aids to QCA." Presented at the COMPASSS Launching Conference, Louvain-La-Neuve and Leuven, Belgium, September 16–17. Available at http://www.compasss.org/wpseries/Cronqvist2004.pdf.

Cutright, Phillips. 1963. "National Political Development: Measurement and Analysis." *American Sociological Review* 28(2): 253–64.

Dahl, Robert A. 1971. *Polyarchy: Participation and Opposition.* New Haven, CT: Yale University Press.

1989. *Democracy and Its Critics.* New Haven, CT: Yale University Press.

Dalton, Russell J. 1985. "Political Parties and Political Representation: Party Supporters and Party Elites in Nine Nations." *Comparative Political Studies* 18(3): 267–99.

Darden, Keith, and Anna Grzymala-Busse. 2006. "The Great Divide: Literacy, Nationalism, and the Communist Collapse." *World Politics* 59(1): 83–115.

Debray, Régis. 1967. *Revolution in the Revolution? Armed Struggle and Political Struggle in Latin America.* New York: Grove Press.

Deere, Carmen Diana. 1982. "A Comparative Analysis of Agrarian Reform in El Salvador and Nicaragua." *Development and Change* 13(1): 1–41.

Deininger, Klaus, and Lyn Squire. 1996. "A New Dataset Measuring Income Inequality." *The World Bank Economic Review* 10(3): 565–91.

1998. "New Ways of Looking at Old Issues: Inequality and Growth." *Journal of Development Economics* 57: 259–87.

de Ipola, Emilio. 1987. "La difícil apuesta del peronismo democrático." In José Nun and Juan Carlos Portantiero, eds., *Ensayos sobre la transición democrática en la Argentina*, pp. 333–74. Buenos Aires: Puntosur Editores.

de Kadt, Emanuel. 1970. *Catholic Radicals in Brazil.* Oxford: Oxford University Press.

De Riz, Liliana. 1987. *Retorno y derrumbe: el último gobierno peronista.* Buenos Aires: Hyspamérica.

2000. *La política en suspenso, 1966–1976.* Buenos Aires: Paidós.

Derby, Lauren. 2009. *The Dictator's Seduction: Politics and the Popular Imagination in the Era of Trujillo.* Durham, NC: Duke University Press.

Diamint, Rut. 2006. "Crisis, Democracy, and the Military in Argentina." In Edward Epstein and David Pion-Berlin, eds., *Broken Promises? The Argentine Crisis and Argentine Democracy*, pp. 163–79. Lanham, MD: Lexington Books.

Diamond, Larry. 1988. *Class, Ethnicity and Democracy in Nigeria: The Failure of the First Republic.* Syracuse, NY: Syracuse University Press.

1992. "Economic Development and Democracy Reconsidered." In Gary Marks and Larry Diamond, eds., *Reexamining Democracy: Essays in Honor of Seymour Martin Lipset*, pp. 93–139. Newbury Park, CA: Sage.

1999. *Developing Democracy: Toward Consolidation.* Baltimore: Johns Hopkins University Press.

2002. "Thinking about Hybrid Regimes." *Journal of Democracy* 13(2): 21–35.

Diamond, Larry, and Juan J. Linz. 1989. "Introduction: Politics, Society, and Democracy in Latin America." In Larry Diamond, Juan J. Linz, and Seymour Martin Lipset, eds., *Democracy in Developing Countries: Latin America*, pp. 1–58. Boulder, CO: Lynne Rienner.

Di Palma, Giuseppe. 1990. *To Craft Democracies: An Essay on Democratic Transitions.* Berkeley: University of California Press.

Disi Pavlic, Rodolfo. 2011. "*A Puzzling Agent and its Changing Principal: Analyzing the Organization of American States' Fluctuating Democracy Promotion in Latin America, 1948–2011.*" Senior honors thesis, University of Notre Dame.

Domínguez, Jorge I. 1998. *Democratic Politics in Latin America and the Caribbean.* Baltimore: Johns Hopkins University Press.

Domínguez, Jorge I., and James A. McCann. 1996. *Democratizing Mexico: Public Opinion and Electoral Choices.* Baltimore: Johns Hopkins University Press.

Doorenspleet, Renske. 2000. "Reassessing the Three Waves of Democratization." *World Politics* 52(3): 384–406.

Downs, Anthony. 1957. *An Economic Theory of Democracy.* New York: Harper and Row.

Doyon, Louise M. 1988. "El crecimiento sindical bajo el peronismo." In Juan C. Torre, ed., *La formación del sindicalismo peronista*, pp. 169–81. Buenos Aires: Legasa.

2006. *Perón y los trabajadores. Los orígenes del sindicalismo peronista, 1943–1955.* Buenos Aires: Siglo XXI Editores.

Drake, Paul W. 2009. *Between Tyranny and Anarchy: A History of Democracy in Latin America, 1800–2006.* Stanford, CA: Stanford University Press.

Dulles, John W. F. 1970. *Unrest in Brazil: Political-Military Crises 1955–1964.* Austin: University of Texas Press.

Dunkerley, James. 1982. *The Long War: Dictatorship and Revolution in El Salvador.* London: Junction Books.

Eckstein, Harry. 1966. *Division and Cohesion in Democracy: A Study of Norway.* Princeton, NJ: Princeton University Press.

1975. "Case Studies and Theory in Political Science." In Fred I. Greenstein, and Nelson Polsby, eds., *Handbook of Political Science*, vol. 7., pp. 94–137. Reading: Addison-Wesley.

Economic Commission for Latin America and the Caribbean (ECLAC). 1992. *Preliminary Overview of the Latin American and Caribbean Economy.* Santiago, Chile: United Nations, CEPAL.

1994. *Social Panorama of Latin America.* Available from http://www.eclac.cl/.

1995. *Social Panorama of Latin America.* Available from http://www.eclac.cl/.

2001. *Economic Survey of Latin America and the Caribbean. Current Conditions and Outlook.* Santiago, Chile: United Nations, CEPAL.

2005. *Social Panorama of Latin America.* Available from http://www.eclac.cl/.

2006. *Preliminary Overview of the Economies of Latin America and the Caribbean.* Available from: http://www.eclac.org/cgi-bin/getProd.asp?xml=/publicaciones/xml/3/27543/P27543.xml&xsl=/de/tpl-i/p9f.xsl&base=/tpl-i/top-bottom.xslt (accessed November 2012).

2008. *Public sector statistics: Tax revenue.* Available from http://websie.eclac.cl/infest/ajax/cepalstat.asp?idioma=i.

2009. *Social Panorama of Latin America.* Available from http://www.eclac.cl/.

2010. *Social Panorama of Latin America*. Available from http://www.eclac.cl/.

2011. *Anuario Estadístico de América Latina y el Caribe*. Available from http://www.
eclac.cl/publicaciones/xml/7/45607/LCG2513b.pdf (accessed November 2012).

Ellner, Steve. 2001. "The Radical Potential of Chavismo in Venezuela. The First Year and
a Half in Power." *Latin American Perspectives* 28(5): 5–32.

Elster, Jon. 1989a. "Social Norms and Economic Theory." *Journal of Economic
Perspectives* 3 No. 4 (Fall): 99–117.

1989b. *Solomonic Judgments: Studies in the Limitations of Rationality*. Cambridge
and New York: Cambridge University Press.

Epstein, David L., Robert Bates, Jack Goldstone, Ida Kristensen, and Sharyn O'Halloran.
2006. "Democratic Transitions." *American Journal of Political Science* 50 (3):
551–69.

Farer, Tom, ed. 1996. *Beyond Sovereignty: Collectively Defending Democracy in the
Americas*. Baltimore: Johns Hopkins University Press.

Ferejohn, John, and Debra Satz. 1995." Unification, Universalism, and Rational Choice
Theory." *Critical Review* 9(1–2): 71–84.

Figueiredo, Argelina Cheibub. 1993. *Democracia ou Reformas: Alternativas
Democráticas à Crise Política*. Rio de Janeiro: Paz e Terra.

Figueiredo, Argelina Cheibub, and Fernando Limongi. 1999. *Executivo e Legislativo na
Nova Ordem Constitucional*. Rio de Janeiro: Editora FGV.

Finkel, Steven, Aníbal Pérez-Liñán, and Mitchell A. Seligson. 2007. "Effects of U.S.
Foreign Assistance on Democracy Building, 1990–2003." *World Politics* 59(3):
404–39.

Finnemore, Martha. 1998. *National Interests in International Society*. Ithaca, NY:
Cornell University Press.

Fish, M. Steven. 2006. "Stronger Legislatures, Stronger Democracies." *Journal of
Democracy* 17(1): 5–20.

Fishman, Robert. 1990a. "Rethinking State and Regime: Southern Europe's Transition to
Democracy." *World Politics* 42(3): 422–40.

1990b. *Working-Class Organization and the Return to Democracy in Spain*. Ithaca,
NY: Cornell University Press.

2011. "Democratic Practice after the Revolution: The Case of Portugal and Beyond."
Politics & Society 39(2): 233–67.

Fontana, Andrés. 1987. "La política militar del gobierno constitucional argentino." In
José Nun, and Juan Carlos Portantiero, eds., *Ensayos sobre la transición
democrática en la Argentina*, pp. 375–418. Buenos Aires: Puntosur Editores.

Forsythe, David P. 1989. *Human Rights and World Politics*. Lincoln: University of
Nebraska Press.

Foucault, Michel. 1972. *The Archaeology of Knowledge*. New York: Pantheon.

Freedom House. 2002. *Freedom of the Press – Argentina*. Available from http://www.
freedomhouse.org (accessed April 16, 2009).

2007. "Freedom in the World." Available from http://www.freedomhouse.org/report/
freedom-world/freedom-world-2007

Frey, Bruno, Matthias Benz, and Alois Stutzer. 2004. "Introducing Procedural Utility:
Not Only What, but Also How Matters." *Journal of Institutional and Theoretical
Economics* 160: 377–401.

Frey, Bruno, Marcel Kucher, and Alois Stutzer. 2001. "Outcome, Process and Power in
Direct Democracy." *Public Choice* 107: 271–93.

Frey, Bruno, and Alois Stutzer. 2005. "Beyond Outcomes: Measuring Procedural Utility." *Oxford Economic Papers* 57: 90–111.

Friedman, Milton. 1953. *Essays in Positive Economics*. Chicago: University of Chicago Press.

Fukuyama, Francis. 1992. *The End of History and the Last Man*. New York: Free Press.

Gangl, Amy. 2003. "Justice Theory and Evaluations of the Lawmaking Process." *Political Behavior* 25(2): 119–49.

García Lerena, Roberto. 2007. *Saúl Ubaldini: Crónicas de un militante obrero peronista*. Buenos Aires: Ediciones Runa Comunicaciones.

Gasiorowski, Mark J. 1995. "Economic Crisis and Political Regime Change: An Event History Analysis." *American Political Science Review* 89(4): 882–97.

    2000. "Democracy and Macroeconomic Performance in Underdeveloped Countries: An Empirical Analysis." *Comparative Political Studies* 33(3): 319–49.

Gaspar Tapia, Gabriel. 1989. *El Salvador: El ascenso de la nueva derecha*. San Salvador: Centro de Investigación y Acción Social.

Gasparini, Leonardo, and Nora Lustig. 2011. "The Rise and Fall of Income Inequality in Latin America." In José A. Ocampo and Jaime Ros, eds., *The Oxford Handbook of Latin American Economics*, pp. 691–714. Oxford: Oxford University Press.

Geddes, Barbara. 1999. "What Do We Know about Democratization after Twenty Years?" *Annual Review of Political Science* 2: 115–44.

    2003. *Paradigms and Sand Castles: Theory Building and Research Design in Comparative Politics*. Ann Arbor: University of Michigan Press.

George, Alexander L., and Andrew Bennett. 2004. *Case Studies and Theory Development in the Social Sciences*. Cambridge, MA: MIT Press.

Germani, Gino. 1974. *Política y sociedad en una época de transición*, 5th edition. Buenos Aires: Paidós.

Gerring, John. 2007. *Case Study Research: Principles and Practices*. Cambridge: Cambridge University Press.

Gerring, John, Phillip J. Bond, William T. Barndt, and Carola Moreno. 2005. "Democracy and Economic Growth: A Historical Perspective." *World Politics* 57(3): 323–64.

Gibson, Edward L. 1996. *Class and Conservative Parties: Argentina in Comparative Perspective*. Baltimore: Johns Hopkins University Press.

Gill, Anthony. 1998. *Rendering unto Caesar: The Catholic Church and the State in Latin America*. Chicago: University of Chicago Press.

Gillespie, Richard. 1982. *Soldiers of Perón: Argentina's Montoneros*. Oxford: Clarendon Press.

Glaeser, Edward L., Rafael La Porta, Florencio Lopez-de-Silanes, and Andrei Shleifer. 2004. "Do Institutions Cause Growth?" *Journal of Economic Growth* 9(3): 271–303.

Gleditsch, Kristian Skrede. 2002. *All International Politics Is Local: The Diffusion of Conflict, Integration, and Democratization*. Ann Arbor: University of Michigan Press.

Gleditsch, Kristian Skrede, and Michael D. Ward. 2006. "Diffusion and the International Context of Democratization." *International Organization* 60(4): 911–33.

Glynn, Adam N. 2012. "The Product and Difference Fallacies for Indirect Effects." *American Journal of Political Science* 56(1): 257–69.

Godio, Julio. 2006. *El tiempo de Kirchner. El devenir de una "revolución desde arriba."* Buenos Aires: Ediciones Letra Grifa.

Goldstein, Judith. 1993. *Ideas, Interests, and American Trade Policy.* Ithaca, NY: Cornell University Press.

Goldstein, Judith, and Robert O. Keohane. 1993. "Ideas and Foreign Policy: An Analytical Framework." In Judith Goldstein and Robert O. Keohane, eds., *Ideas and Foreign Policy: Beliefs, Institutions, and Political Change,* pp. 3–30. Ithaca, NY: Cornell University Press.

Goldthorpe, John H. 1991. "The Uses of History in Sociology: Reflections on Some Recent Tendencies." *British Journal of Sociology* 42(2): 211–30.

Gómez, José María, and Eduardo Viola. 1984. "Transición desde el autoritarismo y potencialidades de invención democrática en la Argentina de 1983." In Oscar Oszlak et al., eds., *"Proceso," crisis y transición democrática,* Vol. 2, pp. 29–42. Buenos Aires: Centro Editor de América Latina.

Gómez de Souza, Luis Alberto. 1984. *A JUC: Os Estudantes Católicos e a Política.* Petrópolis: Vozes.

González, Luis Armando. 2003a. "De la ideología al pragmatismo: Ensayo sobre las trayectorias ideológicas de ARENA y el FMLN." *Estudios Centroamericanos* 58(661–62): 1173–1200.

  2003b. "Anticomunismo sin fundamento." *Estudios Centroamericanos* 58(656): 605–11.

Grosso, Juan Carlos. 1968. "Los problemas económicos y sociales y la respuesta radical en el gobierno (1916–1930)." In Luis A. Romero et al., eds., *El Radicalismo,* pp. 125–73. Buenos Aires: C. Pérez Editor.

Guadagni, Alieto Aldo. 2007. *Braden o Perón.* Buenos Aires: Sudamericana.

Guevara, Ernesto (Che). 1961. *On Guerrilla Warfare.* New York: Frederick A. Praeger.

Guido Béjar, Rafael. 1996. "La izquierda en crisis." In Rafael Guido Béjar and Stefan Roggenbuck, eds., *Partidos y actores políticos en la transición: La derecha, la izquierda y el centro en El Salvador,* pp. 53–78. San Salvador: Fundación Konrad Adenauer.

Guidos Béjar, José Rafael. 1988. "El estado en el proceso de la revolución." In Jorge Cáceres P., Rafael Guidos Béjar, and Rafael Menjívar Larín, *El Salvador: Una historia sin lecciones,* pp. 131–228. San José, Costa Rica: FLACSO.

Gurr, Ted Robert, Keith Jaggers, and Will Moore. 1990. "The Transformation of the Western State: The Growth of Democracy, Autocracy, and State Power since 1800." *Studies in Comparative International Development* 25(1): 73–108.

Haber, Stephen, and Victor Menaldo. 2011. "Do Natural Resources Fuel Authoritarianism? A Reappraisal of the Resource Curse." *American Political Science Review* 105(1): 1–26.

Haggard, Stephan, and Robert R. Kaufman 1995. *The Political Economy of Democratic Transitions.* Princeton: Princeton University Press.

  2012. "Inequality and Regime Change: Democratic Transitions and the Stability of Democratic Rule." *American Political Science Review* 106 No. 3 (August): 495–516.

Hagopian, Frances. 1996a. *Traditional Politics and Regime Change in Brazil.* Cambridge: Cambridge University Press.

  1996b. "Traditional Power Structures and Democratic Governance in Latin America." In Jorge I. Domínguez and Abraham F. Lowenthal, eds., *Constructing Democratic*

Governance: Latin America and the Caribbean in the 1990s-Themes and Issues, pp. 64–86. Baltimore: Johns Hopkins University Press.

2009. "The Catholic Church in a Plural Latin America." In Frances Hagopian, ed., *Religious Pluralism, Democracy, and the Catholic Church in Latin America*, pp. 429–66. Notre Dame, IN: University of Notre Dame Press.

Hall, Peter A. 1989. *The Political Power of Economic Ideas: Keynesianism across Nations*. Princeton, NJ: Princeton University Press.

Halperín Donghi, Tulio. 1995. *Argentina en el callejón*. Buenos Aires: Ariel.

Handy, Jim. 1984. *Gift of the Devil: A History of Guatemala*. Boston: South End Press.

Harnecker, Marta. 1988. *El Salvador: Partido Comunista y guerra revolucionaria: entrevista a Schafik Jorge Handal, febrero 1985-febrero 1988*. Buenos Aires: Dialéctica.

ed. 1993. *Con la Mirada en alto: Historia de las Fuerzas Populares de Liberación Farabundo Martí a través de entrevistas con sus dirigentes*. San Salvador: UCA Editores.

Harsanyi, John C. 1982. "Morality and the Theory of Rational Behaviour." In Amartya Sen and Bernard Williams, eds. *Utilitarianism and Beyond*, pp. 39–62. Cambridge: Cambridge University Press.

Hartlyn, Jonathan. 1984. "Military Governments and the Transition to Civilian Rule: The Colombian Experience of 1957–1958." *Journal of Interamerican Studies and World Affairs* 26(2): 245–81.

1988. *The Politics of Coalition Rule in Colombia*. Cambridge: Cambridge University Press.

1991. "The Dominican Republic: The Legacy of Intermittent Engagement." In Abraham Lowenthal, ed., *Exporting Democracy: The United States and Latin America*, Case Studies, pp. 53–92. Baltimore: Johns Hopkins University Press.

1998. "Political Continuities, Missed Opportunities, and Institutional Rigidities: Another Look at Democratic Transitions in Latin America." In Scott Mainwaring and Arturo Valenzuela, eds., *Politics, Society, and Democracy: Latin America*, pp. 101–20. Boulder, CO: Westview Press.

Hartlyn, Jonathan, and Arturo Valenzuela. 1994. "Democracy in Latin America since 1930." In Leslie Bethell, ed., *The Cambridge History of Latin America, Vol. 6 Part 2, Latin America since 1930: Economy, Society, and Politics*. Cambridge: Cambridge University Press.

Hawkins, Kirk A. 2010. *Venezuela's Chavismo and Populism in Comparative Perspective*. New York: Cambridge University Press.

Helmke, Gretchen. 2005. *Courts under Constraints: Judges, Generals, and Presidents in Argentina*. New York: Cambridge University Press.

Heston, Alan, Robert Summers, and Bettina Aten. 2006. Penn World Table Version 6.2. Center for International Comparisons of Production, Income and Prices at the University of Pennsylvania. Available from http://pwt.econ.upenn.edu/.

Hibbing, John R., and Elizabeth Theiss-Morse. 2001. "Process Preferences and American Politics: What the People Want Government to Be." *American Political Science Review* 95(1): 145–53.

Hirschman, Albert O. 1982. *Shifting Involvements: Private Interest and Public Action*. Princeton, NJ: Princeton University Press.

Hofferbert, Richard I., and Hans Dieter Klingemann. 1999. "Remembering the Bad Old Days: Human Rights, Economic Conditions, and Democratic Performance in Transitional Regimes." *European Journal of Political Research* 36: 155–74.

Hox, Joop J. 2010. *Multilevel Analysis: Techniques and Applications*. 2nd ed. New York: Routledge.

Hsieh, Chang Tai, Edward Miguel, Daniel Ortega, and Francisco Rodríguez. 2007. "The Price of Political Opposition: Evidence from Venezuela's *Misanta*." *American Economic Journal: Applied Economics* 3: 196–214.

Htun, Mala. 2003. *Sex and the State: Abortion, Divorce, and the Family Under Latin American Dictatorships and Democracies*. Cambridge: Cambridge University Press.

Huber, Evelyne, and John D. Stephens. 2012. *Democracy and the Left: Social Policy and Inequality in Latin America*. Chicago: The University of Chicago Press.

Human Rights Watch. 2004. *Rigging the Rule of Law: Judicial Independence under Siege in Venezuela*. Available from http://www.hrw.org/en/node/12011/section/1 (accessed July 2009).

2012. *Tightening the Grip: Concentration and the Abuse of Power in Chávez's Venezuela*. Available from http://www.hrw.org/news/2012/07/17/venezuela-concentration-and-abuse-power-under-ch-vez (accessed November 2012).

Huntington, Samuel P. 1968. *Political Order in Changing Societies*. New Haven, CT: Yale University Press.

1984. "Will More Countries Become Democratic?" *Political Science Quarterly* 99(2): 193–218.

1991. *The Third Wave: Democratization in the Late Twentieth Century*. Norman: University of Oklahoma Press.

1996. *The Clash of Civilizations and the Remaking of World Order*. New York: Simon & Schuster.

Inglehart, Ronald. 1990. *Culture Shift in Advanced Industrial Society*. Princeton, NJ: Princeton University Press.

1997. *Modernization and Postmodernization: Cultural, Economic, and Political Change in 43 Societies*. Princeton, NJ: Princeton University Press.

Inglehart, Ronald, and Christian Welzel. 2005. *Modernization, Cultural Change, and Democracy: The Human Development Sequence*. New York: Cambridge University Press.

Instituto Nacional de Estadísticas y Censos (INDEC). 2009. *Encuesta Nacional a Grandes Empresas (ENGE)*. Available from http://www.indec.mecon.ar/nueva-web/cuadros/16/engeo51501.xls (accessed November 2012).

International Labour Office (ILO). Yearbooks of Labour Statistics 1955, 1960, 1965, 1970, 1975, 1980. Geneva.

2002. *Panorama laboral 2002: América Latina y el Caribe*. Lima.

2009. *Labour Statistics Database*. Available from http://laborsta.ilo.org/.

Iversen, Torben. 1994. "Political Leadership and Representation in Western European Democracies." *American Journal of Political Science* 38: 46–74.

Jackman, Robert 1973. "On the Relation of Economic Development to Democratic Performance." *American Journal of Political Science* 17: 611–21.

Jaggers, Keith, and Ted Robert Gurr. 1995. "Tracking Democracy's Third Wave with the Polity III Data." *Journal of Peace Research* 32(4): 469–82.

James, Daniel. 1990. *Resistencia e integración. El peronismo y la clase trabajadora argentina, 1946–1976*. Buenos Aires: Editorial Sudamericana.

Jaunarena, Horacio. 2011. *La casa está en orden: memoria de la transición*. Buenos Aires: Taeda Editora.

Johnson, Kenneth L. 1993. *Between Revolution and Democracy: Business Elites and the State in the 80s*. PhD Dissertation, Tulane University.

Kahneman, Daniel, and Amos Tversky. 1979. "Prospect Theory: An Analysis of Decision under Risk." *Econometrica* 47 (2):263–91.

Kapstein, Ethan B., and Nathan Converse. 2008. "Why Democracies Fail." *Journal of Democracy* 19(4): 57–68.

Karl, Terry L. 1986. "Imposing Consent? Electoralism versus Democratization in El Salvador." In Paul W. Drake and Eduardo Silva, eds., *Elections and Democratization in Latin America, 1980–1985*, pp. 9–36. San Diego: Center for Iberian and Latin American Studies.

   1987. "Petroleum and Political Pacts: The Transition to Democracy in Venezuela." *Latin American Research Review* 22(1): 63–94.

   1990. "Dilemmas of Democratization in Latin America." *Comparative Politics* 23(1): 1–21.

   1995. "The Hybrid Regimes of Central America." *Journal of Democracy* 6(3): 72–87.

   1997. *The Paradox of Plenty: Oil Booms and Petro-States*. Berkeley: University of California Press.

Keck, Margaret E., and Kathryn Sikkink. 1998. *Activists beyond Borders: Advocacy Networks in International Politics*. Ithaca, NY: Cornell University Press

Kenney, Charles D. 1998. "Outsider and Anti-Party Politicians in Power: New Conceptual Strategies and Empirical Evidence from Peru." *Party Politics* 4(1): 57–75.

   2004. *Fujimori's Coup and the Breakdown of Democracy in Latin America*. Notre Dame, IN: University of Notre Dame Press.

King, Gary, Robert O. Keohand, and Sidney Verba. 1994. *Designing Social Inquiry: Scientific Inquiry in Qualitative Research*. Princeton, NJ: Princeton University Press.

Kitschelt, Herbert. 1994. *The Transformation of European Social Democracy*. Cambridge: Cambridge University Press.

Kitschelt, Herbert, Zdenka Mansfeldova, Rodoslaw Markowski, and Gábor Tóka. 1999. *Post-Communist Party Systems: Competition, Representation, and Inter-Party Cooperation*. Cambridge: Cambridge University Press.

Klesner, Joseph L. 2004. "The Structure of the Mexican Electorate: Social, Attitudinal, and Partisan Bases of Vicente Fox's Victory." In Jorge I. Domínguez and Chappell Lawson, eds., *Mexico's Pivotal Democratic Election: Candidates, Voters, and the Presidential Campaign of 2000*, pp. 91–122. Stanford, CA: Stanford University Press.

Koivumaeki, Riitta-Ilona. 2010. "Business, Economic Experts, and Conservative Party Building in Latin America: The Case of El Salvador." *Journal of Politics in Latin America* 2(1): 79–106.

Konder, Leandro. 1980. *A Democracia e os Comunistas no Brasil*. Rio de Janeiro: Graal.

Kornblith, Miriam. 2005. "Elections versus Democracy: The Referendum in Venezuela." *Journal of Democracy* 16(1): 124–37.

Kuran, Timur. 1989. "Sparks and Prairie Fires: A Theory of Unanticipated Political Revolution." *Public Choice* 61(1): 41–74.

   1991. "Now Out of Never: The Element of Surprise in the East European Revolution of 1989." *World Politics* 44(1): 7–48.

Kvaternik, Eugenio. 1987. *Crisis sin salvaje: La crisis político-militar de 1962–63.* Buenos Aires: Ediciones del IDES.

Laakso, Markku, and Rein Taagepera. 1979. "'Effective' Number of Parties: A Measure with Application to Western Europe." *Comparative Political Studies* 12(1): 3–27.

Lamounier, Bolivar. 1981. "Representação Política: A Importância de Certos Formalismos." In Bolivar Lamounier, Francisco C. Weffort, and Maria Victoria Benevides, eds., *Direito, Cidadania e Participação*, pp. 230–57. São Paulo: T. A. Queiroz, Editor.

Landman, Todd. 1999. "Economic Development and Democracy: The View from Latin America." *Political Studies* 47: 607–26.

Lanusse, Alejandro. 1988. "Entrevista al Tte. Gral. Alejandro Agustín Lanusse por Gregorio A. Caro Figueroa." *Todo es Historia* 253(July): 58–63.

Latin American Public Opinion Project (LAPOP). 2008. *AmericasBarometer.* Nashville, TN: Vanderbilt University.

2010. *AmericasBarometer.* Nashville, TN: Vanderbilt University.

Latinobarómetro. 2007. "Latinobarómetro Report 2007." Available from http://www. latinobarometro.org (accessed November 2011).

2011. "Latinobarómetro Report 2011." Available from http://www.latinobarometro. org (accessed September 2012).

Lauria-Santiago, Aldo A. 1999. *An Agrarian Republic: Commercial Agriculture and the Politics of Peasant Communities in El Salvador, 1823–1914.* Pittsburgh, PA: University of Pittsburgh Press.

Leis, Héctor Ricardo. 2012. *Testamento de los años 70.* Buenos Aires: Fundación TD. Available from http://www.clubpoliticoargentino.org/wp-content/uploads/2012/09/testamento-de-los-70-leis.pdf.

Legler, Thomas, Sharon Lean, and Dexter Boniface 2007. *Promoting Democracy in the Americas.* Baltimore: Johns Hopkins University Press.

Lehoucq, Fabrice. 2012. *The Politics of Modern Central America: Civil War, Democratization, and Underdevelopment.* New York: Cambridge University Press.

LeoGrande, William M. 1998. *Our Own Backyard: The United States in Central America, 1977–1992.* Chapel Hill: University of North Carolina Press.

Lepsius, M. Rainer. 1978. "From Fragmented Party Democracy to Government by Emergency Decree and National Socialist Takeover: Germany." In Juan J. Linz and Alfred Stepan, *The Breakdown of Democratic Regimes: Europe*, pp. 34–79. Baltimore: Johns Hopkins University Press.

Levi, Margaret, Audrey Sacks, and Tom Tyler. 2009. "Conceptualizing Legitimacy, Measuring Legitimacy Beliefs." *American Behavioral Scientist* 53(3): 354–75.

Levine, Daniel H. 1973. *Conflict and Political Change in Venezuela.* Princeton, NJ: Princeton University Press.

1978. "Venezuela since 1958: The Consolidation of Democratic Politics." In Juan J. Linz and Alfred Stepan, eds., *The Breakdown of Democratic Regimes*, Vol. 3, *Latin America*, pp. 82–109. Baltimore: Johns Hopkins University Press.

1981. *Religion and Politics in Latin America: The Catholic Church in Venezuela and Colombia.* Princeton, NJ: Princeton University Press.

1989. "Venezuela: The Nature, Sources, and Future Prospects of Democracy." In Larry Diamond, Juan J. Linz, and Seymour Martin Lipset, eds., *Democracy in Developing Countries: Latin America*, pp. 247–89. Boulder, CO: Lynne Rienner.

1992. *Popular Voices in Latin American Catholicism*. Princeton, NJ: Princeton University Press.

Levitsky, Steven. 2003. *Transforming Labor-Based Parties in Latin America: Argentine Peronism in Comparative Perspective*. Cambridge: Cambridge University Press.

Levitsky, Steven, and Scott Mainwaring. 2006. "Organized Labor and Democracy in Latin America." *Comparative Politics* 39(1): 21–42.

Levitsky, Steven and María Victoria Murillo. 2005. "Building Castles in the Sand? The Politics of Institutional Weakness in Argentina." In Steven Levitsky, and María Victoria Murillo, eds., *Argentine Democracy: The Politics of Institutional Weakness*, pp. 21–44. University Park: Pennsylvania State University Press.

Levitsky, Steven, and Kenneth Roberts. 2011. *The Resurgence of the Latin American Left*. Baltimore: Johns Hopkins University Press.

Levitsky, Steven, and Lucan Way. 2002. "The Rise of Competitive Authoritarianism." *Journal of Democracy* 12(2): 51–66.

2010. *Competitive Authoritarianism: Hybrid Regimes After the Cold War*. Cambridge: Cambridge University Press.

Lieberson, Stanley. 1991. "Small N's and Big Conclusions: An Examination of the Reasoning in Comparative Studies Based on a Small Number of Cases." *Social Forces* 70(2): 307–20.

Lijphart, Arend. 1971. "Comparative Politics and the Comparative Method." *American Political Science Review* 65: 682–93.

1977. *Democracy in Plural Societies: A Comparative Exploration*. New Haven, CT: Yale University Press.

Lind, E. Allan, Carol T. Kulik, Maureen Ambrose, and Maria V. de Vera Park. 1993. "Individual and Corporate Dispute Resolution: Using Procedural Fairnesss as a Decision Heuristic." *Administrative Science Quarterly* 38(2): 224–41.

Linz, Juan J. 1978a. "The Breakdown of Democracy in Spain." In Juan J. Linz and Alfred Stepan, eds., *The Breakdown of Democratic Regimes: Europe*, pp. 142–215. Baltimore: Johns Hopkins University Press.

1978b. *The Breakdown of Democratic Regimes: Crisis, Breakdown, and Reequilibration*. Baltimore: Johns Hopkins University Press.

1988. "Legitimacy of Democracy and the Socioeconomic System." In Mattei Dogan, ed., *Comparing Pluralist Democracies: Strains on Legitimacy*, pp. 65–97. Boulder, CO: Westview Press.

1991. "Church and State in Spain from the Civil War to the Return of Democracy." *Daedalus* 120(3): 159–78.

1994. "Presidential or Parliamentary Democracy: Does It Make a Difference?" In Juan J. Linz and Arturo Valenzuela, eds., *The Failure of Presidential Democracy. The Case of Latin America*, pp. 3–87. Baltimore: Johns Hopkins University Press.

1997. "Democracy, Multinationalism, and Federalism." Instituto Juan March de Estudios e Investigaciones Working Paper 1997/103 (June).

2000. *Totalitarian and Authoritarian Regimes*. Boulder, CO: Lynne Rienner.

Linz, Juan J., and Alfred Stepan, eds. 1978. *The Breakdown of Democratic Regimes*. Baltimore: Johns Hopkins University Press.

1989. "Political Crafting of Democratic Consolidation or Destruction: European and South American Comparisons." In Robert A. Pastor, ed., *Democracy in the Americas: Stopping the Pendulum*, pp. 41–61. New York: Holmes and Meier.

1996. *Problems of Democratic Transition and Consolidation.* Baltimore: Johns Hopkins University Press.

Lipset, Seymour M. 1959. "Some Social Requisites of Democracy: Economic Development and Political Legitimacy." *American Political Science Review* 53(1): 69–105.

1960. *Political Man: The Social Bases of Politics.* Garden City, NY: Anchor.

Lipset, Seymour Martin, and Stein Rokkan. 1967. "Cleavage Structures, Party Systems, and Voter Alignments: An Introduction." In Seymour Martin Lipset and Stein Rokkan, eds., *Party Systems and Voter Alignments: Cross-National Perspectives*, pp. 1–64. New York: Free Press.

Lipset, Seymour Martin, Kyoung-Ryung Seong, and John C. Torres. 1993. "A Comparative Analysis of the Social Requisites of Democracy." *International Social Science Journal* 136: 155–75.

Llanos, Mariana. 1998. "El presidente, el Congreso y la política de privatizaciones en la Argentina (1989–1997)." *Desarrollo Económico* 38(151): 743–70.

Lohmann, Susanne. 1994. "The Dynamics of Information Cascades: The Monday Demonstrations in Leipzig, East Germany, 1989–91." *World Politics* 47(1): 42–101.

Londregan, John B., and Keith T. Poole. 1996. "Does High Income Promote Democracy?" *World Politics* 49(1): 1–30.

López Maya, Margarita. 2005. *Del viernes negro al referendo revocatorio.* Caracas: Alfadil.

Lowenthal, Abraham F. 1991. "The United States and Latin American Democracy: Learning from History." In Abraham F. Lowenthal, ed., *Exporting Democracy: The United States and Latin America, Themes and Issues*, pp. 243–65. Baltimore: Johns Hopkins University.

Luna, Félix. 1975. *El '45.* Buenos Aires: Editorial Sudamericana.

1988. *Yrigoyen.* Buenos Aires: Editorial Sudamericana.

Lustick, Ian S. 1996. "History, Historiography, and Political Science: Multiple Historical Records and the Problem of Selection Bias." *American Political Science Review* 90(3): 605–18.

Lutz, Ellen L., and Kathryn Sikkink. 2001. "The International Dimension of Democratization and Human Rights in Latin America." In Manuel Antonio Garretón and Edward Newman, eds., *Democracy in Latin America: (Re) Constructing Political Society*, pp. 278–300. New York: United Nations University.

Lynch, Cecelia. 1999. *Beyond Appeasement: Interpreting Interwar Peace Agreements in World Politics.* Ithaca, NY: Cornell University Press.

Mackie, Gerry. 2003. *Democracy Defended.* Cambridge: Cambridge University Press.

Maddison, Angus. 1989. *The World Economy in the 20th Century.* Paris: Organisation for Economic Co-Operation and Development.

2003. *The World Economy: Historical Statistics.* Paris, France: Development Centre of the Organisation for Economic Co-operation and Development.

Magaloni, Beatriz. 1999. "Is the PRI Fading? Economic Performance, Electoral Accountability, and Voting Behavior in the 1994 and 1997 Elecctions." In Jorge I. Domínguez and Alejandro Poiré, eds., *Toward Mexico's Democratization: Parties, Campaigns, Elections, and Public Opinion*, pp. 203–36. New York: Routledge.

2006. *Voting for Autocracy: Hegemonic Party Survival and Its Demise in Mexico.* Cambridge: Cambridge University Press.

Magaloni, Beatriz and Alejandro Moreno. 2003. "Catching All Souls: The Partido Acción Nacional and the Politics of Religion in Mexico." In Scott Mainwaring and Timothy R. Scully, eds. *Christian Democracy in Latin America: Electoral Competition and Regime Conflicts*, pp. 247–72. Stanford, CA: Stanford University Press.

Mahoney, James. 2001. *The Legacies of Liberalism: Path Dependence and Political Regimes in Central America*. Baltimore: Johns Hopkins University Press.

2003. "Strategies of Causal Assessment in Comparative Historical Analysis." In James Mahoney and Dietrich Rueschemeyer, eds., *Comparative Historical Analysis in the Social Sciences*, pp. 337–72. Cambridge: Cambridge University Press.

Mainwaring, Scott. 1986. *The Catholic Church and Politics in Brazil, 1916–1985*. Stanford, CA: Stanford University Press.

1993. "Presidentialism, Multipartism, and Democracy: The Difficult Combination." *Comparative Political Studies* 26(2): 198–228.

1999a. "Democratic Survivability in Latin America." In Howard Handelman and Mark A. Tessler, eds., *Democracy and Its Limits: Lessons from Asia, Latin America, and the Middle East*, pp. 11–68. Notre Dame, IN: University of Notre Dame Press.

1999b. "The Surprising Resilience of Latin America's Elected Governments." *Journal of Democracy* 10(3): 101–14.

2006. "State Deficiencies, Party Competition, and Confidence in Democratic Representation in the Andes." In Scott Mainwaring, Ana María Bejarano, and Eduardo Pizarro, eds., *The Crisis of Democratic Representation in the Andes*, pp. 295–345. Stanford, CA: Stanford University Press.

Mainwaring, Scott, Daniel Brinks, and Aníbal Pérez-Liñán. 2001. "Classifying Political Regimes in Latin America, 1945–1999." *Studies in Comparative International Development* 36(1): 37–65.

2007. "Classifying Political Regimes in Latin America, 1945–2004." In Gerardo L. Munck, ed., *Regimes and Democracy in Latin America: Theories and Methods*, pp. 123–60. Oxford: Oxford University Press.

Mainwaring, Scott, and Aníbal Pérez-Liñán. 2003. "Level of Development and Democracy: Latin American Exceptionalism, 1945–1996." *Comparative Political Studies* 36(9): 1031–67.

2005. "Latin American Democratization since 1978: Democratic Transitions, Breakdowns, and Erosions." In Frances Hagopian and Scott Mainwaring, eds., *The Third Wave of Democratization in Latin America: Advances and Setbacks*, pp. 14–59. Cambridge: Cambridge University Press.

2007. "Why Regions of the World Are Important: Regional Specificities and Region-Wide Diffusion of Democracy." In Gerardo L. Munck, ed., *Regimes and Democracy in Latin America: Theories and Methods*, pp. 199–229. Oxford: Oxford University Press.

2013. "Democratic Breakdown and Survival" *Journal of Democracy* 24 (2): 123–137.

Malefakis, Edward. 1996. "Balance Final." In Edward Malefakis, ed., *La Guerra de España, 1936–1939*, pp. 635–64. Madrid: Taurus.

Markoff, John. 1996. *Waves of Democracy: Social Movements and Political Change*. Thousand Oaks, CA: Pine Forge Press.

1999. "Where and When Was Democracy Invented?" *Comparative Studies in Society and History* 41(4): 660–90.

Marshall, Adriana. 2006. *Efectos de las regulaciones del trabajo sobre la afiliación sindical: Estudio comparativo de Argentina, Chile y México*. Cuadernos del IDES N. 8. Buenos Aires: Instituto de Desarrollo Económico y Social.

Mattes, Robert, and Michael Bratton. 2007. "Learning about Democracy in Africa: Awareness, Performance, and Experience." *American Journal of Political Science* 51(1): 192–217.

Mayhew, David R. 1974. *Congress: The Electoral Connection*. New Haven, CT: Yale University Press.

Mayorga, René A. 1991. *¿De la anomia política al orden democrático?: Democracia, estado y movimiento sindical en Bolivia*. La Paz: Centro Boliviano de Estudios Multidisciplinarios.

1997. "Bolivia's Silent Revolution." *Journal of Democracy* 8(1): 142–56.

2005. "Bolivia's Democracy at the Crossroads." In Frances Hagopian and Scott Mainwaring, eds., *The Third Wave of Democratization in Latin America: Advances and Setbacks*, pp. 149–78. Cambridge: Cambridge University Press.

2006. "Outsiders and Neopopulism: The Road to Plebiscitary Democracy." In Scott Mainwaring, Ana María Bejarano, and Eduardo Pizarro, eds., *The Crisis of Democratic Representation in the Andes*, pp. 132–69. Stanford, CA: Stanford University Press.

Forthcoming. "Populismo radical y el desmontaje de la democracia."

McClintock, Cynthia. 1998. *Revolutionary Movements in Latin America: El Salvador's FMLN and Peru's Shining Path*. Washington, DC: United States Institute of Peace Press.

McClintock, Michael. 1985. *The American Connection: State Terror and Popular Resistance in El Salvador*. London: Zed Books.

McCoy, Jennifer L. 2006. "International Response to Democratic Crisis in the Americas, 1990–2005." *Democratization* 13(5): 756–75.

McCoy, Jennifer L., Larry Garber, and Robert Pastor. 1991. "Pollwatching and Peacemaking." *Journal of Democracy* 2(4): 102–14.

McGee Deutsch, Sandra. 1993. "The Right under Radicalism." In Sandra McGee Deutsch and Ronald Dolkart, eds., *The Argentine Right: Its History and Intellectual Origins, 1910 to the Present*, pp. 35–64. Wilmington, DE: SR Books.

McGuire, James W. 1997. *Peronism without Perón: Unions, Parties, and Democracy in Argentina*. Stanford, CA: Stanford University Press.

Merkel, Wolfgang. 2004. "Embedded and Defective Democracies." *Democratization* 11 (5): 33–58.

Merkx, Gilbert W. 1973. "Recessions and Rebellions in Argentina, 1870–1970." *The Hispanic American Historical Review* 53(2): 285–95.

Meseguer Yebra, Covadonga. 2002. *Bayesian Learning About Policies*. Madrid: Centro de Estudios Avanzados en Ciencias Sociales.

Mignone, Emilio F. 1986. *Iglesia y dictadura: El papel de la Iglesia a la luz de sus relaciones con el régimen militar*. Buenos Aires: Ediciones del Pensamiento Militar.

Mill, John Stuart. 1859. *A System of Logic: Ratiocinative and Inductive*. New York: Harper and Brothers.

Monza, Alfredo. 1966. *"Estimación Indirecta del Producto Trimestral."* Buenos Aires: Presidencia de la Nación, Consejo Nacional de Desarrollo (November), mimeo.

Moore Jr., Barrington. 1966. *Social Origins of Dictatorship and Democracy: Lord and Peasant in the Making of the Modern World*. Boston: Beacon.
1978. *Injustice: The Social Bases of Obedience and Revolt*. White Plains, NY: M.E. Sharpe.
Moreno, Alejandro. 1999. *Political Cleavages: Issues, Parties, and the Consolidation of Democracy*. Boulder, CO: Westview Press.
Morgan, Jana. 2011. *Bankrupt Representation and Party System Collapse*. University Park: Pennsylvania State University Press.
Morlino, Leonardo. 2008. "Democracy and Changes: How Research Tails Reality." *West European Politics* 31(1–2): 40–59.
Moyano, María José. 1995. *Argentina's Lost Patrol: Armed Struggle, 1969–1979*. New Haven, CT: Yale University Press.
Muller, Edward N. 1988. "Democracy, Economic Development, and Income Inequality." *American Sociological Review* 53(1): 50–68.
Muller, Edward N., and Mitchell Seligson. 1994. "Civic Culture and Democracy: The Question of Causal Relationships." *American Political Science Review* 88(3): 635–52.
Mulligan, Casey B., Ricard Gil, and Xavier Sala-i-Martin. 2004. "Do Democracies Have Different Public Policies Than Nondemocracies?" *Journal of Economic Perspectives* 18(1): 51–74.
Munck, Gerardo L. 2001. "The Regime Question: Theory Building in Democracy Studies." *World Politics* 54(1): 119–44.
2009. *Measuring Democracy: A Bridge between Scholarship and Politics*. Baltimore: Johns Hopkins University Press.
Munck, Gerardo L., and Jay Verkuilen. 2002. "Conceptualizing and Measuring Democracy: Evaluating Alternative Indices." *Comparative Political Studies* 35(1): 5–34.
Munro, Dana Gardner. 1964. *Intervention and Dollar Diplomacy in the Caribbean 1900–1921*. Princeton, NJ: Princeton University Press.
Mustapic, Ana María. 1984. "Conflictos institucionales durante el primer gobierno radical, 1916-1922." *Desarrollo Económico* 24(93): 85–108.
2005. "Inestabilidad sin colapso. La renuncia de los presidentes: Argentina en el año 2001." *Desarrollo Económico* 45(178): 263–80.
Nef, Jorge. 1983. "Political Democracy in Latin America: An Exploration into the Nature of Two Political Projects." In Archibald Ritter and David Pollock, eds. *Latin American Prospects for the 1980s. Equity, Democratization, and Development*, pp. 161–81. New York: Praeger.
Negretto, Gabriel L. 2009. "Political Parties and Institutional Design: Explaining Constitutional Choice in Latin America." *British Journal of Political Science* 39(1): 117–39.
2013. *Making Constitutions: Presidents, Parties, and Institutional Choice in Latin America*. Cambridge: Cambridge University Press.
Nelson, Joan M. 2007. "Elections, Democracy, and Social Services." *Studies in Comparative International Development* 41(4): 79–97.
Nohlen, Dieter. 1993. *Enciclopedia electoral de América Latina y el Caribe*. San José, Costa Rica: Instituto Interamericano de Derechos Humanos.
Norden, Deborah L. 1996. *Military Rebellion in Argentina: Between Coups and Consolidation*. Lincoln: University of Nebraska Press.

North, Liisa. 1985. *Bitter Grounds: Roots of Revolt in El Salvador*. Westport, CT: Lawrence-Hill.

Novaro, Marcos. 2002. "La Alianza, de la gloria del llano a la debacle del gobierno." In Marcos Novaro, ed., *El derrumbe político en el ocaso de la convertibilidad*, pp. 31–105. Buenos Aires: Grupo Editorial Norma.

2006. *Historia de la Argentina contemporánea. De Perón a Kirchner*. Buenos Aires: Edhasa.

Novaro, Marcos, and Vicente Palermo. 2004. "Introducción. Las ideas de la época entre la invención de una tradición y el eterno retorno de la crisis." In Marcos Novaro and Vicente Palermo, eds., *Historia reciente: Argentina en democracia*, pp. 11–33. Buenos Aires: Edhasa.

O'Donnell, Guillermo. 1973. *Modernization and Bureaucratic-Authoritarianism: Studies in South American Politics*. Berkeley: Institute for International Studies, University of California.

1978. "Permanent Crisis and the Failure to Create a Democratic Regime." In Juan J. Linz and Alfred Stepan, eds., *The Breakdown of Democratic Regimes, Vol. 3, Latin America*, pp. 138–77. Baltimore: Johns Hopkins University Press.

1979. "Tensions in the Bureaucratic-Authoritarian State and the Question of Democracy." In David Collier, ed., *The New Authoritarianism in Latin America*, pp. 285–318. Princeton, NJ: Princeton University Press.

1982. *El estado burocrático autoritario*. Buenos Aires: Editorial de Belgrano.

1986. "Introduction to the Latin American Cases." In Guillermo O'Donnell, Philippe Schmitter, and Laurence Whitehead, eds., *Transitions from Authoritarian Rule: Prospects for Democracy*, Vol. II (*Latin America*), pp. 3–18. Baltimore: Johns Hopkins University Press.

1991. "Argentina, de nuevo." Working Paper No. 152, The Helen Kellogg Institute for International Studies, University of Notre Dame.

1993. "On the State, Democratization and Some Conceptual Problems: A Latin-American View with Glances at Some Postcommunist Countries." *World Development* 21(8): 1355–69.

1994. "Delegative Democracy." *Journal of Democracy* 5(1): 55–69.

2010. *Democracy, Agency and the State: Theory with Comparative Intent*. Oxford: Oxford University Press.

O'Donnell, Guillermo, and Philippe Schmitter. 1986. *Transitions from Authoritarian Rule, Vol. 4: Tentative Conclusions about Uncertain Democracies*. Baltimore: Johns Hopkins University Press.

O'Donnell, Guillermo, Philippe Schmitter, and Laurence Whitehead, eds. 1986. *Transitions from Authoritarian Rule: Prospect for Democracy*. Baltimore: Johns Hopkins University Press.

Ojo Electoral. 2008. *Informe final: Observación referendo sobre la propuesta de Reforma Constitucional, 2 de diciembre de 2007*. Caracas: Ojo Electoral. Available from http://www.ojoelectoral.org/comunicados.php (accessed July 2009).

2009. *Informe final: Observación referendo sobre la propuesta de enmienda constitucional, 15 de febrero 2009*. Caracas: Ojo Electoral. Available from http://www. ojoelectoral.org/comunicados.php (accessed July 2009).

O'Laughlin, John, Michael Ward, Corey Lofdahl, Ordin Cohen, David Brown, David Reilly, Kristian Gleditsch, and Michael Sin. 1998. "The Diffusion of

Democracy, 1946–1994." *Annals of the Association of American Geographers* 88(4): 545–74.

Ollier, María Matilde. 1986. *El fenómeno insurreccional y la cultura política (1969–1973)*. Buenos Aires: Centro Editor de América Latina.

1989. *Orden, poder y violencia (1968–73)*. 2 volumes. Buenos Aires: Centro Editor de América Latina.

1998. *La creencia y la pasión: Privado, público y político en la izquierda revolucionaria*. Buenos Aires: Ariel.

2009. *De la revolución a la democracia: Cambios privados, públicos y políticos de la izquierda argentina*. Buenos Aires: Siglo XXI/Universidad Nacional de San Martín.

Olson, Mancur. 1965. *The Logic of Collective Action: Public Goods and the Theory of Group*. Cambridge, MA: Harvard University Press.

Ostiguy, Pierre. 2009. "Argentina's Double Political Spectrum: Party System, Political Identities, and Strategy, 1944–2007." Kellogg Institute Working Paper #361, University of Notre Dame (October).

Oszlak, Oscar, et al. 1984. *"Proceso", crisis y transición democrática*. 2 volumes. Buenos Aires: Centro Editor de América Latina.

Ottaway, Marina. 2003. *Democracy Challenged: The Rise of Semi-Authoritarianism*. Washington, DC: Carnegie Endowment for International Peace.

Pachano, Simón. 2011. *Calidad de la democracia e instituciones políticas en Bolivia, Ecuador y Perú*. Quito: FLACSO.

Packenham, Robert A. 1973. *Liberal America and the Third World: Political Development Ideas in Foreign Aid and Social Science*. Princeton, NJ: Princeton University Press.

1986. "The Changing Political Discourse in Brazil." In Wayne Selcher, ed., *Political Liberalization in Brazil: Dynamics, Dilemmas, and Future Prospects*, pp. 135–73. Boulder, CO: Westview.

Paige, Jeffery M. 1997. *Coffee and Power: Revolution and the Rise of Democracy in Central America*. Cambridge, MA: Harvard University Press.

Palermo, Vicente, and Marcos Novaro. 1996. *Política y poder en el gobierno de Menem*. Buenos Aires: Grupo Editorial Norma.

Pan American Health Organization (PAHO). 2007. Available from http://new.paho.org/hq/index.php?option=com_content&view=article&id=2470&Itemid=2003&lang=en

Pásara, Luis. 1989. "Peru: The Leftist Angels." In Scott Mainwaring and Alexander Wilde, eds., *The Progressive Church in Latin America*, pp. 276–327. Notre Dame, IN: University of Notre Dame Press.

Pastor, Robert A. 1989. "How to Reinforce Democracy in the Americas: Seven Proposals." In Robert A. Pastor, ed., *Democracy in the Americas: Stopping the Pendulum*, pp. 139–55. New York: Holmes and Meier.

Payne, Leigh. 1994. *Brazilian Industrialists and Democratic Change*. Baltimore: Johns Hopkins University Press.

2000. *Uncivil Movements: The Armed Right Wing and Democracy in Latin America*. Baltimore: Johns Hopkins University Press.

Payne, Stanley G. 2006. *The Collapse of the Spanish Republic, 1933–1936*. New Haven, CT: Yale University Press.

Pearson, Paul. 2003. *Politics in Time: History, Institutions, and Social Analysis*. Princeton, CT: Princeton University Press.

Pedrosa, Fernando. 2012. *La otra izquierda. La socialdemocracia en América Latina.* Buenos Aires: Capital Intelectual.

Pérez-Díaz, Víctor M. 1993. *The Return of Civil Society: The Emergence of Democratic Spain.* Cambridge, MA: Harvard University Press.

Pérez-Liñán, Aníbal. 2007. *Presidential Impeachment and the New Political Instability in Latin America.* Cambridge: Cambridge University Press.

Pérez-Liñán, Aníbal, and Scott Mainwaring. 2013. "Regime Legacies and Levels of Democracy: Evidence from Latin America." *Comparative Politics* 45(4): forthcoming.

Perina, Rubén M. 2000. "El régimen democrático interamericano: El papel de la OEA." In Arlene B. Tickner, ed., *Sistema interamericano y democracia: Antecedentes históricos y tendencias futuras*, pp. 311–76. Bogotá: Ediciones Uniandes.

Peruzzotti, Enrique. 2005. "Demanding Accountable Government: Citizens, Politicians, and the Perils of Representative Democracy in Argentina." In Steven Levitsky and María Victoria Murillo, eds., *Argentine Democracy: The Politics of Institutional Weakness*, pp. 229–49. University Park: Pennsylvania State University Press.

Pevehouse, Jon C. 2002a. "With a Little Help from My Friends? Regional Organizations and the Consolidation of Democracy." *American Journal of Political Science* 46(3): 611–26.

2002b. "Democracy from the Outside-In? International Organizations and Democratization." *International Organization* 56(3): 515–49.

2005. *Democracy from Above? Regional Organizations and Democratization.* Cambridge: Cambridge University Press.

Philpott, Daniel. 2001. *Revolutions in Sovereignty: How Ideas Shaped Modern International Relations.* Princeton, NJ: Princeton University Press.

Plattner, Marc F. 1998. "Liberalism and Democracy: Can't Have One without the Other." *Foreign Affairs* 77(2): 171–80.

Plotkin, Mariano Ben. 1994. *Mañana es San Perón: propaganda, rituales políticos y educación en el régimen peronista (1946–1955).* Buenos Aires: Ariel.

Poggi, Gianfranco. 1967. *Catholic Action in Italy: The Sociology of a Sponsored Organization.* Stanford, CA: Stanford University Press.

Policzer, Pablo. 2003. "The Charter vs. Constitutional Military Involvement in Politics." *Canadian Foreign Policy* 10(3): 75–86.

Polity IV Project. 2012. *Polity IV. Political Regime Characteristics and Transitions, 1800–2010.* Available from http://www.systemicpeace.org/polity/polity4.htm.

Portantiero, Juan Carlos. 1987a. "La transición entre la confrontación y el acuerdo." In José Nun and Juan Carlos Portantiero, eds., *Ensayos sobre la transición democrática en la Argentina*, pp. 257–93. Buenos Aires: Puntosur.

1987b. "La concertación que no fue: de la ley Mucci al Plan Austral." In José Nun and Juan Carlos Portantiero, eds., *Ensayos sobre la transición democrática en la Argentina*, pp. 139–73. Buenos Aires: Puntosur.

Portes, Alejandro. 1971. "Political Primitivism, Differential Socialization, and Lower-Class Leftist Radicalism." *American Sociological Review* 36(5): 820–35.

Potash, Robert A. 1983. *El ejército y la política en la Argentina. 1928–1945: De Yrigoyen a Perón.* Buenos Aires: Editorial Sudamericana.

Potter, Anne L. 1981. "The Failure of Democracy in Argentina 1916–1930: An Institutional Perspective." *Journal of Latin American Studies* 13(1): 83–109.

Power, Margaret. 2002. *Right-Wing Women in Chile: Feminine Power and the Struggle against Allende 1964–1973*. University Park: Pennsylvania State University Press.

Powers, Nancy R. 2001. *Grassroots Expectations of Democracy and Economy: Argentina in Comparative Perspective*. Pittsburgh, PA: University of Pittsburgh Press.

Preacher, Kristopher J. 2008. *Latent Growth Curve Modeling*. Quantitative Applications in the Social Sciences, 157. Los Angeles: Sage.

Preston, Paul. 2006. *La Guerra civil española*. Barcelona: Random House Mondadori.

Pridham, Geoffrey, ed. 1991. *Encouraging Democracy: The International Context of Regime Transition in Southern Europe*. New York: St. Martin's.

　1997. *Building Democracy? The International Dimension of Democratisation in Eastern Europe*. New York: Leicester University Press.

Primo, David M. 2002. "Rethinking Political Bargaining: Policymaking with a Single Proposer." *Journal of Law, Economics, and Organization* 18(2): 411–27.

Przeworski, Adam. 1986. "Problems in the Study of Transition to Democracy." In Guillermo O'Donnell, Philippe Schmitter, and Laurence Whitehead, eds., *Transitions from Authoritarian Rule: Prospects for Democracy*, Part III, pp. 47–63. Baltimore: Johns Hopkins University Press.

　1991. *Democracy and the Market: Political and Economic Reforms in Eastern Europe and Latin America*. Cambridge: Cambridge University Press.

　1999. "Minimalist Conception of Democracy: A Defense." In Ian Shapiro and Casiano Hacker-Cordón, eds., *Democracy's Value*, pp. 23–55. Cambridge: Cambridge University Press.

　2006. "Democracy as an Equilibrium." *Public Choice* 123: 253–73.

Przeworski, Adam, Susan C. Stokes, and Bernard Manin, eds. 1999. *Democracy, Accountability, and Representation*. Cambridge and New York: Cambridge University Press.

Przeworski, Adam, Michael E. Alvarez, José Antonio Cheibub, and Fernando Limongi. 2000. *Democracy and Development: Political Institutions and Well-Being in the World, 1950–1990*. Cambridge: Cambridge University Press.

Przeworski, Adam and John Sprague. 1986. *Paper Stones: A History of Electoral Socialism*. Chicago: University of Chicago Press.

Rabushka, Alvin, and Kenneth Shepsle. 1972. *Politics in Plural Societies: A Theory of Democratic Instability*. Columbus, OH: Charles E. Merrill.

Ragin, Charles C. 1987. *The Comparative Method: Moving Beyond Qualitative and Quantitative Strategies*. Berkeley: University of California Press.

　2000. *Fuzzy Set Social Science*. Chicago: The University of Chicago Press.

　2006. "Set Relations in Social Research: Evaluating Their Consistency and Coverage." *Political Analysis* 14(3): 291–310.

　2008. *Redisigning Social Inquiry: Fuzzy Sets and Beyond*. Chicago: The University of Chicago Press.

Ragin, Charles C., and John Sonnett. 2005. "Between Complexity and Parsimony: Limited Diversity, Counterfactual Cases, and Comparative Analysis." In Sabine Kropp, and Michael Minkenberg, eds., *Vergleichen in der Politikwissenschaft*, pp. 180–97. Wiesbaden: Verlag für Sozialwissenschaften.

Rama, Angel. 1996. *The Lettered City*. Durham, NC: Duke University Press.

Ranis, Peter. 1992. *Argentine Workers: Peronism and Contemporary Class Consciousness*. Pittsburgh, PA: University of Pittsburgh Press.

Rapoport, Mario. 2003. *Historia económica, política y social de la Argentina (1880–2000)*, 2nd ed. Buenos Aires: Ediciones Macchi.

Raudenbush, Stephen W., and Anthony S. Bryk. 2002. *Hierarchical Linear Models: Applications and Data Analysis Methods.* 2nd ed. Thousand Oaks, CA: Sage Publications.

Remmer, Karen. 1984. *Party Competition in Argentina and Chile: Political Recruitment and Public Policy, 1890–1930.* Lincoln: University of Nebraska Press.

   1996. "The Sustainability of Political Democracy: Lessons from South America." *Comparative Political Studies* 29(6): 611–34.

Ribera Sala, Ricardo. 1996. *Los partidos políticos en El Salvador entre 1979 y 1992: Evolución y cambios.* Colección Aportes No. 3. San Salvador: FLACSO.

Rihoux, Benoît, and Charles C. Ragin, eds. 2009. *Configurational Comparative Methods.* Los Angeles: Sage Publications.

Risse, Thomas, Stephen C. Ropp, and Kathryn Sikkink, eds. 1999. *The Power of Human Rights: International Norms and Domestic Change.* Cambridge: Cambridge University Press.

Roberts, Kenneth. 1998. *Deepening Democracy? The Modern Left and Social Movements in Chile and Peru.* Stanford, CA: Stanford University Press.

Robinson, William I. 1996. *Promoting Polyarchy: Globalization, US Intervention, and Hegemony.* Cambridge: Cambridge University Press.

Rock, David. 1975. *Politics in Argentina, 1890–1930: The Rise and Fall of Radicalism.* Cambridge: Cambridge University Press.

   1985. *Argentina 1516–1982. From Spanish Colonization to the Falklands War.* Berkeley: University of California Press.

Romero, Catalina. 1989. "The Peruvian Church: Change and Continuity." In Scott Mainwaring and Alexander Wilde, eds., *The Progressive Church in Latin America*, pp. 253–75. Notre Dame, IN: University of Notre Dame Press.

Romero, Luis Alberto. 2002. *A History of Argentina in the Twentieth Century.* University Park: Pennsylvania State University Press.

   2004. *Sociedad Democrática y política democrática en la Argentina del siglo XX.* Buenos Aires: Editorial de la Universidad Nacional de Quilmes.

Rose, Richard, and William Mishler. 1996. "Testing the Churchill Hypothesis: Popular Support for Democracy and Its Alterntives." *Journal of Public Policy* 16(1): 29–58.

Ross, Michael L. 2001. "Does Oil Hinder Democracy?" *World Politics* 53(3): 325–61.

Rouquié, Alain. 1982a. *Poder militar y sociedad política en la Argentina, hasta 1943.* Buenos Aires: Emecé.

   1982b. *Poder militar y sociedad política en la Argentina, 1943–1973.* Buenos Aires: Emecé.

Rubinstein, Ariel. 1982. "Perfect Equilibrium in a Bargaining Model." *Econometrica* 50 (1): 97–109.

Rueschemeyer, Dietrich, Evelyne Huber Stephens, and John D. Stephens. 1992. *Capitalist Development and Democracy.* Chicago: University of Chicago Press.

Ruhl, J. Mark. 2010. "Trouble in Central America: Honduras Unravels." *Journal of Democracy* 21 No. 2 (April): 93–107.

Rustow, Dankwart A. 1970. "Transitions to Democracy: Toward a Dynamic Model." *Comparative Politics* 2(3): 337–63.

Sahlins, Marshall D. 1976. *Culture and Practical Reason*. Chicago: University of Chicago Press.

Sanchez, Peter M. 2003. "Bringing the International Back In: US Hegemonic Maintenance and Latin America's Democratic Breakdown in the 1960s and 1970s." *International Politics* 40: 223–47.

Sánchez Cuenca, Ignacio. 2008. "A Preference for Selfish Preferences." *Philosophy of the Social Sciences* 38(3): 361–78.

Sani, Giacomo and Giovanni Sartori. 1983. "Polarization, Fragmentation, and Competition in Western Democracies." In Hans Daalder and Peter Mair, eds., *Western European Party Systems*, pp. 307–40. Beverly Hills, CA: Sage.

Santos, Wanderley Guilherme dos. 1986. *Sessenta e Quatro: Anatomia da Crise*. São Paulo: Vértice.

Sartori, Giovanni. 1969. "From the Sociology of Politics to Political Sociology." In Seymour Martin Lipset, ed., *Politics and the Social Sciences*, pp. 65–95. Oxford: Oxford University Press.

   1976. *Parties and Party Systems: A Framework for Analysis*. Cambridge: Cambridge University Press.

Schedler, Andreas. 2002. "The Menu of Manipulation." *Journal of Democracy* 13(2): 36–50.

   ed. 2007. *Electoral Authoritarianism: The Dynamics of Unfree Competition*. Boulder, CO: Lynne Rienner.

Schelling, Thomas C. 1978. *Micromotives and Macrobehavior*. New York: Norton.

Schoultz, Lars. 1981. *Human Rights and United States Policy toward Latin America*. Princeton, NJ: Princeton University Press.

   1998. *Beneath the United States: A History of U.S. Policy Toward Latin America*. Cambridge, MA: Harvard University Press.

Schwartzberg, Steven. 2003. *Democracy and US Policy in Latin America during the Truman Years*. Gainesville: University of Florida Press.

Scully, Timothy R. 1992. *Rethinking the Center: Party Politics in Nineteenth and Twentieth Century Chile*. Stanford, CA: Stanford University Press.

Seawright, Jason. 2005. "Qualitative Comparative Analysis vis-à-vis Regression." *Studies in Comparative International Development* 40 No. 1 (Spring): 3–26.

   2012. *Party-System Collapse: The Roots of Crisis in Peru and Venezuela*. Stanford, CA: Stanford University Press.

Segura-Ubiergo, Alex. 2007. *The Political Economy of the Welfare State in Latin America: Globalization, Development, and Democracy*. Cambridge: Cambridge University Press.

Seligson, Mitchell A. 2002. "The Renaissance of Political Culture or the Renaissance of the Ecological Fallacy?" *Comparative Politics* 34(2): 273–92.

Sen, Amartya. 1995. "Rationality and Social Choice." *American Economic Review* 85(1): 1–24.

   1997. "Maximization and the Act of Choice." *Econometrica* 65(4): 745–79.

Shapiro, Michael J. 1969. "Rational Political Man: A Synthesis of Economic and Social-Psychological Perspectives." *The American Political Science Review* 63(4):1106–19.

Share, Donald. 1986. *The Making of Spanish Democracy*. New York: Praeger.

Shugart, Matthew S., and John M. Carey. 1992. *Presidents and Assemblies. Constitutional Design and Electoral Dynamics*. Cambridge: Cambridge University Press.

Sigal, Silvia, and Eliseo Verón. 1982. "Perón: Discurso político e ideología." In Alain Rouquié, ed., *Argentina, hoy*, pp. 151–205. Buenos Aires: Siglo XXI.

1986. *Perón o muerte. Los fundamentos discursivos del fenómeno peronista*. Buenos Aires: Editorial Legasa.

Sikkink, Kathryn. 1991. *Ideas and Institutions: Developmentalism in Brazil and Argentina*. Ithaca, NY: Cornell University Press.

1993. "The Power of Principled Ideas: Human Rights Policies in the United States and Western Europe." In Judith Goldstein and Robert Keohane, eds., *Ideas and Foreign Policy: Beliefs, Institutions, and Political Change*, pp. 139–70. Ithaca, NY: Cornell University Press.

2004. *Mixed Signals: U.S. Human Rights Policy and Latin America*. Ithaca, NY: Cornell University Press.

2011. *The Justice Cascade: How Human Rights Violations are Changing the World*. New York: W. W. Norton.

Skidmore, Thomas. 1988. *The Politics of Military Rule in Brazil, 1964–1985*. Oxford: Oxford University Press.

Skocpol, Theda. 1979. *States and Social Revolutions: A Comparative Analysis of France, Russia, and China*. Cambridge: Cambridge University Press.

Skocpol, Theda, and Margaret Somers. 1980. "The Uses of Comparative History in Macrosocial Inquiry." *Comparative Studies in Society and History* 22(2): 174–97.

Smilde, David, and Daniel Hellinger, eds. 2011. *Venezuela's Bolivarian Democracy: Participation, Politics, and Culture under Chávez*. Durham, NC: Duke University Press.

Smith, Brian H. 1982. *The Church and Politics in Chile: Challenges to Modern Catholicism*. Princeton, NJ: Princeton University Press.

Smith, Peter H. 1974. *Argentina and the Failure of Democracy: Conflict among Political Elites, 1904–1955*. Madison: University of Wisconsin Press.

1978. "The Breakdown of Democracy in Argentina, 1916–30." In Juan J. Linz and Alfred Stepan, eds., *The Breakdown of Democratic Regimes: Latin America*, pp. 3–27. Baltimore: Johns Hopkins University Press.

2000. *Talons of the Eagle: Dynamics of U.S.-Latin American Relations*. New York: Oxford University Press.

2005. *Democracy in Latin America: Political Change in Comparative Perspective*. Oxford: Oxford University Press.

Smith, William C. 1989. *Authoritarianism and the Crisis of the Argentine Political Economy*. Stanford, CA: Stanford University Press.

Smulovitz, Catalina. 1988. *Oposición y gobierno: los años de Frondizi*. 2 volumes. Buenos Aires: Centro Editor de América Latina.

Snyder, Jack. 2000. *From Voting to Violence: Democratization and Nationalist Conflict*. New York: W. W. Norton.

Souza Lima, Luis Gonzaga de. 1980. *Evolução Política dos Católicos e da Igreja no Brasil: Hipóteses para uma Interpretação*. Petrópolis: Vozes.

Stanley, William D. 1996. *The Protection Racket State: Elite Politics, Military Extortion, and Civil War in El Salvador*. Philadelphia: Temple University Press.

Starr, Harvey. 1991. "Democratic Dominoes: Diffusion Approaches to the Spread of Democracy in the International System." *Journal of Conflict Resolution* 35(2): 356–81.

Stepan, Alfred. 1971. *The Military in Politics: Changing Patterns in Brazil*. Princeton, NJ: Princeton University Press.

1978. "Political Leadership and Regime Breakdown: Brazil." In Juan J. Linz and Alfred Stepan, eds., *The Breakdown of Democratic Regimes*, Vol. 3, *Latin America*, pp. 110–37. Baltimore: Johns Hopkins University Press.

1986. "Paths toward Redemocratization: Theoretical and Comparative Considerations." In Guillermo O'Donnell, Philippe C. Schmitter, and Laurence Whitehead, eds., *Transitions from Authoritarian Rule: Prospects for Democracy*, Part 3, pp. 64–84. Baltimore: Johns Hopkins University Press.

1994. "When Democracy and the Nation-State Are Competing Logics: Reflections on Estonia." *European Journal of Sociology* 35: 127–41.

2001. *Arguing Comparative Politics*. Oxford: Oxford University Press.

Stepan, Alfred, Juan Linz, and Yogendra Yadav. 2011. *Crafting State-Nations: India and Other Multinational Democracies*. Baltimore: Johns Hopkins University Press.

Stepan, Alfred, and Cindy Skach. 1994. "Presidentialism and Parliamentarism in Comparative Perspective." In Juan J. Linz and Arturo Valenzuela, eds., *The Failure of Presidential Democracy*, Vol. 1, *Comparative Perspectives*, pp. 119–36. Baltimore: Johns Hopkins University Press.

Stokes, Susan C. 2001. *Mandates and Democracy: Neoliberalism by Surprise in Latin America*. Cambridge: Cambridge University Press.

Stutzer, Alois, and Bruno S. Frey. 2006. "Political Participation and Procedural Utility: An Empirical Study." *European Journal of Political Research* 45: 391–418.

Sutton, John. 1986. "Non-Cooperative Bargaining Theory: An Introduction." *The Review of Economic Studies* 53 (5): 709–724

Tanaka, Martín. 1998. *Los espejismos de la democracia: El colapso del sistema de partidos en el Perú*. Lima: Instituto de Estudios Peruanos.

2006. "From Crisis to Collapse of the Party Systems and Dilemmas of Democratic Representation: Peru and Venezuela." In Scott Mainwaring, Ana María Bejarano, and Eduardo Pizarro, eds., *The Crisis of Democratic Representation in the Andes*, pp. 47–77. Stanford, CA: Stanford University Press.

Tarrow, Sidney. 2010. "The Strategy of Paired Comparison: Toward a Theory of Practice." *Comparative Political Studies* 43 (February): 230–59.

Tcach, César, and Hugo Quiroga. 2006. "Prólogo: a treinta años del golpe." In César Tcach and Hugo Quiroga, eds., *Argentina 1976–2006: entre la sombra de la dictadura y el futuro de la democracia*, pp. 11–14. Rosario: Homo Sapiens.

Teorell, Jan. 2010. *Determinants of Democratization: Explaining Regime Change in the World, 1972–2006*. Cambridge: Cambridge University Press.

Thelen, Kathleen. 1999. "Historical Institutionalism in Comparative Politics." *Annual Review of Political Science* 2: 369–404.

2004. *How Institutions Evolve: The Political Economy of Skills in Germany, Britain, the United States, and Japan*. Cambridge: Cambridge University Press.

Torcal, Mariano, and Scott Mainwaring. 2003. "The Political Recrafting of Social Bases of Party Competition: Chile, 1973–95." *British Journal of Political Science* 33: 55–84.

Torre, Juan Carlos. 1989. *Los sindicatos en el gobierno, 1973–1976*. Buenos Aires: Centro Editor de América Latina.

Torre, Juan Carlos, and Liliana De Riz. 1993. "Argentina since 1946." In Leslie Bethell, ed., *Argentina since Independence*, pp. 243–363. Cambridge: Cambridge University Press.

Tulchin, Joseph S. 1971. *The Aftermath of War: World War I and U.S. Policy toward Latin America.* New York: New York University Press.

Tussell, Javier. 2005. *Dictadura franquista y democracia.* Barcelona: Crítica.

Tyler, Tom R. 1990. *Why People Obey the Law.* New Haven, CT: Yale University Press.

United Nations Development Programme (UNDP). 2011. *Human Development Report.* Available from http://hdr.undp.org/en/reports/global/hdr2011/ (accessed October 2012).

United Nations University - World Institute for Development Economic Research. 2007. *World Income Inequality Database.* Available from http://www.wider.unu.edu/.

U.S. Department of State. 2002. *2001 Country Reports on Human Rights Practices: Argentina*, March 4. Available from http://www.state.gov/g/drl/rls/hrrpt/2001/wha/8278.htm (accessed November 2012).

——— 2006. *2005 Country Reports on Human Rights Practices: Argentina*, March 8. Available from http://www.state.gov/g/drl/rls/hrrpt/2005/61713.htm (accessed November 2012).

——— 2007. *2006 Country Reports on Human Rights Practices: Argentina*, March 6. Available from http://www.state.gov/g/drl/rls/hrrpt/2006/78877.htm (accessed November 2012).

U.S. Senate. 1975. Covert Action in Chile 1963–1973. (Also known as the Church Report.) Available from http://foia.state.gov/reports/churchreport.asp.

Vaillancourt, Jean-Guy. 1980. *Papal Power: A Study of Vatican Control over Lay Catholic Elites.* Berkeley: University of California Press.

Valenzuela, Arturo. 1978. *The Breakdown of Democratic Regimes: Chile.* Baltimore: Johns Hopkins University Press.

Valenzuela, J. Samuel. 1985. *Democratización vía reforma: la expansión del sufragio en Chile.* Buenos Aires: Ediciones del IDES.

——— 1992. "Democratic Consolidation in Post-Transitional Settings: Notion, Process, and Facilitating Conditions." In Scott Mainwaring, Guillermo O'Donnell, and J. Samuel Valenzuela, eds., *Issues in Democratic Consolidation: The New South American Democracies in Comparative Perspective*, pp. 57–104. Notre Dame, IN: University of Notre Dame Press.

——— 2001. "Class Relations and Democratization: A Reassessment of Barrington's Model." In Miguel Ángel Centeno and Fernando López-Alves, eds., *The Other Mirror: Grand Theory through the Lens of Latin America*, pp. 240–86. Princeton, NJ: Princeton University Press.

——— 2011. "Transición por Redemocratización: El Frente Nacional Colombiano en una reflexión teórica y comparativa." Working Paper No. 380, The Helen Kellogg Institute for International Studies, University of Notre Dame. Available from http://kellogg.nd.edu/publications/workingpapers/index.shtml

Villalobos, Joaquín. 1989a. "A Democratic Revolution for El Salvador." *Foreign Affairs* 74 (Spring): 107.

——— 1989b. "Perspectivas de victoria y proyecto revolucionario." *Estudios Centroamericanos* 483–484(January–February): 11–52.

——— 1992. *Una revolución en la izquierda para una revolución democrática.* San Salvador: Arcoiris.

Vinhas, Moisés. 1982. *O Partidão: A Luta por um Partido de Massas 1922–1974.* São Paulo: Editora Hucitec.

Viola, Eduardo. 1982. "Democracia e Autoritarismo na Argentina Contemporânea." PhD dissertation, University of São Paulo.

Viola, Eduardo, and Scott Mainwaring. 1984. "New Social Movements, Political Culture, and Democracy: Brazil and Argentina in the 1980s." *Telos* 61: 17–52.

Waisman, Carlos H. 1987. *Reversal of Development in Argentina: Postwar Counterrevolutionary Policies and Their Structural Consequences*. Princeton, NJ: Princeton University Press.

1989. "Argentina: Autarkic Industrialization and Illegitimacy." In Larry Diamond, Juan J. Linz, and Seymour Martin Lipset, eds., *Democracy in Developing Countries: Latin America*, pp. 59–109. Boulder, CO: Lynne Rienner.

Waldmann, Peter. 1982. "Anomia social y violencia." In Alain Rouquié, ed., *Argentina, hoy*, pp. 206–48. Buenos Aires: Siglo XXI.

Walker, Ignacio. 1990. *Socialismo y democracia: Chile y Europa en perspectiva comparada*. Santiago: CIEPLAN/Hachette.

Weber, Max. 1978 [1925]. *Economy and Society: An Outline of Interpretive Sociology*. 2 volumes. Berkeley: University of California Press.

Webre, Stephen A. 1979. *José Napoleón and the Christian Democratic Party in Salvadoran Politics 1960–1972*. Baton Rouge: Louisiana State University Press.

Weffort, Francisco C. 1984. *Por Que Democracia?* São Paulo: Brasiliense.

1989. "Why Democracy?" In Alfred Stepan, ed., *Democratizing Brazil: Problems of Transition and Consolidation*, pp. 327–50. Oxford: Oxford University Press.

Weitz, Eric D. 2007. *Weimar Germany: Promise and Tragedy*. Princeton, NJ: Princeton University Press.

Wendt, Alexander. 1999. *Social Theory of International Politics*. Cambridge: Cambridge University Press.

Weyland, Kurt. 2002. *The Politics of Market Reform in Fragile Democracies: Argentina, Brazil, Peru, and Venezuela*. Princeton, NJ: Princeton University Press.

2005. "Theories of Policy Diffusion: Lessons from Latin American Pension Reform." *World Politics* 57(2): 262–95.

2006. *Bounded Rationality and Policy Diffusion*. Princeton, NJ: Princeton University Press.

2009. "Institutional Change in Latin America: External Models and their Unintended Consequences." *Journal of Politics in Latin America* 1(1): 37–66.

2010. "The Diffusion of Regime Contention in European Democratization, 1830–1940." *Comparative Political Studies* 43(8–9): 1148–76.

Forthcoming. *Making Waves: Democratic Contention in Europe and Latin America*.

Weyland, Kurt, Raúl Madrid, and Wendy Hunter 2010. *Leftist Governments in Latin America: Successes and Shortcomings*. New York: Cambridge University Press.

Whitehead, Laurence. 1986a. "Bolivia's Failed Democratization, 1977–1980." In Guillermo O'Donnell, Philippe Schmitter, and Laurence Whitehead, eds., *Transitions from Authoritarian Rule: Prospects for Democracy*, Part II, pp. 49–71. Baltimore: Johns Hopkins University Press.

1986b. "International Aspects of Democratization." In Guillermo O'Donnell, Philippe Schmitter, and Laurence Whitehead, eds., *Transitions from Authoritarian Rule: Prospects for Democracy*, Part III, pp. 3–46. Baltimore: Johns Hopkins University Press.

1991. "Democracy by Convergence and Southern Europe: A Comparative Politics Perspective." In Geoffrey Pridham, ed., *Encouraging Democracy: The International Context of Regime Transition in Southern Europe*, pp. 45–61. New York: St. Martin's Press.

ed. 1996. *The International Dimensions of Democratization: Europe and the Americas*. Oxford: Oxford University Press.

Wiarda, Howard J. 1986. "Can Democracy Be Exported? The Quest for Democracy in US-Latin American Policy." In Kevin Middlebrook and Carlos Rico, eds., *The United States and Latin America in the 1980s: Contending Perspectives on a Decade of Crisis*, pp. 325–52. Pittsburgh, PA: University of Pittsburgh Press.

2001. *The Soul of Latin America: The Cultural and Political Tradition*. New Haven, CT: Yale University Press.

Wickham-Crowley, Timothy P. 1992. *Guerrillas and Revolution in Latin America: A Comparative Study of Insurgents and Regimes since 1956*. Princeton, NJ: Princeton University Press.

Wilde, Alexander W. 1978. "Conversations among Gentlemen: Oligarchical Democracy in Colombia." In Juan J. Linz and Alfred Stepan, eds., *The Breakdown of Democratic Regimes: Latin America*, pp. 28–81. Baltimore: Johns Hopkins University Press.

Williams, Philip, and Guillermina Seri. 2003. "The Limits of Reformism: The Rise and Fall of Christian Democracy in El Salvador and Guatemala". In Scott Mainwaring, and Timothy Scully, eds., *Christian Democracy in Latin America: Electoral Competition and Regime Conflicts*, pp. 301–29. Stanford, CA: Stanford University Press.

Williams, Philip J. 1989. "The Catholic Church in the Nicaraguan Revolution: Differing Responses and New Challenges." In Scott Mainwaring and Alexander Wilde, eds., *The Progressive Church in Latin America*, pp. 64–102. Notre Dame, IN: University of Notre Dame Press.

Williams, Philip J., and Knut Walter. 1997. *Militarization and Demilitarization in El Salvador's Transition to Democracy*. Pittsburgh, PA: University of Pittsburgh Press.

Williamson, John. 2003. "An Agenda for Restarting Growth and Reform." In Pedro-Pablo Kuczynski and John Williamson, eds., *After the Washington Consensus: Restarting Growth and Reform in Latin America*, pp. 1–19. Washington, DC: Institute for International Economics.

Wood, Elisabeth Jean. 2000a. *Forging Democracy from Below: Insurgent Transitions in South Africa and El Salvador*. Cambridge: Cambridge University Press.

2000b. "The Transformation of Elite Representation in El Salvador." In Kevin Middlebrook, ed., *Conservative Parties, the Right, and Democracy in Latin America*, pp. 223–54. Baltimore: Johns Hopkins University Press.

2003. *Insurgent Collective Action and Civil War in El Salvador*. New York: Cambridge University Press.

2005. "Challenges to Political Democracy in El Salvador." In Frances Hagopian and Scott Mainwaring, eds., *The Third Wave of Democratization in Latin America: Advances and Setbacks*, pp. 179–201. Cambridge: Cambridge University Press.

World Bank, The. 2007. *World Development Indicators On-Line*. Available from http://databank.worldbank.org/ddp/home.do?Step=1&id=4 (accessed November 2012).

Wright, Joseph. 2008. "To Invest or Insure? How Authoritarian Time Horizons Impact Foreign Aid Effectiveness." *Comparative Political Studies* 41(7): 971–1000.

Wright, Thomas C. 1991. *Latin America in the Era of the Cuban Revolution.* New York: Praeger.

Yashar, Deborah. 1997. *Demanding Democracy: Reform and Reaction in Costa Rica and Guatemala, 1870s-1950s.* Cambridge: Cambridge University Press.

Yee, Albert S. 1996. "The Causal Effects of Ideas on Policies." *International Organization* 50(1): 69–108.

Zakaria, Fareed. 1997. "The Rise of Illiberal Democracy." *Foreign Affairs* 76: 22–43.

Zamora, Rubén. 1998. *El Salvador, heridas que no cierran: Los partidos políticos en la post-guerra.* San Salvador: FLACSO.

—— 2001. "Participación y democracia en El Salvador." In Ricardo Córdova Macías, Günther Maihold, and Sabine Kurtenbach, eds., *Pasos hacia una nueva convivencia: Democracia y participación en Centroamérica,* pp. 57–94. San Salvador: FUNDAUNGO.

—— 2003. *La izquierda partidaria salvadoreña: Entre la identidad y el poder.* San Salvador: FLACSO.

Index

348 Index

El Salvador (cont.)
  authoritarianism in, 25, 67t, 173–83, 231
  big business in, 11n14, 170–1, 173–5, 177,
    181–5, 188–9, 191–3, 196–7, 200–1, 203,
    308–9
  civil war in, 170–1, 175, 181, 184–6, 188,
    190–3, 195–200, 203–4
  coalitions in, 27, 33, 170–1, 173, 175, 183–4,
    188, 201–3, 213, 236
  coffee-based agriculture in, 178–83
  coups in, 175, 183, 185–6, 192
  death squads in, 50, 174–5, 183–4, 187, 189,
    191–3, 196, 308–9
  democracy in, 23, 67t, 184, 187, 198–9,
    202–4, 233, 245–6, 247t
  democratic survival in, 170–1, 199–201, 279
  de-radicalization in, 52, 177, 188, 200–2
  economic performance in, 171, 177, 178t,
    188, 196, 198–9
  electoral fraud in, 174, 176, 201
  governing parties in, 170, 173–6, 201
  human rights record in, 186–7, 190, 193,
    199–200, 214
  labor unions in, 174, 176
  landed/coffee elite in, 11n14, 173–5, 181,
    184, 193, 198, 308–9
  military in, 170, 173–7, 181–93,
    196–7, 199–201, 203, 213–14, 231, 308–9
  normative preferences in, 56, 59, 129,
    170–1, 174, 182, 188–91, 193–5, 200–1,
    203, 224
  peace accords in, 52, 75, 184–5, 193, 196,
    199, 202–4, 226
  peasant groups in, 174, 176
  polarization in, 171, 175
  policy preferences in, 170–1, 192
  radicalism/radicalization in, 174–6, 182–3,
    189, 201–2
  regional/international influences in, 156, 171,
    175, 181–2, 195, 200–1
  revolutionary left in, 177, 183, 185, 201, 213,
    226–7, 308
  revolutionary socialism in, 174, 182, 188,
    193–6
  semi-democracy in, 22, 66, 67t, 183, 187,
    198, 202–3
  structural factors in, 172t, 176, 178, 180,
    197, 201
  transition in, 126, 170, 183–99, 197, 202,
    204, 229n12, 232, 284
  U.S. in, 185–8, 191, 195, 197–8, 201–3,
    213–14

endogeneity, 20, 31, 88, 106–7, 112, 121, 296
Enlightenment, the, 60, 84
Europe, 132, 225, 227
  authoritarian ideologies in, 132, 168
  Central, 39, 41, 213
  Eastern, 14, 39, 41, 212–13
  Southern, 85, 130–2, 213
  Western, 38, 60, 128, 155, 168, 225–6, 240,
    283, 285, 168
European Union, 46, 213, 266, 277, 285–6, 294

Falkland Islands (Malvinas) war, 146, 153–5, 231
Farabundo Martí National Liberation Front
    (FMLN, El Salvador), 59, 170–1, 174n3,
    183n6, 184–88, 190, 192–6, 308–9
Fernández de Kirchner, Cristina (Argentina),
    149–51, 157t, 158t, 166t
Finland, 38, 159
Ford, Gerald, 146, 218, 230
France, 38, 45, 159
Franco, Francisco (Spain), 147t, 235–6, 276
Freedom House scores, 4, 63, 246–9, 252–5,
    258, 261, 290
French revolution, 84, 235
FREPASO (Argentina), 149n10, 157t
Frondizi, Arturo (Argentina), 139–42, 147t,
    158t, 166t, 167, 305t, 306
Fujimori, Alberto (Peru), 34n5, 264
Funes, Mauricio (El Salvador), 195, 198, 200,
    309
FUSADES (Fundación Salvadoreña para el
    Desarrollo Económico y Social), 185, 187,
    190, 309

Germany, 14
  Weimar Republic, 33
  democratic breakdown, 269, 275–6
Gini index. See income inequality; landholding
    inequality
Gómez, Juan Vicente (Venezuela), 42n14, 57
Great Depression, the, 72, 84, 131–2,
    133t, 161
Guatemala, 22, 37n11, 66, 67t, 75, 119, 126,
    156, 172–3, 178t, 179, 213, 216, 224,
    231–3, 244, 250
  Catholic Church in, 236–7
  democratic breakdowns in, 132, 215–16,
    230, 233
  level of democracy in, 242, 245, 247t, 248–9,
    256
  revolutionary left in, 226–7
Guevara, Ernesto (Che), 221, 223